Animal Cognition

Also by Clive D. L. Wynne

Do Animals Think? (2004)

Animal Cognition

Evolution, Behavior and Cognition

2nd edition

Clive D. L. Wynne, Ph.D.
Professor of Psychology, Arizona State University

Monique A. R. Udell, Ph.D.
Assistant Professor of Animal Sciences, Oregon State University

palgrave
macmillan

First edition published 2001
Second edition published 2013 by
PALGRAVE MACMILLAN

100807295

Palgrave Macmillan in the UK is an imprint of Macmillan Publishers Limited,
registered in England, company number 785998, of 4 Crinan Street,
London N1 9XW.

Palgrave® and Macmillan® are registered trademarks in the United States,
the United Kingdom, Europe and other countries

ISBN: 978–0–230–29422–6 hardback
ISBN: 978–0–230–29423–3 paperback

This book is printed on paper suitable for recycling and made from fully
managed and sustained forest sources. Logging, pulping and manufacturing
processes are expected to conform to the environmental regulations of the
country of origin.

A catalogue record for this book is available from the British Library.

A catalog record for this book is available from the Library of Congress.

For my mother, and in memory of my father
– Clive D. L. Wynne

For my parents, and my husband Chet
– Monique A. R. Udell

Contents

List of Figures

Preface to the Second Edition

It has been over a decade since the first edition of *Animal Cognition* appeared, and a lot has happened in the sciences of animal behavior and cognition in that time. Ten years ago, nobody guessed that a dog would be found that knew the names of over a thousand objects (meet Chaser in Chapter 12) or that a crow would be found on a South Pacific island that could create tools out of pieces of wire (meet Betty in Chapter 6). Some people might have suspected that evidence of culture would be found in chimpanzees (see Chapter 9) and that pigeons would show that they can generalize from experience of pictures of people with no heads to pictures of heads without bodies (Chapter 3) – these latter two discoveries may not be as surprising, but they are nonetheless fascinating. The 2000s were a busy decade for animal cognition, and a new edition was overdue.

In addition to a general updating to reflect advances in the field, this new edition of *Animal Cognition* also makes a few other changes. This edition has a new subtitle: *Evolution, Behavior and Cognition*. The original subtitle (*The Mental Lives of Animals*) suggested a sympathy with mentalistic accounts of animal cognition that does not accurately reflect the authors' views. The new subtitle aims to be more descriptive and give prospective readers a better idea of what to expect in these pages. This new edition also introduces a new type of box in each content chapter – Focus on the data. This addition is our compromise between the desire for a flowing text that is easy to read and a suitable emphasis on the importance of data in the science of animal cognition. It is, after all, the collection of empirical data that makes the difference between a science of animal cognition and the collection of subjective impressions about animals.

The most significant innovation in this new edition is the introduction of a coauthor, Monique Udell, to the project started by Clive Wynne. The addition of a second author ensured that the new edition could be completed in a timely fashion, even though the text is now enlarged by the addition of four new chapters. The new edition's 13 chapters enable it to fit better into a semester rather than a trimester – which was the system Clive was teaching under when the first edition was written.

The addition of a new author brought with it a dilemma: how to deal with first-person anecdotes. Sybille (mentioned in several chapters) was Clive's cat, not Monique's. The pet ferrets in Chapter 7 are Monique's, not Clive's. Because these and other anecdotes belong to only one of us, we decided not to switch to the plural pronoun 'we' in telling them, and having made that decision, we thought it would sound strange if we used plural pronouns in other contexts. Therefore, with the exception of situations where we mean to include the reader in our purview, we have stuck to the singular personal pronoun 'I'. If a reader would like to know whose pets are whose and which of us had which of the experiences described in this book, he or she only needs to ask us.

The preface for the first edition of this book stated the aims of that volume, aims that remain true in this new edition:

> This book wants to convert you to a different way of looking at animals. It wants you to be amazed at what animals can do – but amazed with a critical glint in your eye. This book wants to convince more people to find out what makes animals tick.
>
> If you have an interest in animal cognition but have not studied animal behavior before, then this book is for you. You may be studying psychology and wondering how much of our human cognition is shared by other species. Or you may be studying biology and wondering how complex animal behavior can get. Or you may just be curious about the animals you see around you or hear about through TV documentaries. Though I have assumed no specific prior knowledge of psychology or biology, the tone I have adopted is a somewhat critical one. I think the truth about animal minds is interesting enough without having to embellish it with fanciful stories that are unlikely to stand closer scrutiny.

Some other points made in the preface to the earlier edition remain valid here. This book is intended as a text for students in the first three years of undergraduate degrees. It can function as a stand-alone text for a class on animal cognition – probably with the inclusion of some of the papers listed as further reading. It can also serve as a component of a broader class, perhaps entitled 'Animal Learning and Cognition', 'Animal Behavior and Cognition', or 'Comparative Psychology'. More advanced students can use the chapters of this book as springing-off points to pursue the topics covered here in the primary research literature.

Finally, it is our pleasure to acknowledge the help of those who have made this book possible. We thank three anonymous reviewers who read the whole book in draft form and made highly constructive comments. Our thanks also to Paul Stevens and Jenny Hindley at Palgrave Macmillan, who shepherded the book so skillfully. Of course, responsibility for the errors that remain rests with us.

Clive D. L. Wynne
Arizona State University, Arizona
and
Monique A. R. Udell
Oregon State University, Corvallis, Oregon

Acknowledgements

Figure 1.1 Reprinted courtesy of Kai Lindstrom.

Figure 2.2 Copyright (1976) APA, reprinted with permission from Delius, J. D., Perchard, R. J., & Emmerton, J. (1976). Polarized light discrimination by pigeons and an electroretinographic correlate. *Journal of Comparative and Physiological Psychology*, 90, 560–571.

Figure 2.3 Copyright (1998) Springer and the Psychonomic Society with kind permission from Springer Science and Business Media, Reid, S. L., & Spetch, M. L. (1998). Perception of pictorial depth cues by pigeons. *Psychonomic Bulletin and Review*, 5, 698–704, figure 1.

Figure 2.4 Reprinted courtesy of Robert Cook.

Figure 2.5 Reprinted courtesy of Marcia Spetch.

Figure 2.6 Copyright (2008) National Academy of Sciences, U.S.A., from Begall, S., Cerveny, J., Neef, J., Vojtech, O., & Burda, H. (2008). Magnetic alignment in grazing and resting cattle and deer. *Proceedings of the National Academy of Sciences of the United States*, 105(36), 13451–13455.

Figure 2.7 Reprinted courtesy of Gerhard von der Emde.

Figure 3.1 Reprinted courtesy of Peter A. de Villiers.

Figure 3.2 Copyright (1988) APA, reprinted with permission from Bhatt, R. S., Wasserman, E. A., Reynolds, W. F., & Knauss, K. S. (1988). Conceptual behavior in pigeons: categorization of both familiar and novel examples from four classes of natural and artificial stimuli. *Journal of Experimental Psychology: Animal Behavior Processes*, 13, 219–234.

Figure 3.4 Reprinted courtesy of S. E. G. Lea.

Figure 3.5 Reprinted courtesy of Evelyn B. Hanggi.

Figure 3.6 Copyright (1994) APA, reprinted with permission from Gagnon, S., & Doré, F. Y. (1994). Cross-sectional study of object permanence in domestic puppies (Canis familiaris). *Journal of Comparative Psychology*, 108, 220–232.

Figure 3.7 Reprinted courtesy of Libbye Miller.

Figure 3.8 Copyright (1988) Springer and the Psychonomic Society with kind permission from Springer Science and Business Media, Wright, A. A., Cook, R. G., Rivera, J. J., Sands, S. F., & Delius, J. J. (1988) Concept learning by pigeons: matching-to-sample with trial-unique video picture stimuli. *Animal Learning and Behavior*, 16, 436–444, figure 1.

Figure 3.9 Copyright (1988) Springer and the Psychonomic Society, with kind permission from Springer Science and Business Media, Wright, A. A., Cook, R. G., Rivera, J. J., Sands, S. F., & Delius, J. J. (1988) Concept learning by pigeons: matching-to-sample with trial-unique video picture stimuli. *Animal Learning and Behavior*, 16, 436–444, figure 7.

Figure 4.1 Copyright (2006) reprinted with permission from Elsevier, Henderson, J., Hurly, T. A., Bateson, M., & Healy, S. D. (2006) Timing in free-living Rufous Hummingbirds, Selasphorusrufus. *Current Biology*, 16, 512–515.

Figures 4.4 and 4.5 Reprinted courtesy of Hank Davis.

Figure 4.6 Reprinted courtesy of Elizabeth M. Brannon.

Figure 4.7 Reprinted with permission by Taylor & Francis, Boysen, S. T. (1992) Counting as the Chimpanzee views it. In W. K. Honig, & Gregor Fetterman (Eds), *Cognition Aspects of Stimulus Control*. L. Erlbaum Associates.

Figure 4.8 Copyright (1989) APA, reprinted with permission from Boysen, S. T., & Berntson, G. G. (1989). Numerical competence in a chimpanzee (Pan troglodytes). *Journal of Comparative Psychology*, 103, 23–31.

Figure 5.11 Copyright (2009) *Society for the Experimental Analysis of Behavior, Inc.,* Dorey, N. R., Rosales-Ruiz, J., Smith, R., & Lovelace, B. (2009). Functional analysis and treatment of self-injury in a captive olive baboon. *Journal of Applied Behavior Analysis*, 42(4), 785–794, figure 2. doi:10.1901/jaba.2009.42–785.

Figure 6.1 Copyright (2012) Royal Society Publishing, reprinted with permission from Taylor, A. H., Hunt, G. R., &Gray, R. D. (2012). Context-dependent tool use in New Caledonian crows. *Biology Letters*, 8(2), 205–207.

Figure 6.2 Copyright (1925) Springer-verlag with kind permission of Springer ScienceandBusinessMedia, Kohler, W. (1925) *IntelligenzprufungenbeiMenschenaffen*, Tafel IV, figure 5, p. 96.

Figure 6.3 Reprinted courtesy of E. Visalberghi.

Figure 6.6 Reprinted courtesy of Nathan Emery.

Figure 6.7 Copyright (1981) APA, adapted with permission from Gillan, D. J., Premack, D., & Woodruff, G. (1981). Reasoning in the chimpanzee: I. Analogical reasoning. *Journal of Experimental Psychology: Animal Behavior Processes*, 7, 1–17.

Figure 7.3 Copyright (1946) APA. Reprinted with permission from Tolman, E. C., Ritchie, B. F., & Kalish, D. (1946). Studies in spatial learning. I. Orientation and the short-cut. *Journal of Experimental Psychology*, 36, 13–24.

Figure 7.4 Copyright (1987) Taylor & Francis, reprinted with permission from Chapuis, N., & Varlet, C. (1987). Short cuts by dogs in natural surroundings.

Quarterly Journal of Experimental Psychology. B, Comparative and Physiological Psychology, 39B, 49–64.

Figure 7.5 Copyright (1980) Springer. Reprinted with kind permission from Springer Science and Business Media, Wallraff, H. G. (1980) Olfaction and homing in pigeons: nerve-section experiments, critique, hypotheses. *Journal of Comparative Physiology*, 139, 209–224, figure 6: Maps showing the recovery sites-connected with the respective release site- of CPs and EPs (s > 10km). The home loft is in the center of the circle whose radius is 180 km (scale units (20 km)). The borders of the Federal Republic of Germany are indicated.

Figure 7.6 Reprinted with permission from AAAS, Baker, R. R. (1980). Goal orientation by blindfolded humans after long-distance displacement: possible involvement of a magnetic sense. *Science*, 210(4469), 555–557.

Figure 7.7 Copyright (1990) Taylor & Francis, reprinted by permission of the publisher Taylor & Francis Ltd, http://www.tandf.co.uk/journals, Wallraff, H. G. (1990). Navigation by homing pigeons. *Ethology, Ecology and Evolution*, 2, 81–115.

Figure 7.8 Copyright (1991) Elsevier, reprinted with permission from Dyer (1991). Bees acquire route-based memories but not cognitive maps in familiar landscape. *Animal Behavior*, 41, 239–246.

Figure 7.9 Reprinted with kind permission of Springer Science and Business Media, Köhler, W. (1921). *IntelligenzprüfungenbeiMenschnaffen*, Skizzen 3 and 4.

Figure 7.10 Copyright (1983) Elsevier, adapted with permission from Poucet, B., Thinus-Blanc, C., and Chapuis, N. (1983) Route planning in cats, in relation to the visibility of the goal. *Animal Behavior*, 31, 594–599.

Figure 7.11 Copyright (2012) Royal Society Publishing, reprinted from Baum, K. A., & Sharber, W. V. (2012). Fire creates host plant patches for monarch butterflies. *Biology Letters*, figure 2.

Figure 7.12 Copyright (1996) Company of Biologists Ltd, reprinted with permission from Papi, F., and Luschi, P. (1996). Pinpointing 'Isla Meta': the case of sea turtles and albatrosses. *Journal of Experimental Biology*, 199, 65–71;

Figure 8.2 Copyright (1985) APA, reprinted from Menzel, E. W., Savage-Rumbaugh, E. S., & Lawson, J. (1985). Chimpanzee (Pan troglodytes) spatial problem solving with the use of mirrors and televised equivalents of mirrors. *Journal of Comparative Psychology*, 99(2), 211–217.

Figure 8.3 Reprinted courtesy of Nathaniel Hall.

Figure 8.4 Reprinted from Trut, L. (1999). Early Canid domestication: the farm-fox experiment. *American Scientist*, 87(2), 160, figure 6. doi:10.1511/1999.2.160 (Edward Roberts)

Figure 9.3 Copyright (2003) APA, reprinted from Wrenn, C. C., Harris, A. P., Saavedra, M. C., & Crawley, J. N. (2003). Social transmission of food preference in mice: methodology and application to galanin-overexpressing transgenic mice. *Behavioral Neuroscience*, 117(1), 21–31. doi:10.1037/0735–7044.117.1.21

Figure 9.4 Reprinted courtesy of F. Kanchi.

Figure 9.6 Copyright (2005) Springer, reprinted with kind permission from Springer Science and Business Media, Horner, V., & Whiten, A. (2005). Causal knowledge and imitation/emulation switching in chimpanzees (Pan troglodytes) and children (Homo sapiens). *Animal cognition*, 8(3), 164–181, figure 3(a) Subject inserts tool into the top irrelevant hole of the opaque apparatus (b) Subject inserts tool into front relevant hole of the clear apparatus to retrieve the food reward.

Figure 9.7 Reprinted courtesy of Nicole Dorey.

Figure 10.4 Copyright (1988) Springer, reprinted with kind permission from Springer Science and Business Media, Spetch, M. L., and Honig, W. K. (1988). Characteristics of pigeons' spatial working memory in an open field task. *Animal Learning and Behavior*, 16, 123–131.

Figure 10.5 Copyright (1992) APA, reprinted from Castro, C. A., & Larsen, T. (1992). Primacy and recency effects in nonhuman primates. *Journal of Experimental Psychology: Animal Behavior Processes*, 18(4), 335–340. doi:10.1037/0097–7403.18.4.335

Figure 10.6 Copyright (1992) Taylor & Francis, reprinted with permission from Sherry, D. F. (1992) Landmarks, the hippocampus, and spatial search in food-storing birds. In W. K. Honig and J. G. Fetterman (Eds), *Cognitive Aspects of Stimulus Control* (pp. 184–201). Mahwab, NJ: Lawrence Erlbaum.

Figure 10.8 Reprinted by permission of Blackwell Wissenschafts- Verlag Berlin, GmbH from Fersen, L. von, and Delius, J. D. (1989) Long-term retention of many visual patterns by pigeons. *Ethology*, 82, 141–155, figure 2, p. 145.

Figure 11.3 Copyright (2005) Macmillan Publishers Ltd, reprinted with permission from Riley, J. R., Greggers, U., Smith, A. D., Reynolds, D. R., & Menzel, R. (2005). The flight paths of honeybees recruited by the waggle dance. *Nature*, 435, 205–207.

Figure 11.4 Reprinted with permission from John Wiley and Sons, Konishi, M. (1965). The role of auditory feedback in the control of vocalization in the White Crowned Sparrow. *Ethology*, 770–783, Blackwell Verlag GmbH.

Figure 11.5 Copyright (1994) Elsevier and the Animal Behavior Society, reprinted with permission from Evans, C. S., & Marler, P. (1994). Food calling and audience effects in male chickens, Gallus gallus: their relationships to food availability, courtship and social facilitation. *Animal Behaviour*, 47, 1159–1170.

Figure 12.1 Reprinted courtesy of Herbert Terrace.

Figure 12.2 Reprinted courtesy of D. Rumbaugh.

Figure 12.4 Reprinted courtesy of Robin Pilley.

Figure 12.6 Reprinted from Pilley, J., & Reid, A. (2011). Border collie comprehends object names as verbal referents. *Behavioural Processes*, 86(2), 184–195.

Figure 12.7 Copyright (1984) Elsevier, reprinted with permission from Herman,
L. M., Richards, D. G., & Wolz, J. P. (1984). Comprehension of sentences by bottlenosed dolphins. *Cognition*, 16, 129–219.

Figure 13.1 Reprinted with permission from Elsevier, Jerison, H. (1973). *Evolution
of the Brain and Intelligence*.

Figure 13.4 Reprinted with permission of the Zoological Society of London.

Author Biographies

Clive Wynne, Ph.D., is Professor of Psychology at the Arizona State University. In addition, he is Research Director at Wolf Park in Indiana. In recent years, Clive's research interests have focused on dogs and their wild relatives, but over the last 30 years he has studied the behavior of animals ranging from pigeons to dunnarts (a mouse-sized marsupial) and from bats to Galápagos tortoises. He received his Ph.D. from the University of Edinburgh. Always fascinated by the things animals do, in recent years he has developed an additional interest in how people relate to animals. When not working, he talks to his dog – even though research from his own lab suggests dogs are quite indifferent to what people say to them.

Monique Udell, Ph.D., is an Assistant Professor of Animal Sciences at Oregon State University. She has a special interest in the role of experience and environment in the development of cross-species interactions and bonds, including those between humans and domestic dogs. She also investigates how animal cognition and behavior are influenced by the unique evolutionary and lifetime histories of individuals and species. Dr. Udell received her Ph.D. in Psychology from the University of Florida. Her work on the social cognition of dogs and wolves has resulted in numerous scientific publications as well as national and international speaking opportunities. In her spare time she can be found exploring the diverse terrain of Oregon with her husband and border collie.

1 Evolution, Adaptation, Cognition, and Behavior: An Introduction

Let man visit Ourang-outang in domestication, hear expressive whine, see its intel-ligence when spoken; as if it understood every word said – see its affection – to those it knew – see its passion and rage, sulkiness, and very actions of despair; and then let him dare to boast of his proud pre-eminence.

Charles Darwin, Notebook C, p. 79, 1987

We live with animals[1] – we always have, and we probably always will. As a city dweller at the start of the twenty-first century, I share my home with a dog (elegant and loving), a cat (sweet and cuddly), occasional mice (shy and fast), regular spiders (unsettling but harmless), cockroaches (I don't want to think about), and many other smaller hopping, scurrying, and biting things. Farmers and agriculturists over the last few thousand years have lived with many large domesticated mammals and a few birds. Before agriculture, humans hunted and were in their turn preyed upon by the various beasts that surrounded them. No matter our attitude toward animals, they are always among us.

But what are we to make of them? Do they think? Do they have minds? Are they conscious? What is it like to be a bat (as the philosopher Thomas Nagel famously asked in 1974)? Or a cat? Or an ant? Going back as far as records can show, people have treated animals as if they were people. Simple people, per-haps, but people nonetheless. This tendency to view animals as people is called *anthropomorphism* (from the Greek *anthropos*, human, and *morph*, form), and it seems to be an ancient and irresistible urge. Some of the earliest artworks in the world – paintings on the walls of caves in southern France that date back 30,000 years – depict human bodies with an animal head, suggesting that the people of those times viewed animals as having human-like qualities. I defy anyone, no matter how hard-nosed, not to adopt an attitude to my cat, Sybille, that involves treating her as a small child. I believe I could write a computer program (and not a very long program at that) that could convincingly simu-late Sybille's behavior (to be called SimSybille), and yet I could never for one moment treat her with the same attitude I adopt towards a computer. The tug of anthropomorphism is just too strong.

1

Anthropomorphism, then, is our most natural, spontaneous, and everyday way of considering animals. And yet anyone who has ever observed and reflected on the behavior of an animal for a little while knows this cannot be right. Animals are not little people. Sybille is not a baby; a dog with a gray beard is not a wise old man (or even a foolish old man). It may be emotionally satisfying to treat them that way, but we know it cannot be true. Cats and dogs and all other animals have their own mental lives to lead. In the case of domesticated species, these may overlap quite satisfactorily with the roles we have created for them, but reflection tells us naive anthropomorphism must be wrong. We must consider the psychology of animals in their own right. Box 1.1 considers one example of anthropomorphic projection onto animal behavior: the case of sexual pleasure.

BOX 1.1   THE POPULAR VIEW OF ANIMALS

The other day, a friend came to me with a story he had read in the newspaper. Dolphins, chimpanzees, and humans are the only species to indulge in sexual activity solely for pleasure, not for procreation, said the newspaper report. Had I heard of this, my friend wanted to know, and was it true? As so often, I was astonished at the absurdity of the popular presentation of animal minds. What does it mean to say that some species indulge in sex for recreation not procreation? It would seem to imply that all the other species of animals on this planet engage in sexual activity only when they want to have offspring – that they know the connection between sex and pregnancy – surely a wildly improbable conjecture.

What is known of sexual activity among dolphins? In bottlenose dolphins, male groups of typically two or three individuals harass groups of females and young until they can separate a female from the group. They then keep this female captive, taking it in turns to have sex with her over a period of several days or weeks. In an in-depth study of 255 cases of dolphin mating behavior in Western Australia, Richard Connor and colleagues (1996) reported that 82 percent of these involved coercion on the part of the male dolphins. Of the remaining 18 percent they could not be certain; some coercion may have taken place beneath the water's surface where they could not see it.

It would be anthropomorphic to claim that female dolphins do *not* experience pleasure in sex under these circumstances just because human females would not, but Connor and colleagues' results do not encourage the belief that female dolphins are uniquely privileged in terms of their opportunities for sexual pleasure.

When we look at animals, having recognized that they are not people, we still can't help seeing them from our human perspective – this is called anthropocentrism. Just as tourists visiting a new country make the foreign more manageable by making comparisons with home, so, in considering animal psychology, we inevitably start with our human minds and compare what animals do with what we do. Are they intelligent or conscious? Do they think or feel? All these are anthropocentric questions. We know we are intelligent and conscious, and we think and feel; therefore we ask whether other species share these states. Anthropocentrism is a more subtle problem than anthropomorphism. Since we are human, we can probably never be entirely free from anthropocentrism. But just as astronomers gradually came to recognize that Earth is not at the center of the solar system and developed a cosmology that places our planet appropriately, at a particular point in the solar system in a certain galaxy, so we may hope that we can develop an animal psychology that moves humans from the central position and that sees each species as at the center of its own world.

ON MINDS, THOUGHT, AND INTELLIGENCE IN ANIMALS

So what of 'minds', 'mental life', 'thought', and 'intelligence'? Are these anthropocentric terms, to be avoided by a mature animal psychology? That depends on what these words mean. If by 'mind' you mean something different from your body, something like a nonphysical soul in which your intimate essence resides even beyond the death of your body, then the question of whether animals can have minds becomes one for your spiritual adviser, not an animal psychologist. In this book, however, I use the terms 'mind' and 'mental life' in a more down to earth manner. Here they refer simply to the totality of the behavior of an animal and the operations it performs to create those behaviors. That includes perception: seeing, hearing, and senses we do not share (like the magnetic sense of pigeons); simple behaviors (like having a sense of when dinner is coming); through to the most complex cognitions, such as what psychologists call 'theory of mind' – an individual's understanding that other beings have minds, too.

I am less convinced that the term 'thought' can be made to do useful work for a modern animal psychology. Though others who have considered this question disagree (e.g., Marc Hauser, 2000), to me 'thought' implies language. Though there are certainly mental operations that do not involve language, I would not consider these as thought. Furthermore, my assessment of the attempts to teach language to apes is that this enterprise has been unsuccessful (see Chapter 12). Consequently, I do not believe that animals think in the way we mean that word when we apply it to members of our own species. It is in my view unhelpful anthropocentrism, verging on anthropomorphism, to talk of thought in nonhumans. Talking about 'thinking' animals tricks us into believing we understand animal mental life better than we really do. (For more of my views on animal thinking, see Wynne, 2004).

'Intelligence' is another problematic term for animal psychology. Even in our own species, arguments rage over what constitutes intelligence, where it comes from, and how to measure it. But even if we accept that, for humans, there exists a package of problem-solving skills that can be effectively measured and labeled 'intelligence', it is not clear what this means for nonhumans. Talk of intelligence is often linked to attempts to form a single scale of intelligence, with some species at the top (humans, inevitably) and others at the bottom (marsupials, perhaps, or insects). Modern comparative psychologists take the more Darwinian view that each species has its own problems to solve and has therefore evolved its own skills to solve them. All the species that we see around us today have evolved for exactly the same length of time, and each has adapted to a unique niche. As we shall see in the chapters that follow, different niches make different demands on their occupants, and these include different cognitive demands.

To take an example from the Australian bush, are rabbits more intelligent than wallabies because they are smarter at evading foxes? A fox is a very unfair challenge to a wallaby. Australian marsupials have had only 200 years to try and figure out how to evade foxes, after millions of years adapting to the challenges of a climate that, though often harsh and very dry, was without foxlike creatures. Should we call the wallaby smarter than the rabbit because it can go longer without water and feed on dryer foods?

However, so long as we stay away from attempts to rank-order the intelligence of different species, the term might still be a useful one. Used carefully, as a shorthand term meaning 'wide ranging problem-solving abilities', intelligence seems like a very natural way of describing an important aspect of behavior.

Finally, what about 'cognition' – what does that term mean? In this text, 'animal cognition' simply means the full richness and complexity of animal behavior. To many psychologists, 'cognition' implies behavior driven by internal representations of the world. I prefer to remain agnostic on the question of internal representations because I believe that seeking simple parsimonious explanations is central to the scientific approach. That means that I look for ways of explaining complex behavior in terms of the simplest possible behavioral rules. This is particularly apparent in Chapter 6 of the present text, where I consider animal reasoning. But even if it can be demonstrated that a particular, apparently complex, behavior can be explained with simple behavioral rules, I still believe it is reasonable to call that behavior cognitive. Therefore, 'cognition' will not be defined here in a way that demands the involvement of internal representations.

HISTORICAL BACKGROUND: DARWIN, WALLACE, AND THE MINDS OF BEASTS

Though, as we have seen above, an interest in the behavior of animals is evident in the earliest human artworks, the modern study of animal behavior began with Charles Darwin and his theory of evolution (1859). Darwin's originality lay not so much in arguing that all living things had evolved from earlier forms – others, including his own grandfather Erasmus Darwin, had suggested as much before. Darwin's breakthrough was to propose a plausible mechanism for how such evolution could have taken place. In each generation, Darwin observed, more young are born than can survive to have offspring of their own. These young are very variable – they are not simple clones of their parents. Inevitably, some of the offspring vary in ways that make them more or less likely to survive and have young of their own. In modern terms, they vary in fitness. Darwin reasoned that if some of the qualities that make some individuals better able to have offspring are inherited, then we have a mechanism for evolution. Those individuals with higher fitness will tend to leave the most offspring, and consequently the species will change to contain more fit individuals. Of course, just as in any game of chance, the environmental conditions can change abruptly so that those who were previously less fit suddenly find themselves better suited to the environment. But, on average, over long periods of time natural selection ensures that the most fit organisms survive and have young.

In general, we can say that the Darwinian mechanism for evolution is a process of variation (many different offspring are born), selection (some of these offspring survive to have young of their own), and variation again (the survivors from one generation are the parents of the next). The outcome of this process is a species continually improving its suitability to the environment around it. This suitability is technically known as 'adaptation', and it is a central tenant of modern biology that organisms are adapted to their environments. Box 1.2 explores the power of the adaptionist approach to animal behavior.

BOX 1.2   CAN IT BE RIGHT TO EAT YOUR OWN YOUNG?

The power of a scientific approach lies not just in explaining the obvious cases but in dealing with situations that at first blush seem impossible for a theory to account for.

The cornerstone of the adaptive approach to animal behavior is that animals act to perpetuate their genes into future generations. Broadly speaking, they do this by ensuring their own survival so that they can find mates and then by rearing their offspring. The amount of energy different species put into different aspects of this project vary greatly, but the theme is clear – animals strive to get their genes into future generations.

The real test of this theory lies in trying to explain situations where an animal seems to act to *prevent* its genes from passing forward into future generations.

One especially challenging case is that of animals that, far from caring for their young, actually eat their own offspring. The technical name for this phenomenon is filial cannibalism, and it is quite widespread in the animal kingdom. Filial cannibalism has been observed in a number of species, including hamsters, cats, dolphins – and several species of fish. Eating one's own young happens often enough that it cannot simply be dismissed as some kind of rare and anomalous behavior, and it does not just involve the eating of already dead or perhaps diseased offspring.

How might an adaptive approach account for such a strange course of action by such diverse animals?

Figure 1.1   *Sand goby*

Source: Courtesy of Kai Lindstrom.

Hope Klug and colleagues (2006) made a detailed study of the reasons why the sand goby, a small sandy-colored fish that lives in European waters from the Baltic to the Mediterranean, eats its own eggs (Figure 1.1). In sand gobies it is the males that care for the eggs.

How might eating one's eggs leave a father fish with a net adaptive benefit? There are several possibilities: Perhaps the energy gained by eating the eggs could aid future survival or reproduction; perhaps the fish eat inferior eggs and will invest the energy they gain in the upkeep of superior eggs; or perhaps the parents weed out slower-developing young and thereby give themselves time to have another clutch of eggs before the breeding season is over.

Klug and colleagues (2006) tested one hypothesis: an excessive density of eggs leads to such a high rate of egg death that eating some – and thereby reducing the density – actually enables more eggs to survive. Klug and colleagues found that the father fish did indeed eat more of their young if the eggs were packed in a high density rather than a low density. This effect was strongest when there was a lack of oxygen in the water. In another experiment they simulated the impact of cannibalism by removing some of the eggs themselves so that they could see whether it was really the case that if some of the eggs were removed, the total number surviving would increase or at least not decrease. This was indeed what they found – again especially under conditions of low oxygen in the water. Overall, then, Klug and colleagues were able to demonstrate that by removing some of their eggs, father fish were able to obtain an energetic benefit for themselves with no decrease in the number of their offspring that survived.

From the beginning, Darwin believed that behavior and psychology were part of the evolutionary process too. He expanded on these thoughts in his private notebooks and letters (see Box 1.3), in *The Expression of the Emotions in Man and Animals* (1872), and in *The Descent of Man, and Selection in Relation to Sex* (1877). What struck Darwin were the commonalties between human and nonhuman psychology. In his private notebooks he allowed his feelings to show more than in the works he prepared for publication. The quote at the start of this chapter shows how impressed Darwin was by the human-like behaviors of the first orangutan displayed at the London zoo.

Darwin's proposal of a plausible mechanism for evolution, his detailed analysis of how evolution could account for the then-known facts of biology, and his belief that human psychology was also an evolved trait in which some commonalities with other species could be expected combined to launch a new science of comparative psychology, 'comparative' here meaning the comparison of different species.

One of the first to pick up the challenge of studying the psychology of nonhuman animals from a Darwinian evolutionary perspective was one of Darwin's closest followers, George Romanes. Unfortunately, rather than develop controlled ways to study animal behavior, Romanes relied on anecdotes collected from others' observations. Where Darwin was a masterful compiler of observations from correspondents all around the world, Romanes was far more gullible. At the start of his 1884 book, *Animal Intelligence*, Romanes described how he had considered restricting himself only to anecdotes about animal intelligence that had been recorded by 'observers well known as competent'. This essential constraint, however, he dismissed as too limiting; 'I usually found', Romanes continued, 'that the most remarkable instances of the display of intelligence were recorded by persons bearing names more or less unknown to fame.'

Not surprisingly, Romanes's claims of fellow feeling among ants, fetishism in dogs, and intelligence throughout the animal kingdom raised hackles among his more careful contemporaries. In 1894 another early British animal psychologist, Conwy Lloyd Morgan, published his *Introduction to Comparative Psychology*. In it, Lloyd Morgan dismissed Romanes's over vivid interpretations and argued for more careful interpretations of animal behavior. It fell to an American, however, Edward Thorndike, in his 1898 volume, *Animal Intelligence: An Experimental Study of the Associative Process in Animals,* to introduce the experimental method into the study of animal psychology. Just two years before the start of the twentieth century, with the introduction of experimental rigor, animal psychology became a science.

BOX 1.3   CHARLES DARWIN, ALFRED RUSSEL WALLACE, AND MENTAL CONTINUITY

Darwin would never have thrived in the 'publish or perish' atmosphere of contemporary academia. Between his first sketch of the theory of evolution by natural selection in 1842 and the publication of *On the Origin of Species* in 1859 lies a gap of 17 years (Brown, 2003). In that time, Darwin disclosed his theory to only a handful of his closest confidants. Historians wonder when Darwin would finally have found the courage to publish his theory had it not been for a letter he received from another biologist and explorer, Alfred Russel Wallace, in 1858. Wallace was recovering from malaria in the Spice Islands in Indonesia when the idea of evolution by natural selection came to him. He immediately wrote Darwin, who was stunned by the similarities between his own theory and Wallace's and overcome with anxiety as to how to deal with the difficulty he now faced. How could Darwin be fair to Wallace and yet maintain his own position as the originator of the theory of natural selection? Two of Darwin's friends, to whom he had shown earlier drafts of his theory, proposed that Darwin and Wallace jointly present their theory to a scientific society in London. This was done; though neither Darwin nor Wallace was present in person at the meeting: Wallace was still overseas, and Darwin was mourning the loss of a son to scarlet fever.

In most accounts of the origin of the theory of evolution by natural selection, this is where Alfred Russel Wallace disappears from the story. It is less widely known that in at least one crucial respect Darwin and Wallace differed in their thoughts on evolution. Darwin, as the quote from his notebooks at the beginning of this chapter makes clear, believed that the theory of evolution by natural selection applied to humans. And not just to our physical characters, but to our thoughts and feelings as well: to our minds. Wallace on the other hand drew a line at humanity. He wrote:

Neither natural selection nor the more general theory of evolution can give any account whatever of the origin of sensational or conscious life. The moral and higher intellectual nature of man is as unique a phenomenon as was conscious life on its first appearance in the world, and the one is almost as difficult to conceive as originating by any law of evolution as the other.

Wallace, 1869, p. 391

We know that Darwin disagreed with this statement because the letter he wrote to Wallace to say so has survived:

If you had not told me I should have thought that they [Wallace's remarks on the evolution of the human mind] had been added by someone else. As you expected, I differ grievously from you, and am very sorry for it. I can see no necessity for calling in an additional and proximate cause in regard to Man.

Darwin, in Marchant, J. (1975), Vol. 1, p. 243

Wallace's position that the theory of evolution can tell us nothing about the interesting psychological qualities that human beings have is the dominant position among academic psychologists and lay people today. Take, for example, this introductory statement from a textbook on cognitive psychology:

Whenever higher mental processes are involved, we heartily disagree that human and animal behaviour are necessarily governed by the same principles.

> We regard the human as a specialized product of evolution, as an animal whose cognition is also specialized.
>
> Lachman, Lachman & Butterfield, 1979, p. 42,
> cited in Wasserman, 1993

This was not Darwin's view, and it is not the view we will be pursuing here. The evidence gathered in this book indicates that the mind has evolved and is evolving. Sure enough, there are differences between the minds of humans and those of other animals – just as there are differences between the mind of the mother digger wasp that supplies her eggs with a stunned, but not dead, cricket for them to feed on once they hatch and the mind of the pigeon that finds its way home after a displacement of hundreds of miles from its home loft. There are differences between the minds of different species, just as there are differences between the heads, arms, and feet of different species. But the minds of animals, just like their bodies, are adapted to the environments in which they live. Minds, just like bodies, are the product of evolution by natural selection.

The story of animal psychology in the twentieth century can be told in two parts. For the first half of the century, psychologists in the English-speaking countries developed the laboratory experimental method for studying animal behavior that had originated with Thorndike. They took a particular interest in the kinds of animal cognition covered in Chapter 5 – learning about cause and effect. They found that many species' abilities in this domain were remarkably similar, and so they concentrated on a limited number of species that were easy to work with, particularly rats and pigeons. It was during this period that behaviorism came to the fore. Behaviorists believe that a science of psychology must confine itself to the study of the only thing that can be observed – behavior. Some behaviorists go farther and prohibit all forms of speculation about anything other than observable behavior, thereby excluding from consideration even concepts such as 'memory' or 'attention'. Meanwhile, especially in continental Europe, other scientists were taking an interest in more complex behaviors such as counting (Chapter 4) and reasoning (Chapter 6). In addition, it was particularly the Europeans who developed an interest in studying animal behavior in the wild. Strong fieldwork-based traditions developed in Germany, Austria, and the Netherlands. It was through this tradition that great discoveries were made, such as the dance language by which honeybees communicate the locations of good sources of nectar to each other (Chapter 11). The Europeans' interest in complex behaviors and field studies led to an emphasis on the variety of behavior in different species and a diversity of theoretical approaches. The school of animal psychology that grew out of the fieldwork tradition is known as ethology.

One of the most important insights to come out of ethology are four questions proposed by founder ethologist Niko Tinbergen in 1963. Tinbergen (1907–1988) was a Dutch behavioral biologist who moved to the University of Oxford in England after the Second World War. From there he played a pivotal role in defining the discipline of ethology and disseminating it to the English-speaking world. Tinbergen's insight was recognizing that there are several directions from which behavior must be studied if it is to be fully understood. Specifically, Tinbergen identified four different questions that must be asked and answered about behavior for a complete explanation.

The first is the function of a behavior. Function is meant here in an evolutionary sense as a consideration of the adaptive purpose of behavior. Often the adaptive advantage of a behavior is straightforward, as when a mother wolf suckles her young. But in other cases the function of a behavior in preserving an animal and its offspring may be difficult to uncover. The example of fish that eat their own eggs, described in Box 1.2, is one that was particularly difficult to understand from a functional perspective.

Tinbergen's second question is the evolution – technically 'phylogeny' – of behavior. That is to say, how does the behavior vary among more or less related species? This can help us to understand how the behavior evolved.

The third of Tinbergen's questions concerns the development of behavior in an individual's lifetime – technically 'ontogeny'. This includes consideration of the conditions in early life that are necessary for a behavior to develop and how the behavior changes as the animal ages. It also includes a consideration of learning, such as the learning about cause and effect (considered in Chapter 5) and reasoning (Chapter 6).

Finally, Tinbergen insisted that behavioral scientists must consider mechanism – how a behavior is caused in an animal's brain and how it is caused by its ability to learn from experience.

Few behavioral scientists can claim to address all four of Tinbergen's questions at any one time but an awareness that behavior is a function of multiple levels of causation and that we should not lose sight of any them is a powerful legacy of this original thinker.

The development of animal psychology in the second half of the twentieth century is a story of an opening of communication between the two originally distinct traditions. Behaviorism lost its preeminent position in animal psychology in the 1960s. Scientists studying animal behavior in laboratories in the English-speaking countries began to absorb the more biologically informed views of their continental cousins. Around this time cognitive psychology began to take center stage from behaviorism. The rise of a cognitive approach freed animal psychologists from a concern mainly with learning (in the sense of learning about cause and effect, as in Chapter 5) and enabled them to study a much wider range of phenomena.

Many who work in animal cognition feel the need to line up with one school of animal psychology or another. They may be behaviorists, who disparage the wild speculations of those who call themselves cognitive psychologists or object to the relative lack of control in most field studies carried out by ethologists. Or they may be cognitive psychologists, who criticize behaviorists for not permitting themselves to look at the more interesting and complex aspects of animal behavior. For their part, ethologists sometimes argue as though only their work, because it observes animals in their natural habitats, can be considered to be the 'true' science of animal psychology. But science is not sports. We do not have to cheer for one team or another. On the contrary, this tribal attitude is quite antithetical to a scientific frame of mind. Since the purpose of this book is to come to a well-rounded appreciation of the minds of animals, I borrow what I find useful from all three schools of animal psychology. From the behaviorists, I take a concern with finding watertight experimental designs and an impatience with unnecessarily complex explanations. From the cognitive psychologists, I take a willingness to consider very complex behaviors as part of my field of interest. Finally, the ethologists make me aware that behavior is part of a toolkit of adaptations that animals use in the wild in the daily struggle for survival.

A CAUTIONARY TALE AND A CANON

Clever Hans: the horse with the intelligence of a 14-year-old child

Clever Hans was a horse who lived in Germany at the end of the nineteenth century. Hans's trainer was a schoolteacher, Mr. von Osten. Under von Osten's tutelage, Hans was able to answer a great variety of questions put to him by von Osten and other interested people. Hans was most famous for his ability to answer arithmetical questions. By stomping his foot the appropriate number of times, Hans was able to answer questions involving addition, subtraction, multiplication, and division, with both integers and fractions. Asked, for example, 'what is 2/5 plus ½?', Hans stomped his foot 9 times, followed after a pause by 10, to indicate 9/10. Hans's mathematical abilities went beyond simple arithmetic to include calendar reckoning ('If the eighth day of a month comes on Tuesday, what is the date for the following Friday?') and clock reckoning ('How many minutes has the large hand to travel between seven minutes after a quarter past the hour and three quarters past?'), and he could also answer questions requiring words as answers, such as 'What is this lady holding in her hand?' and 'What does this picture represent?' Hans provided word answers by reference to a table of letters. In this table, each letter of the alphabet could be identified by Hans stomping his foot the requisite number of times to indicate the column and row of the letter required. Clever Hans, Mr. von Osten, and the table of letters are shown in Figure 1.2.

Hans was no fairground spectacle trained for profit to hoodwink the unwary. A group of experts called on the schoolteacher von Osten and his horse, put them through their paces, and declared there was no trickery involved – Hans the horse had the intelligence of a 13- or 14-year-old child. This committee of

Figure 1.2   *Clever Hans with his trainer Mr. von Osten*

Notes: Examples of the kinds of arithmetic problems Hans could solve are shown on the small board in the bottom left corner. The larger board behind it is the table of letters of the alphabet Hans used to answer questions requiring a word answer.
Source: Pfungst (1911/1965).

experts included an African explorer, the director of the Hannover zoo, the leading psychologist of the day (Professor Stumpf of the University of Berlin), and two experts on horses from the Prussian cavalry. All were convinced of the horse's ability to count and solve arithmetical problems. Professor Stumpf was interviewed in the newspaper:

> Concerning the question whether the horse was given some sort of aid, Prof. Stumpf expressed himself freely. He said: 'We were careful to state in our report that the intentional use of the means of training, on the part of the horse's teacher, is out of the question, ... nor are there involved any of the known kinds of unconscious, involuntary aids'.
>
> Frankfurter Zeitung, Sept. 22, 1904

Despite the unanimous acclamation of this committee of experts, some were still suspicious. Oskar Pfungst, a research student with Stumpf, decided to make a detailed study of Hans and his trainer. Pretty soon, Pfungst began to notice some strange aspects of Hans's performances. For one thing, although Hans could answer questions put to him by many different people (which was one of the aspects of Hans's performance that had convinced the commission that his feats were genuine), he could do so only if that person already knew the answer and if the person putting the question was visible to him. Pfungst put von Osten in a tent to question Hans, and Hans's performance collapsed. These observations led Pfungst to the idea that the horse was relying on visual cues from his interrogator. Careful investigation of the behavior of the person testing Hans led Pfungst to this conclusion:

> As soon as the experimenter had given a problem to the horse, he, involuntarily, bent his head and trunk slightly forward and the horse would then put the right foot forward and begin to tap, without, however, returning it each time to its original position. As soon as the desired number of taps was given, the questioner would make a slight upward jerk of the head. Thereupon the horse would immediately swing his foot in a wide circle, bringing it back to its original position.
>
> Pfungst, 1911/1965, p. 47

The crucial detail here is the 'involuntarily' in the first sentence. It is not surprising or remarkable that a horse could be trained to tap his foot in response to very slight movements on the part of the questioner – circus animals are routinely trained in this way. What is remarkable and important about Hans is that there was no suggestion that von Osten knew he was making these signals, nor did the many other people who questioned Hans successfully. The horse was picking up on very slight movements of the head that his questioners did not even realize they were making.

The involuntary, unconscious nature of the signals that Hans's questioners gave the horse is very important for two reasons. First, it shows that Hans really was very clever – just not clever in the way von Osten believed. Hans's ingenuity lay not in understanding arithmetic, spelling, the calendar, and so forth but in an astonishingly acute eye for the body language of the people around him. Who would have guessed that the way one nods one's head gently while watching a horse tap its foot could be used by that animal to guess how many taps are required? This was indeed a clever horse. The second reason that what has become known as the 'Clever Hans Phenomenon' is important to anyone interested in animal cognition is what it implies about studying animals. Whenever a human experimenter gets together with an animal subject to test some aspect of that animal's cognition, steps must be taken to ensure that the animal does not have the opportunity to pick up on signals that the experimenter gives off unintentionally. It is not enough for the experimenter to go into the experiment with the honest intention of not giving any signals – the story of clever Hans tells us that for a signal to be picked up on by an animal, it is not necessary that the experimenter intend to give this signal or even know he is giving it. The only conditions where we can be certain that unintentional cueing is ruled out are where the experimenter cannot be seen (or heard, or picked up in any other way) by the subject and where the experimenter does not know the correct answer. Nowadays, these conditions are usually built into the critical tests in any experiment, but this cannot simply be assumed, and it is always important to check.

Lloyd Morgan's canon: the most awesome weapon in animal psychology

Conwy Lloyd Morgan published his *Introduction to Comparative Psychology* in 1894 in response to Romanes's *Animal Intelligence* of ten years earlier. Morgan was concerned that Romanes's rich interpretation of fanciful anecdotes was getting the fledgling science of comparative psychology off to a bad start. For one thing, no science can be based on facts that are unreliable. Furthermore, it is a principle of science that simpler explanations are always preferred to more complex ones. The reason for this is that an unlimited number of more complex explanations always exist for any observation. The trick is to find the most parsimonious explanation for what we see – the one based on the fewest principles. It may seem easier at first to use richer, more complex explanations for what animals do. However, if these turn out to be red herrings, so much time will have been lost. It is far better in the long run to be safe, secure, plodding, and confident that the knowledge we have amassed so far is reliable.

> In no case may we interpret an action as the outcome of the exercise of a higher psychical faculty, if it can be interpreted as the outcome of the exercise of one which stands lower in the psychological scale.
>
> Morgan, 1894, p. 53

This statement has become known as Lloyd Morgan's canon or principle. It is certainly not without problems of its own. How, for example, can we tell what is a 'higher psychical faculty' and one 'lower in the psychological scale'? The whole notion of a psychological scale is now considered outdated. Nonetheless, if we take Lloyd Morgan to be saying that we should not get carried away with what look superficially like astonishing animal performances but experiment carefully to find the quite possibly simple explanation underlying the behavior, then his canon can continue to do useful work in comparative psychology.

NOW AND THE FUTURE

As Thorndike complained over a century ago, if one poor dog finds its way home from twenty or thirty miles away, you can be sure that the story will be all over the papers and the evening news. Every weekend pigeon fanciers release thousands of pigeons over much greater distances, the majority find their way home, and nobody sees any need to comment on it. Stories about animals in the media emphasize the improbable, the rare, and the downright untrue. And yet, as I hope this book will show, the truth is often far stranger than fiction. The amazing skills pigeons use to find their way home are just one example of that.

Animal cognition – the study of the mental lives of animals – is a very new science. Unlike the older sciences, there is no great mass of accepted fact through which a student must wade before she can hope to make a novel contribution. There is no reason why any reader of this book could not expect to make a contribution to our understanding of the minds of animals. I hope that reading this book will inspire some to do so.

FURTHER READING

Desmond, A. & Moore, M. (1994) *Darwin*. London: Michael Joseph.
Darwin's life, including the dispute between Darwin and Wallace mentioned here, is recounted in this book.
For a more extended account of Darwin's life, see Browne, J. (1996) *Charles Darwin: A Biography, Vol. 1 – Voyaging*, and (2003) *Charles Darwin: A Biography, Vol. 2 – The Power of Place*. Princeton, NJ: Princeton University Press.
Plotkin, H. (2004) *Evolutionary Thought in Psychology: A Brief History*. Oxford: Wiley-Blackwell.
This book offers an excellent brief introduction to the history of evolution and psychology.
Wynne, C. D. L. (2004) *Do Animals Think?* Princeton, NJ: Princeton University Press.
One of the present author's further thoughts on animal minds.

Web sources

http://www.pbs.org/wnet/nature/animalmind/intelligence.html
This attractive multimedia site considers different forms of animal intelligence.

http://wallacefund.info/
This fascinating site attempts to restore a higher profile to the life of Alfred Russel Wallace.

http://www.pigeon.psy.tufts.edu/psych26/history.htm
Robert Cook's site contains carefully selected readings from important historical figures.

2 Other Ways of Seeing the World

A fox invited a Crane to supper and provided nothing for his entertainment but some soup made of pulse, which was poured out into a broad flat stone dish. The soup fell out of the long bill of the Crane at every mouthful, and his vexation at not being able to eat afforded the Fox much amusement. The Crane, in his turn, asked the Fox to sup with him, and set before her a flagon with a long narrow mouth, so that he could easily insert his neck and enjoy its contents at his leisure. The Fox, unable even to taste it, met with a fitting requital, after the fashion of her own hospitality.

Aesop's Fables, translated by G. F. Townsend

The world that we sense around us seems complete – and yet physicists tell us that there are many aspects of our environment of which we have no awareness. As I look out my office window, I have no sense of the polarization of the sun's light in the sky. I do not experience the magnetic fields generated by the computer I'm typing on and the electrical wiring of the house. My ears fail to register the many sounds of pitch higher than about 18 kHz[1] around me. Any number of chemicals in the air do not prompt my nose to register any sensation of smell. And the same is true of any other species we care to think about. My cat may hear higher-pitched sounds than I can, but her daytime vision is considerably less acute than mine.

The pioneer behavioral biologist Jakob von Uexküll was the first to suggest that the world around an animal (what he, being German, called its *Umwelt* – the surrounding world or environment) is not the same as its *Innenwelt* – its world as perceived and internalized (von Uexküll, 1934/1957). He expressed this idea in quite poetic terms:

Here we may glimpse the worlds of the lowly dwellers of the meadow. To do so, we must first blow, in fancy, a soap bubble around each creature to represent its own world, filled with the perceptions which it alone knows. When we ourselves then step into one of these bubbles, the familiar meadow is transformed. Many of its colourful features disappear; others no longer belong together but appear in new relationships. A new world comes into being. Through the bubble we see the world of the burrowing worm, of the

17

butterfly, or of the field mouse; the world as it appears to the animals themselves, not as it appears to us.

Jakob von Uexküll, 1934/1957

This is as true for us as it is for the tick that von Uexküll took as his example. A
female tick sits waiting on a blade of grass for a mammal to go by so that she can
pounce and get the meal of blood she needs to feed her eggs and complete her
life cycle. But the tick does not recognize a mammal as we might from its size,
four-leggedness, or furriness. Just one thing tells the mother tick that a mammal
is passing by – the odor of butyric acid. This acid emanates from the skin of all
mammals and is therefore a reliable sign that the right type of beast is close by.
Having fallen onto a mammal, the tick then searches for a clear patch of skin
so that she can burrow into her prey for a blood meal. At this stage, it is warmth
alone that tells the tick she is heading in the right direction. For the tick, the
rich world surrounding her is reduced to just a couple of signs: the butyric acid
that denotes a mammal and the warmth that implies blood beneath the skin.
As von Uexküll puts it, 'the very poverty of this world guarantees the unfailing
certainty of her actions, and security is more important than wealth'.

Every species, not just simple ones, has a unique perceptual world that has evolved
out of the demands of the life it leads. These perceptual worlds are astonishingly
varied – as varied as the niches that their possessors inhabit. There are birds that
see ultraviolet, insects that see infrared, many animals that see the polarization of
sunlight, bats that hear sounds three octaves higher in pitch than the highest we
can hear and use sonar to 'see' the flapping of an insect's wings. But in the interest
of gaining some depth of understanding, rather than just scratching the surface
in many places, I have chosen to emphasize as much as possible the sensory world
of one species – the pigeon. Pigeons have been more extensively studied than any
other species, they are to be found in most of the countries where this book is
likely to be read, and they have a surprisingly rich perceptual world.

First, we discuss vision and then smell, hearing, the magnetic sense, the electric sense, and finally air pressure perception. We should not forget that perception is not a toolkit of odd pieces but an integrated package working as the
handmaiden of action – action directed toward solving the problems of life that
an animal faces. In subsequent chapters we shall see how different species of
animal utilize their senses to solve problems that are crucial to their survival.

VISION

We do not see the world we look at: our view of the world is limited by our eyes'
and brain's ability to perceive what is around us. What we see as light physicists
understand to be electromagnetic radiation. Our eyes permit us to see only a
small part of the electromagnetic spectrum, wavelengths from about 420 nm[2]
(violet; see Figure 2.1) to about 700 nm (red). Light from the sun includes

Figure 2.1   *Diagram of the electromagnetic spectrum showing human and pigeon zones of sensitivity*

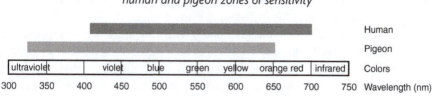

wavelengths both shorter and longer than those we can see. Longer ones are called infrared; these are responsible for the warming effect of sunlight (still longer wavelengths are radio waves). Shorter wavelengths are ultraviolet; for humans, overexposure to these rays can cause skin cancer. Other species can see into both the infrared and ultraviolet parts of the spectrum. In addition, our eyes do not report directly the wavelengths of light that impact on them. Rather we have just three types of color receptors – each tuned for a different wavelength. That is why two colors mixed together look like a single color rather than a mixture. A mixture of red and green may stimulate two of our color receptors in just the same way as the color yellow, which lies between red and green in the color spectrum (see Figure 2.1). Consequently we see the mixture as the intermediate color. Red and green do not *become* yellow – they only *seem* yellow. A physicist with a sensitive instrument would be able to distinguish a mixture of red and green from 'real' yellow. Some species have more of these color receptors than we do and can consequently distinguish between mixtures of colors and pure colors that to us are indistinguishable. Fish and reptiles, for example, appear to have four color receptors; birds have as many as six. Other species have fewer color receptors than our three and thus experience many more potential color confusions than most of us. Dogs, along with most other mammals except primates, have only two color channels, and therefore the world of color presents itself to them something like the way it appears to color-blind people.

The sun's light has another dimension of which we are completely ignorant – polarity. (This is not quite true. Under special conditions some people can see a faint colored pattern. The orientation of this pattern depends on the polarization of the light.) Electromagnetic radiation can be thought of as waves passing through space. These waves can oscillate predominately horizontally, vertically, or at any intermediate orientation. This is their polarity. The only time most of us have any awareness of the polarity of light is when wearing polarized sunglasses. Light reflected from water or glass tends to be horizontally polarized, and so by blocking light polarized in this direction only, polarized sunglasses block the glare of reflections. Other species, however, are able to directly detect the polarization of sunlight. This can be useful in finding your way because the polarization of sunlight changes depending on the sun's position in the sky. Over 90 species of invertebrates, particularly arthropods (insects, spiders, crustaceans, and so on) have been shown to be sensitive to the polarization of sunlight, as have fish and some species of birds.

Since the polarization of sunlight changes with the position of the sun, it can be used as a compass. To do this, it is not necessary to see the sun itself – any patch of blue sky will suffice. This makes polarization a powerful aid to orientation even on largely overcast days. Orientation and navigation are the focus of Chapter 7.

BOX 2.1   HOW TO INVESTIGATE
THE PERCEPTUAL WORLD OF ANIMALS

The development in the mid-twentieth century of methods of animal training using pigeons in small boxes known as 'operant chambers' – or more colloquially as Skinner boxes – provided a great boost to the study of the perceptual world of animals.

One flexible and powerful procedure used in an operant chamber is called the 'Go/Nogo' discrimination. Monika Remy and Jacky Emmerton utilized this method to investigate what wavelengths of light pigeons could see (Remy & Emmerton, 1989). Thirsty birds were trained to mandibulate (open and close their beak) in return for water only if a light was on. The light came on for 30 seconds and then went off for the same period of time. This pattern of light on followed by light off was repeated 20 times. If the pigeons mandibulated in the light, they received water, but if they mandibulated in the dark, they received no water, and in addition, the period of time they had to wait until the light came back on again was extended by 10 seconds. The pigeons easily learned this discrimination and within a couple of days were reliably moving their beaks only when the light was on. Obviously, this discrimination of 'light on' compared with 'light off' can be learned only if the pigeon can see the light that is being shone at it. If the light is of a wavelength to which the pigeon's eye is not sensitive, then the birds will fail the task. By testing the pigeons with light of different wavelengths, Remy and Emmerton were able to uncover the ultraviolet sensitivity of the pigeon's eye.

Another popular procedure used in the operant chamber is the concurrent operant discrimination. In this situation the subject is given a choice of two (or more) possible responses. For example, Juan Delius and colleagues (1976) presented hungry pigeons with a choice of four plastic keys that they could peck to obtain food. As shown in Figure 2.2, the four pecking keys were arranged at 90 degree intervals around the box. In the roof of the box was a light fixed with a polarizing filter so that the polarization of the light crossed only one of the two pairs of pecking keys. In order to obtain food reward, the pigeon had to peck on one of the two keys that were lined up with the polarization of the light – responses on the other keys produced no food reward. The polarization of the light changed randomly from trial to trial. The pigeons learned this problem in around 15 to 20 days of training, showing that they were sensitive to the polarization of the light.

In a later experiment with a slightly different design, Marc Coemans and colleagues (1990) presented pigeons in a Go/Nogo procedure with light of different polarizations that shone from a single location. The pigeons had to

Figure 2.2 *View from above of the apparatus used by Delius and colleagues to assess pigeons' sensitivity to the polarization of light*

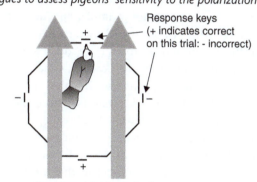

Response keys
(+ indicates correct
on this trial: - incorrect)

Direction of light polarization

Notes: The arrows indicate the direction of polarization of light during the current trial. This changed randomly from trial to trial.

Source: From Delius et al. (1976).

peck on a key if the light coming from it had certain angles of polarization but not if it was polarized in the opposite direction. Coemans and colleagues found that even after two months of daily training, their pigeons were completely unable to discriminate the light of differing polarization.

These contradictory results from Delius's and Coemans's laboratories show the difficulties of working with stimuli that we as humans are unable to perceive. It is possible that stray reflections, not polarization, cued the pigeons in Delius and colleagues' experiment or that the sounds of the equipment used to shift the light of different polarizations to different keys gave the pigeons unintended cues about which key to peck. On the other hand, it is just as possible that the pigeons in Delius's laboratory really do see the polarization of light and that some detail of the procedure used in Coemans's laboratory obscured the pigeons' true abilities.

The pigeon's eye view of the world: a case study in animal vision

The human eye is certainly a wonderful instrument, but there is another eye that has been well studied that has some capabilities even beyond our own – the eye of the pigeon. Box 2.1 outlines some of the methods that have been developed that are particularly useful in assessing the visual abilities of pigeons.

The first thing to notice in the pigeon is that the arrangement of its two eyes is quite different from our own. Where we see most of what we look at with *both* eyes and thus with stereo depth, pigeons have very poor stereovision. Our binocular visual field – the area we see with both eyes – is about 120 degrees out of our total 200-degree field of view. Pigeons' eyes only overlap in what they see for about 35 degrees, but they have a much larger total visual field – around 340 degrees. They use this small stereo part of their visual field only when considering things close up – when feeding, for example. But the large area off to each side that the pigeon sees with just one eye (the lateral field) means that a pigeon can see almost all the way around behind it (McFadden & Reymond, 1985).

Pigeons can also see into the ultraviolet domain. When looking into the distance (as they do when flying), pigeons use the large nonoverlapping, lateral fields of their eyes. It is these lateral fields that have been shown to be sensitive to ultraviolet light (Remy & Emmerton, 1989).

When it comes to visual acuity, pigeons are able to resolve a seed of about 0.3 millimeters at a distance of 50 centimeters. This acuity is only about half as good as the human case (and only one-tenth what a predator bird such as a hawk or eagle can achieve) but is excellent compared with that of many other species (Bloch & Martinoya, 1982).

When looking upward and to the sides with their large lateral fields, pigeons have normal or long-sighted vision. When attending to the ground with the frontal field of the eye, however, there is good evidence that the pigeon is short-sighted. This combination of short-sightedness for the frontal field and normal or slightly long-sighted vision for the lateral fields means that the eye of the pigeon is perfectly graded so that the bird can see simultaneously, in focus, the ground it is standing on and the sky above it (Bloch & Martinoya, 1982; Fitzke et al., 1985). At one and the same time the pigeon can see the grains on the ground in front of it, the distant horizon, and most of what is going on behind it clearly without having to change the focus of the eye.

As discussed in Box 2.1, some evidence suggests that the pigeon eye can perceive the polarization of light. In the real world outside the laboratory, the polarization of sunlight changes as the sun moves across the sky from dawn to dusk. Because all areas of blue sky are polarized, pigeons may be able to use polarization to figure out the position of the sun even when it is invisible, so long as there is sunlight anywhere in the sky. This would be very useful on largely (though not completely) overcast days and at dusk. The sun-compass – the trick of using the position of the sun and time of day to find compass directions – is discussed in Chapter 7. An awareness of the polarization of sunlight would make it possible for pigeons to use the sun-compass even when the sun itself is not visible.

We humans are trichromats – that is to say, we have three kinds of color receptors. In essence, we have one receptor sensitive to red light (a peak receptivity around 564 nm; see Figure 2.1), one sensitive to green (534 nm), and another sensitive to blue (420 nm). We perceive all the hues in between these values because colored light stimulates more than one of these receptors. A wavelength of around 600 nm, which we perceive as an orange light, for example, stimulates both the green and red receptors. This is why a mixture of yellow and red can appear indistinguishable from orange – the mixture stimulates the green and red receptors to the same extent as does 'true' orange light. If we had more than just these three color receptors, we wouldn't necessarily be fooled by mixtures of primary colors in this way.

The retina of the pigeon contains at least six different kinds of color receptors. This is partially how they are be able to see in the ultraviolet range, but it also means that color mixtures do not so easily confuse them. Using a Go/Nogo method (see Box 2.1) Adrián Palacios and Francisco Varela (1992) were able to show that there was no mixture of 470 nm (blue) and 560 nm (yellow) that pigeons would accept as being identical to light of 520 nm (green).

Patterns and pictures

It is all very well to look at the ability of the pigeon eye to perceive different aspects of light, but that still leaves open the question of what a pigeon actually sees when it looks at something.

Several studies have shown that pigeons can perceive three-dimensional objects and recognize photographs and other two-dimensional images as being the same as the three-dimensional items they represent. In one interesting study, Cheri Reid and Marcia Spetch were able to ascertain what kinds of depth information pigeons could extract from two-dimensional images (Reid & Spetch, 1998). The pigeons were shown a large number of pairs of computer-generated images of three-dimensional objects. Some of these images are shown in Figure 2.3. For each pair of images, one represents a three-dimensional object with appropriate shading and perspective information (larger at the front than at the back). The other image in each pair was a two-dimensional outline, a shape with appropriate shading but no perspective information or a shape with the correct perspective but no shading. Reid and Spetch were able to show, using a concurrent discrimination technique (see Box 2.1), that pigeons use both perspective and shading information to recognize the three-dimensionality of two-dimensional images. This suggests that three-dimensional objects look to pigeons much as they do to us.

Apart from the shading and perspective of static objects, we also pick up information about how far away a moving object is from the way it appears to get larger as it approaches or smaller as it moves away. You can get this same impression by staring into a rotating spiral. An inward rotating spiral appears to recede away, an outward rotating spiral looms toward you. In an ingenious study, Carlos Martinoya and Juan Delius (1990) investigated whether pigeons are also prone to this illusion. Using a concurrent discrimination procedure (see Box 2.1) and precision computer-drawn spirals with windings of several different degrees of tightness that were then spun at different speeds, Martinoya and Delius were able to establish that pigeons can discriminate apparently approaching from apparently retreating visual patterns.

Robert Cook has also investigated whether pigeons perceive patterns similarly to the way humans do. One striking aspect of our perception of the visual world is how certain features tend to jump out from their background.

Figure 2.3   *Examples of the stimuli used by Reid and Spetch (1988)*

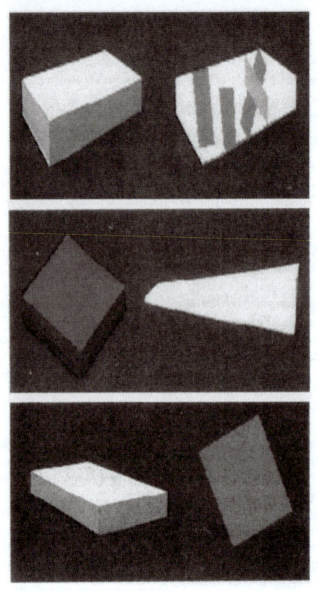

Notes: In each pair of objects, one is a three-dimensional representation,
the other is either an altered three-dimensional image or
a two-dimensional object.

In Figure 2.4, for example, the figure on the left clearly shows a square area of different color that comes out from the background. The figure on the right also contains a square area different from the background in exactly the same position, but it is very difficult to spot. This is because the square area in the

Figure 2.4 *Two representative displays used by Robert Cook*

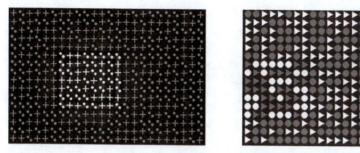

Notes: The left figure shows a clear square area that jumps out from the background. The equivalent area in the right figure is very difficult to spot.
Source: From Cook (1992).

left panel is made up of elements that are of different color – the square area in the right panel is made up of elements that are a different combination of form and color than the background items (the background elements are empty circles and filled triangles; the square area is composed of filled circles and empty triangles). Just like people, pigeons find it more difficult to find the special square area in the right panel than in the left one (Cook, 1992).

How can we tell if the world looks to pigeons as it does to us? One thing to look for is whether pigeons confuse similar items. Donald and Patricia Blough trained pigeons to discriminate the various letters of the alphabet and then looked at which ones the pigeons found easy to discriminate and which were more difficult. They found that the pigeons' difficulties lay mainly with the same letters (such as *A* versus *R* and *B* versus *P*) that people are also most likely to confuse (Blough & Blough, 1997).

Although many studies carried out for different purposes have utilized two-dimensional visual scenes in pigeon research (we shall see some of these in Chapter 10), it has not proven easy to demonstrate that pigeons actually perceive a two-dimensional image as a representation of a three-dimensional object in the way that a human does. In an ingenious study, Marcia Spetch and Alinda Friedman (2006) were able to prove that pigeons can indeed perceive two-dimensional pictures as three-dimensional objects. Spetch and Friedman trained pigeons to discriminate between two objects of different shape that were identical in color (Figure 2.5). Each pigeon had to peck at a screen in front of one object but not at the screen in front of the other object. Some pigeons were trained on digital photographs of the objects, and the other pigeons were trained on three-dimensional models. Once all the pigeons had learned their discrimination, they were swapped over so that those that had been trained on the three-dimensional objects were now confronted by the photographs, and those that had been trained on the photographs were now confronted by the

Figure 2.5   *A pigeon choosing between two objects in Spetch and Friedman's (2006) experiment*

Source: Courtesy Marcia Spetch.

objects. All the birds spontaneously transferred their experience either from photographs to objects or the other way round. This shows that pigeons do recognize a correspondence between a picture and the thing pictured.

Even though pigeons can generalize from two-dimensional images to three-dimensional objects in the way we do, it would still be a mistake to assume that pigeons perceive the visual world the same way as humans. One suggestion that pigeons' visual experience may differ from our own comes from an interesting study by Juan Delius and Valerie Hollard (1987). Objects in the world around us present themselves at many different angles. A chair with its back to you is a very different thing to look at than the same chair with the seat toward you, and yet both are recognized as the same object – a chair. Delius and Hollard demonstrated that pigeons could also recognize rotated objects as being the same item, no matter what the angle of rotation. The difference from the human case lies in the length of time it takes to make the recognition decision. Humans asked to identify whether two items that look similar are really the same or different take longer to make this decision the farther around one object has been rotated relative to the other. In pigeons, however, the time taken to make the recognition decision does not depend on the angle of rotation. Perhaps the pigeon's avian lifestyle has led to the development of a different system for recognizing objects. It is possible that the view of a flying animal more often contains rotated objects and that therefore birds recognize rotated forms more quickly. Whatever the fate of this hypothesis – a more recent study with a different procedure (Hamm et al., 1997) suggests that pigeons *are* influenced in their recognition decision by the angle of rotation of a stimulus – the pigeon has provided many hints of a quite different perceptual world from our own.

Another study that has shed interesting light on possible differences between pigeons' and peoples' perception of the world utilized images from the *Peanuts* cartoon strip. John Cerella trained pigeons using a Go/Nogo method (see Box 2.1) to distinguish images including the main character Charlie Brown from other panels of the *Peanuts* cartoon that did not contain Charlie Brown (Cerella, 1980). Pigeons were readily able to carry out this discrimination. The aspect of the study that suggested that pigeons' perceptions of the drawings may differ from the way humans perceive them occurred when Cerella took various images of characters in the *Peanuts* cartoon strip, chopped them up, and rearranged the pieces. Unlike human beings, the pigeons in Cerella's experiment were just as capable of discriminating Charlie Brown from other characters when his various body parts were jumbled as they had been when his head was on his torso and his arms and legs connected to it in the normal way.

Michael Young and colleagues carried out experiments that add to a sense that the pigeon's perception of pictures of objects is not identical to our own. They trained pigeons to peck in different locations on a computer-controlled touch screen, depending on which of four different objects was presented: an arch, a barrel, a brick, and a triangular wedge (Young et al., 2001). The objects were initially presented to the pigeons as images shaded to suggest light shining on them from one direction. Next, Young and colleagues tested the pigeons with pictures of the same objects, but this time illuminated from a different direction, or simple unshaded outline drawings of the objects. To the experimenters' surprise, the pigeons' ability to recognize the objects was disturbed by changes in lighting that human observers were barely able to perceive, and when the shaded pictures were replaced by simple outline drawings, the pigeons showed no sign of recognizing the objects at all.

SMELL

Smell is not usually a particularly salient dimension of perceptual experience for us, but for other species it can be very important indeed. The sense of smell enables animals to pick up low concentrations of chemicals in the air. This ability is useful for finding food (either other animals, in the case of predators, or vegetable matter for herbivores) or to avoid becoming food (by smelling the approach of a predator). But smell can also function as a simple form of communication, as when one member of a species releases a chemical that then influences the behavior of other members of that species. In Chapter 7 we consider the evidence that pigeons use smell when homing from distant release sites. There is also evidence that other species of bird use smell when young to find their nests. Eduardo Mínguez (1997) studied British storm petrel chicks at their nesting sites on Benidorm Island. Mínguez moved young chicks a little way from their nests, blocked their noses, and then observed whether they were able to find their way back or not. With blocked noses, not one of the chicks could find its nest, whereas with their noses open they all found their way home.

Many insects use chemicals, known as pheromones, as a means of communication. Male currant clearwings, for example, are attracted to the pheromone emitted by females of their species, as are male American cockroaches and many other insect species. Pheromones with a variety of functions have been identified in the fruit fly. These range from those that act to attract other fruit flies to others that make the fruit fly jump. Bumblebees may construct odor trails from nest entrance to the nest core: Termites also follow odor trails. Digger wasps recognize prey using chemical cues picked up on their antennae. Several species of fish use pheromones to attract sex partners in a similar manner to that of insects (Wyatt, 2003).

Mammals of many species are able to recognize specific individuals on the basis of their smells. Turkish hamsters, for example, are able to discriminate even the subtle odor differences between brothers (Heth et al., 1999). Giant pandas have also been shown capable of discriminating the odor of different individuals of their species. In an experimental study, both male and female giant pandas were able to discriminate different male giant panda urine odors, but neither sex could reliably discriminate different female urine odors (Swaisgood et al., 1999).

Female house mice kept in seminatural enclosures prefer the odor of adult male mice to that of juvenile male mice, and they also prefer the odor of male mice captured within 20 meters of their own nests to the odors of more distant males. When they are at their most sexually receptive, the female mice also prefer the odor of dominant male mice; but at other times in their sexual cycle they exhibit no such preference (Mossman & Drickamer, 1996).

Pregnancy in female bank voles can be blocked if the females are exposed early in the pregnancy to the pheromones from a male bank vole that is not the father. Malgorzata Kruczek (1998) demonstrated that female bank voles during this vulnerable early phase of pregnancy prefer the odor of their mate to that of another male bank vole. Later in pregnancy this preference wanes, but it returns during lactation.

Not only do predator mammals find their prey by smell, but prey mammals also know to avoid areas on the basis of predator smell. Hedgehogs prefer to forage at sites contaminated with the odor of animals that do not prey on them (such as chipmunks) rather than at sites smelling of a predator (badger) (Ward et al., 1997). Water voles avoid cages containing the odor of predators (American mink and brown rat) but show no aversion to cages with a novel control odor (sheep) (Barreto & MacDonald, 1999). Interestingly, the voles in these experiments had never had experience with American mink, so their response was largely innate. Mice show stronger reactions to the odors of cat feces when the cats have been feeding on mice than when the cats have been fed a vegetarian diet (Berton et al., 1998).

It used to be believed that birds were almost without any sense of smell. However, research from the 1960s onward has definitively shown that this earlier view was false. It seems likely that all birds have some sense of smell, and some, particularly ground-nesting water-associated birds, have exceptionally large olfactory bulbs in their brains, suggesting a major role for smell in their lives. Despite this suggestive evidence, few species of birds have had their sense of smell studied to any great degree. Evidence of the importance of the sense of smell to homing pigeons is discussed in Chapter 7, 'Navigation'.

Another species of bird that has had its sense of smell investigated is the domestic fowl. Individually housed chicks prefer the smell of the wood shavings that served as their own bedding to that of clean wood shavings or those soiled by another chick. They also prefer orange oil odor if they have been brought up with that odor in their home cages, but not if they have not experienced the orange odor early in life. Male and female seven-day-old chicks avoided a cloth that had been rubbed over a cat as opposed to a cloth treated with water or disinfectant. Rather strangely, however, older chicks did not show this aversion. Similar results were found with a cloth stained with blood. In general, chickens show a preference for familiar odors over novel ones (Jones & Roper, 1997).

Dogs, of course, are famous for their sense of smell and ability to identify distinct odors to the benefit of humanity. Dogs are ubiquitous in security and border-control contexts, where they are employed in detecting explosives, firearms, and contraband ranging from illegal drugs to prohibited fresh produce. Of many possible examples, I have chosen a study by Margie Pfiester and colleagues that demonstrated dogs could be trained to signal the presence of live bedbugs and viable bedbug eggs to a human handler (Pfiester et al., 2008). Pfiester and colleagues used food and verbal reward to train the dogs and then tested them in a hotel room. In the hotel, the dogs were 98 percent accurate in locating the live bugs and viable eggs. The dogs did not make a single false positive identification. That is to say, they never indicated that a location contained bedbugs or eggs when it was in fact devoid of these pests. In the commercial environment in which these dogs will be put to work, this is a very important detail. Once bedbugs are detected, a hotel has to destroy bedding and mattresses and perhaps even rip into walls to fully eradicate these pests. Dogs that make false positive identifications can cause a great deal of unnecessary expense.

HEARING

Many animals use sound to detect predators or prey, and some, including birds, humans, and many other mammals, also communicate with sound. Most animals that use sound to find objects in the world around them rely on the sounds that others make – either intentionally or despite their best efforts to remain silent. A few, however, like some bats and dolphins, orient themselves by listening for the return echo from sounds that they produce themselves especially for that purpose.

Humans and birds that are specialized for locating prey with sound, such as owls and harriers, can locate the position of a sound source to within 2 degrees. Barn owls have been found capable of estimating the distance between themselves and a simulated mouse target with an error of about 10 percent (Konishi, 1973). It is possible to locate the source of a sound because the signal that reaches each of two ears is slightly different, depending on where the sound originates. The farther apart an animal's ears are, the easier it is to locate the sound source. Smaller birds should therefore have more difficulty identifying the location of a sound source than larger birds because their ears are closer together. Brian Nelson and Philip Stoddard (1998) found that, in a natural habitat, eastern towhees, a North American passerine (perching bird) were able to estimate distance with an error of just 7 percent and direction with an error of about 9 degrees. The success of these birds, whose ears are only about 1 centimeter apart, may have been because the experimenters played male towhees the calls of other male towhees. Since these birds are highly territorial, locating the calls of other members of their species is extremely important to them.

Sound is waves of pressure going through the air. Human hearing covers a range from around 100 Hz to nearly 20 kHz. Many species of rodents have good low-frequency hearing (below 150 Hz). Bats that echolocate using clicks they generate either with their tongue or in the throat have the ability to hear much higher frequencies than other animals (Box 2.2). Egyptian fruit bats, which make their echolocating clicks with their tongue, can hear sounds up to 64 kHz (Koay et al., 1998). This is around two octaves higher than humans are capable of perceiving. Bats that use clicks made in their throat for echolocation, such as the big and the little brown bat, the Indian false vampire bat, the fish-catching bat, and the greater horseshoe bat, can hear sounds up to 100 kHz – about three octaves higher than the highest tones audible to humans. Dolphins of several echolocating species can also hear sounds up to 100 kHz.

BOX 2.2   BAT ECHOLOCATION

For centuries, the ability of bats to fly in complete darkness without bashing into things and even to catch flying insects on the wing was a deep mystery. Back in the eighteenth century, experiments with blind and deaf bats had suggested that hearing, not vision, was the critical sense that bats were using. However, in the absence of any sounds audible to the human ear and due to the difficulties in imagining how the sense of hearing could be of any use in navigation, the bat's ability to fly in the dark remained mysterious.

Only in 1941, with the publication of a series of simple but elegant experiments by Donald Griffin and Robert Galambos, did it become clear that bats produce ultrasound (sounds of higher pitch than humans can hear) and listen to the echoes in order to perceive the world around them. Griffin and Galambos temporarily covered the ears, mouth, or eyes of several species of bats and set them the task of flying through a room containing several vertical wires. Whereas bats with their eyes covered were unperturbed, bats with their ears or mouth covered were reluctant to fly at all and, if forced to fly, were quite unable to fly around the wires in the room. Using what were for their time high-tech recording devices, Griffin and Galambos were able to determine that the bats were emitting ultrasonic vocalizations while flying.

A blindfolded person can reliably tell if she is in a large or small room or outdoors on the basis of the quality of the echoes of footsteps and other noises. Further studies with ultrasonic recording devices soon made clear, however, that the abilities of bats went way beyond anything a human could do. By the late 1950s Griffin and his associates demonstrated that bats can locate, track, and capture flying moths, small flies, and mosquitoes using their sonar system. The bats emit ultrasonic 'chirps' lasting about 15 milliseconds when searching, which then change to a continuous 'buzz' when attacking or avoiding an obstacle (Griffin, 1986). But the evolutionary arms race of predator and prey is seldom one-sided, and in 1961 Kenneth Roeder and Asher Treat demonstrated that the noctuid moth, a species regularly preyed upon by North American bats, has a specialized tympanic organ for the detection of bat ultrasound (Roeder & Treat, 1961).

Research continuing in Europe and North America on several different species of bats indicates that they typically echolocate their prey within 2 meters, accurately correcting the tone of the sounds they emit to allow for distortion created by their own movement through the environment.

The echolocating abilities of at least some species of bats are so finely tuned that they can perceive the texture of a surface or the change in wing beat of a moth. James Simmons and colleagues (1998) report that big brown bats can detect a difference of just 0.3 millimeters in two surfaces. Anne Grossetête and Cynthia Moss (1998) reported that the same species of bat could also discriminate between an artificial moth wing beating 50 and 41 times per second.

What is becoming clear from the more recent work on bat echolocation is that the phenomenon has been misnamed: we are not dealing here with a system simply of location, but of perception. Echo-perception enables bats to 'see' the world – not just avoid obstacles but also perceive the position, shape, and texture of objects, 'see' the beating wings of an insect and presumably the wing flaps of other bats. Though the nature of their nighttime world is hard for us to imagine, it must be a very rich sensory world indeed, not like the blank darkness that we perceive at all.

But as our understanding of the echo-world of the bat has developed, so too has our awareness of the lengths that their prey can take to avoid capture. After it was discovered that moths could hear bat echo signals, it was also found that these moths actually emit ultrasound clicks of their own. James Fullard and colleagues (1994) demonstrated that the moths hold off making their own clicks until the bat has shifted from its searching phase to the terminal attack phase. Aaron Corcoran and colleagues in 2011 reported an ingenious study in which they analyzed the full impact of the moths' blocking signal on the bats' hunting activity. Corcoran and colleagues found that the bats did not act as if the moths' clicks were phantom echoes from other objects, nor did the clicks seem to mask the moth entirely and make it 'invisible' to the bat. Rather, the bats consistently misjudged their distance away from the moth and so failed to catch it in seven cases out of ten. This led Corcoran and colleagues to conclude that the moths' clicks interfere with the precise localization of the prey that bats rely on during the last 400 milliseconds of their attack.

The war between predator and prey never ends. Holger Goerlitz and colleagues reported that one species of bat, the barbastelle, has evolved the ability to emit sonar pulses that are 10 to 100 times quieter than those of other moth-hunting bats (Goerlitz et al., 2010). These quieter calls mean that the barbastelle bat can detect a moth only when the bat is close to it, but they reduce the chances that the moth will hear the bat's attack.

Several species of dolphins have also been shown, by similar methods to those developed with bats, to be capable of echolocation. The sensitivity of the dolphins studied thus far does not quite match that of bats, but nonetheless, Atlantic bottlenose dolphin have been found to be capable of discriminating differences in the thickness of objects of about 3 millimeters, and they can discriminate the distance of an object from themselves with an accuracy of around 1 centimeter at a distance of 1 meter (Au, 1997).

MAGNETIC SENSITIVITY

The possibility that there could be species sensitive to magnetic fields was for a long time a controversial one. Modern techniques of analysis have clarified that several species of mammals, birds, and insects are sensitive to magnetic fields. Homing pigeons use of the earth's magnetic field to find their way home is discussed in Chapter 7. Richard Holland and colleagues demonstrated that it is a mineral substance in the brain of big brown bats that enables them to detect the earth's magnetic field (Holland et al., 2008). Like pigeons, bats use this sensitivity to orient and navigate. Migrating fish (see Chapter 7) may also depend on magnetic fields to aid in finding direction, as may rats and other rodents.

Shifting from birds and mammals to insects, it is now well established that honeybees are sensitive to magnetic fields. The waggle dance with which they communicate to fellow foragers the direction and distance from the hive of sources of food (see Chapter 11) can be disrupted by changes in magnetic fields

(Gould, 1980). Bees can also be trained to choose the food source placed on top of a magnet in preference to a less rich (but otherwise identical seeming) food source not placed on a magnet (Walker & Bitterman, 1985, 1989a, 1989b). Magnetic material has even been found in the bodies of monarch butterflies, though whether it enables them to use magnetic fields to navigate remains controversial (Mouritsen & Frost, 2002). Back in the 1950s, David Vowles demonstrated that ants were sensitive to magnetic fields by putting iron filings on their antennae (Vowles, 1954). More recently, a research group from Turkey led by Yilmaz Camlitepe demonstrated sensitivity to magnetic fields in ants by first training them to retrieve honey from the north-pointing arm of a maze that had four arms, one pointing in each cardinal compass direction (Camlitepe et al., 2005). Camlitepe and colleagues then used a solenoid to change the magnetic field around the maze and found that the ants' search for the honey shifted in accord with the changes to the magnetic field.

One remarkable demonstration of the sensitivity of cattle and deer to the earth's magnetic field utilized satellite images from Google Earth. Sabine Begall and colleagues at Princeton University pored over thousands of images of resting cattle and deer visible in satellite photographs. They found that the overwhelming majority of these animals aligned themselves along a north–south axis with their heads pointing north. The researchers were able to exclude wind and other factors and observed that in areas around magnetic anomalies in the earth's crust, where magnetic north and true north diverged substantially, magnetic north was a better predictor of the animals' resting position than true geographic north (Begall et al., 2008).

FOCUS ON THE DATA

Begall and colleagues (2008) analyzed many thousands of satellite images of cattle (panel A), roe deer (B), and red deer (C) to determine the compass direction in which the animals were resting (Figure 2.6). They plotted their results in these circular spaces with north at the top. Each pair of dots on

Figure 2.6   *Resting orientations of cattle (A), roe deer (B), and red deer (C)*

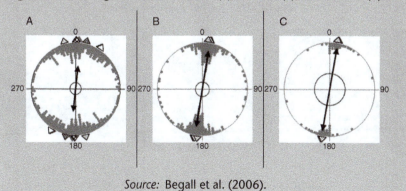

Source: Begall et al. (2006).

opposite sides of each circle shows the resting direction of animals at one location somewhere on the earth's surface. The double-headed arrow in the middle of the circle shows the average resting direction of that species, with the length of the arrow proportional to the consistency of the animals at different locations. Red deer are the most consistent animals, roe deer are a little less consistent, and cattle are the least consistent. In addition, Sabine and colleagues included in this figure the average orientation of animals resting in different parts of the world. The triangles on the outside of the circles show the mean resting orientations of animals in North America (dotted), Asia (gray), Europe (checkered), Australia (striped), Africa (black), and South America (white). In most cases these are not very discriminable, showing that animals all around the world orient themselves to the same north–south dimension.

ELECTRIC SENSE

Several species of fish, some amphibians, and even a few mammals such as the platypus and star-nosed mole are sensitive to electric fields. Weak electric fields are generated by the muscles in an animal's body and vary as the animal moves. Consequently, a sensitivity to electric fields can help a predator animal find its prey in situations where other senses are not much help; for example, it can help a fish catch crayfish lurking in silty river beds.

Where most animals are content to use the energy already in the world around them to find things, a few produce some signal of their own whose echo tells them about the state of the world. Echolocating bats have already been mentioned (in Box 2.2). Though we may not use echoes much – especially not in the very high frequency range utilized by bats – we have all heard echoes at some time, so the notion is not completely alien to us. Harder to imagine, however, is what the world must feel like to those animals that perceive the world by 'listening' for the electric echo produced by the reflection of electric fields they have produced themselves.

Weakly electric African fish are nocturnal animals from South America and Africa. They produce weak electric fields using an organ in their tail and possess

Figure 2.7   *Weakly electric African fish*

Source: Photograph courtesy of G. von der Emde.

sensor organs under the skin along both sides of the body. By attending to the electric field reflected back onto their body from the objects around them, they are able to form an impression of what surrounds them in the dark water. These fish are confronted with a special problem if they want to find out how far away an object is. For the senses most commonly used to find distance information (hearing and vision), animals have a pair of receptors separated by some distance. The animal can estimate how far away an object is from the difference in signal strength received by these two receptors (ears or eyes). The weakly electric African fish cannot do this, however, because the electric field reflected off an object will fall only on one side of the fish. Furthermore, the size of the reflected electric field cannot be used as a cue to find distance, because a close-up large object will reflect a similar-sized electric field to a distant small object (the electric reflections, like shadows, get larger the farther away the object is).

A report by Gerhard von der Emde and colleagues (1998) demonstrated not only that these fish are capable of estimating distances but also how they do so. Figure 2.7 shows one of these fish. What changes as the object moves closer, apart from the size of the electric reflection, is also the sharpness of the edges of the reflection. A closer object has a sharper-edged electric reflection than a more distant object. Von der Emde and colleagues tricked the electric fish with objects at the same distance from the fish but that differed in the sharpness of their electrical reflections and were thereby able to confirm that the edge sharpness of the reflected electric field was the critical factor that enabled the fish to determine distance.

SENSITIVITY TO AIR PRESSURE

One species – the pigeon again – has been shown to be sensitive to changes in air pressure (Kreithen & Keeton, 1974). These changes were equivalent to differences in altitude of just 10 meters (about 33 feet). As well as providing altitude information to a flying animal, air pressure also changes with the weather (which is what is shown by barometers) and could therefore indicate to a migrating animal when the season has come to begin its journey.

CONCLUSIONS

Taken as a grab bag of almost magical abilities, the perceptual worlds of animals are like something out of science fiction. But we can be sure that what we are considering here are solutions to various problems that have come up during evolution. Color vision, for example, is what enables us and birds to differentiate ripe berries from unripe ones – food from poison. The hearing of bats, specialized to pick up very high frequencies, is essential to their echolocation system, itself a solution to the problem of orientation at night. Fine-tuned hearing is also central to the evolutionary arms race between predators and prey: predators use their ears to find prey, and prey use theirs to spot the predators first.

Often though, we see the solution – the perceptual ability – and can only guess at what the problem might be that it is solving. Why, for example, do pigeons have six color receptor channels and the ability to see ultraviolet? Francisco Varela and colleagues (1993), in considering the question of why pigeons (and other birds) can see ultraviolet, turned the question on its head and asked, '[T]he question is not "Why do many animals see ultraviolet?" but rather "Why is it that most mammals do not?"' Ultraviolet light shows up more pattern in the coats of animals, in flowers, and in blue sky than we can see. Varela and colleagues suggested that mammals lack ultraviolet sensitivity, not because they lack a use for such vision, but because a long evolutionary history of nocturnal habits has limited the functionality of the mammalian eye in daylight. Thus evolution not only solves problems, but because of its historical nature, it is also constrained in how it can go about solving them.

FURTHER READING

Gould, J. L. & Gould, C. G. (1995) *The Honey Bee*. New York: Scientific American Library.
This entertainingly written book contains a wealth of information on honeybee perception and navigation.

Griffin, D. R. (1986) *Listening in the Dark: The Acoustic Orientation of Bats and Men*. Ithaca, NY: Cornell University Press.
A fascinating personal account of the discovery of echolocation in bats.

Schiller, C. H. (ed. and trans.) (1957) *Instinctive Behavior: The Development of a Modern Concept*. New York: International Universities Press.
This volume contains an English translation of Jakob von Uexküll's (1934) *Streifzüge durch die Umwelten von Tieren und Menschen*, 'A stroll through the worlds of animals and men', from which the quote and example at the beginning of this chapter are taken.

Thomas, J. A., Moss, C. F. & Vater, M. (2002) *Echolocation in Bats and Dolphins*. University of Chicago Press.
This volume has an enormous scope. There is unlikely to be any question within its remit not covered here. More suitable for the advanced student.

Wajnberg, E., Acosta-Avalos, D., Alves, O. C., De Oliveira, J. F., Srygley, R. B. & Esquivel, D. M. S. (2010) Magnetoreception in eusocial insects: an update. *Journal of the Royal Society Interface*, 7 (SUPPL. 2), S207–S225.
An up-to-date survey of the abilities of insects to detect and respond to magnetic fields.

Wyatt, T. D. (2003) *Pheromones and Animal Behaviour: Communication by Smell and Taste*. Cambridge, U.K.: Cambridge University Press.
A wide-ranging survey of the roles of pheromones in animals' lives.

Web sources

http://www.pbs.org/wgbh/nova/sharks/hotsciencesharks/
This excellent site describes the perceptual world of the shark.

http://andygiger.com/science/beye/beyehome.html
This site makes a simultaneously serious and entertaining attempt to show the world through the eyes of a bee.

http://alumnus.caltech.edu/~rasnow/
This is a good site on weakly electric fish.

http://www.pigeon.psy.tufts.edu/avc/toc.htm
This site is a scholarly book by multiple expert authors on the visual system of birds.

3 Concept Formation

'What sort of insects do you rejoice in, where you come from?' the Gnat inquired.

'I don't rejoice in insects at all,' Alice explained, 'because I'm rather afraid of them – at least the large kinds. But I can tell you the names of some of them.'

'Of course they answer to their names?' the Gnat remarked carelessly.

'I never knew them do it.'

'What's the use of their having names,' the Gnat said, 'if they won't answer to them?'

'No use to them,' said Alice; 'but it's useful to the people who name them, I suppose. If not, why do things have names at all?'

'I can't say,' the Gnat replied.

Lewis Carroll, *Through the Looking Glass*, 1871

The way the world appears to an animal is not just a question of the animal's perceptual abilities – what it can hear, see, smell, or sense in any other way – but also of how the pieces of experience can be put together to organize the relationship between raw perceptual experience and what is going on in the world. It is this more abstract level of conceptualization that is the subject of this chapter.

Research on the ability of animals to form concepts is, with a few worthy exceptions, a product of just the last few decades. Consequently, it is not surprising that most of the research carried out so far has taken human conceptual abilities as its starting point. While there is a danger here in failing to take an appropriately species-centered point of view, on the other hand, experimental tasks used in human psychology, particularly those designed by developmental psychologists, have certainly proven useful.

We start this chapter with a discussion of a very simple extension from direct perceptual experience – the ability to form perceptual concepts. That is to say, to recognize, for example, that all trees have something in common that distinguishes them from nontrees. Fish, people, and chairs are further examples of these perceptual concepts. Although this is one of the older branches of research in animal concept formation, the evidence is still controversial as to whether other species form perceptual concepts the same way we do.

Next we consider another simple-seeming aspect of experience: the question of object permanence. Can an animal understand that a hidden object continues to exist even when it is out of sight? This apparently straightforward concept does not appear to be clear to most of the species that have been tested. A handful of not very closely related species (dogs, chimpanzees, and gorillas) can solve even the most difficult object permanence tasks, while others such as birds and cats fail consistently.

This leads to consideration of some other, to us very simple concepts, such as recognizing what is 'same' and what is 'different'. These matters are so deeply engrained in us that it is surprising to find that it has proven difficult to demonstrate that animal species can learn to discriminate objects on the basis of whether they are the same or different from each other.

Research on animals' conceptual abilities is still at an early stage, but there is already evidence both of commonality and of diversity across species.

We start with the most direct extension from direct perceptual experience, perceptual concepts.

PERCEPTUAL CONCEPTS

A perceptual concept is a grouping together of items that share common features or functionality. The concept of a chair, for example, groups together as equivalent a great many objects that differ in any number of ways but share a certain functionality – they can all be sat on. The concept of fish groups together all animals that live in water and have a backbone, gills, and various other qualities that biologists have determined qualify them as fish. Some simple concepts, like triangles, may be defined by certain common features that all triangles share (three straight edges intersecting in three angles). With such natural concepts as chairs and fish, however, the boundaries of the category may be much fuzzier. There is probably no single feature common to all chairs. Concepts like this can be called perceptual concepts because they group together some objects and differentiate them from others on the basis of certain properties that are available to our senses.

Over 30 years ago Richard Herrnstein and colleagues (Herrnstein et al., 1976) performed a simple but very interesting experiment on pigeons. These birds were presented with slides of photographs – many hundreds of them – one at a time. Some of the photographs contained images of people; in others there were no people present. If the photograph contained a person, the pigeon could earn a food reward by pecking at it; if there was no person present, the pigeon had to withhold its responses or the delay to the next rewarded picture would be lengthened (the Go/Nogo method: see Box 2.1). Even though the photographs varied substantially, the pigeons gradually mastered this discrimination. In subsequent experiments, Herrnstein and colleagues explored pigeons' ability to categorize photographs containing trees, bodies of water, fish (Herrnstein & De Villiers, 1980), and even a specific person. Even though thousands of pictures were used in these experiments (making memorization of individual pictures highly unlikely), the pigeons learned to discriminate between them and achieved considerable success when a novel example from the category was presented to them for the first time.

These early demonstrations of perceptual concepts in pigeons inspired a number of imitations. Pigeons have been found capable of discriminating between the locations used in pictures. They can form concepts of cats, flowers, oak leaves, other pigeons, cars, and chairs and correctly generalize to examples of these concepts they have never seen before. In a study by Shigeru Watanabe and his colleagues (Watanabe et al., 1995), pigeons were even able to discriminate paintings by Monet and Picasso. The pigeons also correctly identified novel paintings by these two artists. In the first study of the categorization of schools of art by a nonhuman subject, paintings by Cézanne and Renoir were spontaneously categorized as belonging to the Monet school, while paintings by Braque and Matisse were categorized as belonging to the Picasso school.

Several of these studies compared pigeons' success in categorizing stimuli grouped together according to concepts that arise naturally in human language (e.g., chair, fish, and so on) with their performance with groups of stimuli formed according to no specific rule – just a random conglomeration of items. This kind of comparison serves two functions. First, it ensures that the pigeons are not just memorizing all the stimuli and learning what to do to obtain reward when they come along – in other words, it acts as a control for rote learning (pigeons have a prodigious capacity for rote learning; see Chapter 10). The second and more interesting function of these so-called pseudo-category tasks is that they test the thesis that conceptualization requires language. It has been argued that we need the word 'tree' to conceptualize trees successfully. The fact, however, that pigeons more successfully categorize pictures containing trees than two random groups of pictures suggests that they have also formed a concept of a tree. Since pigeons do not have language, this implies that there is something about the visual image of trees that enables them to be conceptualized as a group of similar objects even without the need for the linguistic term 'tree'.

Less research has been performed on perceptual concepts in species other than pigeons. Monkeys have been shown to be able to form the concept of a person using person and nonperson photographs and methods broadly similar to those employed with pigeons. Monkeys have also successfully classified pictures of other people and monkeys (Schrier et al., 1984). Likewise, blue jays can classify pictures of cryptic moths and leaves that were damaged by cryptic caterpillars (Real et al., 1984).

But how do we know that these animals are really learning *concepts* and not just noticing features that the positive slides (and negative slides) have in common? We know that many animals have astonishingly good abilities to memorize many hundreds of slides (see Chapter 10). In addition, it has been known since the early days of psychological study on animals that they can *generalize*. As we discuss in Chapter 5, generalization is the ability of animals, having been trained to respond to one stimulus, to then respond similarly to other stimuli that are comparable in some way. As already mentioned, Herrnstein and the other researchers who performed the original studies on conceptualization in pigeons included a *pseudo-concept* control – a condition in which a random half of the slides were considered positive and the other half negative. The pigeons were unsuccessful in this condition, suggesting that there was something about the sorting of the slides into those containing the concept under training and those without it that made the slides easier to learn for the pigeons. This control condition, however, and the pigeons' failure to learn it do not guarantee that when the pigeons do learn to discriminate the person from nonperson slides (to take just one example), what they have learned is really the concept of a person as we understand it.

It must first be admitted that even among psychologists who study concept learning in human beings, there is no consensus about what it is that makes a concept a concept. There are, however, results from animal research that strongly suggest that, whatever a concept may be to a human being, pigeons and monkeys are not learning concepts in the same way.

Michael D'Amato and Paul van Sant (1988) trained *Cebus apella* monkeys to discriminate slides containing people from those that did not. The monkeys readily learned to do this. Then the monkeys were presented with novel slides they had never seen before which contained either scenes with people or similar scenes with no people in them. Here also the monkeys spontaneously classified the majority of slides correctly. So far, so good – clear evidence that the monkeys had not just learned the particular slides they had been trained on but had abstracted a person concept from those slides that they then successfully applied to pictures they had never seen before.

Or had they? D'Amato and van Sant did not stop their analysis simply with the observation that the monkeys had successfully transferred their learning to novel slides – rather they went on to look carefully at the kinds of errors the monkeys had made. Although largely successful with the novel slides, the monkeys made some very puzzling mistakes. For example, one of the person slides that the monkeys had failed to recognize as a picture of a human being had been a head and shoulders portrait – which, to another human, is a classic image of a person. One of the slides that the monkeys had incorrectly classified as containing a human had actually been a shot of a jackal carrying a dead flamingo in its mouth; both the jackal and its prey were also reflected in the water beneath them. What person in her right mind could possible confuse a jackal with a flamingo in its mouth with another human being?

The explanation for both these mistakes is the same: the monkeys had generalized on the basis of the particular features contained in the slides they had been trained with rather than learning the more abstract concept that the experimenters had intended. The head and shoulders portrait of a person lacked the head-torso-arms-legs body shape that had been most common among the images that the monkeys had been trained with, and consequently, they had rejected it as not similar enough to the positive image they were looking for. Similarly, during training, the only slides that had contained flashes of red happened to be those of people. Three of the training slides had contained people wearing a piece of red clothing, whereas none of the nonperson slides had contained the color red. Consequently, when the jackal with prey slide came along during testing, it contained the color red, and so the monkeys classified it as a person slide. Richard Herrnstein and Peter de Villiers drew similar conclusions from a detailed analysis of the errors pigeons made when categorizing slides of fish such as those shown in Figure 3.1 (Herrnstein & De Villiers, 1980).

The findings above may suggest that nonhuman species learn to categorize images by relying more on particular features in the images than humans do. This, however, is to overlook the fact that, in the human case, perceptual categorization takes a very long time to develop. Young children commonly make misclassifications for many years, such as calling all four-legged animals sheep (to the amusement of those around them). The fine distinctions of adulthood take a long time to develop. Although experiments on perceptual categorization with non-humans use hundreds of images and may involve a year or more of training, that is very little compared with a child's continuous experience with an almost limitless set of perceptual encounters. The child's experience involves real three-dimensional objects viewed from many angles, not just the flat images used in animal studies. The richness of the three-dimensional world may discourage learning based on individual features and encourage a more holistic view. Perhaps future experiments on animal conceptualization may find ways to capture more of the real-world experience of learning about concepts and answer the question of whether

Figure 3.1 *Examples of stimuli readily classified by pigeons as fish (left) and a picture commonly misclassified (right) in Herrnstein and de Villiers's experiment*

Source: Courtesy of P. de Villiers.

animals are really able to generalize more from individual features when they learn perceptual concepts.

Ramesh Bhatt, Edward Wasserman, and colleagues suggested that the standard method used in many of these studies of perceptual concepts may fail to capture a large aspect of how animals conceptualize in the real world. Their point was that binary classification such as trees / not trees, fish / not fish, and so forth fails to capture how conceptualization occurs in the real world (Bhatt et al., 1988). In reality animals and people need to be able to classify objects into multiple categories simultaneously, not just one at a time.

Bhatt and colleagues (1988) developed a specially modified pigeon Skinner box so that they could project a slide onto a central screen surrounded by four pecking keys (see Figure 3.2). The pigeon saw projected onto the central screen slides of people, flowers, cars, and chairs. First, the bird had to peck onto the image screen to indicate that it was paying attention, and then it had to peck one of the pecking keys arranged around the slide to identify which class of object had appeared on the screen. For example, Bhatt and colleagues trained one pigeon to respond to the top left key if the image showed a person, the top right key if the image showed a flower, the bottom right for a car, and the bottom left for a chair. Other pigeons in the experiment were trained to peck different keys to indicate what they saw so that preference for any one key could not taint the results.

Figure 3.2   *Apparatus used by Bhatt and colleagues (1988) to train pigeons to classify each of 40 pictures into one of four categories. Note the four pecking keys, one at each corner of the screen showing the image*

With extensive training, the pigeons in this experiment gradually learned to classify which of the four categories of object 40 slides contained to levels of accuracy above 80 percent for each category.

Having shown that their pigeons could learn this discrimination on 40 slides (10 for each category), Bhatt and colleagues decided to test how the birds would perform if shown completely novel pictures of objects belonging to the same categories. They found that, although the pigeons' performance on novel slides was generally worse than on slides they had seen repeatedly, they were able to categorize images of people, flowers, cars, and chairs that they had never seen before at levels above chance.

This demonstration brings our understanding of animal conceptualization in the laboratory closer to what animals must need in their daily lives: it is not enough just to form binary categorizations, they must also categorize objects along multiple dimensions simultaneously.

All of the studies on animal concept formation described so far have relied on two-dimensional pictures as their stimulus materials. How can we be sure that when we show animals photographs of objects in the real world, they see these flat pictures as depicting the things we know they represent? In fact, it is probably best to assume that other species do not see pictures as representations of the real world. However, one very ingenious experiment was carried out on ten pigeons by Ulrike Aust and Ludwig Huber with results that indicate that these birds may see images as representing the world around them. Aust and Huber's study shared much of its methodology with one of the original studies by Herrnstein and colleagues: Pigeons were trained to discriminate pictures of people from pictures that did not contain people (Aust & Huber, 2006). The twist in Aust and Huber's study was that the slides of people were always missing a body part; thus the pigeons were shown headless people and handless people in the slides (Figure 3.3 shows pictures similar to those used by Aust and Huber, 2006). If the pigeons had simply been learning to classify blobs of color that were meaningless to them, then having once been trained on the headless people, if they were shown heads, they should have viewed these as completely unrelated slides and not generalized their responses to them. On the other hand, if they recognized the photographs of headless people as representing people, such as those they saw around them every day, then they should have generalized to slides of heads – because heads belong to people, too. Aust and Huber found that the birds did indeed generalize to slides of people's heads and hands, having been trained on images of people without heads and hands. Control tests with arbitrary shaped patches of skin did not produce the same generalization. This suggests that these pigeons did perceive the slides as representations of objects in the real world.

In a follow-up study, Aust and Huber (2010) repeated their experiment, this time with a group of pigeons that were raised in a special aviary that prevented

Figure 3.3 *Images similar to those used in Aust and Huber's studies of the ability of pigeons to recognize pictures as real objects*

Notes: The three images in the top row are disembodied heads; and the three images in the bottom row are examples of headless people. Pigeons trained to discriminate the headless images from pictures that did not contain people successfully generalized their training to images of disembodied heads – indicating that they generalized from the image to the real object it represents.

them ever seeing a human being. This group was able to learn to discriminate slides containing people (without heads or hands) from slides not containing people at all. However, when tested with pictures of just heads, they failed to generalize their training. This result appears to indicate that experience with the real object is necessary to correctly generalize when looking at pictures, but the force of this conclusion is diluted by the observation that the same result was not found for the group of pigeons reared without exposure to human beings and trained on pictures of people with no hands. That group of pigeons, even though they had never seen a human being, generalized their training on handless people to pictures of disembodied hands. These results suggest that there is still much to be understood about how animals perceive pictures. Another aspect of how animals learn about concepts, the possibility that pigeons form prototypes, is considered in Box 3.1.

Some researchers have taken the question of how animals perceive static pictures and extended it to the study of moving images. Alexander Ophir and Bennett Galef Jr. (2003) capitalized on the fact that female Japanese quail show a preference for male quail that they have seen courting and mating with another female. They found that female quail showed just as much attraction toward male quail that they had seen courting and mating for five minutes on video as to male quail that they had observed mating live.

BOX 3.1   CAN PIGEONS LEARN PROTOTYPES?

One theory of how humans learn perceptual concepts is that they do so by recognizing a prototype of the concept under consideration. A prototype is the perfect embodiment of a concept. For example, in one study people had to classify cartoon drawings into one of two categories. In one cartoon category, the faces had small foreheads, short noses, and closely spaced eyes. In the other category, the faces had larger foreheads, longer noses, and more widely spaced eyes. Once the subjects had passed this test, they were introduced to new cartoons. The novel test cartoons that were most successfully classified represented the averages of all the training cartoons in each category. The average cartoons were the easiest to categorize, it is argued, because they were representative of the prototype of each class of cartoons.

Lorenzo von Fersen and Stephen Lea (1990) trained pigeons to discriminate sets of photographs of outdoor scenes to see if they did this by forming prototypes. These photographs differed from each other in five ways. First, they were of two different scenes (a pub in the town or a university building). Second, they were photographed under two different weather conditions (sunny or cloudy). Third, the photos were taken at two different camera distances (near or far). Fourth, there were two different camera orientations (horizontal or oblique). And, fifth, there were two different camera heights (ground level or 20 meters above the ground). Two sample images from this study are shown in Figure 3.4. For each of these five

Figure 3.4   *Two sample images from the experiment by Fersen and Lea*

Notes: The image on the left shows the university building, photographed from street level on an overcast day with the camera on an oblique angle. The right image shows the exact opposite. It is a photograph of the pub, taken on a sunny day, from 20 meters above the ground and with the camera on the level.

Source: Courtesy of S. E. G. Lea and L. von Fersen.

dimensions, one value was arbitrarily designated as positive. If an image had three or more positive qualities, then pecks at that image were rewarded with food. If an image had three or more negative qualities, then pecks to it were not rewarded (the Go/Nogo method; see Box 2.1). The image with all five positive qualities can be considered the positive prototype, and the image with all five negative qualities was deemed the negative prototype. Fersen and Lea found that their pigeons responded fastest to the positive prototype. This result cannot, however, be seen as strong evidence that the pigeons had formed a prototype to solve the discrimination – they may simply have been responding on the basis of the features individually. The positive prototype image may have been responded to fastest just because it contained more of the features that were individually associated with reward.

A stronger demonstration that pigeons form prototypes comes from an experiment by Aydan Aydin and John Pearce (1994). These investigators also showed pigeons images that contained features whose discrimination would be followed by reward or nonreward. In this case, the images were made up of three bars of different colors and patterns placed together on a computer screen. There were six different types of bars altogether, which for simplicity were designated as A, B, C, D, E, and F. Bars A, B, and C were positive; bars D, E, and F were negative. On any given trial the pigeons saw three bars, and these were always either two positive and one negative (responses to these patterns were followed by a food reward) or one positive with two negative (no reward). Once the pigeons had learned this discrimination exercise, they were tested on the pattern of wholly positive bars (A, B, and C) and the pattern of wholly negative bars (D, E, and F), which had never been presented during the training period. These patterns could be considered the prototypes of the concepts the pigeons had learned during training, and sure enough, they responded at a higher rate to the positive prototype and at a lower rate to the negative prototype than they had for any of the patterns they had been trained with. This suggests they had conceptualized the prototype during training, even though they had never seen it.

Aydin and Pearce go on to suggest, however, that prototype extraction, in humans as well as animals, can be explained with simple learning rules and the laws of generalization. In essence their argument is that the prototype, even though it had never been seen during training, contained more of elements associated with reward than did any of the training patterns.

Although the range of species that has been studied for their conceptual abilities is not large, Evelyn Hanggi (1999) has reported on the categorization abilities of horses. Two horses were trained to select a black circle stimulus with an open center in preference to a solid black circle stimulus. Once this discrimination had been mastered, the horses were trained on additional, similar stimuli – selection of the stimulus with the contrasting center always being rewarded. (One of Hanggi's horses is shown making a choice in Figure 3.5). By the end of their exposure to a series of 15 pairs of items, the horses were making very few errors when presented with a novel pair of items, indicating that they had abstracted the concept of always choosing the stimulus with the contrasting center.

Figure 3.5 *One of Hanggi's horses choosing between a filled and an open sunlike stimulus*

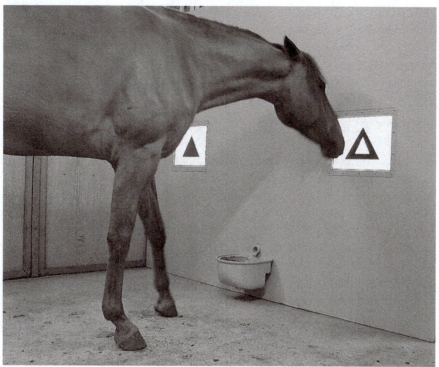

Source: Courtesy of E. Hanggi.

Hank Davis and colleagues (1997) carried out an interesting series of studies on the question of whether different species can recognize individual people. In one study they found that rats, given just one ten-minute opportunity to interact with a specific human being, would later choose that person when given a choice between two different people seated at a table. In subsequent studies, Davis and colleagues found similar abilities to discriminate individual people in chickens, rabbits, sheep, cows, seals, llamas, and even penguins.

Most studies on concept formation in animals have had to be carried out in the laboratory in order to fully control the stimuli that are presented to the subjects. But in one particularly creative study Douglas Levey and colleagues (2009) succeeded in demonstrating that northern mockingbirds on a university campus could form a concept of particular people. Mockingbirds learned to assess the threat posed by different individuals. People who threatened a nest on four successive days were much more likely to be intercepted and squawked at than a novel person who had never interfered with the nest before. In all cases, the people carrying out the experiment did no harm to the nest.

Research on perceptual concepts in a number of species indicates that the ability to categorize objects – even quite abstract objects such as paintings by different artists – is widespread among mammals and birds. The evidence from more detailed studies of just *how* animals achieve these feats of conceptual learning suggests that the mechanisms may be relatively simple forms of associative learning and generalization. Complex behavior can often arise as the outcome of relatively simple underlying principles.

OBJECT PERMANENCE

If I take a chocolate in one hand, pass my hand behind a box, and stop for a moment before bringing my hand out and showing you that it is empty, where would you expect to find the chocolate? Most likely behind the box. You saw everything that happened: if the chocolate is not in my hand then it must be behind the box. Your ability to reason in this way is known as 'object permanence' – you have a concept that objects continue to exist even when they disappear from sight. Object permanence was recognized by the famous child psychologist Jean Piaget (1952), who found that small children below about 12 to 18 months of age do not yet appreciate that objects that disappear from view continue to exist.

Testing for object permanence can be straightforward. One test is simply to make a desired object disappear from view and ask whether the subject searches for it in the spot where it was placed – just as in the example with the chocolate behind the box. A task of this type is known as a 'visible displacement'. There is no trick – everything that happens to the object is clearly visible to the subject (adult human, child, or animal). Somewhat more complex is the 'invisible displacement' task. In this case, a desired object is first placed in a container, which is then taken behind a screen, out of the subject's sight, where the object is removed from the container. Finally, the empty container is shown to the subject, who is then free to search for the desired object. An individual capable of object permanence will recognize that if the object is no longer in the container, then it must have been removed while it was behind the screen. Consequently, this subject will search for the object behind the screen. Children can solve the simpler task, the visible displacement, at around 12 months of age. Only children above about 18 months are able to solve invisible displacement problems.

Figure 3.6 shows a typical arrangement for studying object permanence in animals. In this study of the development of object permanence in puppies, Sylvain Gagnon and François Doré (1994) allowed a puppy to watch as an experimenter placed a favorite toy behind one of the three boxes. Once the object was hidden, the puppy was released and allowed to search for the toy. The puppy was scored as successful on this visible displacement task if it went straight to the box where the toy was hidden. Gagnon and Doré found that puppies started to master this test at around seven weeks of age.

For an invisible displacement test, the experimenters placed the toy into a small opaque container in full view of the puppy. The container with the toy was then placed behind one of the boxes shown in Figure 3.6. While out of sight behind the box, the toy was removed from the container. Next the now empty container was removed from behind the box and shown to the puppy so that it could see that the container was empty. Where would the puppy search for the missing toy? Very few of even the oldest puppies showed any inclination to search for the toy behind the box where it had been left. After several tests, some of the dogs did search in the right place, but it seems likely this was just trial and error learning. With repeated testing using the same target box, the puppies simply learned to go to that box to get their toy. There was no evidence that they understood the sequence of events that had led to the toy ending up in that box and not another. Gagnon and Doré found adult dogs to be successful on the invisible displacement task only after about one year of age.

The visible displacement task has been tested with a wide range of species, all of which have solved the task and found the hidden object. These include great apes (chimpanzees: Call, 2001; gorillas: Natale et al., 1986; orangutans: Call, 2001), monkeys of many kinds (De Blois & Novak, 1994; Neiworth et al., 2003),

Figure 3.6   *Gagnon and Doré's testing arena for dogs*

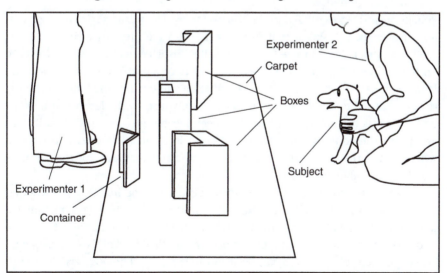

Note: Experimenter 2 holds the dog while Experimenter 1 moves the desired object.

Source: Gagnon & Doré (1994).

other mammals (cats: Goulet et al., 1994; dogs: Gagnon and Doré, 1994; hamsters: Thinus-Blanc & Scardigli, 1981), and birds (chickens: Vallortigara et al., 1998; doves: Dumas & Wilkie, 1995; parrots: Pepperberg et al., 1997).

Success on the invisible displacement task has been far more difficult to demonstrate unequivocally. Three species of great apes have passed the invisible displacement task (chimpanzees: Call, 2001; gorillas: Natale et al., 1986; orangutans: de Blois et al., 1998). Initial apparent successes by cats and dogs have not withstood further scrutiny.

Sonia Goulet and colleagues (1994, 1996) studied the factors that lead to apparent success on invisible displacement tasks in cats. They found that the cats were more successful in finding a hidden toy if they were prevented from looking for it until 20 seconds had elapsed since the placing of the toy. Why should these cats have been *more* successful if they were forced to wait 20 seconds before making their response? Surely with time their memory for where the toy was placed should have decayed – not improved (see Chapter 10 for more on animal memory)? Indeed, a cat's memory does decay, and this is precisely why the cat does better after 20 seconds than if it is free to make a response immediately. The cat's memory for where the toy is fails to take account of the toy's invisible displacement and is therefore incorrect. After 20 seconds, the cat has forgotten where it last saw the toy and therefore makes fewer incorrect choices. In Goulet and colleagues' study, by making fewer incorrect responses, there was an inevitable but purely coincidental increase in the incidence of the cats searching behind the box where the toy had indeed been hidden.

Gagnon and Doré (1994) reported that puppies were unsuccessful on the invisible displacement task but that full-grown dogs were the only animals outside the great ape clade to succeed on an invisible displacement problem. However, Emma Collier-Baker and colleagues (2004) noticed a problem with Gagnon and Doré's experimental design. Gagnon and Doré had been in the habit of leaving the device used to move the toy from box to box next to the last box it had visited. This was the box that the toy had been left behind. When Collier-Baker's group left the container in various different locations, the dogs had no idea where to find the toy. Thus, it seemed clear that the dogs had not really understood the invisible displacement.

Holly Miller and colleagues (2009) introduced a new method to assess whether dogs are capable of following invisible movements of objects. They confronted a dog with a wooden beam nearly 2 meters long. The beam was supported in the middle so that it could be rotated and had an identical bucket fixed at each end. The experimental apparatus can be seen in Figure 3.7. The dog was allowed to see the experimenter place a piece of food in one of the buckets, and then the beam was slowly rotated in front of the dog. Miller and colleagues found that if the beam was rotated through 180 degrees so that it ended up looking identical to how it had appeared before it was rotated, the dogs were confused and could

Figure 3.7 *A dog in Miller and colleagues' (2009) experiment*

Notes: The top panel shows the beam with two buckets after an object has been placed in one of the buckets but before the beam is rotated. The middle panel shows the beam with buckets after a 90-degree rotation. The bottom panel shows the beam after a 180-degree rotation and the dog has been released to make its choice.

Source: Photos courtesy of Libbye Miller.

not locate the bucket containing the hidden item. However, if the beam was rotated only 90 degrees, the dogs performed well at locating the hidden toy. When children and apes were tested with the 180-degree rotation, they also found it very difficult (Barth & Call, 2006). It may well be that because a rotation of 180 degrees returns the beam with the buckets to a position in which it looks identical to its appearance before the rotation started, it confuses subjects. The success of Miller and colleagues' dogs on the 90-degree rotation is certainly interesting evidence that dogs may understand invisible displacements under certain conditions after all (see Box 3.2).

BOX 3.2   HOW TO TEST YOUR DOG OR CAT FOR OBJECT PERMANENCE

While much contemporary animal cognition research is carried out on rats and pigeons – excellent lab species, but not common pets – considerable research on object permanence has also been performed on dogs and cats. Since the research requires no special equipment and is completely harmless, there is no reason why you should not test your own dog or cat for object permanence. In my experience there is considerable variation between individual dogs and cats, making the results of these tests by no means a foregone conclusion.

You will need a human assistant, three boxes (cardboard grocery boxes are excellent), your subject's favorite toy (it's probably worth washing it!), and a container large enough for the toy (an empty yogurt or ice cream container will do nicely).

First, catch your dog or cat. Make sure he or she is in an alert but not too boisterous mood. Just before a regular feeding time is better than just after; and it is wise to maintain a sober demeanor so as not to overexcite your animal.

While your assistant holds the cat or dog, arrange the three boxes about 20 centimeters apart in a semicircle about 1 meter from your animal. Lay the boxes on one side so that the open edge faces toward you and away from the animal (see Figure 3.6).

To ensure that your dog's or cat's motivation and general sensory abilities are up to the task, show him the toy and let him go. Check that he can find the toy by sight alone (many older dogs and cats have poor eyesight, in which case the experiment is impossible for them). Once he has found the toy, praise him and let him enjoy it for a moment. If it seems necessary to maintain motivation, you might want to give him a small treat.

Assuming that your dog or cat has passed this preliminary test, start the visible displacement task. One of you (Experimenter 2, from Figure 3.6) holds your subject, while the other one (Experimenter 1) visibly places the toy clearly in one of the three boxes. Place it deep inside so that it can be seen only by going right into the box. While you are doing this, maintain eye contact with the other experimenter – don't follow the toy with your eyes or your animal may follow your eyes instead of the toy. Now, Experimenter 2, let your subject go and see where he searches for the toy. If he heads straight for the box containing the toy, score that as a successful trial. If the first box he searches out is any other, score that as a failure. Try this a few times, selecting a different box each time.

If your dog or cat succeeds at the visible displacement test, it is time to try invisible displacement. To do this, set up the boxes and subject as at the beginning of the visible displacement experiment (Figure 3.6). Place the toy inside the yogurt carton (or other container) in full view of your subject. Now move the container with the toy behind one of the boxes and quietly empty the container into the box. Move the now empty container back out from behind the box and show your subject that it is empty (turn the container to face your subject). Finally, Experimenter 2, let your dog or cat loose to see where he searches for the object. A success is scored only if he heads straight for the box containing the toy. It does not count as a success if your subject gradually improves over several trials with the toy hidden behind the same box – he could be learning by trial and error always to go to that box. If you perform multiple trials, you must choose a different box each time.

If your dog or cat is successful on the invisible displacement test, you might want to try a better-controlled version of the task. Instead of leaning in and removing the toy from the container, set up a container that makes it possible for the toy to be removed without any movement by the experimenter that is visible to the subject. Figure 3.6 shows a V-shaped container on a pole. With this set-up, Gagnon and Doré were able to release the toy simply by twisting the pole to which the container was attached – an operation that could not be seen by the animal being tested. You could construct a V-shaped container of your own out of cardboard.

With this very simple testing arrangement many of the controversies in the literature can be re-created in your own home. Is it the case, for example, as Goulet and colleagues claimed, that performance on the invisible displacement improves if a delay is imposed before the animal is given an opportunity to fetch the toy? Or does your dog or cat perform better if he is already moving toward the toy at the point when it disappears?

It would also not require much expertise to build the apparatus used by Miller and colleagues (2009), shown in Figure 3.7, in order to test for object permanence using Miller and colleagues' methods.

Just why should so many species be capable of solving visible displacement tasks, and so few succeed on invisible displacements? Possibly visible displacements represent more ecologically meaningful problems than invisible displacements. Visible displacement is the sort of thing any predator animal has to put up with. A hunted prey animal disappears behind a rock. Clearly there is an adaptive advantage to be had from looking behind the rock. Conversely, invisible displacements may not correspond to any problem that an animal would confront in its daily life. Consider again the predator searching for prey. The prey slips behind a stone and then, invisible to the predator, leaves that stone for the next one. Our predator goes up to the first stone and fails to find its prey. In the design of invisible displacement experiments this would be counted as an error. To be scored as successful, the subject must *not* look behind the first stone where the prey animal disappeared. It would typically make sense for a predator to first search for prey in the last place where the prey was seen for sure, before widening the search to places to which it may have moved. This makes the task a rather unrealistic one compared with the demands of life outside of psychological experiments.

A further difficulty with invisible displacement tasks is that they contain many components. To be successful, the subject must understand that an object can be carried by another object (the toy is carried inside a container). The subject must also appreciate that the object can be removed from the container without any obvious intervention. Since the object in these tests is inanimate, there is no strong reason why the subject should appreciate that it can leave the container without any visible intervention. Then, on being shown the empty container, the subject must remember where the container has been. This form of memory may be difficult for many subjects because they are given no cue that they are going to have to remember where the container has gone.

Given the many cognitive demands made by the invisible displacement task, it is perhaps not surprising that most species tested have failed. As so often in the study of animal cognition, these failures raise many more questions than they answer. For example, would a cat be more successful at the task if the hidden object were animate (a mouse, say)? Would subjects be more successful if they were given some kind of cue to encourage memorization of the pattern of movement of the container? While it is refreshing to see different species from the standard rats and pigeons being tested, it would be valuable to assess object permanence in these more commonly studied species. We have far more knowledge of the abilities of rats and pigeons in the domains of memory and attention (see Chapter 10). Now that we are armed with this knowledge, interpretation of success and failure on invisible displacement tasks might be easier.

RELATIONAL CONCEPTS

Some concepts have nothing to do with individual objects at all but say something about the relationships between objects. Consider the concept 'same'. How do we know what counts as the same as what? This may sound like a very trivial question, but it turns out to be by no means a straightforward issue. For humans, for example, notions of same and different can vary between different cultures. Where English speakers consider objects on one side of them (left, say) to be in the same position no matter where they are standing, native speakers of Guugu-Yimithirr (a language of the native peoples of northeastern Australia) only consider objects placed at the same point of the compass to be in the same position, independent of where they are standing and whether the object is on their left or right.

Same-different

One of the first demonstrations that any animal species can learn to identify objects as the same or different was carried out by Anthony Wright and colleagues (1988). Wright's group trained pigeons to identify pairs of pictures presented on a computer screen as either the same or different. The apparatus used in this study is shown in Figure 3.8. Each trial started with the presentation of a stimulus that the pigeon had to peck a couple of times (this is known as the 'sample' stimulus). As soon as it had done this, two comparison stimuli were presented next to the original stimulus. One of the comparison stimuli was the same as the original stimulus – the other was different. The pigeon's task was to peck on the comparison stimulus that was identical to the original stimulus (known as the 'matching' stimulus). One group of pigeons was trained with just two sample stimuli; these pigeons mastered the problem in little more than two weeks. A second group of pigeons was trained with 152 sample stimuli that

Figure 3.8 *Apparatus used by Wright and colleagues to study pigeons' comprehension of the same-different concept*

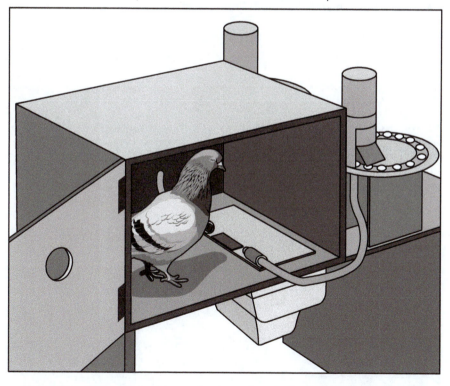

Notes: The pigeon pecked onto a horizontally mounted computer screen, and correct responses were rewarded with food grains dropped onto the screen from food hoppers mounted on top of the testing chamber.

Source: Image based on Wright et al. (1988).

were presented only once in each daily training session. These subjects required 18 months to master the same task.

The critical question in concept learning, however, is not just whether the subjects can learn to respond to the correct stimuli during training but whether they have abstracted the conceptual rule under investigation. To test whether the two groups of pigeons had abstracted the same-different concept, Wright and colleagues presented each group of pigeons with a completely new set of stimuli they had never seen before. The question now was whether they would apply the same-different rule to these new stimuli. Wright and coworkers found that the pigeons that had been trained with just two stimuli, although they had learned quickly, had not abstracted any kind of rule – they were completely stumped by the novel stimuli. The pigeons that had been trained with 152 stimuli, on the other hand, although they had learned very slowly, were much better able to categorize the novel stimuli as either the same or different. This indicates that they had learned an abstract rule.

Successful tests of the same-different concept have been made with rhesus monkeys (Wright et al. 1990), chimpanzees (Parr et al., 2000), and California sea lions (Schusterman & Kastak, 1998).

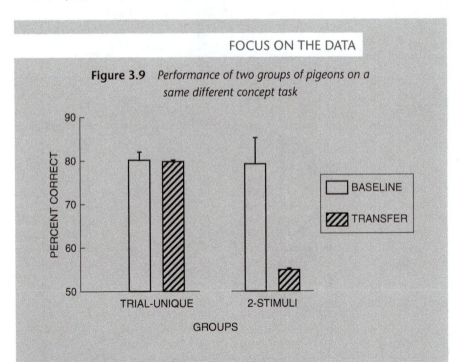

FOCUS ON THE DATA

Figure 3.9 *Performance of two groups of pigeons on a same different concept task*

Figure 3.9, from Wright and colleagues (1988), shows the performance of two groups of pigeons trained to discriminate same from different pictures. The group whose performance is presented on the left were trained with 152 different stimuli, each presented once per day. They achieved correct levels of around 80 percent during their baseline training, and they also maintained that level of performance when they were tested in transfer tests with stimuli they had never seen before. The group whose data is presented on the right were trained with just two pictures. They performed very similarly to the first group for those two training stimuli, but when they were shown new stimuli, their performance collapsed to close to chance levels.

Stimulus equivalence

A more extended notion of 'sameness' is the recognition that although some things are not the same, they may share certain properties that make them equivalent. A picture of an apple comes to have some of the same significance for a child as the spoken word 'apple' and, later, as the written word. An apple is a red or green spherical object that can be eaten; the word 'apple' – spoken or written – has none of these qualities, and yet it functions in some of the same ways as the object it names. This ability of objects to substitute for each other under certain conditions, known as 'stimulus equivalence', is an important pre-requisite for symbolic thought.

Attempts to demonstrate stimulus equivalence in animals have been made with several methods.

Edward Wasserman and Bhatt (1992) used the apparatus shown in Figure 3.2 with a modified procedure to show that having to make the same response to diverse stimuli could cause different objects to be considered as equivalent stimuli. Wasserman and colleagues showed pigeons 12 color pictures, each from one of four different categories: people, cars, chairs, and flowers. Unlike the Bhatt and colleagues (1988) study, in which the pigeons pecked on one of four keys around the picture area in order to indicate which of the four categories each picture belonged to, in this study only two of the pecking keys were operational, and the pigeons had to peck one key (say the top left one) for both cars and flowers and the other key (bottom right) for slides containing both people and chairs. This is termed 'common response' training: one response for one pair of categories, another response for the other pair.

Once this training was mastered, Wasserman and colleagues retrained the pigeons to make new responses but with only half the pictures. The pigeons were trained to respond on the bottom left key for pictures of chairs and the top right key for pictures of flowers. At this stage the pictures of cars and people were not presented.

After the pigeons had learned the new key assignments for the pictures of chairs and flowers, pictures of cars and people were reintroduced. Where would the pigeons peck for these images? Would they appreciate, since chairs are equivalent stimuli to people and they now had to respond on the bottom left key for chairs, that they should therefore also respond on the bottom left for people? Likewise, that they should respond top right for cars?

During tests in which reward and nonreward were administered independently of how the birds responded (so as not to bias their responses), the pigeons showed a clear tendency to assign the stimuli that had not been retrained (in this example, the cars and people) to the same response keys as the stimuli that had been retrained (the flowers and chairs, respectively). Performance was not perfect, but it was clearly above chance. This indicates that having a common response for diverse stimuli can prompt pigeons to recognize that the images are equivalent stimuli.

Another approach to stimulus equivalence in animals is to ask whether having similar consequences can cause stimuli to be considered equivalent. Peter Urcuioli and colleagues presented pigeons first with a single stimulus alone (the sample stimulus) and then followed it with two simultaneously presented comparison stimuli. Depending on which sample stimulus was presented, one or the other of the comparison stimuli was rewarded. Thus, a pigeon could be trained to respond on a circle stimulus after presentation of a red sample, but it had to respond on a dot stimulus after presentation of a green line sample. This was the Phase 1 training. In Phase 2 the pigeon was trained to expect new comparison stimuli based on some of the familiar sample stimuli. In the example shown in Figure 3.10, the pigeon learned that the red sample goes with a blue comparison stimulus and the green sample goes with a white comparison stimulus. The question of interest is what will the pigeons make of the vertical and horizontal sample stimuli when they are given blue and white comparison stimuli? Will the pigeons recognize that because red and vertical (and green and horizontal) stimuli had similar consequences in the original training and red and green now have new consequences, those new consequences will also apply to the vertical and horizontal stimuli, or will they simply be confused when they are

Figure 3.10   *Design of Urcuioli and colleagues' (1989) stimulus equivalence experiment*

Phase 1: Original Trraning

Sample Stimulus	Comparison stimulus
Red	Circle (not Dot)
Vertical	Circle (not Dot)
Green	Dot (not Circle)
Horizontal	Dot (not Circle)

Phase 2: Equivalence Traning

Sample Stimulus	Comparison stimulus
Red	Blue (not White)
Green	White (not)

Phase 3: Test for equivalence

Sample Stimulus	Comparison stimulus
Red	Blue or White??
Horizontal	White or Blue??

given sample stimuli followed by comparison stimuli that they had not been trained to expect? Urcuioli and colleagues (1989) found that pigeons tended to choose the blue comparison after the vertical sample and the white comparison after the horizontal comparison. This suggests that the pigeons treated the red and vertical (and green and horizontal) stimuli as equivalent because they had had the same consequences in the first phase of training. Figure 3.10 shows the outline of this experiment.

Consequences can also mean the reward that a hungry pigeon receives for making its response. Charles Edwards and colleagues (1982) explored stimulus equivalence by first training pigeons to respond on a red key (instead of a green one) after they had been shown a red sample stimulus. They also trained the pigeons to respond on the green key (instead of a red one) after the green sample stimulus. The same pigeons were also trained to respond on a black plus symbol (instead of a circle) after a plus had been presented and to respond on the circle (instead of a plus) after a circle had been presented. Thus these pigeons had learned two sets of matching to sample stimuli: one set of colors and one set of shapes. For these pigeons, a correct response to the green and plus matching tasks produced wheat as a reinforcer; correct responses to the red and circle matching tasks produced peas as the reinforcer. Other groups of pigeons were trained similarly but received rewards for their responses that did not differ depending on what stimulus they saw on each trial.

In critical tests, the samples and the choice stimuli from the color and the shape tasks were crossed over. Thus the birds now had to respond to the red comparison stimulus after seeing the circle sample and the plus comparison stimulus after the seeing the green sample stimulus. For the birds in the group that in initial training had received different rewards (wheat and peas), these different rewards were continued during testing so that they still received whatever type of reward had been associated with the sample and comparison stimuli during training. In other words, green and plus still led to wheat; red and circle to peas.

Edwards and colleagues observed that the birds in the group that experienced distinct outcomes with the different stimuli performed above chance on the first test with the crossed-over stimuli. The other group's performance was only at about chance levels.

These results suggest that the stimuli that led to the identical outcomes were grouped together by the birds as equivalent stimuli.

I will illustrate one final approach to stimulus equivalence in animals with an experiment on an animal other than a pigeon: the dolphin.

Lorenzo von Fersen and Juan Delius (2000) initially trained two dolphins to make a response to the left after two different tones (we'll call them T1 and T3). The dolphins were trained to go right after two other tones, T2 and T4. Once the dolphins had mastered this discrimination, it was reversed, starting just with T1 and T2. The dolphins now had to go right for T1 and left for T2. After ten trials with this reversal, the same reversal training was carried out with T3 and T4. For the first three trials with T3 and T4, the dolphins were given no feedback as to whether they had performed the task correctly so that Fersen and Delius could assess how much the training on T1 and T2 had affected the dolphin's assessment of what to do with T3 and T4. In this way Fersen and Delius could check whether the training with T1 and T2 led to faster acquisition of the reversed discrimination with T3 and T4.

Fersen and Delius repeated these reversals 14 times and observed that indeed, with practice, the dolphins performed consistently better on each new reversal with T3 and T4 than with T1 and T2. In other words, the reversal training caused the stimuli T1 and T3 (and T2 and T4) to be treated as equivalent stimuli.

Overall then, there is convergent evidence from several experimental designs showing that animals are capable of treating diverse stimuli as equivalent. This can occur because the stimuli require similar responses, because they lead to similar outcomes, or because their outcomes stay together when they are changed.

Most of the studies in this domain have been carried out on pigeons, but there are also some experiments on dolphins, sea lions (Kastak et al., 2001), and a chimpanzee (Tomonaga, 1999).

CONCLUSIONS

In Chapter 2 we saw that the perceptual worlds of other species can be very different from our own. Many animals can see ultraviolet and infrared radiation that is invisible to us or hear tones that are too high or low for us to hear or perceive electric fields. In the realm of the more abstract aspects of experience that are the subject of this chapter, there does not seem to have been the same uncovering of 'superhuman' abilities in other species. This may be because we cannot conceive of how to look for conceptual skills that we do not have. Nonetheless, the experiments reviewed in this chapter have shown that several species share aspects of human conceptual experience. Various forms of perceptual categorization have been shown in some mammals and birds. An understanding of the permanency of hidden objects has been shown in adult dogs and some apes. Perhaps it will be found in other species as better means of testing are developed.

FURTHER READING

Urcuioli, P. (2012) Stimulus control and stimulus class formation. In G. J. Madden, W. V. Dube, T. D. Hackenberg, G. P. Hanley, & K. A. Lattal (Eds), *APA Handbook of Behavior Analysis, Vol. 1: Methods and Principles* (pp. 361–386). Washington, DC, US: American Psychological Association.

Urcuioli offers a comprehensive summary of research on concept formation.

Wasserman, E. A. & Young, M. E. (2010) Same-different discrimination: the keel and backbone of thought and reasoning. *Journal of Experimental Psychology: Animal Behavior Processes,* 36, 3–22.

A wide-ranging thoughtful discussion of the importance of the same-different concept as a foundation of reasoning.

Zentall, T. R. (2000) Symbolic representation by pigeons. *Current Directions in Psychological Science,* 9, 118–122.

Zentall summarizes the results of many experiments on stimulus equivalence.

Web sources

http://www.equineresearch.org/
Evelyn Hanggi's research on horse cognition is summarized at this site.

http://biosci-labs.unl.edu/avcog/research/bjay.htm
Interesting research on how blue jays learn to find moths and how moths evolve to be more cryptic is summarized here.

4   Time and Number

The Lion went once a-hunting along with the Fox, the Jackal, and the Wolf. They hunted and they hunted till at last they surprised a Stag, and soon took its life. Then came the question how the spoil should be divided. 'Quarter me this Stag,' roared the Lion; so the other animals skinned it and cut it into four parts. Then the Lion took his stand in front of the carcass and pronounced judgment: 'The first quarter is for me in my capacity as King of Beasts; the second is mine as arbiter; another share comes to me for my part in the chase; and as for the fourth quarter, well, as for that, I should like to see which of you will dare to lay a paw upon it.'

Aesop's Fables, translated by G. F. Townsend

An awareness that animals have a sensitivity to the passage of time probably predates recorded history. Our hunting and gathering ancestors surely noticed that some of their prey were active during the day, others at night, and still others only at dawn and dusk. The patterns of daily activity that we notice in ourselves and in species that have sleeping and waking patterns so different from our own, such as bats, indicate an underlying sensitivity to intervals of time of about 24 hours. But sensitivity to the rhythms of the day is not the only way that animals are responsive to time. Research that started in Ivan Pavlov's laboratory at the end of the nineteenth century has shown that many animal species are also sensitive to short and arbitrary time intervals. Pavlov's students found that if dry food is put into a dog's mouth at regular intervals of a few minutes, after a few repeated presentations, the dog will start salivating just before the food is going into its mouth even though there is no explicit conditioned stimulus present. Time itself was the conditioned stimulus in this case.

Many species have been shown to have a strong sense of time of day, as well as the ability to learn about shorter and variable intervals between important events.

The study of animals' sense of numbers does not have such a long history, and as we learned in Chapter 1, its beginnings were not auspicious. Though the study of animal numerical abilities got off to a bad start in the nineteenth century with Clever Hans – the horse who had everybody fooled into thinking that he could perform advanced mathematical functions – more recent studies have uncovered some important evidence for basic numerical abilities in a range of species.

TIME

Learning about time of day

Most animals and many plants show typical daily rhythms of activity. Bean seedlings open out their leaves each morning to catch the sun and close them again in the evening. Many flowers also open during the day and close at night. Many animals are more active during the day than the night, but many others are more active during the night than the day; hamsters, rats, and cockroaches, for example, all engage in more movement during the night. Some animals, such as fiddler crabs and some lizards, change their body color from day to night. Sparrows, like most birds, are more active during the day than during the night for the simple reason that they would probably bump into things if they tried to fly in the dark. Bees can learn that certain sources of food are available at certain hours of the day and not others. Humans have these circadian (approximately day-length) rhythms, too – as anyone who has flown more than a couple of time zones east or west can attest (Mistleberger & Rusak, 2004).

As the experience of jet lag suggests, we and other species do not simply become active because the sun has risen. There is an internal component to circadian cycles of activity. Experiments in which animals were left in an environment that did not change in lighting or any other way over the 24-hour period shed light on this internal component. Despite the lack of external stimulation, the animals in these studies developed a pattern of waking and sleeping, activity and inactivity, flying and not flying, or whatever other behavior was being measured that approximated the 24-hour cycle of the normal earth day. Sparrows left in the dark, for example, generated a spontaneous rhythm of hopping and not hopping that repeated approximately every 24 hours (Mistlberger & Rusak, 2004, give many more examples).

Although jet lag shows us that our pattern of waking and sleeping has an inborn, endogenous component, the fact that jet lag ultimately passes and we become accustomed to the new day and night cycle in the time zone we have moved to shows that circadian rhythms are entrainable. Factors that can entrain the natural daily rhythm of an animal's activity are given the German name *Zeitgeber* – literally 'time giver'. Although the natural daily rhythm is one of 24 hours, many animals will entrain to shorter or longer periods of time given the right *Zeitgeber*. Light is a very important *Zeitgeber*. Other signals that animals use to set their circadian rhythm include temperature (it is usually cooler at night than during the day); social factors (two sparrows in adjacent cages entrain each other to the same circadian rhythm); and feeding (delivery of food at regular times can entrain the circadian rhythm even when other *Zeitgeber* are absent). With suitable entrainment, many animals can adapt to cycles of activity of less than 24 hours (in some cases as short as 16 hours, but most animals cannot adapt to cycles shorter than 20 or 22 hours). The upper limit in plants as well as animals is around 28 to 30 hours although entrainment to such extreme values requires bright light.

The circadian clock is also very accurate. Bees and rats, to take two random examples, can regulate their daily activity patterns with an accuracy of between five and ten minutes. This is an error of around half a percent.

Unlike animals in captivity and pets in homes where food is often left out all day, animals in the real world often have to do different things at different times of day in order to find food. Circadian timing enables animals to forage effectively. In an early laboratory demonstration of what is called 'time and place learning', Herbert Biebach and colleagues (1989) gave garden warblers (a small brown bird with a pleasant song, common in Europe) feeders in four different rooms to eat at. The feeder in the first room was open for three hours early in the morning, the second feeder was available for three hours in late morning, and the final two feeders were operational in the early and late afternoon, respectively. The garden warblers readily learned to go to the correct feeding location for the time of day. In tests in which all the feeders were available all the time, the birds persisted in going to each feeder primarily at the time that it had been operational during the training phase. This indicates that the birds could use their circadian clock to time their visits to match when the food was available. A further test of this notion came when the experimenters blocked access to the rooms containing the feeders during a three-hour period when one feeder would have been active. When the rooms were opened again, the birds went to the correct room to obtain food at that time of day rather than simply going to the next feeder in sequence. This demonstrates that they were not just going to one feeder after another but had learned that a particular feeder was the appropriate place to find food at a certain time of day.

In another informative time and place learning experiment, Matthew Pizzo and Jonathon Crystal (2002) offered rats food in three different locations at three different times of day. One group of rats found food once in the morning and twice in the afternoon; another group found food twice in the morning and just once in the afternoon. Once the rats had learned this distribution of food – as shown by their tendency to show up at the correct feeder at the correct time – Pizzo and Crystal switched the time of the second feeding. For rats that had been accustomed to finding food in the late morning, this feeding was shifted to the early afternoon, and vice versa for the rats that had been finding food in the early afternoon. If the rats were simply slowly traipsing from one feeding location to the next in order, this switching of the time of the middle feeding of the day should not have made much difference to them. If, on the other hand, they were using their circadian clock to regulate their presence at the different feeding locations, the switching of the time of the second feeding should have thrown them off the scent. Pizzo and Crystal found that the latter was the case – the changed timing confused the rats, indicating that they had been relying on their circadian clocks.

The importance of circadian rhythms is not just that they ensure that an animal's activity is suited to the environment in which it lives, though that is certainly important, but an internal sense of time of day is also extremely useful to animals that have to navigate. As we will see in Chapter 7, pigeons, bees, and other homing animals combine their sense of time of day with the position of the sun in order to establish their bearings. It is not known how many species use this trick, but its presence in two such unrelated species suggests it may be quite widespread.

Learning about short time intervals

The ability to accurately gauge time of day – circadian timing – is without doubt highly useful to animals. It enables them to structure effectively their patterns of activity through the day, as well as providing the basis for sun-compass orientation. Circadian timing, however, has two limitations. The first is that it is restricted to time periods of approximately 24 hours. Many of the things that happen in this world at regular intervals of time are not restricted to periods of approximately one day. The arrival of predators, prey, and other important events may reoccur at intervals of seconds, minutes, or hours. The second drawback with circadian timing is that it can be used only to place events within a daily cycle – animals are not able to use the circadian clock to judge arbitrary time intervals.

Long-tailed hermit hummingbirds feed on nectar-bearing flowers in the Costa Rican jungle, where their feeding habits have been studied by Frank Gill (1988). Male hummingbirds need a great deal of energy to survive, but foraging time is scarce; male hummingbirds like to spend as much time as possible trying to impress female hummingbirds. Every moment that the male hummingbird is away looking for nectar is a possible mating opportunity lost. To add to the difficulty of the male hummingbird's situation, flowers are not always full of nectar. After the nectar has been removed, different flowers refill at different rates. The longer the hummingbird waits before going off on a foraging trip, the greater the probability that the flowers he last visited will have refilled with nectar, but there is also an increased risk that another bird will have made off with that nectar. Consequently, the hummingbird is confronted by a difficult timing problem. He needs to time his nectar-foraging trips so that his visits to the flowers coincide as closely as possible with the length of time it takes each flower to refill. Too short a length of time, and he will fail to pick up the maximum amount of nectar from each flower; too long, and there is a risk that another bird will get there first.

Gill (1988) set up some artificial flowers that he could fill with nectar whenever he wanted to in order to test how well the hummingbirds were able to time their flower visits. Just as his field observations had suggested, Gill found that when he refilled the flowers with artificial nectar ten minutes after a bird's last visit, it adjusted the interval between visits to a little longer than the ten-minute refill time. How soon a hummingbird returned to the flowers also depended on whether the bird had exclusive use of that flower or whether other birds were feeding from the same nectar source.

Studies by Jonathan Henderson and colleagues (2006) on another species of hummingbird also utilized artificial flowers, this time to show how the birds could time multiple events simultaneously. Rufous hummingbirds living wild in Alberta, Canada, were offered eight artificial flowers that the experimenters had filled with sugar solution. Four of the flowers were refilled ten minutes after the birds emptied them; the other four flowers were refilled after twenty minutes had passed. Henderson and colleagues found that within two or three days the birds matched the time of their visits to the refill times of the different flowers, showing that they could remember where and when sugar water would be available.

FOCUS ON THE DATA

Figure 4.1 shows the timing behavior of three rufous hummingbirds from Henderson and colleagues' study (2006). Each panel shows the distribution of postreinforcement pauses; that is to say, how long the birds delayed their return to an artificial flower. Flowers that were refilled every 10 minutes are shown in black; those that refilled at 20-minute intervals are shown in gray. It can be seen that the birds most commonly waited 10 to 15 minutes before returning to a flower that refilled every 10 minutes, and they most commonly waited 20 to 25 minutes before returning to flowers that refilled every 20 minutes.

Figure 4.1   *Timing behavior of rufous hummingbirds*

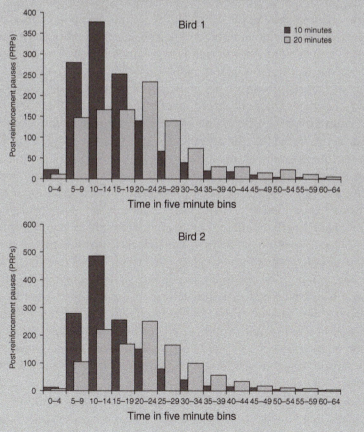

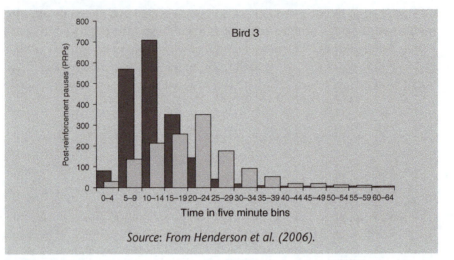

Source: From Henderson et al. (2006).

Sensitivity to time intervals is not an obscure ability of a handful of species that have special timing problems to deal with. One of the most direct ways of ascertaining any animal's sensitivity to time intervals is simply to give it food at regular intervals of time – say once every two minutes. The first couple of times the animal receives the food, it may be surprised, but it will quickly come to expect the food at the two-minute point and will demonstrate this expectation by approaching the feeder about half way through the interval. Other species-specific food-directed behaviors may also develop. A pigeon may peck any foodlike detail in the environment; a rat might gnaw on something near the feeder; a cat may meow and rub itself against a suitable object. Each of these behavioral patterns occurs at characteristic points in the interval, and they indicate that the animal has an ability to time the interval and that this ability is quickly entrained.

An experiment that is only slightly more involved than this requires a rat or pigeon (typically, though many other species have also been used) to make at least one response on a lever (for rats) or pecking key (for pigeons) after a set interval has elapsed. In order to obtain food, a response is required only *after* the interval has elapsed, but hungry pigeons and rats (and other species) start making their lever or key responses well before the interval is up. Typically, for an animal in a box with nothing else to do, responding starts after about one-third of the interval has elapsed and then gradually increases in rate so that the animal is responding very quickly as the interval reaches its end and the reward becomes available. In this situation, known as a fixed-interval schedule, the fact that the pigeon or rat will start responding earlier if the interval is shortened or later if the interval is lengthened is further evidence of these animals' sensitivity to time intervals.

Seth Roberts (1981) introduced a simple modification to the fixed-interval procedure that provides additional insight into the way in which these animals time intervals. Now, although most intervals are just like the intervals in the fixed-interval procedure, occasional intervals do not end with food. Instead they run for three or four times the normal length. Under these conditions Roberts found that, with training, the rate of responding peaks at around the time that food would normally be delivered. For this reason, this modified fixed-interval procedure is known as the 'peak interval' procedure. The fact that the response rate peaks at the time when food would normally be delivered suggests that the animals tested have an expectation of when the food would normally arrive. Figure 4.2 shows a typical pattern of responding from a peak interval experiment with rats.

The fixed interval and peak interval procedures are examples of situations where an animal's sense of time becomes apparent in the patterns that develop in its own behavior. The rats used to compile the data for Figure 4.2 revealed their appreciation that food would normally be delivered after 40 seconds by producing their highest response rate at the 40-second point.

In another type of procedure, animals are presented with stimuli of different durations and indicate their perception of these durations by responding to different alternatives.

Rats can be trained to respond on one lever after a short stimulus (a tone of three seconds' duration, say) and on a different lever after a longer stimulus (a tone of twelve seconds). The same task can be given to pigeons using pecking keys rather

Figure 4.2 *The average rate of lever pressing for a group of rats accustomed to receiving food reward every 40 seconds*

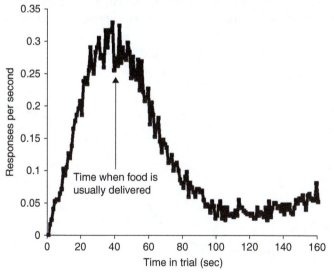

Notes: In this trial the interval has been extended to 160 seconds, but the rats' rate of lever pressing peaks at around 40 seconds – the time when food would normally be delivered.

Source: Data provided by E. Ludvig.

than levers. We can call the alternative that the animal is trained to respond to after the shorter stimulus the 'short' lever or key; the other alternative is then the 'long' lever or key. The first experiment with this procedure was carried out by Russell Church and Marvin Deluty (1977) with rats. Once Church and Deluty had the rats reliably responding to the long lever after the long stimulus and the short lever after the short stimulus, they occasionally exposed the rats to stimuli that varied in duration between the short and long extremes. A similar function obtained from pigeons trained to peck on one pecking key after 2 seconds and then an alternative key after 8 seconds and tested with durations intermediate between 2 and 8 seconds is shown in Figure 4.3. In this figure, the proportion of occasions when the rats responded on the long lever is plotted as a function of the duration of the stimulus. A figure with the same shape, just flipped over, would have been obtained if Church and Deluty had instead plotted the propor-tion of responses to the short lever, since on each trial the rats must respond on one or other lever. Figure 4.3 clearly shows that the pigeons responded to stimuli that were very similar to 3 and 12 seconds mostly on the short and long levers, respectively. It is interesting to consider what stimulus duration the rats treated as psychologically equidistant from 2 and 8 seconds; that is, the stimulus duration to which they made half of their responses on each key (drawn on Figure 4.3 as a dotted line). This duration is not halfway between 2 and 8 seconds (which would be 5 seconds) but slightly shorter – around 4 seconds. Four seconds is the geometric mean of 2 and 8 seconds – that is, the square root of their product: $\sqrt{(2 \times 8)}$.

For many years the dominant theory of how animals time short intervals has assumed that animals possess a sort of internal clock. According to 'scalar tim-ing' theory, proposed by Russell Church (1978), timing in animals is controlled

Figure 4.3   *Proportion of responses to the long key made by pigeons after stimuli of different durations*

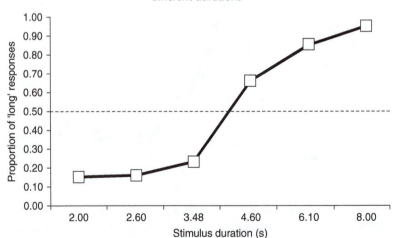

Notes: The pigeons had first been trained to respond to the long key after an 8-second stimulus and to the short key after stimuli lasting 2 seconds.

by something akin to a ticking clock. When an event happens that the animal wishes to time, the ticks of the clock are counted into a short-term memory store. The animal knows that the correct time has elapsed when the number of ticks in the short-term memory matches the number of ticks stored on the basis of previous experience in long-term memory.

Though this theory has been strikingly successful and long-lived, in more recent years alternative theories have been developed.

One alternative theory comes from a behaviorist perspective and eschews all mention of internal clocks. Peter Killeen and Greg Fetterman's (1988) 'Behavioural Theory of Timing' proposes that in a timing experiment such as the fixed-interval procedure, animals progress through a series of different states, visible in different behaviors that they show at different points through the interval. At the beginning of the interval, an animal such as a rat or hamster may spend a lot of time chewing the food it has just received. As the interval progresses, other behaviors, unrelated to the food, may appear – behaviors like grooming and walking about. As the interval nears its end and the opportunity for food gets closer, the animal engages in behaviors that are clearly related to the food delivery –gnawing at the food opening, for example. Though the existence of these diverse behaviors inspired the theory, the underlying hypothesized states are not identical with the observed behaviors, and indeed there can be underlying states that do not show in any obviously visible behavior. Animals come to be able to time intervals because they can associate events in the outside world with their internal states.

When food is more frequent, animals move through their states faster; when food is less frequent they move through their states slower. This accounts for the often observed fact that animals time short intervals more accurately than longer ones.

Another alternative theory that does away with the need for an internal clock was proposed by John Staddon and Jennifer Higa (1999). In Staddon and Higa's theory, timed behavior is controlled by steadily decaying memory traces for salient events. For example, on a fixed-interval schedule (where, as described above, food is given for the first response after an interval of time has elapsed), each food reward sets up a memory trace that gradually decays in the interval until the next food reward is delivered. Animals, it is proposed, can learn to associate a particular level of this memory trace with an action. Once the memory trace decays below that memorized level, the subject starts to make responses.

What this theory implies is that if the food reward is made larger, then the memory trace will start off larger. If the memory trace starts at a high level, then it will take longer to decay to the critical level at which responding commences. Consequently, larger food rewards will lead to delayed responses in fixed-interval experiments. Conversely, the replacement of a food reward with a neutral stimulus of equal duration (e.g., a light) should lead to a shorter response delay in such experiments. Both these findings were observed many years ago (Staddon, 1970) but previously lacked a theoretical explanation.

Although interval timing is far more flexible than circadian timing, that flexibility does come at a cost. Where events of approximately daily frequency can be timed with an accuracy of around 99.5 percent, the accuracy of interval timing decreases with the length of the interval being timed. Consequently, though an interval of seconds or a few minutes can be timed quite effectively, the error in timing an interval of several hours in this way is catastrophic. In a simple but interesting experiment, David Eckerman (1999) compared the ability of pigeons to time intervals from 12 to 48 hours. Just as had been found many times before in experiments on interval timing, accuracy was generally proportional to the duration of the interval – longer intervals were less accurately timed than shorter ones. However, at intervals of 24 hours, and also 12 and 48 hours (simple multiples or subdivisions of 24 hours), an anomaly appeared – the pigeons' timing was much more accurate than at slightly shorter or longer intervals. This must have been because the pigeons switched to their circadian timing ability, which, though less flexible, is far more accurate.

NUMBERS

What does it mean to have a sense of number? At its simplest, it can just mean being aware that ten items are more than five items. This is known as relative number judgment and differs from the (presumably) simpler judgment of amount by virtue of its being the total number of items that are critical in making the judgment – not their total amount. Twenty ants are larger in number than two elephants, despite being much smaller in terms of amount. The next level of complexity in the appreciation of number is the recognition that all quantities of the same number have something in common. This is called absolute number judgment: what it is that three cars have in common with three plums. Counting implies more than just a relative and an absolute sense of number. To count means at least using certain number names in a consistent order to 'tag' groups of items and recognizing that the name of the last item in a counted group is the name for the number of items in the whole group. Counting can also mean using arithmetical operations.

Relative number judgments: more or less

As we saw in Chapter 1, the study of animal cognition started out with a terrible embarrassment in the consideration of animals' numerical perception – the case of Clever Hans. This inhibited research on animals' ability to judge number for close on a century. During this period, however, there were a couple of exceptional individuals who maintained an active interest in animals' perception of number. One of them was Otto Koehler. Koehler (1951), together with his students and colleagues, studied the numerical ability of several species of birds. Jackdaws, crows, budgerigars, ravens, magpies, and pigeons were favored subjects in experiments in which the subject had to pick containers with different numbers of pieces of grain glued to their lids. If the bird chose incorrectly, no food reward was forthcoming from the container, and if necessary it was shooed away verbally, by hand, or, in recalcitrant cases, with something akin to a fly swatter. Koehler and his coworkers were able to demonstrate that pigeons could learn to pick the container with the smaller or larger number of grains glued to its lid. The pigeons found it easier to pick when the alternatives presented to them were farther apart in number (e.g., seven versus four) than when they were consecutive (five versus four).

There was a problem with these early studies, however, of which Koehler was fully aware. How could he be sure that the pigeons and other subjects were attending to the *number* of grains when they made their choices? They could have solved these problems on the basis of some other, perhaps simpler, quality of the containers' grain-covered lids. For one thing, when there were fewer grains on a lid, less of the lid would have been covered over – hence there might have been confusion between number and the area of the lid that was covered. Though Koehler did try to control for this problem in one experiment by using lumps of plasticine instead of grains, the equipment available in his day did not permit wide-ranging control. Another problem with the early studies is that, with such small numbers, the birds may have learned about the characteristic visual patterns that small numbers of items typically make. One item is always just a point; two items form a line; three items typically form a triangle; four items a quadrilateral. With larger numbers this becomes less of an issue, but with small numbers it is a considerable problem, particularly when modern knowledge about the number of visual patterns that animals are able to learn by rote is taken into account (see Chapter 10).

Jacky Emmerton and colleagues adapted Koehler's experiment using modern methods to control for the alternative ways that birds might be choosing between fewer or more items, apart from the control by number of items that we are interested in (Emmerton et al., 1997; Emmerton, 1998). Emmerton's subjects, pigeons, were trained in a Skinner box (see Box 2.1) to respond to slides containing different numbers of dots. During their initial training, the pigeons were rewarded for pecking on one response key if six or seven ('many') dots appeared on a slide and rewarded for pecking on a different response key if one or two ('few') dots appeared. Emmerton's results suggested that the pigeons had abstracted a concept of number because the birds, after their initial training had taught them to discriminate between six or seven dots and one or two, performed correctly when given choices between three, four, or five dots. Unlike Koehler, Emmerton was able to test that it really was the number of dots and not some other factor that was controlling the pigeons' choices by systematically varying other dimensions of the stimuli that might have been important to the pigeons and observing whether these variations had any impact. The factors Emmerton considered included the shape of the dots, their size, their brightness, and how closely packed together they were. Emmerton's results show clearly that pigeons are capable of learning the abstract concept of relative number – that is, they can discriminate 'fewer' from 'more', at least for numbers up to seven. Similar results have been found with monkeys (Jordan & Brannon, 2006) and, using sounds instead of images, with rats (Meck & Church, 1983).

Absolute number

As well as understanding that seven is more than five, using the concept of number effectively also means understanding that every group of five items has something in common. This quality that a certain number of ants shares with the same number of elephants is known as 'absolute number'. Otto Koehler and his students were the first to investigate absolute number in animals. A raven called Jakob was trained to pick a pot with five spots on its lid out of five pots with different numbers of spots on their lids. Jakob succeeded at this task even though the area on the lids that the different numbers of dots occupied varied 50-fold (Koehler, 1951).

In an experiment on a very little-studied species, Hank Davis (1984) made a detailed study of the ability of a raccoon named Rocky to pick the clear plastic cube that contained three objects (grapes or small metal balls) out of a set of plastic cubes containing from one to five items. Only the cube containing three items could be opened. Rocky's reward for a correct choice included being able to eat the grapes or wash the metal balls. In addition, Rocky was given social reward in the form of hugs from the experimenter (see Figure 4.4)

Figure 4.4 *On the left, Rocky the raccoon is selecting the transparent cube containing an object in an early phase of training. On the right, Rocky is receiving social reinforcement*

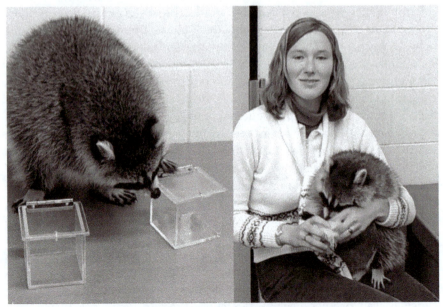

Source: Courtesy of H. Davis.

Davis and his colleagues carried out several other experiments on absolute number using the more familiar rat subjects. In an experiment reminiscent of Monty Python's holy hand grenade ('The number thou shalt count shall be three'), Hank Davis and Melody Albert (1986) demonstrated that rats could learn to make a response only after three bursts of white noise, not two or four. These bursts of noise were of random duration, so the rats could not solve the task using their ability to judge time intervals. In a follow-up experiment, Davis and colleagues (1989) considered whether rats could distinguish three touches to their whiskers from two or four. In this experiment, the timing of the whisker touches was also randomized so that the rats had to discriminate the number of touches, not their timing. Other studies showed that rats could learn to restrict their feeding to a fixed number of food items even if the type of food was shifted after the original training. Different groups of rats were assigned as three-eaters, four-eaters, or five-eaters. If they ate the correct number of items, they were praised verbally and given an extra food item. If, however, they tried to eat too many food items, they were punished with a loud 'no' and a (slightly) frightening hand clap (Davis & Bradford, 1991).

Studies with a quite different design also support the hypothesis that rats can distinguish absolute numbers. Hank Davis and Sheree Bradford (1986) trained rats to take food from the third of six tunnels. All tunnels contained food (so odor cues were controlled), but all except the third tunnel had their doors jammed shut so that the rat could not enter and eat the food within. The exact positions of the tunnels could be moved around so that positional cues were controlled for. Figure 4.5 shows part of the apparatus and a rat choosing the correct tunnel. With training the rats would go directly to the third tunnel, ignoring the others on their way.

Kerrie Lewis and colleagues (2005) used a novel technique to demonstrate sensitivity to number in a little-studied species, the mongoose lemur. The experimenters let the lemurs watch as they dropped grapes into a bucket. On half of the trials, the bucket had a false bottom that trapped some of the grapes so that they disappeared and the lemurs could not obtain them. Lewis and colleagues were interested to see whether the lemurs would recognize that something was wrong and spend longer searching the bucket when grapes that should have been there were missing. The lemurs showed that they had a sense of number by searching longer when grapes had been trapped in the false bottom of the bucket – at least when half the grapes were missing. When only one-third or one-quarter of the grapes deposited in the bucket had disappeared, there was little evidence that the lemurs detected the theft. This suggests the limits of their numerical ability.

Research by other investigators has shown that rats and pigeons can be trained to make a specific number of responses to a response lever. Platt and Johnson (1971), for example, trained rats to make a certain number of responses on a lever in order to earn a reward. When they had completed the required number of responses, the rats had to put their head in the food tray. If the rat broke

Figure 4.5 *One of Davis and Bradford's rats selecting the correct tunnel*

Source: Courtesy of H. Davis.

off making responses and put its head in the food tray prematurely, it had to start over with pressing the lever. Accuracy was high only for small numbers (below 10; Mechner, 1958), but some evidence of a perception of the number of responses made has been demonstrated with numbers up to 50 (Rilling & McDiarmid, 1965).

In the world outside the laboratory, number must often be confused with other aspects of objects, such as size. But some recent studies have shown that animals in the wild can be sensitive to numbers.

David White and colleagues (2007) investigated the behavior of the female brown-headed cowbird. Cowbirds are parasites that lay their eggs in the nests of other birds such as red-winged blackbirds. Ideally, cowbirds should select nests for their eggs that the host bird has only just begun to lay her eggs in. This would ensure that the host mother would carry out the full cycle of incubation on the parasite's egg. Since red-winged blackbirds typically lay about four eggs in a clutch, White and colleagues hypothesized that the brown-headed cow-birds should prefer to lay their eggs in nests that contain two or three eggs. They brought cowbirds into the laboratory, where they prepared nests with different numbers of eggs in them. Their results showed that the cowbirds preferred to lay their own eggs in nests that already contained eggs and that they preferred nests with three eggs to nests containing just one.

Counting

Though some would use the term 'counting' to refer to any ability to perceive number, there is really much more to counting than just the relative and absolute number competencies we have considered so far. In order to count, it is not just necessary to recognize that five items are more than four items (relative number). It is not even enough to recognize that every group of five items has something in common with every other group of five items (absolute number), whatever those items may be. Counting also means recognizing at least two further qualities of numbers:

1. *Tagging*: a certain number name or tag goes with a certain quantity of items. In English the name 'one' or symbol '1' stands for a single item. 'Two' or '2' goes with a pair of items, and so on. These tags must always be applied in the same order.
2. *Cardinality*: the tag applied to the last item of a set is the name for the number of items in that set. Thus, as I tag the pens on my desk, I call the first one 'one', the next one 'two', and the last one 'three'. 'Three' is consequently the correct name for the number of pens on my desk.

Although, as we have just seen, there is some evidence that at least a few species of animals are sensitive to number, evidence that any animals can count is harder to come by. For one thing, to demonstrate an appreciation of tagging and cardinality, a subject has to be able to produce a range of different responses. Without a range of different number tags available to it, an animal could never tell us whether it appreciates that three items deserve the tag 'three' and not 'two' or 'four'.

Some of the strongest evidence for counting comes from an African gray parrot called Alex, trained in a rather original way by Irene Pepperberg (1987, 1994). Box 4.1 outlines the method used with Alex. Alex was trained to respond verbally in English to questions presented to him verbally by an experimenter. He would be presented a tray of several objects and asked 'What's this?' or 'How many?' In tests with novel objects Alex was able to correctly identify the number of items in groups of up to six objects with an accuracy of around 80 percent. Even mixed groups of more than one type of object were not an insurmountable problem for Alex, though his accuracy suffered a little. Although only small numbers were tested, Pepperberg took care to ensure that the objects did not fall into characteristic patterns on the tray. Alex was also able to answer questions such as 'How many purple wood?' when presented with a tray containing pieces of purple wood along with orange wooden items, purple pieces of chalk, and orange chalk all intermixed.

BOX 4.1   HOW TO TRAIN A PARROT TO COUNT

Irene Pepperberg (1987, 1994) developed a unique training procedure that takes advantage of the enthusiasm of Africa gray parrots to imitate human sounds. During training the parrot is encouraged to answer questions put to him by the experimenter using the model-rival technique. In this method humans demonstrate the required response. A human acts as a model for the parrot by answering the experimenter's questions and as the parrot's rival for the experimenter's attention.

During training the experimenter might present a tray of objects to the parrot and the human subject and ask 'What color?' If the parrot shows no inclination to answer, the human will give a response and receive praise and reward from the experimenter if correct. The human subject sometimes makes errors, copying the kinds of mistakes the parrot might make. Errors are 'punished' with disapproval from the experimenter, who removes the materials, shakes her head, and says 'No' emphatically. The parrot's natural desire for attention and the opportunity to play with the objects presented is enough to encourage him to attempt to answer the question himself the next time it is asked. Thus, the human subject acts both as a model for the parrot to attempt to copy and as a rival for the rewards the experimenter is offering. Reward for the parrot typically takes the form of an opportunity to play with the objects presented (which ensures he makes a detailed inspection of the objects) or a nut. To encourage the parrot to keep working even when he is no longer interested in the objects being presented, he is also permitted to ask for and play with a more preferred object after he has answered a question correctly.

To test what the parrot has learned, a different experimenter is brought in to ask questions. The primary trainer now sits facing away from the parrot and acts solely as an interpreter, repeating to an assistant the words the parrot has said (which can be difficult for an untrained ear to understand).

Using this method, one parrot, Alex, was trained to produce over 100 English words, and he could answer questions about several qualities of the objects presented to him, including their color, shape, and material, as well as number.

More evidence for counting comes from the chimpanzee Ai. Ai was trained by Tetsuro Matsuzawa and coworkers to touch numerals on a computer screen in ascending numerical order (Biro & Matsuzawa, 1999, 2001; Kawai & Matsuzawa, 2000). Up to five numerals, selected at random from the range zero to nine, appeared simultaneously in randomized positions on the computer screen. Ai first had to touch the lowest numeral, which then disappeared. Then she had to pick the lowest of the remaining numerals, and it too disappeared. This process was repeated until, finally, Ai touched the only remaining numeral (the highest number in the original set), and she received a small food reward. Ai succeeded at this task even when all the remaining numerals were replaced by white squares after the first numeral had been touched.

Masaki Tomonaga and Tetsuro Matsuzawa (2002) compared the performance of chimpanzees with that of humans. In their study, up to ten numerals (from zero to nine) were presented on a computer touch screen for just one-tenth of a second before being replaced by white squares. The subjects had to touch the white squares in the order of the numbers that had briefly been visible in their place on the screen. Tomonaga and Matsuzawa found that the chimpanzee Ai was far better at this task than were four graduate students at Kyoto University. Though it should be noted that she had also received much more practice than the students. Sana Inoue and Matsuzawa (2007) extended this work to the next generation of chimpanzees. They tested three mother–offspring pairs of chimps and found, perhaps not surprisingly, that the more briefly the numerals were presented on the screen, the less successful the subjects were at the task. Interestingly, however, this was true only of the college students and the adult chimpanzees. Ayumu, Ai's son, who at the time of the study was four years old, performed equally well no matter how quickly the stimuli were presented. This, the authors suggested, might be evidence that Ayumu possesses 'eidetic imagery'. Eidetic imagery, sometimes known colloquially as a 'photographic memory', is an ability to remember a complex pattern with high precision. In humans, this ability is present to a higher degree in children than in adults.

Experiments by Elizabeth Brannon and Herb Terrace (2000) on three macaque monkeys shared some of the design features of the research on Ai the chimpanzee. Brannon and Terrace's monkeys learned to touch stimuli on a computer screen in order of numerosity. In Brannon and Terrace's experiments, however, the stimuli were not numerals (as Ai's had been) but different numbers of objects. These objects could be simple squares or circles of differing sizes or items selected from clip art software or even objects that differed in size, shape, and color. An example array is shown in Figure 4.6. The monkeys were well able to select quantities from one to four in ascending or descending order even though the stimuli used varied greatly throughout training.

Brannon and Terrace point out that it is not particularly difficult to train a monkey to respond to any series of four arbitrary items in a specific order. Their success in training monkeys to select quantities from one to four in certain orders might therefore have nothing to do with counting and could just be evidence of this ability to order arbitrary stimuli and responses. In a follow-up experiment to test for this possibility, the monkeys were shown two groups of two quantities at a time. The correct response was to select the groups of items in either ascending or descending order, depending on which type of training the monkey had experienced in the first experiment. Some of these stimuli involved quantities from the one-to-four range, which were familiar from earlier training; others contained quantities from five to nine, which the monkeys had not previously experienced. Tests involving novel quantities were not rewarded and therefore served as a test of whether the monkeys really had abstracted the rules involved in counting objects or had just learned certain sequences of responding. All three monkeys performed at very high levels in choosing quantities from one to four, for which they had previously been rewarded. Choice in the five-to-nine range was less reliable but exceeded chance levels for two of the three monkeys – the two who had been trained to select quantities in ascending order. The third monkey, who had been trained to select quantities in descending order, was completely unsuccessful with the new quantities of five to nine. However, all three improved in their performance on the novel quantities once reward for correct choices was introduced.

Jessica Cantlon and Elizabeth Brannon (2006) extended this research by training two more rhesus macaques with numerical discriminations from 1 to 9 and then testing them on novel displays of up to 30 items. They presented pairs of arrays of items, and the monkeys had to touch the array with the smallest number of items first. The results from monkeys compared very favorably with those from people tested under similar circumstances. The monkeys performed just as well when they had to respond to two familiar arrays (of 9 or fewer items) and when

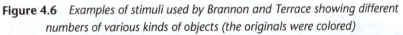

Figure 4.6 *Examples of stimuli used by Brannon and Terrace showing different numbers of various kinds of objects (the originals were colored)*

Source: Courtesy of E. Brannon.

they had to choose between one familiar and one unfamiliar array (of 10, 15, 20, or 30 items). When the monkeys had to determine which was the smaller of two unfamiliar arrays, their performance declined slightly but was still clearly above chance. For both the monkeys and the people, reaction times were longer when attempting to distinguish quantities more nearly alike (though the monkeys were consistently faster than the people!). This study indicates that there is likely no upper limit to the monkeys' abilities to form numerical discriminations.

Numbers are useful to us for more than just counting objects; they can also be used to add and subtract quantities of items. One of the few suggestions that an animal can use numbers in this way comes from one of Sarah Boysen's chimpanzees, Sheba. Boysen (1992) first trained a group of chimpanzees to match cards with Arabic numerals on them to numbers of objects presented on a tray. As shown in Figure 4.7, the chimps were given cards bearing the numbers 1, 2, and 3, and they then had to choose the correct one to go with a tray containing three treats. Once this had been mastered, the task was reversed and the chimpanzees were required to pick the correct tray of items to match an Arabic numeral.

Sheba was then given further training on an arithmetical problem (Boysen & Berntson, 1989). Sheba was trained to make a circuit around three different places in her training environment (Figure 4.8). On any one trial, two out of three of these places contained oranges. After Sheba had made a circuit of the room, cards containing the Arabic numerals from zero to four were placed on a wooden platform. Sheba's task was to select the Arabic numeral that matched the total number of oranges she had seen on her trip around the training area. Sheba quickly learned, for example, that if there was one orange on the tree stump and two more in the plastic dishpan, the numeral she must select was '3'. Sheba's next task was to solve the same problem but now with the oranges replaced with cards with Arabic numerals on them. She was immediately able to transfer what she had learned with oranges to the numerals, correctly performing three-quarters of the first tests given to her.

Figure 4.7 *Sarah Boysen's chimp Sheba selecting the set of items that match the numeral shown on the screen*

Source: From Boysen (1992).

Figure 4.8 *The room in which Sheba carried out the adding task*

Notes: Dots mark the three places where Sheba might find oranges. She then had
to pick the numeral that corresponded to the total number of
oranges she had seen.

Source: From Boysen & Berntson (1989).

Intriguing as this apparent demonstration of addition may be, it needs to be
kept in mind that Sheba was tested only with numbers up to four. To make totals
of up to four from two quantities requires very few combinations. A total of zero
can be made only by two quantities of zero. Likewise a total of one can also be
achieved only one way, by adding zero and one. Two can be constructed two
ways (zero plus two or one plus one), as can three (zero plus three or one plus
two). Even a total of four can be constructed only three ways (zero plus four;
one plus three, or two plus two). Consequently, the five possible totals can be
achieved in just nine different ways. It is not inconceivable that a chimpanzee
might learn these nine different alternatives by rote memorization.

More recently, Jessica Cantlon and Elizabeth Brannon (2007) showed that rhesus monkeys could add together the number of dots on a video screen. The monkeys sat at a screen and watched as first one and then a second set of dots was
presented quite quickly (about half a second each). Then they saw on the screen
two different quantities of dots: one in a white square on the left of the screen, the
other in a square on the right side of the screen. One of the squares contained the
number of dots that was the sum of what they had seen on the first two screens,

the other was a distractor. The monkeys were rewarded if they touched the square that contained the total number of dots shown in the prior two screens.

With extensive training, the monkeys became adept at making correct choices with all possible combinations of the integers that add up to 2, 4, 8, 12, and 16. Although the monkeys were generally able to perform above chance, Cantlon and Brannon observed that the monkeys' accuracy depended on the ratio of the numbers of dots in the first two screens. Thus if the monkeys had seen 1 + 7, they were more likely to select 8 than if they had been shown 4 + 4. This same pattern of results was also obtained in college students, suggesting that the basic processes that underlie addition may be the same in monkeys and people.

CONCLUSIONS

Widespread evidence is available to demonstrate that animals have both a sense of time of day and an ability to learn about short, arbitrary time intervals. Some aspects of the sense of number, including the ability to discriminate relative and absolute numbers, have been shown in some birds and mammals. Some components of the more advanced aspects of number sense that contribute toward the ability we call counting have been shown in nonhuman primate species, as well as an African gray parrot. That these abilities should be found in such a disparate group of animals suggests that further studies on other species may also produce successful results.

FURTHER READING

Brannon, E. & Cantlon, J. F. (2009) A comparative perspective on the origin of numerical thinking. In L. Tommasi, M. A. Peterson & L. Nadel (Eds), *Cognitive Biology: Evolutionary and Developmental Perspectives on Mind, Brain and Behavior* (pp. 191–219). Cambridge MA: MIT Press.
An excellent and wide-ranging chapter on number ability in people and animals.

Koehler, O. (1951) The ability of birds to 'count'. *Bulletin of Animal Behaviour*, 9, 41–45.
This article is the only account of Otto Koehler's classic research in English.

Web sources

http://alexfoundation.org/
This website is the official site of Irene Pepperberg's foundation to support research on parrot intelligence. It provides excellent background on Alex and the other parrots she has worked with and includes interesting pictures of Alex at work.

http://www.pri.kyoto-u.ac.jp/ai/
Tetsuro Matsuzawa of Kyoto University features his star subject, Ai, at this website.

5 Cause and Effect

A prince had some monkeys trained to dance. Being naturally great mimics of men's actions, they showed themselves most apt pupils, and when arrayed in their rich clothes and masks, they danced as well as any of the courtiers. The spectacle was often repeated with great applause, till on one occasion a courtier, bent on mischief, took from his pocket a handful of nuts and threw them upon the stage. The monkeys at the sight of the nuts forgot their dancing and became (as indeed they were) monkeys instead of actors. Pulling off their masks and tearing their robes, they fought with one another for the nuts.

Aesop's Fables, translated by G. F. Townsend

An animal's ability to recognize causes and effects in the world around it is a simple but at times very powerful mechanism that many species use extensively to steer themselves through life. The same ability underlies an animal's sensitivity to the meaning of signals that predict when and where significant events will occur. This form of learning is known as 'associative learning' and is one of the best researched topics in animal psychology. Indeed to most academic psychologists, associative learning is all they understand as belonging under the heading 'animal learning'. An interest in associative learning predates even Darwin and stems from the empirical tradition in British philosophy; a tradition enriched by the contributions of David Hume and John Locke in the eighteenth century before being folded into the nascent discipline of psychology in the nineteenth century by Herbert Spencer, William James, and others.

Our purpose here in considering associative learning (or 'conditioning', as it is also often called) is to explore the sensitivity of different species to the association of causes and effects in their environment. We will also cover cases where there is no real causation involved but where one stimulus reliably signals that another is coming up. We shall also look at a little of what is understood about how animals learn about associations in the world around them. In Chapter 6 we will look at what role associative learning might play in more complex behaviors, such as reasoning. In Chapter 10, where memory is under discussion, associative learning will be mentioned as a simple form of memory, and in Chapter 12 we explore the possibility that associative learning underlies some of the abilities that have been termed 'language learning' in several species.

A sensitivity to causes and effects, to warnings, signals, portents, harbingers, and the like, can be of use to any animal in almost any environment. There is no point to a tree learning to fear the sound of the chain saw, but for any being that can move (and that covers the vast majority of animals), there is usually an advantage in being able to learn about signals and their consequences. The animal that can recognize a rustle in the undergrowth as the approach of either predator or prey will be more likely to leave offspring in the next generation than one that cannot. An animal that can learn which flavors are likely to lead to sickness and which to good nutrition will probably lead a longer and healthier life than one that cannot. Similarly, an individual that can learn which of its own actions will enable it to escape from a dangerous situation, how to capture prey, and even how to fashion tools will be more likely to see its genes continue into future generations. Furthermore, while evolution allows for changes to a species' behavior or form over generations, associative learning allows for adaptive changes during the lifetime of a single organism – a very powerful tool in a quickly changing world. And while both evolutionary and learning selection processes work together to shape the behavior of the individual animal, the ability to learn is itself an important adaptation that can be credited to an evolutionary history that favored it. The ubiquity of situations in which a sensitivity to causes and effects in the environment would be valuable is at least part of the reason why this ability has been found almost everywhere that animal psychologists have looked for it, from bees and snails to mankind itself.

Before we go on, it is worth mentioning that I am not here talking about the extent to which different animals *understand* the relation between cause and effect. I am attempting to demonstrate only sensitivity to signals and causes – the question of how much an animal understands about them is trickier and is discussed in other chapters (including Chapters 8 and 11). You can no doubt activate a television set by pressing the power button; but do you understand the processes that lead from pressing that button to getting a moving image on the screen? Clearly a full understanding is not necessary for successful operation in the world in most cases. Therefore, following Lloyd Morgan's canon (Chapter 1), we will be careful not to assume that just because animals are sensitive to the relationship of cause and effect between two events in the world around them, they therefore understand what underlies that relationship.

As we shall see, the detection of cause and effect is the success story of the animal kingdom as far as psychological abilities are concerned. While other aspects of animal psychology may be controversial (e.g., animal language; see Chapter 12) or marginal, at least at the present state of our knowledge (e.g., about animal reasoning; see Chapter 6), the detection of causation by animals is a very well-established phenomenon. Sensitivity to the relationship of cause and effect was first demonstrated by Ivan Pavlov and Edward Thorndike toward the end of the nineteenth century and has been replicated in almost every species for which it has been attempted, from bees through fish and several species of birds and mammals, including of course humans (from infants upward).

The processes of associative learning (or conditioning) are traditionally split into two classes, and I will follow that division here. First, there is the question of how an animal learns which signals herald or cause the appearance of things that are important to it, such as food, a sex partner, or danger. This process is named Pavlovian conditioning in honor of its discoverer, Ivan Pavlov. Second, there is the question of how an animal learns which of its own actions cause important things to happen (such as getting food or sex or avoiding danger). This is known as instrumental conditioning. Pavlovian and instrumental conditioning will be the subject of the two main sections of this chapter.

PAVLOVIAN CONDITIONING

Outline

Ivan P. Pavlov (Figure 5.1) was originally a physiologist – not a psychologist. In 1904, for his work on the physiology of digestion, he received only the fourth Nobel Prize in medicine ever awarded. The physiology of digestion may seem mundane now, but at the time it was by no means clear how the body turned food into useful nutrients. Pavlov was particularly interested in what fluids were secreted in the body during different stages of the digestion process. This research involved dogs that were strapped into harnesses so that their secretion of bodily fluids could be measured. Pavlov clearly had a great affection for his dogs. Very late in life, when he was asked about experiments that he had performed over half a century earlier, he had trouble remembering the names of his students and collaborators, but the names of the dogs were still quite clear to him!

At one stage Pavlov and his assistants were interested in the production of saliva in the mouth. They put a dog in a harness and inserted a tube into its mouth to enable them to measure how much saliva was produced in response to pieces of dried dog food. An assistant in a white laboratory coat would put food in the dog's mouth, and the dog would salivate. This had been going on for a long time when Pavlov noticed something very strange – the dog would start salivating when a scientist in a white coat entered the room. There was no food in the dog's mouth, but it was salivating. Pavlov labeled this 'psychic secretions' – clearly they had something to do with a psychological stimulus (the scientist in the white coat) rather than the physical stimulus that had previously caused salivation (meat).

The astonishing thing about Pavlov is that he was so taken by this discovery that he turned around his well-established research operation on the physiology of digestion to uncover what was going on with his psychic secretions. He soon discovered that there are four critical components to this situation:

1. A stimulus that already produces a response. In the dog's case this was the dried dog food. Try this yourself: put some dry food into your mouth (it

doesn't have to be dog food!), and you will notice the production of saliva. This is usually termed the 'unconditioned stimulus'.

2. The response to that stimulus – often a reflex or a biologically predisposed reaction. In the dog's case (and yours too, if you try it) this was salivation. This response is termed the 'unconditioned response'.

3. Some other stimulus that did not already produce the unconditioned response. In Pavlov's dog's case, this was initially the white lab coat, though Pavlov quickly turned to more controllable stimuli such as the ticking of a metronome or the sound of a tuning fork. (Although tradition says that Pavlov used a bell, it now seems highly unlikely that he ever used one in his experiments; the sound emitted from a bell would have been too variable for Pavlov's taste in tightly controlled experimental conditions.) If you

Figure 5.1　 *I. P. Pavlov (1849–1936)*

Source: From Pavlov (1954).

have to queue up for lunch, you may notice that you salivate as you are waiting; the sights, sounds, and smells around you as you wait for your lunch have come to function as 'conditioned stimuli', just as the lab coat did for Pavlov's dogs.

4. Finally, there was the response to the conditioned stimulus. For Pavlov's dogs, this was salivation. For you, as you wait for your lunch, it may be salivation, too. This response is known as the 'conditioned response'. (These terms have come down to us from the first English translations of Pavlov's work. Terms that better capture the sense here would be unconditional stimulus, unconditional response, conditional stimulus, and conditional response. These better express the idea that one stimulus–response pair does not depend on any training [i.e., is *unconditional*], whereas the other stimulus–response pair is *conditional* on a process of training.)

Before we go on to look at the wide range of species in which Pavlovian conditioning has been demonstrated, let me emphasize a couple of points of procedure. Prior to training, the unconditioned stimulus evokes the unconditioned response (being stung by a bee [unconditioned stimulus] may cause a fox, attracted to a log by the smell of honey, to run for cover [unconditioned response]). The conditioned stimulus (buzzing sound of the bee) initially has no effect – it is a neutral stimulus. The conditioned stimulus is then repeatedly presented just before the unconditioned stimulus (there is a buzzing sound just before each bee sting – this is called training), and after a while it is found that there is a response to the conditioned stimulus as well as to the unconditioned stimulus (the fox runs for cover when it hears the bee's buzz). This response to the conditioned stimulus is called the conditioned response.

In the classic example of salivation by Pavlov's dogs (just as in the example with the bee and the fox), the conditioned response (salivation) appeared to be the same as the unconditioned response (also salivation) – but this is by no means the general case. What is generally true is that the conditioned response shows that the animal has learned to expect the unconditioned stimulus. If the unconditioned stimulus is something good, then the response to the conditioned stimulus is likely to be a preparation for that good thing (salivation for food, sexual arousal for a sexual opportunity, and so on). If the unconditioned stimulus is something bad, then the conditioned response is usually some kind of protective response (blinking to protect the eyes, cowering, running away, and so on). The key point about Pavlovian conditioning is that it shows that animals learn about stimuli that signal or cause important events in their environment.

Pavlovian conditioning through the animal kingdom

The ability to respond appropriately to a stimulus that is innocuous in itself but signals that something important is going to happen has been demonstrated in an astonishing number of species, ranging from snails and other mollusks through to human beings. In fact, no animal that has been tested thoroughly has been found incapable of this type of learning. The touch of Pavlovian conditioning even seems to extend outside the animal kingdom. Slime mold, a protist, has been the focus of research in recent years for its ability to form associations between stimuli and future environmental events, adjusting its behavior accordingly (Saigusa et al., 2008). Before considering just what it is that animals are learning in these situations, however, let us take a quick tour through the many examples of Pavlovian conditioning.

One of the smallest animals in which Pavlovian conditioning has been demonstrated is the marine snail, Aplysia (Box 5.1). Similar work has been done on at least two species of mollusks.

BOX 5.1   CONDITIONING IN THE SEA SLUG

The marine snail, Aplysia, is an animal with very few senses and few behavioral options, so how can one test it for Pavlovian conditioning? One of the most important organs of the Aplysia is its gill, which it uses to 'breathe'. Usually water is drawn in through the mantle, which protects the gill, and expelled through an organ called the siphon (Figure 5.2). Any sufficiently strong shock to the animal's tail causes the mantle to be pulled closed in order to protect the delicate and important gill. Thus the shock to the tail can be considered an unconditioned stimulus that produces gill closure as the unconditioned response. The problem is, what could function as a conditioned stimulus? Eric Kandel and colleagues (Carew et al., 1983) found that a light touch to the mantle had no effect on its own. But if the animal was touched lightly on the mantle and each mantle touch was followed rapidly by a shock to the tail, then – after some training – the animal started to close the gill flap when just the mantle was touched. In other words, it had learned that the innocuous mantle touch meant that a potentially dangerous tail shock was going to occur, and so it took evasive action.

In this simple form of Pavlovian conditioning it may appear that the conditioned response and the unconditioned response are the same (both

Figure 5.2   *Sketch of Aplysia showing siphon, mantle, and gill*

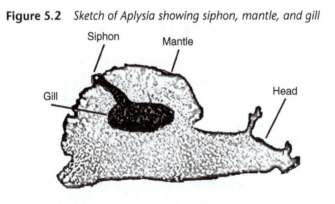

involve closure of the mantle to protect the gill). Closer examination, however, shows that these responses differed in detail. For one thing, the unconditioned response was much more powerful and lasted longer than the response to the conditioned stimulus. For another, the unconditioned response usually included the release of 'ink' (a purple defensive material) – inking has never been reported as a response to the conditioned stimulus.

In the case of bees, it has been shown that Pavlovian conditioning enables them to learn about colors that signify the availability of food (which, from a bee's perspective, is why flowers are colored).

Among fishes, lemon sharks have learned to blink to a light that heralds a mild electric shock close to the eye. The shock causes them to blink, and after a little training they blink to the light that precedes (and therefore warns of) the shock. The light comes to function as a conditioned stimulus that warns of the unconditioned stimulus, the mild electric shock. Several studies have been carried out on Pavlovian conditioning in goldfish. In one of these studies the fish were exposed to a neutral stimulus that predicted a mild electric shock. After a series of exposures it, became clear that the fish had learned that the neutral stimulus would be followed by a shock as they produced general body movements in response to the stimulus. Here again the neutral stimulus acted as the conditioned stimulus, warning of the unconditioned stimulus – the electric shock (see Box 5.2).

BOX 5.2   ELECTRIC SHOCK

Mention of electric shock in animal research may conjure up frightening images: the electric chair or horror movie scenes of electrodes and dials marked '500 volts'. The reality is that electric shock is often used in animal studies because it is the most controllable and therefore most humane form of mildly unpleasant stimulus. There is value in finding out whether animals can learn about signals that predict unpleasant events. For example, several studies have looked at whether animals can learn about stimuli that give warning of the need to blink. In order to do this, it is necessary to find a stimulus that prompts the animal to blink. This is sometimes achieved with a little hammer set up to tap the animal's head close to the eye. The problem with this is that if the apparatus were to come out of alignment, it could hit the animal's eye and injure it. A blink can also be produced with a puff of air to the eye, but over time the animal's eye dries out, and there is an increased risk of infection. The most humane method is to apply a mild electric shock to the cheek, close to the eye. Exactly the same method can be used on human beings, and people describe the sensation as a mild tingle, nothing like the vicious zapping in horror movies.

Siamese fighting fish perceive their own image in a mirror as a threatening intruder and react aggressively (see Chapter 8 for more about animals' reactions to themselves in mirrors). In an experiment in which a red light was lit just before the introduction of a mirror, the fish eventually produced elements of their aggressive display in response to the red light, which had become a conditioned stimulus that warned of the threatening intruder – the unconditioned stimulus. A similar method has been implemented with blue gourami fish (Hollis et al., 1995). In this case the red stimulus predicted the introduction of an actual competitor. An early start of the aggressive display, made possible by the conditioned response to this stimulus, not only placed the forewarned fish at a significant advantage in the following competition but increased its success in subsequent fights as well. This is an outcome that could lead to an important fitness advantage in the wild – allowing the fish to secure and defend better territory and acquire mates. Although in a natural setting fish would likely not have the benefit of scientists warning them of potential challengers with penlights and red panels, these findings suggest that beyond brute force or body size, individuals who are more sensitive to environmental stimuli – stimuli that predict the presence of a potential challenger before it arrives by smell, changes in water current, and the like – may win more fights and come out ahead in the long run. See also Box 5.3 for another example of Pavlovian conditioning in fish.

A few studies have demonstrated Pavlovian conditioning in amphibians. Leopard frogs blink in response to a touch to the eye but not a light touch on the nostril. After several pairings of a nostril touch followed by an eye touch, the frogs came to blink to the light touch on the nostril that signaled the light touch to the eye. A similar approach was taken in a study on toads. A light touch to the head region, which would normally not produce a blink, came to do so after it had been paired repeatedly with a light touch closer to the eye.

BOX 5.3   PAVLOVIAN CONDITIONING IN MALE BLUE GOURAMI

Male blue gourami are freshwater tropical fish with difficult lives. On the one hand, in order to impress the females of their species, they must hold and defend a good nest site – one that protects from predators as well as offering good freshwater for the optimal development of eggs and young. This involves forcibly repelling other male blue gourami that may be after the same spot, but not defending the territory so aggressively that female blue gourami are afraid to approach. Researchers studying these fish have determined that males holding better quality nest sites are more likely to mate with females than are males who do not possess a territory. But it has also been found that the territory-holding males react aggressively to all visitors, even egg-bearing females. On occasion, females are attacked to the point that they leave the male's territory without mating with him.

Karen Hollis and colleagues (Hollis et al., 1997) have determined that male blue gourami fish are able to learn, through Pavlovian conditioning, that they should not attack a female fish.

First, the male fish were exposed to a 10-second presentation of a white light. This was followed immediately by a 5-minute exposure to a female fish (unconditioned stimulus). Over the course of 18 days of training, it was found that the light (now a conditioned stimulus) caused the male fish to show more and more mating displays and they were aggressive toward the female fish far less often than a control group of fish that did not experience the Pavlovian conditioning (conditioned response). At the end of the experiment, the group of male fish experiencing Pavlovian conditioning had mated far more with the females than had the control group of fish. The proof of the effectiveness of Pavlovian conditioning is that each conditioned male fish had a total of over 1,000 offspring by the end of the experiment; the control group of male fish sired an average of fewer than 50 each.

Among reptiles, Bengal monitor lizards learned that a flickering light predicted the arrival of food and came to attack the light with bites or pecks. Collard lizards changed their breathing, pulse, and leg movements in response to a sound and a light that together predicted an electric shock. Red-eared turtles learned to pull their heads in to the onset of a light that warned of a hammer tap on their shell. Garter snakes learned that eating worms treated with a toxin would be followed by a feeling of sickness and were reluctant to attack worms or other pieces of food that had been dipped in worm juice.

Some studies on Pavlovian conditioning have been performed on birds, especially on pigeons. Trained responses include blinking, swallowing, changes in heart rate and respiration, and pecking an illuminated plastic disk. These were responses to stimuli that predicted food, water, and shock.

Most of the animals in which Pavlovian conditioning has been studied are mammals. Standard laboratory species such as rats, mice, and rabbits have been studied extensively, as have household pets like cats and (of course) dogs (Dickinson & Mackintosh, 1978). Farm animals have been conditioned (Nicol, 1996), as have several species of nonhuman primates (humans, too; Miskovic & Keil, 2012). Even those forgotten mammalian cousins, the marsupials, have been tested and found capable of Pavlovian conditioning (McLean et al., 2000).

What is learned in Pavlovian conditioning?

I have already said that I am not suggesting that animals learn about causes and effects in Pavlovian conditioning just because they respond to the relationship between the signal (the conditioned stimulus) and the thing it signifies (the unconditioned stimulus). But how much knowledge of the relationship between signal and thing signified do they have? Pavlov himself, and other early theorists, believed that animals learned about the relationship between the conditioned and the unconditioned stimulus solely because they were close together in time and space. This closeness together is known as contiguity. Pavlovian conditioning, it was believed, depended solely on contiguity. Certainly contiguity is important: if the conditioned and uncondi-tioned stimuli are not fairly close together no learning will take place. Just how close depends on the exact situation. In eye-blink conditioning, the uncondi-tioned stimulus must usually occur within about half a second of the condi-tioned stimulus. In taste-aversion learning, on the other hand (where an animal learns that a novel flavor leads to sickness), the interval between the condi-tioned stimulus and the unconditioned stimulus can be as much as 24 hours. But is contiguity alone enough? In 1967 Robert Rescorla reported an ingenious experiment that demonstrated that contiguity alone cannot fully account for Pavlovian conditioning (see Box 5.4).

BOX 5.4   RESCORLA'S TRULY RANDOM CONTROL EXPERIMENT

To test the importance of contiguity in Pavlovian conditioning, Robert Rescorla (1967) developed a truly random control procedure. One group of rats experienced conditioned stimuli that were followed by unconditioned stimuli in the normal way. Every so often a conditioned stimulus (light) was followed immediately by an unconditioned stimulus (a mild electric shock to the feet) (see the left panel of Figure 5.3). A second group of rats experienced the same number of conditioned stimuli and the same number of unconditioned stimuli with the same average spacing between them, but their order was jumbled up. No longer were the conditioned stimuli followed immediately and regularly by unconditioned stimuli; instead the condi-tioned and unconditioned stimuli could come at any time (see the right panel of Figure 5.3). Thus in the first group there was an orderly predictive relationship between the conditioned and the unconditioned stimuli, but in the second group there was not. Rescorla found that only the first group developed conditioned responses – the group that was exposed to jumbled

Figure 5.3   *The standard (left) and jumbled (right) groups from Rescorla's truly random control experiment*

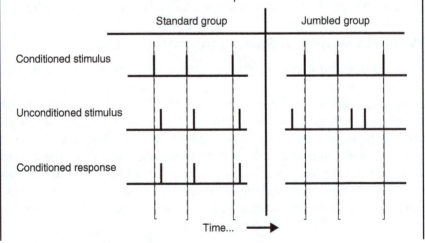

conditioned and unconditioned stimuli did not. This result proves that contiguity alone is not sufficient for Pavlovian conditioning to occur; there must also be a regular predictive relationship between the conditioned and unconditioned stimuli – this relationship is called a contingency.

Rescorla showed the necessity of a contingency between the conditioned and unconditioned stimuli (a contingency between the two items means that one necessarily follows from the other). Quite soon after Rescorla's experiment, other researchers began to ask whether the presence of a contingency might be enough to guarantee that Pavlovian conditioning would take place. Leon Kamin (1968) developed a very ingenious experiment to test this. As outlined in Figure 5.4, he took two groups of rats. The first group (the experimental group) was trained by Pavlovian conditioning to expect an electric shock every time a buzzer sounded. During this time the second group (the control group) was given no training. Next Kamin trained both groups of rats with a buzzer and a

Figure 5.4   *Design of Kamin's blocking experiment*

Group	Phase 1	Phase 2	Phase 3
Experimental	Train buzzer → shock	Train light + buzzer → shock	Test light? No conditioning
Control	Nothing	Train light + buzzer → shock	Test light? Conditioned fear

light that together predicted an electric shock. The question Kamin was interested in was, what would the two groups of rats have learned about the light? In order to ascertain this, both groups were given a final test with just the light stimulus – would they have learned that the light predicted shock? The control group, which had not had any experience with the buzzer on its own, learned quite readily that the light indicated that an electric shock would follow – they stopped what they were doing when they saw the light and waited for the shock. The really interesting result was the case of the experimental group – the group that in the first phase had experienced the buzzer on its own followed by the shock. The experimental group failed to show any fear of the light – they had not become conditioned to it. For both groups there was a perfectly good contingency between the light and the shock – every time the light came on it was followed by the shock. For the experimental group, however, the light was redundant; it only doubled up what they already knew from attending to the buzzer. Kamin concluded that contingency was not enough for Pavlovian conditioning to take place; prior associations could block a second association between stimulus and outcome, even when contingency was present.

Much contemporary research on Pavlovian conditioning is dedicated to finding out what, in addition to contingency and contiguity, is necessary for conditioning to occur. Some researchers believe that the unconditioned stimulus must be surprising for learning to occur; others emphasize that the subject must attend to the conditioned stimulus. Within these camps there are arguments about what makes a stimulus 'surprising' or 'attended to' and so on. For our purposes what is interesting here is that, although animals may not understand cause and effect in a deep way (just as I don't understand in any deep way the relationship between pressing these keys and seeing my words appear on the screen in front of me), they are not just responding to the fact that the conditioned and unconditioned stimuli tend to be close together (contiguity) or that one tends to follow the other reliably (contingency). Learning in Pavlovian conditioning may not be deep, but it is not as superficial as was at first supposed. However it is achieved, Pavlovian conditioning is an evolved mechanism that enables animals to be sensitive to environmental signals that are important to their lives.

INSTRUMENTAL CONDITIONING

Outline

One part of learning about causes and effects is the case where both signal and thing signified are events in the outside world – this is the case with which Pavlovian conditioning is concerned. The other side of the coin is the situation where an animal's own behavior is the cause of an event in the environment – this is called instrumental conditioning. Instrumental conditioning (also known as operant or Type II conditioning) is so called because the animal's behavior is instrumental to obtaining some outcome: the cat pounces on the dove feeding on the ground; the chimp signs 'gimme' to obtain a toy or food; I turn on the kettle to make a cup of tea. Instrumental conditioning can also result in complex and even multistep behaviors such as problem solving (see Chapter 6) and communication strategies (Chapters 11 and 12). At the heart of instrumental conditioning, however, animals, including humans, learn to increase the rate of behaviors that result in desired or appetitive environmental changes – consequences – and reduce the rate of behaviors that lead to unwanted or aversive consequences. Unlike Pavlovian conditioning, in instrumental conditioning the consequence or outcome occurs only if the animal engages in a particular behavior first – making the latter a more active form of learning.

Instrumental conditioning was first described by Edward L. Thorndike at the end of the nineteenth century (Thorndike, 1911). For his doctoral thesis, Thorndike studied the behavior of many animals. In those days, the facilities for animal

Figure 5.5   *An example of one of Thorndike's puzzle boxes*

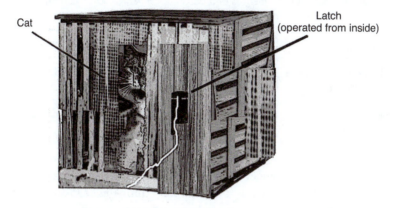

research in psychology departments were very limited; so Thorndike kept his cats, dogs, and a monkey in his lodgings! Although Thorndike experimented on many species, it is his studies on cats that have become the best known. Thorndike built simple cages out of orange crates. He called these cages 'puzzle boxes' (Figure 5.5). Each puzzle box could be opened from the inside with some kind of latch mechanism. In one box, for example, the latch could be opened by pushing against a vertical pole. Thorndike put cats in the boxes one at a time and observed how long it took each one to learn to operate the latch mechanism. At first, Thorndike observed that a cat would just flail around in a fairly directionless manner until ultimately operating the latch by chance. With each return to the box, however, the cat needed a little less time to operate the latch successfully. Ultimately, the cat operated the latch as soon as it entered the box and gained its freedom immediately. Thorndike recorded that he saw no evidence of insight or intelligence in his cats, just blind trial and error learning. Nonetheless, the cats were showing sensitivity to a cause and effect relationship between their own behavior and events in the outside world – the hallmark of instrumental conditioning.

Learning from consequences

Although an action can lead to many outcomes, scientists have defined four broad categories of consequences that work to influence the future behavior of an individual through instrumental conditioning. These can be found in Figure 5.6. There is a simple trick for remembering these categories: When you engage in a behavior (and as a result act on the environment), the consequence may take the form of something being added (+) to your surroundings or taken away (–). For example, if you write a brilliant essay, your teacher might add an A (+) to the top of your paper. If your dog rips all the stuffing out of its new chew toy, creating a big mess, you might remove the toy (–) and take others like it away as well. A consequence that adds something to the environment is termed 'positive'. Like a positive number in

Figure 5.6 *Consequences and outcomes of instrumental conditioning*

	The Behavior Increases In Rate	The Behavior Decreases In Rate
Environmental stimulus added (+)	Positive reinforcement	Positive punishment
Environmental stimulus removed (−)	Negative reinforcement	Negative punishment

mathematics or a positively charged ion, a positive consequence does not imply that something is good (or bad) – only that something has been added. For example, another positive consequence might be a parent who adds more chores to a child's list for talking back. The chores are 'positive' simply because they have been added, but this does not imply they are desired by the child or enjoyed. The same is true for 'negative' consequences. Negative consequences imply only the removal of something, not the nature of the thing being removed. While your dog may not like the removal of its beloved chew toy, the removal of dirt from a hole it just dug in the back yard is also a negative consequence – but this time one that is considerably more rewarding, at least for the dog.

The other half of the equation is the impact that the positive or negative consequence has on the animal's behavior. This concept is fairly straightforward: A behavior that continues in the future or increases in rate is considered reinforced (strengthened), a behavior that decreases in rate due to the consequence is considered punished. It is important to note that the scientific use of the term 'punishment' requires that the behavior decrease in rate. Therefore, a child who is scolded has been punished only if the punishment has the intended effect (a decrease in frequency) on the behavior. If the child continues to throw a tantrum, then the consequence, independent of its form, was not truly punishment.

When these two components are put together, we obtain four possible outcomes for instrumental conditioning: Positive reinforcement, positive punishment, negative reinforcement, and negative punishment. These consequences may be programmed or determined by another individual deliberately, or they may occur naturally as the result of a change in the environment. The majority of the examples thus far have considered programmed consequences (consequences predetermined by scientists or others); the following will provide an example of each outcome as it might relate to an animal in a more naturalistic setting:

Positive reinforcement: A woodpecker taps on a soft spot in a tree and produces (+) a tasty grub; it readily moves to another soft spot and tries again (reinforcement).

Positive punishment: A curious wolf pup approaches a porcupine rustling through the forest. The porcupine releases some of its sharp spines into the wolf's nose (+). The wolf learns to avoid (punishment) approaching porcupines in the future.

Negative reinforcement: Around feeding time, a blue-footed booby hatchling was routinely getting pecked by a slightly older chick in its nest. After slumping into a submissive posture, the pecking subsided (–). The hatchling began to display this submissive posture more often (reinforcement).

Negative punishment: A squirrel buried its nuts in a nearby a tree despite onlooking neighbors. When it returned, the nuts were gone (–). The squirrel reduced the frequency with which it buried its food stores in the presence of others (punishment).

Understanding how specific categories of consequence tend to influence behavior can allow scientists and animal trainers, as well as perceptive parents and teachers, to predict how certain consequences may shape the future behavior of the animal or human in question. In fact, a growing understanding of these relationships has greatly improved animal conservation and welfare efforts by informing the way animals are kept in captivity and the methods of handling animals that might one day be reintroduced into the wild (e.g., establishing proper contingencies needed for survival in an individual's ultimate environment). It can also allow for purposeful modification of behavior toward a desired goal.

In addition to the value of studying instrumental conditioning in its own right, scientists can also use knowledge of this natural learning mechanism to motivate performance on a wide range of scientific tasks, including many of those discussed throughout this book.

Instrumental conditioning throughout the animal kingdom

Instrumental conditioning has been observed in almost as wide a range of species as Pavlovian conditioning.

Just as bees have been successfully conditioned using Pavlovian methods, so they have also proven to be useful subjects in instrumental learning experiments. The dance language of bees (discussed in Chapter 12) is just one example of a behavior that has been shown to be modified through instrumental learning.

Amphibians have not proven easy to condition instrumentally, probably because our understanding of how to motivate them is very poor. It has also been suggested that amphibians may be more prepared to learn to recognize stimuli that they should respond to (as releasers) as opposed to learning new responses in the presence of stimuli (Suboski, 1992). Although adult frogs and toads have proven to be particularly recalcitrant subjects, their larvae have been more cooperative. In a study that combined aspects of Pavlovian and instrumental learning, tadpoles learned to move away from a light in order to avoid a shock (Hoyer, 1973).

Figure 5.7   *Pigeon in an operant chamber*

Among reptiles, in another study combining aspects of Pavlovian and instrumental conditioning, anole lizards learned to escape from an electric shock by running to another part of an apparatus (Powell, 1967). Similar results were obtained with collared lizards and desert iguanas (Bicknell & Richardson, 1973).

Fish species successfully tested for instrumental learning include goldfish, koi, carp, and queen triggerfish. In one study hungry queen triggerfish were trained to press a small plastic rod that was connected to an automatic feeder that dropped food into their tank. Typically these fish needed only about five rewards to learn what they were required to do.

As with Pavlovian conditioning, several species of birds have been popular species in tests of instrumental conditioning. Again, pigeons are the most commonly used (see Box 5.5 for example), but doves, chickens, gulls, and quail have been tested successfully. In a typical instrumental learning experiment with birds, a subject is put in a specially built experimental chamber, known as an operant chamber or Skinner box. This box contains at least one plastic key for the bird to peck and a food hopper to deliver rewards of food grains. The birds are trained to peck at the key in order to obtain rewards according to some program or schedule, usually controlled by a computer. Figure 5.7 shows a pigeon in a typical operant chamber.

Of course, instrumental conditioning is important to birds in the wild as well. A jay may learn to avoid eating certain species of butterflies such as monarchs – who display bright warning colors such as orange and red – after becoming ill following the initial consumption of the butterfly. Bright colors are later avoided due to the bird's association with illness. In this case the bright warning colors become something called a discriminative stimulus, or a stimulus that allows an individual to discriminate between two or more stimuli that predict different outcomes when an action is to be taken. A jay that becomes ill after eating a monarch may not stop eating all butterflies; however, most butterflies serve as a perfectly good meal. Instead, the bright colors of toxic butterflies can come to serve as stimuli that predict the unwanted (or aversive) outcome – illness – if the butterfly were to be eaten, while the dull (gray, brown, black, white) or cool (blue, green, violet) color schemes of other butterflies and moths may predict nutrition in the absence of illness. Jays will learn to avoid eating butterflies that display stimuli that predict illness and instead seek out those with colors that indicate that they are safe to consume (Brower, 1969; Hill, 2006).

A wide range of mammalian species have been tested for instrumental conditioning, including a couple of marsupials, rodents such as rats and mice, rabbits, cats, dogs, raccoons, skunks, ferrets, minks, some farm animals, several primates, and many others. A typical operant chamber in which a small mammal can be tested is shown in Figure 5.8. This is a box similar to that used with birds, but instead of a pecking key, it contains a lever that the animal can press with its forepaws or snout. The food delivery apparatus is modified to deliver a food item attractive to the animal being trained.

A simple instrumental learning experiment with rats might involve making a food reward dependent on pressing the lever in the operant chamber. Similar tests can be done on appropriately scaled equipment for most species. Mazes

Figure 5.8   *Rat in an operant chamber*

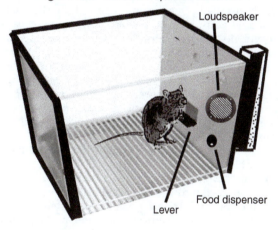

Figure 5.9   *T and radial mazes*

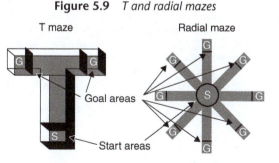

are another popular piece of apparatus for studying instrumental learning in rodents. These usually have a simple T, Y, or star shape. Figure 5.9 shows a couple of alternatives. The animal's task here is to learn which way to run to get a reward. For example, in a T or Y maze, only one arm of the maze may be consistently baited – the left arm perhaps. In the star-shaped maze (usually known as a 'radial maze'), all the arms are baited, but the animal has to collect food from the bottom of each arm without reentering an arm it has already visited. Rats can easily cope with eight arms in this way.

Instrumental conditioning is not just for animals – a large part of learning in human beings is also characterized as behavior controlled by its consequences. This is how we learn as babies to cry to get attention, as children to study in order to get good grades at school, and as parents to praise and scold our children in order to maintain a comfortable family life.

BOX 5.5 THE PING-PONG PIGEONS

The complexity of behavior that can be acquired through instrumental conditioning can be quite dramatic. Although we didn't use this terminology at that point, we in fact already considered one example in Chapter 1 – that of Clever Hans, the horse who appeared to have the intelligence (and knowledge) of a 14-year-old child but was just paying close attention to the body movements of people around him. The most famous proponent of instrumental conditioning in modern times, B. F. Skinner, developed several startling demonstrations of the effectiveness of instrumental conditioning in training animals. One of these was his ping-pong experiment (Skinner, 1962). Pairs of pigeons were taught by means of instrumental conditioning to peck a ping-pong ball back and forth in a form of table tennis. The apparatus Skinner used is shown in Figure 5.10. The playing table had rails around the edges to prevent the ball from falling off, and at each end there was a return trough. If the bird defending a shot failed to peck the ball back to its opponent, the ball would land in this trough and roll into a mechanism that triggered a food reward for the opposing pigeon. In this way each bird was rewarded if it succeeded in pecking the ball past its opponent. After training, Skinner reported the birds were able to maintain rallies of up to six returns, each time pecking the ball back to their opponent.

Training started with each bird individually. First, the bird was rewarded just for pecking a table tennis ball fixed to the edge of the playing table. Once the bird reliably pecked the ball in one position, the ball was moved to another place until the pigeon was willing to peck it wherever it might be found. The next stage was to train the bird to peck the ball when it was free to roll around. The final stage, before introducing each pigeon to its opponent in the game, was to reward the bird only if it succeeded in pecking the ball so that it hit a bar placed across the playing table. Finally, the birds were introduced to each other and rewarded for scoring points past each other.

Today the majority of formal animal training relies on instrumental conditioning. Talking parrots on television, parading elephants and acrobatic

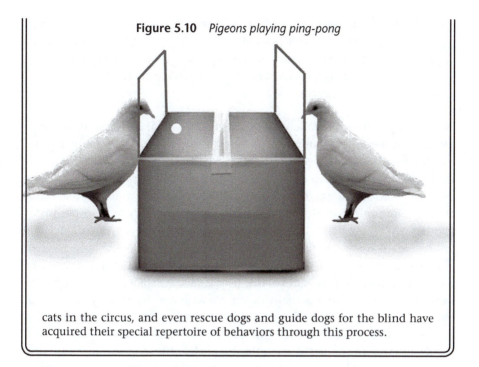

Figure 5.10   *Pigeons playing ping-pong*

cats in the circus, and even rescue dogs and guide dogs for the blind have acquired their special repertoire of behaviors through this process.

What is learned in instrumental conditioning?

As with Pavlovian conditioning, the first explanation that was proposed for instrumental conditioning was that animals pick up the fact that their behavior is causing something to happen just because the behavior is very close in time and space to the outcome it produces. We saw in discussing Pavlovian conditioning that this closeness together in space and time is called contiguity. Contiguity certainly is important – many species are unable to learn in an instrumental conditioning experiment if too long an interval separates their behavior from its consequence. 'Too long' in this context often means as little as a second. For many animals an interval of just a couple of seconds between performing a behavior and experiencing the consequences of that behavior is long enough to ensure they will not learn the relationship between what they did and its consequence.

The view that contiguity between behavior and reward was the key element in animals' learning about instrumental conditioning led to an interesting controversy. Skinner (1948/1972) performed an experiment in which hungry pigeons caged individually were given food at regular intervals of time (every 15 seconds). They did not have to do anything to get this food. Skinner left the pigeons alone for a while and then came back to see what had happened. What Skinner claimed to find was that each pigeon was doing something different in the moment just before food was delivered.

One bird was conditioned to turn counterclockwise about the cage, making two or three turns between [rewards]. Another repeatedly thrust its head into one of the upper corners of the cage. A third developed a 'tossing' response, as if placing its head beneath an invisible bar and lifting it repeatedly. (Skinner, 1948/1972)

Skinner argued that the following development had taken place. At first, each pigeon had been quietly minding its own business, preening, walking around, or whatever. Then, unexpectedly, food was delivered. The closeness together in time (contiguity) between the action the pigeon had been performing and the delivery of food led the pigeon to react as if it had been rewarded for that action and therefore to repeat that action more often in the future. In other words, Skinner was arguing that contiguity alone was a complete explanation of how animals learn about instrumental conditioning.

This account stood until, in 1971, John Staddon and Virginia Simmelhag repeated Skinner's experiment but this time with much more detailed recording of what the pigeons were actually doing. Staddon and Simmelhag did not find their pigeons engaging in different, more or less randomly chosen behaviors after a period of regular food deliveries. Rather, just before each food delivery all the pigeons tended to do the same thing – peck at the food magazine. In other words, the pigeons had learned to expect food at regular intervals and therefore, each time food came around, performed actions that were appropriate to trying to get the food (animals' sensitivity to time is covered in Chapter 4). Certainly, contiguity is important in instrumental conditioning, just as it is in Pavlovian conditioning, but it is not the whole story. Animals do not learn what the consequences of their actions are just on the basis of what happens immediately after they perform some action – another factor is necessary.

Part of that something else is contingency – the reliable dependency of one event on another. If a pigeon, or other animal, is going to learn that something it did had a particular consequence in the world around it, then the consequence must reliably follow on the action – a behavior-consequence contingency must exist. The simplest experimental demonstrations of this fact are those in which reward is not delivered for every appropriate response. This breaks up the contingency between behavior and its consequence and makes it more difficult for an animal to learn about the outcomes of its actions. The contingency between behavior and consequence can also be disturbed by giving an animal 'free' rewards – rewards that do not depend on performance of any particular action (this is rather similar to the jumbled condition in Rescorla's truly random control condition; see Box 5.4). Under this condition animals are much less likely to continue performing the intended response. Contingency, however, is once again not the whole story. Much contemporary research in instrumental conditioning is aimed at understanding just how animals come to learn about the relationship between their actions and the consequences of those actions.

It should also be noted that instrumental conditioning can enable an animal to learn more than just the association of action to consequence. An animal may also come to learn that there is only contingency between a response and a particular outcome under specific environmental conditions, at certain times, or in the presence of specific stimuli. As mentioned in Chapter 4, hummingbirds will often return to flowers where they have consumed large amounts of nectar in the past (positive reinforcement). However, some species of hummingbird have been shown to delay their return to the same flower (providing opportunity for the flower to produce more of the sweet liquid), apparently using time as a *discriminative stimulus* that predicts a replenished source of nectar ripe for consumption. Conversely, an animal can apply the experience gained from a single occurrence of an action leading to a consequence to similar occasions in the future (even if the environment or circumstances are not identical). Take the example of the jay that became ill after eating the monarch butterfly. Eating butterflies may most reliably result in an upset stomach when the wings are donned with bright colors, and the jay might learn that this is a reliable stimulus for becoming ill if consumption occurs. However, this may not only allow the jay to *discriminate* toxic butterflies from edible ones but also, with repetition, may allow it to *generalize* the avoidance response to all insects that are brightly colored and thus also potentially hazardous; for example, avoiding yellow jackets and bees in addition to monarchs. In other words, experiencing the consequences for behaving in a specific way in the presence of environmental stimuli can allow animals to respond appropriately in the presence of both old and new stimuli on the basis of their prior experiences, providing versatility and obvious fitness value. An animal does not have to re-live the exact same experiences to benefit; a similar experience under like conditions may be sufficient to produce the modified response.

FOCUS ON THE DATA: SELF-INJURY IN A BABOON

Instrumental conditioning can occur with or without intent, meaning that many of the things animals learn are not the product of scheduled training in a world-sized Skinner box. Instead animals often learn by experiencing the natural consequences of a behavior, as when the jay became ill after consuming a monarch, or from the social consequences of behavior, as when a dog receives a firm swat from a cat after sniffing its rear end too enthusiastically. The behavior of animals that live with or around humans may also be modified when we respond to their actions – even if we have no intention of training them to do anything. Dogs who beg from the dinner table, for example, have likely learned that doing so leads to human provision of food (a positive reinforcer), even though most people claim they wish their dogs would stop begging obnoxiously during meals.

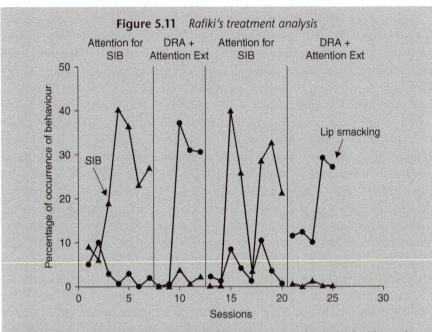

Figure 5.11   *Rafiki's treatment analysis*

Source: Reprinted with permission from Dorey, Rosales-Ruiz, Smith, and Lovelace (2009, figure 2).

In 2009, Nicole Dorey and colleagues demonstrated that some problem behaviors seen in zoo animals might also be explained by this kind of learning. Zookeepers had reported that a 13-year-old baboon named Rafiki was engaging in *self-injurious behavior* – regularly biting her own arms and legs and pulling at her hair until she had created several bald spots. After initial observations and a functional analysis (used to determine the effectiveness of different reinforcers in maintaining or increasing the rate of a behavior), it was suspected that Rafiki's bad behavior might have been unintentionally reinforced by the well-meaning keepers who were trying to stop it. Shouts of protest or attempts at calming Rafiki while she engaged in biting or hair pulling may have provided her with extra attention or resources that she otherwise may not have received in a busy zoo setting; in other words, this may have been Rafiki's version of a child's temper tantrum.

Figure 5.11 illustrates the effect of keeper attention on the frequency of both bad (self-injury) and good (lip-smacking) behaviors made by Rafiki in Dorey, Rosales-Ruiz, Smith, and Lovelace (2009). The black triangles indicate the percentage of time Rafiki was engaged in self-injury (hair pulling or biting) during the session, and the black circles indicate the percentage of time Rafiki was engaged in lip smacking (a healthy behavior) during the session. Each individual circle or triangle corresponds with the data from a single session (one data point). Each session was 10-minutes long. Lines are used to connect each data point to help illustrate overall trends in behavior.

Figure 5.11 is also broken into four panels, in this case each panel represents either a baseline or treatment condition. Because each type of condition is repeated in alternating order, we would call this an ABAB reversal design (baseline, treatment, baseline, treatment), which allows researchers to measure the effect of an independent variable (in this case, selective attention) on the dependent variable (Rafiki's behavior) while also accounting for the passage of time and testing order. During the baseline condition (first and third panels) Rafiki's keepers were told to deliver statements of concern or reprimands (e.g., 'don't do that,' 'don't hurt yourself') each time self-injury (SIB) occurred. As you can see in Figure 5.11, Rafiki's self-injurious behavior increased across sessions in conditions where it resulted in this kind of human attention; thus we can say that keepers' attention served as a positive reinforcer for this behavior. At the same time, very little lip-smacking behavior was seen during baseline (panels 1 and 3), as the keepers were instructed to ignore this behavior. In treatment conditions keepers were instructed to ignore Rafiki's biting and hair pulling (placing it on extinction) and instead differentially reinforce an alternative behavior (DRA+), lip smacking, by providing attention in the form of brief compliments, such as 'You look pretty today,' when it occurred. As predicted, panels 1 and 3 show that the percent of time Rafiki spent engaged in self-injury dropped almost to 0 percent when she no longer received keeper attention for this behavior. Instead the amount of time she spent engaging in the new healthy behavior, lip smacking, increased, allowing her to gain the extra attention she found so reinforcing without continued health risk.

Read the full article: Dorey, N. R., Rosales-Ruiz, J., Smith, R. & Lovelace, B. (2009) Functional analysis and treatment of self-injury in a captive olive baboon. *Journal of Applied Behavior Analysis*, 42(4), 785–794.

Biological predispositions and roadblocks

One caveat about associative conditioning should be mentioned here. Just because an exquisite sensitivity to cause and effect is present in all animals that have been studied, that does not mean that they can learn about all situations with equal ease. If you asked a group of your friends, are you afraid of spiders? How about snakes? There is a good chance at least a few of them would be afraid of one or both animals, even if it is difficult for them to pinpoint what experiences may have led to the conditioning of that fear. Now ask about cars. Despite the fact that the average moving car has much more potential for causing harm than the average spider, we are less likely to fear them. Furthermore, someone who is afraid of cars can usually recall the specific instant or chain of events that led to the fear – typically an accident or some other memorable event. One reason why we might come to fear spiders more readily than cars could be that cars do *good* in our lives as well as pose a threat – by allowing us to get to the store more quickly or providing us with the freedom of the open road. However, spiders often do good as well, even if more subtly, ridding our houses and yards of pesky flies and other unwanted insects.

The distinction between a fear of spiders and a fear of cars may lie deeper than a basic list of pros and cons. There appear to be certain fears that many members of a species share, and research suggests that while specific fears may still be learned through associative conditioning, animals may be predisposed to acquire fear or aversions toward some stimuli more easily than others.

In one now famous study, Tinbergen (1948) discovered that newly hatched turkey chicks with no prior experience would crouch in fear when some overhead objects cast a shadow over them. Using models, he found that they were especially sensitive to the shape of a hawk, running for cover and screeching in fear when presented with this stimulus. They were less sensitive to the shape of a goose, an animal that in fact would be harmless to them. This response is not unique to turkeys, however, as many species, including humans, have been found to show behavioral reactions toward stimuli that might influence their ultimate survival or fitness. When I acquired my first pet ferret, Dakota, I was surprised to see that when taken outdoors and placed in an open field my domesticated weasel, who had no prior experience with birds or the sky, would nonetheless crouch in fear and look up for the talon-bearing predators that were no doubt searching for her. Our next ferret, Bear, had the same reaction to the high-pitched beep of a microwave – that, with some imagination, could sound a bit like a screeching bird of prey. This fear eventually subsided when, over many repeated occasions, the sound of the microwave did not reliably predict the arrival of a hawk but instead produced warm food treats. It took many months, but Bear eventually learned to wait eagerly by the kitchen door when he heard the sound that once inspired such a strong predisposed fear. As with Bear, additional studies have found that predispositions of fear toward stimuli like the ones Tinbergen described were modifiable through experience. However, these tendencies can create an uneven platform on which future associations are formed – making some associations inherently more intuitive than others.

In fact, evolutionary predispositions not only influence how animals initially respond to potentially hazardous stimuli but can also influence how readily they learn new associations through personal or social experiences. In one experiment conducted by Michael Cook and Susan Mineka (1990), young rhesus monkeys with no prior fear of snakes or flowers were shown videotapes of monkeys responding with fear in the presence of a snake but neutrally in the presence of a flower *or* with fear in the presence of a flower but neutrally in the presence of a snake. Monkeys who witnessed a demonstrator behaving fearfully in the presence of a snake readily began to fear snake models. However, those that witnessed a demonstrator displaying fear in the presence of a flower acquired no such fear. The researchers concluded that while even the fear of snakes was learned, an inborn predisposition allowed for a more reliable acquisition of fear toward snakes than for flowers.

Another example, standard in introductory psychology courses, concerns learning about sickness. People, like most animals, are very well able to learn to avoid flavors that are associated with sickness. If the flavor was unfamiliar at the time the person (or animal) first got sick, the aversion may last a lifetime. On the other hand, people and other animals have great difficulty learning that a light or sound is going to make them sick. It makes perfect sense – we are born prepared by evolution to learn that flavors can warn of sickness, but we are unprepared to learn that a sight or sound could be warning us about sickness even though we can learn many other things about sights and sounds.

Biological predispositions are not limited to fears or aversions. For example, in the early years of the twentieth century, a debate developed in Germany over whether bees have color vision or not. One researcher tested to see if bees could learn different colors as signals of the opportunity to escape from a box and concluded that they do not have color vision. Other researchers tested bees' abilities to recognize different colors as cues for food and concluded that bees have excellent color vision – including ultraviolet, which we cannot see. The answer to this riddle is that both were right: Bees can learn colors as signals for where to get food and for the way into the hive; but they do not learn about colors as signals for how to escape. (Subsequent studies have shown that bees are particularly attentive to the colors they see in the three seconds before landing on a food source and that, after just three visits, a bee may remember a color for the rest of its life; for a review of this work, see Menzel & Erber, 1978). This is yet another example of how animals come equipped by evolution to learn about some cause and effect relationships better than others.

To reiterate once again a point that was made earlier in this chapter: The fact that a very wide range of species show evidence of both Pavlovian and instrumental conditioning does not mean that conditioning will take place under all circumstances. Take for example the pigeon, probably the single most popular experimental species in instrumental conditioning. Pigeons have been trained to peck, not peck, hop, not hop, swallow, fly, and do a range of other things in order to get food, water, and shelter or to avoid noxious stimuli like electric shocks. And yet they have never been house-trained! Nobody has ever taught a pigeon to watch out where it defecates. As a bird, the pigeon is supremely indifferent to where it leaves its feces.

In fact, predisposed responses to stimuli can both inhibit learning as well as expedite it. Scientists who work with pigeons often take advantage of a process called autoshaping when training their subjects to learn the basic but necessary response of key pecking. By reinforcing key pecks with birdseed, the researcher is both reinforcing the specific response and eliciting reflexive actions that naturally occur in pigeons in the presence of food – bobbing and pecking. To make this process even easier, some researchers initially glue seeds to the button itself. Because pecking taps into the natural food-getting repertoire of pigeons, it is much easier to train and subsequently test pigeons in a box that requires them to peck at a key to indicate a choice and then, say, to press a lever with their foot.

On the other hand, it is much easier to shape rats to press a lever with their paws than to peck a key. Rats often manipulate food with their paws, thus pressing a lever in anticipation of food is much more intuitive then mashing their sensitive noses onto a hard plastic disk.

The mechanisms responsible for a pigeon's preference to peck and a rat's preference to press a lever lie at the intersection between predisposed and learned responses to an animal's environment. Sometimes an animal's predisposed behavior toward a stimulus is so strong that it can interfere with the conditioning of new behaviors. This has been called *instinctive drift* and refers to an animal's tendency to drift away from what is currently being learned back toward its initial or predisposed response to a stimulus. In an article titled 'The Misbehavior of Organisms', Keller and Marion Breland (1961), students of B. F. Skinner (who at one time championed the idea that any organism could learn any behavior almost without limit), described several scenarios in which they had encountered the strictures imposed on learning by nature. One of the most notable examples was the training of a raccoon named Rocky. The Brelands, who had used their education and expertise in associative processes to start an animal training company, had often been commissioned to prepare animals for performances in commercials for banks and other businesses. On one such occasion they were assigned the seemingly straightforward task of training a raccoon to pick up two coins and deposit them into a piggy bank. The first sign of trouble came when Rocky readily picked up the first coin and walked to the bank but became hesitant to let it go. Instead he dipped the coin into the slot and clung to it for several seconds before dropping it in the bank as required – even though this delayed the receipt of his food reward. Nonetheless, while slow, the behavior was accomplished, and the Brelands moved on to the next step – adding the second coin. This is where the real trouble began. Now Rocky not only dipped and clung to the coins as before but also rubbed them together for minutes on end despite the fact that this behavior was never reinforced. What the Brelands had unwittingly tapped into was the natural feeding repertoire of raccoons, which often involves catching shellfish and other critters near bodies of water where they then dip and wash them before consumption. In fact, this behavior is so characteristic of raccoons that the scientific species name for raccoon, *Procyon lotor*, can literally be translated as 'washer'. Much as pigeons naturally peck at a lit key in the presence of food, the raccoon began to dip and wash not because that was the reinforced behavior but because the presence of food rewards in the training environment elicited this predisposed but unwanted response.

CONCLUSIONS

The relationship of cause and effect is a fundamental feature of the world around us, as is the value of being able to recognize signals for what they predict about consequences (see Box 5.6 for how such relationships influence our daily lives). For any organism that can act on the world, and that covers most animals, the ability to learn about the consequences of its actions must be important and advantageous. Similarly, for any organism that can perceive events in the world around it, the ability to pick up on relationships between those events must be adaptive. The mouse that can hear the sound of the swooping barn owl and run to cover, the dog that comes to understand the word 'walkies', through to the sea snail that can learn what gentle touch is a harbinger of a more painful shock: All of these and myriads more are plausible examples of situations where an ability to detect cause and effect (or signal–signifier) relationships would be highly advantageous. The range of situations where an ability to respond to these relationships would be very useful is matched by the range of species that have been shown to be capable of picking up on these relationships. Examples are most common among birds and mammals, but this is most likely just the preference of the scientists working in this field. Those that have chosen to work with bees, fish, or marsupials, for example, have also been successful in demonstrating both Pavlovian and instrumental forms of conditioning.

BOX 5.6   SYBILLE'S BREAKFAST: A CASE STUDY IN PAVLOVIAN AND INSTRUMENTAL CONDITIONING

In the real world outside the laboratory, it is often difficult to distinguish between Pavlovian and instrumental conditioning. The habits of animals are often not noticed until they have become well established, and we therefore fail to see the process of learning as it happens. With an eye informed about Pavlovian and instrumental conditioning, however, it is often possible to at least make an informed guess about what is going on.

Take my cat Sybille for example. Sybille gets her breakfast every morning at about 7 a.m. She sleeps inside, but unless it is raining, she is fed outside. Like all healthy cats, Sybille takes a very serious interest in mealtimes and does everything in her power to encourage me to remember her needs; she also pays careful attention to any signs that may predict when food is on its way.

The first thing we notice is that she has some sense of the time of day when breakfast is likely to be delivered; this sensitivity of animals to time of day is a form of Pavlovian conditioning that was covered in Chapter 4. For all the animals that have been studied, time of day can function as a conditioned stimulus that they use to predict the occurrence of important events – unconditioned stimuli. Her way of conveying that she knows it is breakfast time is to attempt to wake me up. This she does by jumping on the dressing table and upsetting bottles and other breakable items. Pavlovian conditioning guides her awareness of time of day (conditioned stimulus – time of day; conditioned response – waking and jumping on dressing table; unconditioned stimulus – me waking up and getting her breakfast; unconditioned response – eating breakfast), but instrumental conditioning keeps her jumping onto the dressing table and making a racket (instrumental behavior – making a nuisance of herself; outcome – I wake up). Now that I am awake, the next stage is to get my attention on to her and her needs. This she does by meowing energetically near the bedroom door. Her meows must be an instrumental response, rewarded by my finally getting up from bed. This is the cue for her to run to the back door and meow even stronger – these might be Pavlovian (conditioned stimulus – someone getting up from bed) or instrumental (rewarded by breakfast) behaviors. Only controlled experimentation could tell if they are one or the other or a mixture of both. Finally, I open the back door and provide food.

Most of the research on how animals learn to detect cause and effect relationships has centered on a handful of species that are easy to house in the laboratory, especially rats and pigeons. These studies have found that for both Pavlovian and instrumental forms of conditioning, contiguity (closeness together in space and time) and contingency (reliable dependency of one event on another) are important but may not be the whole story. While it is quite possible that other things may be important in the many other species that have not been studied in such detail, it seems unlikely. On purely logical grounds, contiguity and contingency are the most likely clues to understanding the relationship of cause and effect or signal and thing signified.

Animals certainly differ in what cause and effect relationships they are prepared to learn about, but if they can learn about something, it seems likely that they all do so in much the same way. Furthermore, selectivity of conditioning does not weaken its effectiveness. On the contrary, by preparing animals to learn to associate some things more readily than others, evolution has provided a preliminary focusing of associative learning abilities that is highly efficient. The evolutionary preparedness to learn certain associations rather than others spares animals from getting caught up in 'red herring' associations that are unlikely to be of much use in their daily lives. Next time you wake up feeling unwell, imagine how pointless it would be if you asked yourself, 'I wonder what the decor was like in the restaurant last night?' rather than 'I wonder what it was I ate last night?'

Before we leave Pavlovian and instrumental conditioning, one more point is worth mentioning. This exquisite sensitivity to cause and effect (and signal–signifier) relations that we observe in many species (and assume to be present in the others) offers a mechanism for surprisingly complex learning under certain circumstances. We saw in Chapter 1 how Hans the horse came to appear to be able to perform arithmetic on the basis of attending to the very slight signs that the people around him offered. Hans was detecting causal relationships between their body movements, his foot stomps, and the reward he could get in a very ingenious way. I think I would find it easier to learn arithmetic than to learn to attend to signals people were making that were so subtle they didn't even realize they were making them themselves! We shall discuss in Chapter 6 how, at least under certain conditions, animals' reasoning abilities may be derived from their sensitivity to cause and effect relationships as manifested in Pavlovian and instrumental conditioning. Many of the claims about animal language that we review in Chapter 12 are also reducible to associative learning of these types. In short, the ability to detect the relationship of cause and effect is an immensely powerful tool that at least some species are able to exploit to reach astonishing levels of behavioral complexity.

FURTHER READING

Heyes, C. (2012) Simple minds: a qualified defence of associative learning. *Philosophical Transactions of the Royal Society B: Biological Sciences,* 367(1603), 2695–2703.

A stimulating discussion on the appropriateness of appealing to associative learning and/or cognition when discussing animal behavior.

Skinner, B. F. (1972) *Cumulative Record.* 3rd edn. New York: Appleton Century Crofts.

Several of Skinner's classic experiments, including the ping-pong pigeons and the original superstition experiment, are described in this collection of papers.

Wynne, C. D. L. & McLean, I. G. (1999) The comparative psychology of marsupials. *Australian Journal of Psychology,* 51, 111–116.

This paper offers a recent review of learning in marsupials.

Web sources

http://www.britannica.com/bcom/eb/article/1/0,5716,109611+1,00.html
Read the *Encyclopedia Britannica*'s entry for animal learning at this site.

http://www.nobelprize.org/educational/medicine/pavlov/
This is an interactive site where you can practice classical conditioning techniques with a virtual dog.

http://www.ted.com/talks/joshua_klein_on_the_intelligence_of_crows.html
This interesting talk on the behavior of crows includes great examples of conditioning in the wild (as well as a real-world use for the operant chamber) and videos of amazing corvid feats!

6 Reasoning

A Crow, half-dead with thirst, came upon a Pitcher which had once been full of water; but when the Crow put its beak into the mouth of the Pitcher he found that only very little water was left in it, and that he could not reach far enough down to get at it. He tried, and he tried, but at last had to give up in despair. Then a thought came to him, and he took a pebble and dropped it into the Pitcher. Then he took another pebble and dropped it into the Pitcher. Then he took another pebble and dropped that into the Pitcher. Then he took another pebble and dropped that into the Pitcher. Then he took another pebble and dropped that into the Pitcher. Then he took another pebble and dropped that into the Pitcher. At last, at last, he saw the water mount up near him, and after casting in a few more pebbles he was able to quench his thirst and save his life.

Aesop's Fables, translated by G. F. Townsend

To reason, according to the *Oxford English Dictionary*, is to adapt thought or action to some end. Though the dictionary adds that this intellectual power is usually regarded as characteristic of mankind only, the definition it offers would appear to cover all the forms of behavior considered in this book. Although almost any form of behavior directed toward some end could be considered reasoning, the term is usually reserved for the more complex cases of problem solving – cases that appear to demand drawing conclusions beyond what is immediately available to the senses. Traditionally, these kinds of problems have been considered to involve some kind of mental calculation although more recently it has proven possible to explain behavior with simpler mechanisms than the complex ones that were originally proposed. As we shall see here, many of the examples of behavior that appeared to demand abstract mental calculation for their solution are in fact solved by applying simple rules of association, such as those considered in Chapter 5. Some would say that if these problems can be solved by simple associative rules, then they no longer qualify as 'reasoning'. I think, however, that this is too harsh a position, and I would rather keep these interesting phenomena together – as examples of complex behavior, however achieved.

TOOL USE

Although, like so many cognitive skills, tool use was once considered a uniquely human ability, the use of tools is now understood to be quite widespread among primates and has been demonstrated in several nonprimate species as well. A tool can be defined as an external object used to assist in gaining some desired end. Of course, it must be acknowledged that not all animal behaviors that fulfill this definition can also be considered as cases of 'reasoning'. Take, for example, the behavior of the larvae of a species of Neuroptera. These larvae are called ant lions because of their aggressive character. To capture prey, ant lions make use of the soil in which they live. They excavate a funnel-shaped pit in suitably soft earth. When prey falls in the pit, the ant lion tries to grab it and eat it. If the unfortunate animal so captured tries to escape up the side of the pit, the ant lion will shower it with sand by rapid head and mandible movements in an attempt to hinder its escape. Fascinating as this behavioral pattern certainly is, there is no suggestion that this behavior can be flexibly adapted to circumstances. There is no integration of information going on here that would fit any definition of reasoning.

Many of the most flexible examples of tool use come from primates; for example, many wild primates use objects to threaten outsiders. But there are many cases of tool use in other mammals, as well as in birds and other animals. Tools are used by many species in the capture and preparation of food. Chimpanzees use sticks and poles to fish out ants and termites from their hiding places (Suzuki et al., 1995). Among the most complex tool use observed in the wild is the use of stones by chimpanzees in the Ivory Coast of Africa to crack open nuts (Boesch, 1991; Inoue-Nakamura & Matsuzawa, 1997). They select a large flat stone as an anvil and a smaller stone as a hammer. Stones suitable for use as anvils are not easy to find, and often a chimpanzee may carry a haul of nuts more than 40 meters to find a suitable anvil. There may be cultural implications for this behavior as well, as it is not a universal strategy but appears in isolated groups. The role of social learning in the development of these behaviors is discussed in Chapter 9.

The use of tools by chimpanzees is especially interesting because these animals sometimes modify tools to make them better suited for their intended purpose. To make a twig more effective for fishing out termites, for example, a chimp may first strip it of its leaves.

There are also several species of birds that use sticks to probe holes in search of insects. One of the species of Galapagos finches first noticed by Darwin, the woodpecker finch, and a few species of corvids, most notably the New Caledonian crow, have been shown to pick up or break off an appropriately shaped twig, cactus spine, or leaf stem when hunting for food. This primitive tool is then held in the beak and used to probe holes in trees for insects at depths that the bird could not reach with its beak alone. Birds have been seen to carry twigs from tree to tree searching for prey, and in some cases individuals have been observed shortening a twig or removing pieces that would make it difficult to insert into insect-bearing holes (Hunt & Gray, 2004).

Recently a modification on this procedure was discovered. Instead of stabbing or dragging prey forcefully from their tree dwellings, some New

Caledonian crows instead 'fish' for wood-boring beetle larvae. Again a stick or a twig is used, but in this case the bird uses the tip of the stick to tickle or agitate the larva until, in its own defense, it snaps at the agitator, grabbing on with its hard, mouthlike beak. Once the larva is hooked, the bird can withdraw its twig pole from the wood burrow and consume its meal (Bluff et al., 2010). Researchers have noted that adult birds use these tools much more efficiently than their young, suggesting that this skill is at least in part learned.

In 2002 a crow named Betty surprised the world with an innovative spin on this form of tool use. During participation in a study to assess preference between a hooked or straight wire in a food-retrieval task, Betty found herself with only a straight wire after the male crow in the experiment removed the more effective hooked version. Not to be deterred, Betty spontaneously began to bend the end of the straight wire into a hook, which she then used to successfully retrieve the food reward. To explore this behavior further, a year later Alex Weir, Jackie Chappell, and Alex Kacelnik (2002) gave Betty and her male companion ten trials where food was placed in a small bucket lowered into a pipe. For each trial, the crows were provided with only a straight metal wire. While the male crow did manage to retrieve the food using the straight wire during one trial, he never bent the wire and was generally unsuccessful at the task. Betty, on the other hand, quickly bent the wire into a hook (often in less than 10 seconds), which allowed her to once again retrieve the food from the tube with relative ease. In total, Betty displayed this behavior on nine out of the ten trials, suggesting that at least some crows are capable of novel tool construction even from materials not found in their natural environment.

The need to break open mollusk shells brings out the tool user in two other species. Sea otters smash mollusk shells onto stone anvils that they hold against their chests (Hall & Schaller, 1964), while gulls drop stones onto mollusk shells from a height (Oldham, 1930). A similar technique is used by vultures to crack open ostrich eggs (Thouless, Fanshawe & Bertram, 1989). Other mollusks, such as octopuses, serve not as the prey but as the tool users. Julian Finn, Tom Tregenza, and Mark Norman (2009) reported repeated observations of soft-sediment-dwelling octopuses using coconut shell halves on the seafloor for shelter. These octopuses not only pick up, clean, and climb inside the protective shells, they are also known to carry the shells with them for future use – even though this requires a more awkward and energetically expensive form of locomotion called stilt walking.

Tools may also be used for active defense. Forest-dwelling primates of many species throw objects, including stones, at intruders. Hermit crabs grab sea anemones with their claws, which they then use to repel the crab's enemies. Laboratory studies have demonstrated that crabs can significantly improve their protection against a predator, such as an octopus, with this tactic (Brooks, 1988, 1989).

FOCUS ON THE DATA: FLEXIBLE TOOL USE

The ability of animals to use tools flexibly and appropriately – for example, a crow using a long stick to obtain food when the morsel is out of direct reach of its beak – provides evidence for reasoning skills that extend beyond simpler forms of object use. We have already seen how tools can be used by animals to acquire food or for protection, but a recent study (Taylor et al., 2012) demonstrated that a combination of those objectives can provide yet another outlet for tool use in crows: the selective use of sticks to retrieve close food items positioned near potentially dangerous stimuli. In this study, 11 New Caledonian crows were first assessed for their ability to use sticks as tools in a food-retrieval task. All 11 readily used a stick to retrieve a cube of food placed 15 centimeters behind bars (out of direct reach) but did not use a stick when the food was placed only 1 centimeter behind the bars (from this close distance all crows used their beak to retrieve it). Next the crows experienced a series of trials where a block of food was again placed 1 centimeter behind bars, only this time a familiar feeding bowl, a novel teddy bear, or a novel model snake was placed next to the food item. Again the crows were provided with sticks, and the experimenters recorded the frequency with which the crows handled and utilized these potential tools.

Figure 6.1   *Tool use of crows confronted with a familiar food bowl or novel stimuli in a food retrieval task*

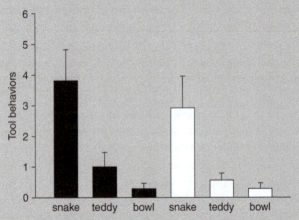

Source: Figure reprinted with permission from Taylor, Hunt, and Gray (2012). Figure 1 ©Royal Society Publishing 2012.

In Figure 6.1, the black bars show the average (mean) number of times that the crows picked up a stick during the first three trials of each condition. The white bars show the average (mean) number of times the crows then used this stick to probe at the food or object behind the bars. As you can see, even though the food was only 1 centimeter away (within reach of their beaks), the crows were now more likely to pick up and/or use a stick (either for possible food retrieval or protection) than in the pretest (where none of the crows used the stick). Crows were also more likely to use a stick when confronted with a novel object (the snake or teddy bear) than when confronted with a familiar one (a food bowl). However, crows on average, were most likely to pick up a stick when confronted with a model snake, resembling a natural predator, than when confronted with either a teddy bear (Wilcoxon signed-rank test: $Z = -2.053$, $p = 0.037$) or the food bowl (Wilcoxon signed-rank test: $Z = -2.527$, $p = 0.008$). They were also most likely to use that stick to probe behind the bars in the snake condition when compared with the bear (Wilcoxon signed-rank test: $Z = -2.254$, $p = 0.023$) and the food bowl conditions (Wilcoxon signed-rank test: $Z = -2.375$, $p = 0.016$). This suggests that crows may take the potential for danger into account when choosing to utilize tools to retrieve food items in addition to the food item's accessibility (Taylor et al., 2012).

The error bars (lines extending upward from the average bars) on the graph show the SEM, or the standard error of the mean. While the error bars in this graph are visible only above the mean value, the SEM actually extends an equal distance above and below this mean. When the error bars for conditions with different means do not overlap, this is one indicator that the differences between these groups may be statistically significant. If you compare the full extension of the error bars for the snake condition with the other two conditions, you will find that they do not overlap (however, those for the teddy bear and bowl conditions do), and indeed this condition alone was significantly different from the others based on the statistical tests run. Read the full article: Taylor, A. H., Hunt, G. R. & Gray, R. D. (2012) Context-dependent tool use in New Caledonian crows. *Biology Letters*, 8(2), 205–207.

As so often in studies of animal behavior, field studies raise the most interesting questions but do not always enable the kind of control necessary to judge just how flexible the observed behavior is. Since flexibility of response is one of the hallmarks of reasoning, we need to measure this property of the behavior to see if it qualifies as reasoning. Some interesting cases of animals manipulating objects in their environment adaptively under controlled conditions are considered in the next section.

INSIGHT

One of the few sets of studies of animal cognition that have made it into almost all introductory psychology textbooks is the one carried out by Wolfgang Köhler (1925) on chimpanzees. Köhler, a German citizen, was trapped by British naval blockade on the island of Tenerife for the duration of the First World War. With his stay at the Prussian Anthropoid Research Station prolonged indefinitely, Köhler set about giving the chimps a series of problems that required reasoning for their solution.

One of the most famous of these problems was the so-called block stacking task. A banana was hung from the roof of an enclosure out of reach of six chimps. The enclosure contained three wooden packing boxes. Köhler describes what happened next:

> All six apes vainly endeavored to reach the fruit by leaping up from the ground. Sultan soon relinquished this attempt, paced restlessly up and down, suddenly stood still in front of the box, seized it, tipped it hastily straight towards the objective, but began to climb upon it at a (horizontal) distance of ½ meter, and springing upwards with all his force, tore down the banana. (Köhler, 1925/1957, p. 41)

Sultan's feat is shown in Figure 6.2.

In another of Köhler's tasks, Sultan was put inside an enclosure, and some pieces of fruit were placed out of reach beyond bars. Sultan was provided with two hollow bamboo sticks, each of which was too short to reach the highly desired food items. At first, Sultan tried to reach the food with his hands and then with each of the sticks separately and then with one stick pushed along by the other stick. All these efforts were futile, and after about an hour Sultan gave up. Sultan's keeper then observed Sultan playing with the two sticks for a while before inserting the thinner of the two inside the thicker stick. With this now lengthened stick, Sultan rushed back to where the fruit was and raked it all in rapidly.

Köhler's emphasis in these studies was on the sudden change in the chimpanzee's behavior from initial failure to sudden success. He felt that the very suddenness of the chimp's solutions to these problems suggested higher mental faculties – in particular insight. One problem with Köhler's interpretation of his results is that we know so little about the animal's prior training. (We also have to contend with the fact that up to six chimps are working on any one problem at one time.) Köhler mentions that the chimpanzees were given many opportunities to play with packing boxes, hollow bamboo sticks, string, and many other things. There is little indication, however, of exactly what the different chimps did with these objects. It is possible, for example, that Sultan had previously stood on packing boxes to reach desired items or had inserted one stick inside another for some other purpose (Köhler does mention that he put his finger into the end of the larger stick to try to suggest to Sultan that objects could be inserted into it). Köhler was impressed that his apes did not seem to be engaging in blind trial and error learning, but we have no way of knowing that the trial and error learning had not taken place earlier, when the apes were playing with boxes and sticks while nobody was looking.

Sixty years after Köhler, Donald Premack and Guy Woodruff (1978) presented a chimpanzee named Sarah with updated versions of some of the problems Sultan had solved. Sarah was put in front of a television monitor to watch videotapes of a person attempting to reach bananas that were out of reach. In none of these brief videos did the person succeed. Having viewed the video, Sarah was offered a choice between two photographs. One showed the person successfully obtaining

Figure 6.2   *Grande completing Köhler's block stacking task while Sultan watches*

Source: From Kohler (1963/1921, figure 5, p. 96).
Copyright Springer-Verlag, Berlin.

the banana with the help of a tool; the other showed the person failing to reach the banana. In one of the videos, for example, Sarah could see a person attempting to reach a banana suspended out of reach from the ceiling – standing nearby was a large box. In this case Sarah chose the photograph that showed the person standing on the box and successfully reaching the banana, not the alternative picture in which the person was unsuccessful. Sarah chose the person successfully reaching the banana in 21 of the 24 tests she was given.

Although Premack and Woodruff's results reinforce Köhler's earlier conclusions that chimpanzees can solve problems of this type, they, too, failed to tell us how such performances are achieved, particularly in terms of the types of prior experience that might enable a chimp or other animal to solve these kinds of reasoning problems.

One important experiment that directly studied the question of what prior experience might lead to success on a task such as the block stacking problem was performed on a species quite distant from the chimpanzee – the pigeon. Robert Epstein and colleagues (1984) trained their pigeons on two tasks. Firstly, the birds were trained to climb on a small box and peck a picture of a banana; they were rewarded with food grains when they did so. Secondly, the pigeons were trained to push the box toward a spot on the wall. The starting position of the box and the position of the spot varied randomly from trial to trial. Here also the pigeons were rewarded with food grains for pushing the box. During the banana-pecking trials pushing the box was not rewarded. During the box-moving trials, attempts to climb on the box were not rewarded. Nonetheless, when the pigeons were introduced to a chamber containing the banana with the box at some distance away and no spot on the wall, the pigeons, after a minute or so's hesitation, pushed the box under the banana, climbed onto it, and pecked the banana.

Epstein and colleagues argued that when the pigeons first saw the box and the banana together in the chamber, there were two possible responses: pecking the banana, and pushing the box. Pecking the banana without standing on the box had never been rewarded in this situation; so that left pushing the box as the only behavior available to them that had been rewarded in the past. The pigeons were observed to line up the box with the banana, just as they had previously been trained to line it up to the spot on the wall. Once they had the box under the banana, it is not surprising that the pigeons then climbed on top of it to peck the banana, since the situation now was the same as one they had previously experienced.

This experiment with pigeons by Epstein and his colleagues has been dismissed as only suggesting a mechanism for how pigeons – a species not noted for its cognitive abilities – can be tricked into doing something that only looks like reasoning. This, however, is to miss the point: here, for once, was complete knowledge of the animals' prior experience with the objects in the task. It is the thorough knowledge of the animals' prior experience that gives the performance less of the almost magical quality we expect of abstract reasoning – not the fact that they were pigeons. More recent studies on insightful reasoning have followed this lead and have better controlled and recorded subjects' prior experiences.

A more recent, well-controlled study on primate tool use failed to reveal such apparently insightful behavior in its subjects. Elisabetta Visalberghi and Luca

Figure 6.3   *A capuchin monkey pushing a pole into Visalberghi and Limongelli's 'trap tube' so as to obtain a candy*

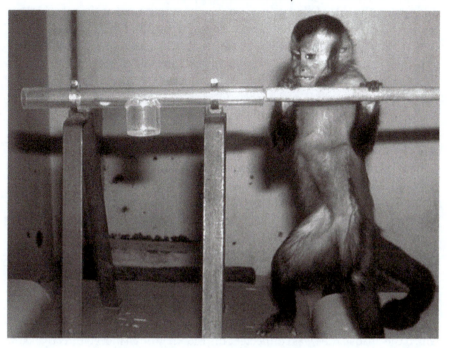

Source: Photograph courtesy of E. Visalberghi.

Limongelli (1994) tested capuchin monkeys on a quite simple task they called the 'trap tube' problem. The trap tube is shown in Figure 6.3 – it is a simple tube with a hole in the middle. A treat was placed in either the right or left end of the tube, and the monkey was provisioned with a stick of just the right thickness to push through the tube and dislodge the treat. If the monkey pushed the treat out either end of the tube, then it was allowed to consume it. If, however, the monkey pushed the treat so that it fell down the hole in the middle, it was lost to the monkey on that trial. In the course of over 140 trials of testing, only one of the four monkeys learned to push the treat consistently from the direction that ensured it would come out of the end and not fall down the 'trap'. Even this monkey's understanding of the task did not appear to have much depth, however, because if the tube was inverted so that the trap pointed upward and was consequently quite harmless, the monkey continued pushing the treat with the stick as if the 'trap' were still dangerous. It was concluded that this monkey had learned by simple conditioning (see Chapter 5) to always push the treat from the end of the tube that was farthest from where the treat was resting.

When the same task was presented to a group of chimpanzees, the performance was a little better; two of the five chimpanzees were successful (Limongelli et al., 1995). These two chimps' understanding of the task was tested by presenting them with a version of the trap tube task where the position of the trap hole was moved closer to one end or the other of the tube. In this version the rule of always inserting the stick at the end of the tube farthest from the food item would sometimes cause the treat to fall through the hole. One of the chimps, Sheba (who, as we saw in Chapter 4, performed well on some numerical reasoning tasks), was consistently able to insert the stick into whichever end of the tube would ensure the food did not fall down the hole. The second chimpanzee was successful most of the time but often achieved his successes by inserting the stick into the wrong end of the tube and then pulling it out and trying from the other end when he could see that the treat was about to fall through the hole.

Another interesting failure to demonstrate insight was reported by Bruce Hood and colleagues (1999). Hood developed a very simple task. Cotton top tamarins were shown objects being dropped down an opaque tube in the apparatus shown in Figure 6.4 As this figure shows, there were three points at the top of the box where the tube could be connected and another three outlet points at the bottom of the box. The crucial feature of this apparatus was that the tube never connected an opening at the top of the box to an outlet directly beneath it. Thus an object dropped through one of the openings at the top would never come out the hole directly below the place where it had been inserted. The tamarins failed to learn this and, as Figure 6.4 shows, seldom chose the outlet to which the opaque tube was connected. Instead, they often looked directly below

Figure 6.4 *Six of the arrangements used by Hood and colleagues (1999) on the gravity task*

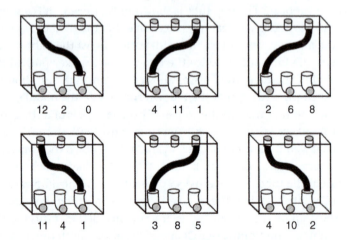

12   2   0   4   11   1   2   6   8

11   4   1   3   8   5   4   10   2

Notes: The numbers beneath each outlet from the box indicate how often a monkey searched at that point for an object introduced at the top of the tube (the object always came out at the point to which the bottom of the tube was connected).

Figure 6.5 *Simple (A) and more complex (B & C) versions of the string-pulling task*

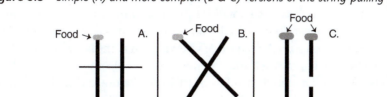

the opening where the object had been dropped, following the path – that in the absence of the tubes rerouting – would have been established by gravity.

A variation on the gravity task is the string-pulling task. Instead of food being dropped down a tube leading to one of several end points, food is now tied to one of several strings laid out horizontally or hung from a platform. In the simplest version of the task, each string is stretched out straight and runs parallel to the other strings. Because there is no overlap, it is quite clear which string the food is attached to. Pulling the end of the rope that lies directly above or in front of the food item will result in its retrieval. However, the real test comes when the strings are crossed or manipulated in a way that requires a more sophisticated understanding of the layout of the ropes. As Figure 6.5 shows, when the strings form an X shape (Panel B), the food is no longer in line with the end of the rope located directly above it. Likewise, a gap in the rope (Panel C) would make pulling on the end fruitless. The correct response is always to pull the rope that will allow the individual to obtain the food, independent of configuration. Several studies have suggested that some corvids, including crows and ravens, may be naturals at this task, able to solve both simple and complex rope arrangements – in some cases with little to no prior experience (Bagotskaia et al., 2010a; Taylor et al., 2010). However, both individual and species variability has been reported (Bagotskaia et al., 2010b). Interestingly, Emma Whitt, Marie Douglas, Britta Osthaus, and Ian Hocking (2009) found that domestic cats were hopeless at this task, failing to choose the correct string even when the two ropes were laid out straight next to each other.

In recent years there has been a resurgence of interest in looking for advanced reasoning skills and insight in nonprimates. The current chapter opened with an Aesop's fable written almost 2,000 years ago. In this fable, a crow dying of thirst encounters a pitcher with a small amount of water located at the bottom, just out of the crow's reach. In a moment of insight the crow begins to drop nearby rocks in the pitcher, raising the level of the water and saving his own life. Given the growing number of reports of tool use and other complex behaviors in crows and other related birds, some scientists questioned whether there might be truth to this old tale. The first study in this line of investigation was conducted by Christopher Bird and Nathan Emery (2009). Four adult hand-raised rooks, a species of corvid that is not known for tool use in the wild, were individually presented with a clear plastic tube holding a waxworm – a preferred food item – that was floating on a small amount of water located at the bottom. As in Aesop's tale the birds could not reach the water or the worm floating upon it. While all subjects had been exposed to tubes of this type before and had encountered gravel stones in their home enclosure, none of the subjects had engaged in a task that required them to add rocks to such a tube previously. Nonetheless, when stones were presented, all four rooks began to drop the rocks in the tube, raising the water level to secure their floating food reward (Figure 6.6). The rooks also demonstrated sensitivity to the number of stones required to raise the water

Figure 6.6　*Illustration of the Pitcher and the Crow based on Aesop's tale, and a photograph of the real-world counterpart as reported by Christopher Bird and Nathan Emery (2009)*

Source: Drawing by Monique Udell, photograph courtesy of Nathan Emery.

level to an appropriate height. When this study was later replicated with New Caledonian crows (Taylor et al., 2011), the crows did not spontaneously make use of the stones to adjust the water level. Instead the stones had to be initially set up on a platform so that they would accidently fall into the water when the bird attempted to reach for the worm. After observing the outcome of several accidental stone drops (a rise in the water level and, in some cases, a reachable worm), all five crows learned to systematically place the stones in the water for themselves. While not all corvids demonstrate the same level of spontaneous insight in this situation as Aesop's thirsty crow, there may nonetheless be some truth to the age-old tale after all.

Examples of both tool use and insightful behavior suggest that animals can sometimes take pieces of experience and put them together in novel ways to obtain desired ends – this is a form of reasoning. When making such claims, however, we must be careful to demonstrate that the animal subject really is using insight and not relying on trial and error learning that took place before or during the experiment. With tool use we likewise need to be sure that the animal is showing a flexible exploitation of the tool that shows an ability to reason and and is not simply instinctive or habitual behavior.

REASONING BY ANALOGY

To recognize that 'dog is to puppy as cat is to kitten' is to reason by analogy. We recognize that a relationship between two objects can imply the same relationship between two other objects. An interesting study was performed by Douglas Gillan and colleagues (1981) on a chimpanzee, Sarah, who had been taught to use a variety of symbols as a means of communication with her trainers (discussed in more detail in Chapter 12). Sarah was trained using pieces of colored plastic. As shown in Figure 6.7, Sarah was shown two pieces that were the same color but different sizes and another piece that was a different shape but the same size as one of the first pair. The pair of pieces and the third piece were separated by a yellow shape bearing an equals sign, which was a sign Sarah had been taught as meaning 'same'. Sarah was then given a choice between two alternative pieces (shown below the line in the left panel of Figure 6.7. The correct response was to choose the piece that was the same shape as the one on the right but the same size as the lower one on the left. Sarah was very successful at selecting the piece that ensured that the pieces in both pairs were in the same relationship to each other.

Sarah's most impressive successes came when she was given real-world objects in the same manner. In the first problem of this type, Sarah was shown a padlock and key and then the 'same' symbol in front of a tin can. As an alternative solutions she was offered a can opener and a paintbrush. Here the correct solution is the can opener ('Padlock is to key as can is to can opener'). Given the same can and alternative solutions but pencil and paper as the premises, Sarah

Figure 6.7   *Examples of the items used to test Sarah's comprehension of analogy*

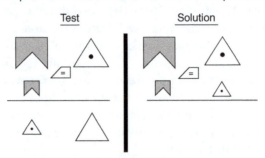

Notes: Sarah had to choose the item below the line that stood in the same relationship to the object on the right as the two objects on the left.
The right side of the figure shows the correct solution.

Source: From Gillan et al. (1981).

now selected the paintbrush because the paintbrush stood in the same relationship to the can as the pencil did to paper. Sarah was correct on 15 out of 18 trials
using a variety of household objects.

SERIES LEARNING I: TRANSITIVE INFERENCE

If Mary is taller than Susan and Susan is taller than Jane, who is the tallest,
Mary, Susan, or Jane? If you answered 'Mary', then you successfully formed a
transitive inference. This form of reasoning is interesting because its successful
solution requires you to go beyond the information given in order to deduce
true relationships about the world. You were not told that Mary is taller than
Jane, and yet you can deduce this relationship.

   Problems of the transitive inference type entered psychology in the early years
of the twentieth century, and for a long time their solution was considered a
uniquely human ability. In the 1970s, however, some developmental psychologists, interested in uncovering the earliest age at which children could solve
these kinds of problems, developed a version of the transitive inference task
that did not rely so heavily on language for its presentation. They did this by
presenting children rods of different lengths and colors and asking the children
which was the longest rod.

   Brendan McGonigle and Margaret Chalmers (1977) recognized that, with
a little more work, a completely nonverbal version of the transitive inference
task could be developed for animals. McGonigle and Chalmers' subjects were
squirrel monkeys. These monkeys were presented with pairs of containers of
different colors placed on a tray (this tray goes by the name of the 'Wisconsin
General Test Apparatus'). For each pair of containers, one had a peanut hidden

underneath it, and the other did not. So, for example, the monkey might be offered a choice between a blue and a red container. If it chose the blue container, it would find the peanut; if it chose the red one, it would get nothing. Once the monkeys knew what to do with the blue and red containers, they were introduced to green and blue containers. The blue container no longer hid the peanut – it was beneath the green container. Once the green-blue problem had been learned, the monkey was introduced to a yellow and green pair. Here it was the yellow and not the green container that hid the peanut. This pattern of training was extended to four overlapping pairs of five colors, as shown below:

Pair 1: Blue-peanut	Red-nothing
Pair 2: Green-peanut	Blue-nothing
Pair 3: Yellow-peanut	Green-nothing
Pair 4: Violet-peanut	Yellow-nothing

Once the monkeys had mastered each of the four problems separately, McGonigle and Chalmers intermixed them thoroughly so that, by the end of training, the monkeys would choose, say, the green container on a green-blue trial but on the very next trial would ignore the green container and choose the yellow one.

The point of this training scheme is that it is a nonverbal equivalent to the 'Mary is taller than Jane' scenario sketched at the beginning of this section. A monkey that chooses the violet container on a yellow–violet trial, the yellow container on a yellow–green trial, the green container on a green–blue trial, and the blue container on a blue-red trial is indicating that violet is better than yellow, yellow is better than green, green is better than blue, and blue is better than red. If this training pattern is equivalent to telling the monkey that 'violet is better than yellow' and so on, what operation is equivalent to tasking the monkey, 'Who is tallest – Mary, Susan, or Jane?' McGonigle and Chalmers reasoned that if the monkeys had perceived the relationship they intended between the different-colored containers, then presenting the yellow and blue containers together would be a valid test of whether the monkeys could form transitive inferences. Both yellow and blue containers had been rewarded with peanuts during training, but each had also, on occasion, been the container without a peanut hidden under it. Consequently, in terms of how often a peanut could be found under each container, they should be equal. If the monkey understood the relationships between the different-colored containers that the experimenters had intended (violet is better than yellow, yellow is better than green, and so on), then it should prefer the yellow container to the blue one. In effect, the monkey should reason, 'Yellow is better than green, and green is better than blue; therefore yellow is better than blue.'

After a lengthy training period, McGonigle and Chalmers performed this test and found that the monkeys showed a spontaneous preference for yellow when presented a choice between the yellow and blue containers. (The reason, by the way, that they trained five colors in four pairs rather than the three objects in two pairs used in tests on human subjects is that tests containing either the first or last items in the series would not be interesting. The monkeys would be expected to select the blue container in any test simply because, during training, it was the only container that *always* had a peanut under it. Similarly, the yellow item would never be chosen during tests just because it had *never* had a peanut under it.)

McGonigle and Chalmers' success in demonstrating transitive inference formation in squirrel monkeys came as a shock. Previously, it had been believed that even children had to have reached a relatively high level of cognitive development before they could solve problems of this type – but now nonverbal monkeys were doing it. Soon after McGonigle and Chalmers' demonstration, other researchers used similar methods to demonstrate transitive inferences in chimpanzees (Gillan et al., 1981).

Lorenzo von Fersen and colleagues (1991) modified McGonigle and Chalmers' methods to make them suitable for pigeons. Using a modified Skinner box (see Chapter 5), their pigeons were trained to peck patterns projected onto two pecking keys. Here, too, when tested on the critical second and fourth item from the implied series of stimuli, the pigeons chose correctly (see also Box 6.1). Hank Davis (1992) demonstrated transitive inference formation in rats using a similar method.

These observations of transitive inferences in such unrelated vertebrate species raise the question of why such animals would need such apparently advanced reasoning skills. Why do pigeons, rats, squirrel monkeys, and chimpanzees need the skill to be able to deduce that Mary is taller than Jane? The answer turns out to be quite simple. The ability to form transitive inferences enables an animal to form rankings, and the need to form rankings is quite widespread in many species. Many social animals, for example, need to be aware of the hierarchy within their group. Figuring out who is dominant to whom is a process fraught with possibly dangerous interactions. An animal unable to form transitive inferences would have to interact with every member of the group to ascertain its own status. In order to understand the status of all members of the group, it would be necessary to observe all possible interactions between the various members. For a group of just 12 members, there would be 66 possible interactions of two individuals. On the other hand, if this animal was capable of forming transitive inferences, then it would be necessary to observe only 11 interactions to deduce the relationships between all the group members. The ranking of other objects – for example, a hierarchy of food preferences – would also be made much more efficient by a transitive inference reasoning process.

BOX 6.1   HOW DO ANIMALS FORM TRANSITIVE INFERENCES?

The ability to form mental representations of complete series of objects seems unlikely in small-brained animals. Furthermore, there is evidence from a different experimental paradigm (see the next section) that suggests that pigeons are unlikely to be able to form mental linear orderings of a series of stimuli. So how do they solve transitive inferences?

Pat Couvillon and Geoff Bitterman (1992) proposed that each stimulus in a transitive inference experiment has a certain value to the animal being tested. Though complex in detail, the principle behind this theory can be easily grasped.

Imagine that you are a pigeon in a transitive inference experiment. To capture the idea that each stimulus in the experiment has a certain value to the pigeon, give yourself 50 Monopoly dollars for each of the five stimuli. Now you are confronted with the stimuli A and B – which should you choose? The usual choice is the stimulus with the highest monetary value attached to it, but at the moment all the stimuli are of equal value ($50), so choose by tossing a coin. If you chose A, you will be rewarded for a correct choice and so you can add $2 from the bank to A's $50. If you chose B, you will get no reward, and so you must return $2 from B's stash to the bank. As long as the difference in value between two stimuli is small (say, less than $9), you should continue to choose between them by tossing a coin. Once, however, the value difference is $10 or more, you should consistently choose whichever stimulus has the most value.

Train yourself first in this way on the AB pair. You should find that a $10 difference in value between A and B develops after five trials. Keep going until you have done ten AB trials. Now train yourself on BC trials. You will notice that when you start on this, the value of B has been reduced by your AB trials. Keep going as before until you have completed ten BC trials. Then proceed with CD trials. Here you may start by making incorrect D responses before picking up the correct, C, response because C's value was depleted from the BC trials. Finally, complete ten DE trials.

The following are the results I obtained at the end of ten training trials of each type:

A – $70
B – $62
C – $54
D – $54
E – $42

Since the stimuli are now ranked in order of value, an individual (person or animal) can always choose correctly whenever two stimuli are offered so long as it always chooses the stimulus with the higher value. The transitive interference problem can thus be solved without any mental ordering beyond the simple one that arises as a consequence of assigning values to stimuli in this way.

In this simplified example, the pairs of stimuli were presented only one at a time. In the full model (Wynne, 1998) the transitive inference problem can be solved no matter which order the stimulus pairs are presented in.

SERIES LEARNING II: LINEAR ORDERING

A form of learning about series that sounds superficially similar to the transitive inference problem but has led to radically different results was developed by Herb Terrace in the 1980s.

Terrace (1993) confronted pigeons with an array of eight pecking keys. Each of these keys could be illuminated with red, green, blue, yellow, or violet light. In any given trial five randomly chosen keys were illuminated, each with a different-colored light. The pigeon's task was to peck the five keys in a fixed order. For example, it might have to peck red first', then green, then blue, then yellow, and finally violet. Since different pigeons were tested with different color sequences, it is easier to denote the colors with letters of the alphabet; so we shall call this the sequence *A-B-C-D-E*. All keys remained lit until the pigeon had successful completed the sequence (when it was given a food reward). If the pigeon made a mistake (such as pecking the same color twice or jumping ahead in the series), all the lights went out, and the pigeon had to wait a few seconds for the trial to start again. Perhaps surprisingly, the pigeons found this task difficult to learn (it took around 120 daily sessions for a group of five pigeons to reach a satisfactory level). A further surprise was that the pigeons performed very poorly when tested on most subsets of stimuli from the original task. Terrace showed the pigeons different pairs of stimuli selected from the original five colors. Though the pigeons were successful on any pair that contained either the first (*A*) or the last (*E*) stimulus, their performance was around chance with any other pair of stimuli. Quite unlike the case with transitive inference, this was as true for pairs that had occurred during training, such as *BC* or *CD*, as it was for the pair *BD*, which the pigeons had not been required to respond to during training.

Michael D'Amato and Michael Colombo (1988) tested cebus monkeys on Terrace's task. The monkeys were required to touch geometric shapes that appeared on a computer screen in a set order. The fact that the monkeys learned the task much faster than Terrace's pigeons had done might be put down to procedural differences (the monkeys' screen had only five possible locations where the five stimuli could appear, compared with the eight response keys that the pigeons had to work with), but more interestingly, the monkeys had little difficulty in solving subcomponents of the problem that did not involve the first (*A*) and last (*E*) stimuli. The monkeys were just as successful on the *BC*, *CD*, and even *BD* pairs as they were on pairs like *AB* and *DE*.

Why should the performance of pigeons and monkeys on this task be so different? One suggestion is that monkeys can form some kind of mental representation of the whole series of stimuli, but pigeons cannot. The way pigeons solve the task, Terrace proposes, is by learning a series of associations that can be expressed as simple rules. The first rule the pigeon learns is 'when the stimulus lights come on – peck stimulus *A*'. The next rule that comes into play is 'when you have pecked stimulus A – peck B'. This is followed by 'when you have pecked stimulus B – peck C', 'when you have pecked stimulus C – peck D', and finally, 'when you have pecked everything else – peck E'. This would explain why the pigeons can respond correctly to any stimulus pair that includes stimuli A or E, because the rules that contain these stimuli do not refer specifically to any other stimuli – they just tell the pigeon to respond to A first and E last.

The difficulties the pigeons have when presented with groups of stimuli that contain just B, C, or D stem from the fact that the simple associative rules that involve these stimuli start with stimulus A, which is not present on these trials. When, for example, the pigeon is confronted with the pair BC, the first rule that is activated is 'when the stimulus lights come on – peck stimulus A'. But stimulus A is not available to be pecked. The only rule that instructs the pigeon to peck stimulus B is the rule 'when you have pecked stimulus A – peck B'. Since there is no stimulus A available, this rule cannot be activated. Consequently, the pigeons' behavior appears consistent with the theory that pigeons are unable to form a mental representation of a series of stimuli and instead act on the basis of simple associative rules.

Cebus monkeys, on the other hand, appear to work with a more structured representation of a series of stimuli – or at least a set of rules that can be applied more flexibly to novel circumstances.

FAIRNESS

While animals may learn to associate symbolic items or characters with value, many appear to have a natural hierarchy or preference for items they routinely encounter. These preferences are often strikingly consistent across presentations and can allow scientists to assess an individual's or a species' aversion to the loss of items of value or even inequity. Such studies have in turn been used by scientists to investigate deeper questions of more theoretical interest. For example, can nonhuman animals reason about the fairness of a situation?

Sarah Brosnan and Frans de Waal (2003) conducted a series of studies to assess how capuchin monkeys would respond to receiving less preferred rewards than a companion under a number of different conditions. Throughout the tests the monkeys received tokens that they could exchange for one of two rewards held by the human: a small piece of cucumber or a grape. Grapes were the preferred food by far, but it was the human that controlled which reward would be given, and in the absence of grapes the monkeys were initially quite willing to accept a piece of cucumber. This continued to be true as long as both subjects were provided with tokens that they could exchange for an equally valued food (both got cucumber or both got grape). However, the researchers found that subjects were less likely to exchange a token for a lower valued food (cucumber) when they witnessed their companion receiving a higher valued food (grape) for the same action. This effect was elevated when the subject was offered the cucumber for a token exchange just after it had witnessed its companion receiving a free grape. After multiple trials of such an injustice the monkeys became less likely to try to exchange their tokens at all. In some cases they responded by throwing their token on the floor or at the experimenter, dramatically refusing the lesser reward.

Because it was possible that the monkeys were responding not to inequity but instead to a devaluation of the reward for their efforts (receiving a cucumber after previously receiving a grape or simply in the presence of grapes), a control condition was conducted. While the monkey received a piece of cucumber in exchange for a token, in alternating trials a grape was placed in an empty spot where the other monkey previously sat. In this condition, the monkey was hesitant to accept the cucumber at first but was more willing to accept this outcome after multiple trials – eventually taking the cucumber in exchange for the token with reduced delay. Therefore the capuchins seemed to be responding to the inequity of the situation, something that Brosnan and de Waal (2003) suggested might be a evolutionary precursor to what humans call fairness. It is harder to judge the degree to which the refusal behavior required reasoning about the relative fairness of the situation. It is also unclear what purpose the refusal of a lesser reward might serve. By refusing the lesser reward, the monkey ends up with nothing – a worse situation than just taking the less preferred reward. In any case, this and other studies suggest that sensitivity to inequity may not be unique to humans or our primate cousins. Similar claims have recently been made about dogs (Range et al., 2008), although in another study dogs appeared unfazed by the unfair behavior of a trainer, appearing to focus more on the potential for maximum reward (Horowitz, 2012). In the later study dogs were asked to sit in pairs (consisting of a control dog and the subject under test) and were rewarded for doing so with a food reward. In some cases a fair trainer provided both dogs with an equal reward, one piece of food for completing the behavior. However, at other times a different, unfair trainer would provide unequal rewards, either in favor of the control dog (three pieces of food given to the control, one given to the subject) or in favor of the subject (zero pieces of food given to the control, one given to the subject). Later, subject dogs were given the chance to approach either the fair or unfair trainer. If dogs showed aversion to inequity, one might expect that the subject dog would prefer the fair trainer in both cases (or minimally, in the case where the subject dog was the one being treated unfairly). Instead the dog subjects showed no strong preference for the fair trainer over the under-rewarding trainer. In fact, the single trainer that was most preferred was the one who had overrewarded the control dog (with three treats compared with the subject's one), putting them at a disadvantage. Thus instead of an aversion to inequity, dogs in this study appeared more concerned with who doled out the greatest number of treats total (even if they were not the initial recipient of most of them). Given the use of different methods and experimental conditions, more research is needed to evaluate how comparable the canine findings are with the capuchin results.

The possibility exists that the behavioral responses involved in inequity tasks may also be learned or influenced by other factors. In fact, Brosnan and de Waal (2003) found that in initial tests only female capuchins demonstrated a strong aversion to inequity; males were less likely to refuse the lesser reward and were subsequently removed from the study. Even human perceptions of equality and fairness can vary greatly by individual, culture, and relative experience. Development also seems to play an important role. Human children in what Piaget called the *pre-operational stage* of cognitive development quickly point out that it is not fair to give their older sibling two cookies if they only have one. However when he split the younger children's cookie in half so that they now had two pieces, the situation resolved itself, and the children were happy despite the fact that the actual quantity of cookie remained the same. This is because before the age of seven many children lack what is called *conservation of mass*, or an understanding that some physical properties of objects remain the same – such as amount or quantity – even though aspects of their physical appearance might change. This in turn may influence a young child's perception of equality. In Chapter 4, it was discussed how similar considerations had to be made by Otto Koehler when assessing numerical competence in birds. Koehler had to ensure that birds were not just responding to the relative surface area covered by more or fewer pieces of grain glued to container lids (physical appearance) as opposed to the actual number of grains present. Similar considerations, including those influenced by developmental and experiential factors, may therefore play a role in other areas of animal reasoning.

CONCLUSIONS

The term 'reasoning' may not seem like a particularly useful one when applied to animal behavior. Many examples of animals acting on the possibilities that are present in a tool use or problem solving situation can be explained by their ability to detect cause and effect relationships according to the widespread rules of associative learning (discussed in Chapter 5). There remains, however, a difference between just detecting cause and effect relationships and applying that sensitivity to complex situations.

As we have seen so often in this book, there is no obvious structure to the pattern of species that show more or less advanced reasoning abilities. In nature, primates, especially chimpanzees, are the most common tools users – tool use being one of the few field observations that occurs frequently and can imply reasoning. In the laboratory, on the other hand, rats and pigeons often perform as well as primates. Dogs and cats also perform excellently. Cases have also been observed of primates failing to reason appropriately, even in a completely natural situation of great adaptive importance to them.

Dorothy Cheney and Robert Seyfarth (1990) have conducted an intensive study of the vervet monkeys of East Africa (their work on the communicative abilities of these animals is discussed in Chapter 12). One of the species that prey on vervet monkeys is the leopard. Leopards have the habit, unique among the species that prey on vervets, of dragging their kill into trees so that they can feed on it without harassment from the other predators of the area. The sight of a carcass in a tree is a clear sign to human observers to be wary because a leopard is in the vicinity. The question is, do vervet monkeys reason in the same way when they see a carcass in a tree? Vervet monkeys certainly know to be afraid of leopards and give a characteristic alarm call when they see one (see Chapter 12).

Each of the vervet monkeys Cheney and Seyfarth studied had had the opportunity to watch a leopard drag its kill into a tree. So to test whether these monkeys had learned the implications of seeing a dead animal in a tree, Cheney and Seyfarth hid a stuffed carcass of a Thompson's gazelle in a tree close by where the vervet monkeys were sleeping at night. Although the dead gazelle fooled a tourist bus driver into thinking a leopard was in the vicinity, the monkeys were completely unfazed by the presence of a carcass so near by. They made no leopard alarm calls; there was not even any increase in vigilance by the group.

The vervet monkeys' failure to reason appropriately in this situation is doubly puzzling. It is puzzling first because of the importance of the task – there is no question here of the experimenters having created an unnatural problem for their subjects. It is additionally puzzling because it is not even a very difficult problem – it amounted to little more than the detection of cause and effect, which we saw in Chapter 5 is a very widespread ability in the animal world.

The reason for the monkeys' failure on this task (a failure that extended to a similar inability to detect signs of other predators and that was also found in baboons living nearby) remains a mystery. It is, however, a healthy reminder that animals do not always do what we expect them to. Just as a relatively small-brained bird like the pigeon can demonstrate the ability to perform well on a test (jumping on a box and pecking a banana) that in chimpanzees is considered a sign of insight, so, too, can large-brained primates, with one of the most elaborate natural communicative systems known to science, fail to pick up on simple yet important signals in their natural environment.

FURTHER READING

Deecke, V. B. (2012) Tool-use in the brown bear (Ursus arctos). *Animal Cognition*, 15(4), 725–730.

Köhler, W. (1925) *The Mentality of Apes*. London: Kegan Paul Trench & Trubner (trans. E. Winter).

Köhler's research on spatial reasoning in a variety of species, as well as his work on insight and problem solving in chimpanzees, is reported in his book.

Schloegl, C., Schmidt, J., Boeckle, M., Weiß, B. M. & Kotrschal, K. (2012) Grey parrots use inferential reasoning based on acoustic cues alone. *Proceedings of the Royal Society B: Biological Sciences*, 279(1745), 4135–4142.

Web sources

http://rspb.royalsocietypublishing.org/content/early/2010/01/05/rspb. 2009.1953/suppl/DC1

This website shows a video of a New Caledonian crow fishing for beetle larvae.

http://www.pbs.org/wnet/nature/animalmind/intelligence.html

This website includes video of a chimpanzee emulating Köhler's chimp Sultan trying to reach a banana by climbing on boxes.

http://www.pbs.org/wgbh/nova/nature/tool-using-animals.html

This website provides information on and examples of tool use in animals.

7 Navigation

A Camel-driver, after harnessing his Camel, asked him which he would like best, to go up hill or down hill. The poor beast replied, not without a touch of reason: 'Why do you ask me? Is it that the level way through the desert is closed?'

Aesop's Fables, translated by G. F. Townsend

Navigation, at its root, involves skillfully getting from one place to another and in some cases returning back to one's starting point again. We have all experienced navigation. We do it each day on our way to work or school, even from our living room to our kitchen. Some of us can navigate great distances from memory; others require detailed instructions or landmarks, and some may use a map, compass, or a GPS. For humans these tools are often external, but we will discuss cases where animals may possess internal tools not unlike our handy maps and compasses. As familiar as the topic of navigation may seem, its true wonder and complexity lies in the details: in the hundreds of kilometers a herd of elephants journeys each year to a known distant water hole, in the long and treacherous swim an adult salmon makes from its saltwater home to the very same freshwater stream where it was born, in the way dogs can track a human for kilometers using a fading scent trail yet hesitate to travel around a fence to obtain a piece of food on the other side (presumably because doing so means first traveling away from the food source). This chapter provides an overview of how the perceptional and cognitive abilities of different species may contribute to the way they navigate the world around them. We will focus first on spatial reasoning, looking at experimental research directed at understanding the physical and cognitive dimensions involved in animal navigation. Next we will look at examples of animal migration in the wild, especially those species for which – given the distance and high stakes involved – navigational abilities are put to the ultimate test.

SPATIAL REASONING

In solving spatial problems many species demonstrate reasoning abilities that are not apparent in other dimensions of experience. How an animal reasons about location and space provides insight into the choices it makes when navigating in its environment.

Dead reckoning

Imagine wandering around a foreign city for the first time. All of the new sights captivate you, so you don't bother to bring a map or take note of landmarks. At the end of the day, you find yourself in a new part of town; the sun is setting, and you are ready to head back to your hotel. You don't speak the language; so you can't ask for directions or read the street signs. How will you find your way home? To many of us this would be cause for some worry, possibly even more so if this scenario were to instead take place on the open ocean or in a dense forest. However, some species would not find this a difficult challenge at all. For example, the mangrove swimming crab, a native of the Kenyan coast, can find its way back to its nest when displaced up to 20 meters from home by an experimenter. Stefano Cannicci and coworkers (1995) removed crabs from their nests and observed if they could find their way back home. The crabs headed straight for home even after displacements that involved a variety of detours. Other species of crabs journey much farther, in some cases over 1,000 meters a day during migrations, and still manage to move in straight lines directly toward their destination (Adamczewska & Morris, 2001). Box 7.1 discusses one way that some species might accomplish this feat.

BOX 7.1   THE BLINDING POWER OF DEAD RECKONING

Owning ferrets provided me with a front-row seat to many new and unusual behaviors that one does not typically encounter even after many years of caring for pet cats or dogs. One relates to the concept of *dead reckoning*. Ferrets are spatially oriented creatures. If you move just one thing in the house while they are asleep, you can be assured that they will investigate it, as well as the place it used to be, the second they wake up. If they find a desirable object in their environment, they will grab it and run directly back to their den to hide the spoils – even from distant or novel locations (ferrets are notorious thieves, taking anything from pens and car keys to shoes; in fact, the ferrets' species name, *Putorius furo*, literally means 'smelly thief' in Latin).

Blindness is also not uncommon in pet ferrets; however, many owners do not even recognize that their ferret is functionally blind for many months or even years because they have an amazing ability to navigate familiar territory, even in the absence of sight. Unlike many other animals, ferrets do not seem to be slowed down at all by this condition. Often the discovery that a ferret is blind is first made when the owner gets a new piece of furniture, and the poor creature runs unsuspectingly straight into it.

When I moved to a new home with my then three-year-old ferret Bear, I noticed his vision was failing. While he maneuvered just fine when walking – likely making good use of his nose and ears – when excited enough to take off in a gallop, he ran straight into the unfamiliar walls. Within a day, however, he was navigating the new territory like a pro at any speed. Ferrets (which are in the weasel family), as well as many rodent species, display dead reckoning skills. This means that they can form an idea about the distance and direction they must travel to return to a home base even in the absence of obvious visual information and even if a more meandering path was taken when traveling to the distant site in search of food or other resources. This is useful for animals that navigate dark tunnels with limited visual landmarks, as well as for those that sometimes cover vast expanses of open area when foraging (such as ants or bees).

One way to determine whether an animal has some internal representation of distance and direction (as opposed to relying solely on external cues) is to let the individual make a journey from its home to a distant site and then capture it just as it is about to return home again. If the animal is now relocated so that it cannot keep track of this movement (e.g., in a slowly rotated opaque box) and is then released, let us say 3 miles to the east, the animal will head *for home* in a straight line at what *would* be the correct direction and for the right distance from the place you captured it. However, the animal would now find itself at a location exactly 3 miles east of home. In other words, when using dead reckoning, an animal is not moving toward a set location in space; instead it is traveling back in the relative direction from which it came (despite the fact that its surroundings may look completely different given the shift in starting point). For my ferret in his new home, his ability to judge the direction and distance to his cage (despite failing vision) was impeccable and automatic. It was his inability to initially avoid new obstacles along the path that gave him away.

However, the fact that an animal is capable of dead reckoning does not automatically imply that it is not also utilizing additional environmental cues to aid its journey. Sight, smell, sound, and even temperature may influence the path an animal chooses to take back home. Furthermore, the primary mode of navigation an animal chooses to rely upon may change with environmental factors (such as the availability of landmarks, sunlight, and smells) or circumstances (the purpose of the trip, distance, and likelihood of predators). For example, some species thought to engage in dead reckoning have also been found to use visual or olfactory landmarks under some circumstances. Pigeons can navigate up to 1,800 kilometers (1,300 miles) back to their home if relocated to a foreign site. However, careful tests have shown that pigeons can find their way home even if they are kept in visual, magnetic, and olfactory isolation on the outward journey, with continuous rotation of their cages so that they cannot keep track of the direction in which they are being taken (Walcott, 1996). We will discuss how this might be possible in a following section. Though bees do not fly the distances that pigeons can cover, their achievements in finding their way back to the same patch of nectar-bearing flowers are no less dramatic on their own scale than is that of pigeons in homing over longer distances. To the skill of homing, bees add the ability to communicate the direction and distances of nectar sites to their hive mates (see Chapter 8). However, research has shown that the directional information bees are providing is dependent on an external environmental cue, the sun (Brines & Gould, 1979). Bee navigation and the use of the sun as a compass will also be discussed in more detail in the following sections.

Routes, landmarks, and beacons

A common method of navigation is *route* formation, in which an animal either learns a chain of responses necessary to get from point A to point B or learns to complete certain navigational maneuvers at specific landmarks along a consistent path. The use of routes is common to many species, including humans. Telltale physical evidence of routes also exists. Animals that regularly travel along paths often trample vegetation or carve depressions into the dirt upon which they walk; from deer and sheep trails to the pacing patterns of captive animals in zoos, well trodden paths are often easy to spot.

One classic example of route use comes from the work of Konrad Lorenz (1952) in his study of the behavior of his pet shrews. Almost entirely blind, some species of shrews develop running trails that they stick to closely, never wavering more than a few centimeters off the path unless disrupted. To test his shrews' reliance on these paths, as well as the importance of landmarks encountered along the route, Lorenz created one running area with stones, which the shrews learned to climb over as they made their way across this familiar stretch of path. One day Lorenz moved the stones and observed the shrews' response. When each shrew came to the location where the first stone should have been, it automatically jumped into the air in preparation to scramble over it as they all had done in the past. However, when the shrews landed – not on the stone but flat on the smooth ground – they froze and began feeling their way around using their whiskers as if they were lost in an entirely new environment. In fact, this same blind reliance on routes by water shrews can sometimes result in injury or death when a shrew hastily leaps into a familiar pond along its path only to find it has recently been drained.

In other cases, beacons or landmarks are used as a guide, independent of a specific route or path. While the term *beacon* (a local cue) is typically used when referring to an object located close to an animal's destination or even a cue associated with the destination itself (e.g., a large oak tree standing over a fox's den or the smell of bedding material in a rat's nest), the term *landmark* (a global cue) is used for environmental features located at a distance (such as a mountain located on the way to a bird's perch or a line of bushes located just past a bee's hive). An animal does not necessarily want to navigate *toward* a landmark (as opposed to a beacon), as it might lie behind or to the side of the actual goal; however, it can nonetheless use it to find its bearings.

The use of beacons could be described as a by-product of Pavlovian conditioning (see Chapter 5): the animal may come to associate objects, sights, and smells around and in its home with the home itself. Therefore, once conditioning has taken place, the use of beacons may not be all that different from the animal moving toward a home that it can actually see – presumably a simple feat. The use of landmarks, however, is a bit more complex. Not only does an animal have to make an association between a landmark and home, it also has to make note of the relative direction of the landmark with respect to its home. While some studies have found that animals will sometimes rely heavily on a single landmark, even when multiple landmarks are available (see Collett et al. [1986] for an example with gerbils), many species tested, including pigeons (Cheng, 1989), chickadees (Cheng & Sherry, 1992), and Clark's nutcrackers (Gould-Beierle & Kamil, 1996), appear to average directional information across multiple landmarks, allowing them to more precisely pinpoint a desired destination (by locating the intersection where multiple points of reference meet). This may help them overcome alterations to individual features in the environment.

Once landmark associations are formed, they can be incredibly strong. In one demonstration by Niko Tinbergen (1972), a circle of pinecones was set out around the nest of a digger wasp, a species that uses visual cues to navigate back to its home after foraging. Members of this species typically circle the entrance to their nest several times before venturing too far away – presumably to get a bearing of the entrance and surrounding objects that could serve as landmarks (in this case, the circle of pinecones). In his experiment, Tinbergen waited for the wasps to emerge and allowed them to survey the area; however, once they were out of sight, he moved the circle of pinecones off to one side of the nest. While the pinecones still formed a circle, they no longer surrounded the entrance. When the wasps returned, they unsuccessfully attempted to locate the entrance of each nest inside the circle of pinecones instead of approaching the actual entrance nearby (Figure 7.1).

Figure 7.1   *A sketch based on Tinburgen's famous digger wasp experiment*

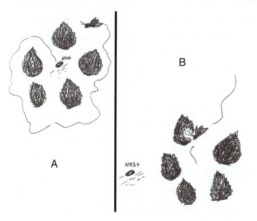

Notes: (A) Wasps surveyed the pinecones before leaving the
proximity of their nest.
(B) While the wasps were away, the pinecones were moved so that they no longer surrounded the nest entrance; however, when the wasps returned, they still attempted to use the pinecones as landmarks, searching for their nest entrance in the center.

Because of the important role memory plays in the use of landmarks, we will revisit this topic again in Chapter 10, along with several additional examples of landmark use in birds and rodents.

The sun-compass

Animals that use the position of the sun or polarized light emanating from the sun as a landmark (more commonly referred to as a *sun-compass*) have an added challenge. While many landmarks such as mountains and buildings remain relatively stable over long periods of time, the sun is continuously moving. Therefore, animals that use the sun as a compass must be aware of this movement and account for it when navigating over a period of time. For example, if a bird flies away from a large mountain to forage in the morning, to return home it might only need to spot the mountain and fly toward it. However, if the same bird (this time with no mountain to rely on) flies away from the rising sun in the morning and then in the evening attempts to return home by flying toward (the now setting) sun, it would find itself terribly lost. However, birds that use the sun as a compass in the real world do not make this mistake (Schmidt-Koenig et al., 1991). Instead of relying solely on the position of the sun itself, they use something called the *sun azimuth* – the angle of the sun from due north in a clockwise direction – which can provide directional information about an observer's location with respect to a target destination (assuming the time of day is known). To some extent, even if the terminology is foreign, this concept is familiar to humans, who recognize some of the larger movements of the sun over time and can make a few basic calculations regarding time of day and directionality without too much effort. For example, our knowledge that the sun rises in the east and sets in the west (along with a basic sensitivity to our own biological clock) would allow us, if nothing else, to gain geographic bearings in the early hours of the day (near sunrise) or in the later hours (near sunset) if needed. However, this means that any animal using the sun as a compass must account for both location and time of day (and possibly the time that has passed since the beginning of its journey as well) to predict the change in the angle of the sun with respect to its destination. Some species can account for changes in the sun's position over a time frame of just minutes or seconds spent foraging (or up to hours and days when needed). While several species of birds and insects seem to do quite well with these cues, over short time spans the movement of the sun would be practically imperceptible to humans, and as discussed in Chapter 2, additional directional cues given off by polarized light would be unavailable to the human eye.

Cognitive maps and shortcuts

A map is one of the most useful tools the average human could ask for when navigating the environment (aside from possibly a commercial GPS, designed to function and look like a digital map). Therefore it comes as no surprise that scientists have spent many years marveling over the fact that many species get around just fine without this handy tool – even over distances of many hundreds of kilometers. Because scientists were pretty sure that animals were not carrying around physical maps, the next step for some was to look for the presence of internal (or cognitive) maps that might serve the same function.

To test this hypothesis, the pioneer of animal cognition, Edward Tolman, gave rats the opportunity to explore a rather complex maze, shown in Figure 7.2 (Tolman & Honzik, 1930). In this maze there were three paths from the start box (where the rat was placed at the start of a trial) to the goal box (where food could be found). Path 1 was the most direct, Path 2 involved a short detour, and Path 3 required a longer detour. By blocking one or more of these paths at a time, the rats were given the opportunity to experience all three paths. Tolman and colleagues found that their rats would first explore the most direct route, Path 1; only if they found that short path blocked would they explore Path 2; and only if that was also blocked would they head down the longest path, Path 3. This suggested that

Figure 7.2   *A sketch of the maze used by Tolman and Honzik to study detour learning in rats*

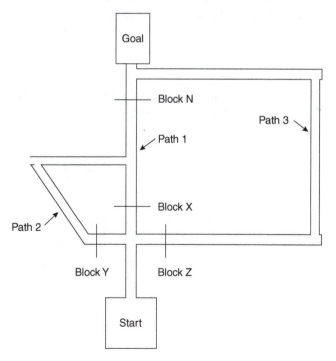

Notes: Blockages could be placed at points X, Y, and Z as well as N.

Source: From Tolman and Honzik (1930).

the rats may have indeed formed some internal representation or map of the maze based on their prior explorations, allowing them to make informed choices about the fastest route to a destination under different conditions. Tolman also noted that the rats' performances – in this study and others like it – were indicative of *latent learning*. Instead of remembering a set route or engaging in a chain of behaviors that had previously led to food reward, the rats in Tolman's study appeared to learn the layout of a maze simply by having the opportunity to explore it prior to the start of an experiment – even in the absence of food. A rat that had the opportunity to explore a maze first was more likely to be able to locate the shortest path to the goal when a food reward was later on the line.

In another of Tolman's experiments (Tolman et al., 1946), rats were given the opportunity to explore the maze shown in the left panel of Figure 7.3. In this maze there was only one path from the start area to the goal box, but this path was rather lengthy and twisted. Once the rats had had sufficient opportunity to explore this route, the apparatus was altered to the configuration shown in the right panel of the figure. Now the original route had been blocked off, and a large area of alternative routes offered in its place. Would the rats pick the alternative route that led most directly to the goal box? Tolman and colleagues found that indeed they did.

Unfortunately for the interpretation of how these rats found the shortest of the alternative routes, Tolman and colleagues made an error in the design of their experiment that simplified the task for the rats. Above the goal box they had fixed a lightbulb. This light was visible to the rats from any position in the maze.

Figure 7.3 *The mazes used in two stages of the experiment described by Tolman and colleagues.*

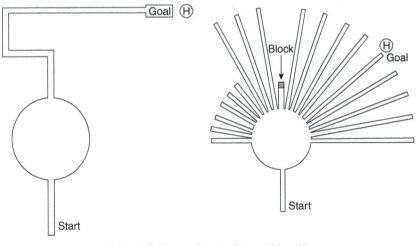

Note: A light was located at position H.

Source: From Tolman et al. (1946).

Figure 7.4   *The triangular test area used by Chapuis and Varlet to test dogs'*
spatial reasoning ability.

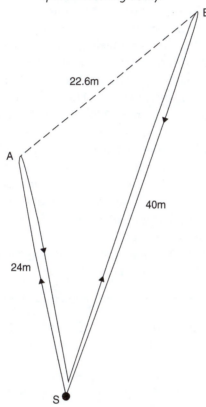

Source: From Chapuis and Varlet (1987).

Consequently, there was no need for them to reason about which alternative was
the shortest way to the goal box; they could simply head straight for the light
(a rather obvious beacon). Attempts by subsequent researchers to replicate these
results without the presence of a light over the goal box have generally not been
successful. One exception might be a study conducted several decades later with
voles (Gaulin & FitzGerald, 1986). Voles reportedly performed well on a replica-
tion of Tolman's task, even in the absence of a light over the goal. However, in
this study an additional scent cue was added away from the reward area to aid in
orientation, introducing another factor that may have altered performance.

Another method of testing for cognitive maps is based on the prediction that
an animal possessing a field map–like representation of an area and the objects
within it should be able to take shortcuts within its environment, even along
paths not previously traveled. Nicole Chapuis and Christian Varlet tested dogs'
spatial reasoning abilities by exploring their skill in making shortcuts in a large

meadow (Chapuis & Varlet, 1987). The task involved the triangular test area shown in Figure 7.4. Food was place in two positions (*A* and *B* in the figure), separated by an angle of 30 degrees when viewed from the starting point (*S*). Food position *A* was 24 meters from the start point, and position *B* was 40 meters from the start point. After an experimenter had placed food at points *A* and *B*, a dog was led around the field from *S* to *A* and back again and then from *S* to *B* and back again (solid lines in the figure). This enabled the dog to see where the food was, but it was not allowed to take it. The critical question was, what would the dog do once it was let loose from *S*? Would it follow the lengthy route it had been led on, or would it make the short cut from *A* directly to *B* (or from *B* down to *A*)? Chapuis and Varlet found that 86 percent of their dogs took the shortcut. On only 1 percent of all trials did the dogs repeat the lengthy route that they had been shown originally (see Box 7.2 to test this for yourself).

Nicole Chapuis and Patricia Scardigli (1993) tested hamsters on more complex versions of the task Chapuis and Varlet had used on dogs. Using an apparatus that permitted a variety of different alternative routes to the same desired goal object, Chapuis and Scardigli found that hamsters were very well able to deduce the shortest route under a variety of conditions.

BOX 7.2   HOW TO TEST THE SPATIAL REASONING ABILITIES OF YOUR DOG OR CAT

Both Poucet and colleagues' and Chapuis and Varlet's methods can very easily be adapted for use at home with your pet dog or cat (or other tame animal).

For Chapuis and Varlet's method, the only requirements are a suitably motivated dog or cat (as mentioned in Box 3.2 on object permanence, when testing your pet's object permanence, it is probably better to try this before a feeding time than after), some suitable food, a fairly large open area (Chapuis and Varlet worked in a three-hectare meadow), and an assistant. Binoculars may help if you choose to work with a particularly large test area.

It is probably wise to get the ground measured out before your subject animal is brought onto the scene. The dimensions shown in Figure 7.4 are the ones that worked well for Chapuis and Varlet in the case of young Alsatian dogs. For other species you would probably want to adjust the scale in proportion to the size and mobility of your animal. In addition, in order to be able to give repeated trials (Chapuis and Varlet tested each of seven animals twice a day for two days), you will need several of these testing triangles (otherwise the tracks left on one trial may tell the subject what to do on the next trial without the need for it to solve the problem anew). Eight of the triangles shown in Figure 7.4 can fit round a circle centered on the same start point.

Be careful in setting up the test area not to walk along any lines except those from *S* to *A* and *S* to *B*, never from *A* to *B*. Once you have your test area set up, walk your animal on a lead from the start point to the first food item (*S* to *A*) and then back to the start point. Immediately set off to the second food point and back to the start area (S to B to S). Without any delay, release your animal and observe where it runs. Without moving from the start point yourself, record your animal's search route in as much detail as possible. Chapuis and Varlet gave their animals a maximum of ten minutes search time. Although you may wish to alter this depending on the speed of your animal, it is wise to set a maximum time for the task, after which the animal is deemed to have failed.

Depending on the success of your animal at this the task, you may wish to explore your animal's spatial reasoning ability in more detail. Theoretically interesting questions include the following: What difference does the angle between food points A and B make? The smaller the angle, the more efficient the shortcut becomes – does this make a difference to your animal's behavior? What about the delay between being led around the two food points and being released to get the food on their own – does increasing this delay improve or worsen your animal's performance? Finally, how would dogs or cats cope with more complex spatial reasoning problems such as those originally set out by Tolman; for example, that shown in Figure 7.3? These problems could also be arranged in an open field using modifications of the method developed by Chapuis and Varlet.

The method used by Poucet and colleagues needs only some suitable barriers in addition to the materials required for Chapuis and Varlet's method. Transparent barriers can be made easily out of chicken wire attached to posts stuck in the ground. Opaque barriers could be made from cardboard (except for taller dogs, in which case it might be better to work around preexisting walls and fences). Interesting modifications to Poucet and colleagues' tests can be achieved by using barriers that present alternative routes of different lengths and that pass closer or farther away from the goal object. Intelligent dogs, for whom this task may be too easy, could be tested on detours that require more substantial backtracking before the goal can be reached, as well as more complicated routes to the goal.

Not all studies have reported equal success, however. Jacques Bovet (1995), in a study of the navigation ability of red squirrels, found that these animals could successfully return to their nests only if they were moved along straight paths. In this study, the squirrels were displaced along routes of approximately 700 meters that involved two right-angled turns. These turns were either both to the left or both to the right, so that the displacement route described three sides of a rectangle – the shortest route home being the remaining fourth side of the rectangle. The squirrels, however, did not pick this shortest route home; instead their return bearings were essentially random.

There has been some debate over whether even successful performance on latent learning and shortcut tasks can actually demonstrate the presence of a cognitive map or whether these results might be explicable by other means. As mentioned, it was later found that rats in one of Tolman's experiments were likely using a beacon (a light over the goal) to guide their path, not a cognitive map. And in many other studies of this type, possible landmark or beacon use cannot be entirely ruled out. Other scientists have defined the term 'cognitive map' more loosely so that other strategies, including landmark use and dead reckoning, count as cognitive mapping as well (Gallistel, 1993). However, if animals do use mental representations of spatial areas or maps to assist in navigation, it seems clear that the amount of detail and accuracy of these maps can vary greatly. In many cases it might be more fruitful to explore an animal's navigation and spatial reasoning strategy in terms of the perceptional world of the species coupled with available external stimuli in the individual's immediate environment rather than relying on presumed internal representations.

Case studies

Scientists most often learn about different navigation techniques by intensely studying the spatial reasoning and navigation skills of model species (especially those that rely heavily on precise navigation for survival or achieve impressive navigational feats on a regular basis). To get a better picture of how a species might utilize different navigational tools (as well as combinations of tools previously discussed in this chapter) to make both long and short voyages in their environment, the next section will provide an overview of two species studied extensively in this area: pigeons and bees.

Pigeon homing

Pigeons have served as a popular subject of study, as well as a source of enjoyment and even companionship, for centuries. Although today many may have a hard time imagining pigeons as prominent contributors to society (beyond painting the sidewalks white), this book demonstrates the important role pigeons continue to play in many areas of science, especially in our understanding of cognitive principles. Pigeon's once served an important role as message carriers in wartime as well, although today homing demonstrations are conducted primarily for sport. We know that the homing abilities – the strong tendency for a displaced pigeon to fly home on a straight and swift trajectory – were recognized by the Romans, as an ancient text records their use as early as 43 B.C. However, this ability was long overlooked by scientists, including Darwin, even though he wrote extensively about the artificial selection of pigeon strains in *On the Origin of Species* (more on this topic can be found in Wynne, 2004). As a result, scientists are still working to understand the mechanisms underlying the pigeon's ability to travel home.

Using the sun-compass

Well-trained Boy Scouts find north by pointing 12 o'clock on their watch at the sun: south is now halfway between the hour hand and the 12 (or north in the Southern Hemisphere). This trick, known as the sun-compass, works because the sun progresses from east to west via south (north in the Southern Hemisphere) in the course of each day. So if you know what time it is and where the sun is, you can figure out compass directions.

In a series of ingenious experiments, pigeons have also been shown to be able to use the Boy Scouts' trick of considering the position of the sun and the time of day to find compass directions. Pigeons, like most animals, have a clear sense of time of day (see Chapter 4), which they then combine with the position of the sun to find any bearing they need. This was demonstrated by training birds in an enclosed box so that they could receive a reward only by responding in a certain compass direction. First, the birds were trained to respond on the pecking key placed in the east corner of the box (say) with normal sunlight coming into the box. It was found that they could learn this without difficulty. Next the birds were trained with sunlight coming into the box as normal but then tested under conditions where the light appeared to come from a different direction because mirrors had been used to shift the apparent light source. It was found that the pigeons were confused about compass direction by an amount dependent on the angle of the mirrors that were used to shift the sun's light (see Schmidt-Koenig et al., 1991).

As we saw in Chapter 2, pigeons are also sensitive to the polarization of sunlight. This means that they can find the sun's position through perception of the polarization of sunlight in any patch of clear sky and utilize the sun-compass even on partially overcast days or at dusk after the sun has dipped below the horizon.

But do pigeons actually use the sun-compass to find their way home when they are displaced hundreds of kilometers from the home loft? To see if this was the case, pigeons were first confused as to the time of day. A pigeon's sense of time of day comes from when the sun rises and when it sets – this entrains its circadian clock (see Chapter 5). So to confuse the birds about time of day, they were kept under conditions where the lights in their home aviary came on and went off six hours earlier than usual (other birds were kept with the lights going on and off six hours later than usual). Birds that had been exposed to days that started and ended six hours earlier than normal chose directions that were 90 degrees off the correct compass directions; in other words, they made the same error that a Boy Scout would who had been given a watch that was six hours off the correct time (Schmidt-Koenig et al., 1991).

More recent studies have indicated that experienced pigeons are not thrown off course by clock shifts as much as they ought to be. Furthermore, homing pigeons can still home successfully on completely overcast days when no blue sky is visible. Both these facts indicate that the sun-compass cannot be the only way that homing pigeons find compass directions.

Magnetic compass
Every Boy Scout true to his creed ('Be Prepared!') would carry with him a proper magnetic compass whenever he was out and about. A magnetic compass works because there is a magnetic field around the whole planet that can be thought of as an ordinary bar magnet with north close to the North Pole and south close by the South Pole. Much controversy surrounds whether pigeons are sensitive enough to the earth's magnetic field to be able to use it to find their way home.

Indirect evidence that pigeons might be using the earth's magnetic field to help them navigate comes from observations that birds home slower when there is high sunspot activity. Sunspots interfere with the magnetic field around the earth. Magnetic storms also disrupt pigeon homing, at least according to some studies. In an extensive series of studies over several years at two sites in North America, William Keeton and colleagues found that the homing directions of a group of pigeons varied according to the amount of background magnetic activity. A more direct test of the hypothesis that pigeons can navigate by the earth's magnetic field is to strap a small magnet onto a pigeon's head – it should create an additional, larger magnetic field that makes magnetic navigation impossible. Keeton's group tried this (Keeton, 1971, and elsewhere) and found a small shift in the pigeons' homing bearings (3° to the left). The small size of this disruption is a little strange since the field created by placing a magnet on the pigeon's head should be large compared with the earth's natural magnetic field. Further studies have also failed to replicate this result. Another study in North America found that a magnet attached to a pigeon's head caused a navigational shift in the opposite direction. Further European studies have found variations in homing direction in the same direction as Keeton's original results (see Wiltschko & Wiltschko, 1996).

The evidence for a magnetic compass in pigeons is mixed. It is quite possible that different pigeons in different places may rely on magnetic information to different degrees. Charles Walcott (1991), for example, reported that areas of magnetic anomaly on the earth's surface confuse the homing of one group of pigeons but not of another group. There may be strain differences between different groups of pigeons, or these birds may rely on different cues depending on the kind of terrain they normally fly over.

Odor maps

But no compass system, sun based or magnetic, can explain how a pigeon, having been transported 600 kilometers (400 miles) in the back of a truck to a place it has never visited before, can find the correct bearing to fly home. For a compass – any kind of compass – to be of use, you need to have at least a rough idea of where you are relative to where you are trying to get to. The biggest unsolved riddle in pigeon navigation is how these birds find the right direction home from places they have never visited before.

Many European researchers are convinced that pigeons use their sense of smell to find how to get home from distant release sites. These scientists propose that even locked up in their home cages, pigeons are exposed to different odors depending on which way the wind is blowing. Subsequently, when inexperienced pigeons are trucked out to an unfamiliar site and released, they can figure out which direction they have come from on the basis of the smells they passed through on their trip out to the release site. This account is supported by experiments in which one group of pigeons was brought up in cages open to the wind around them, and another group was brought up in air-conditioned quarters so that they could never know the direction of odors in the outside world. When these two groups of pigeons were subsequently driven to the same location and released, only those pigeons brought up in cages open to the outside world were able to find their way home. Similarly, pigeons that had been brought up normally but had their noses blocked before being taken out and released had difficulty finding the correct direction home (see Able, 1996; Wiltschko, 1996).

Figure 7.5 compares the homing success of a group of anosmic pigeons (birds that had had their noses blocked so they could not smell anything) and a normal control group of pigeons. All were transported around 180 kilometers from their home loft to sites they had never visited before and then released. Whereas the majority of the control birds found their ways home fairly directly, very few of the anosmic birds were able to home successfully (Wallraff, 1990).

Other experiments suggesting a role for smell in pigeon homing have involved driving two groups of pigeons along different routes on their way to the same release site. Presumably, along these different routes, the two groups of pigeons passed through regions with different smells (see Figure 7.6). Upon release, it was found that the pigeons from the two groups followed different flight paths back toward their home loft – each group of pigeons headed more toward the direction in which they had been brought (Baker, 1980).

Figure 7.5   *Homing of anosmic pigeons*

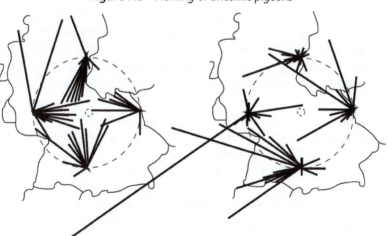

Notes: Naive pigeons released at sites about 180 kilometers distant from their home loft at least head for home in approximately the right direction (left-hand panel), even if they are not always totally successful in getting home. Pigeons deprived of their sense of smell, however (right-hand panel), headed off in random directions. The central dot is the home loft (Würzburg), and the borders of the then West Germany are shown.

Source: From Wallraff (1980).

Figure 7.6   *Pigeons taken out on two routes return by two different paths*

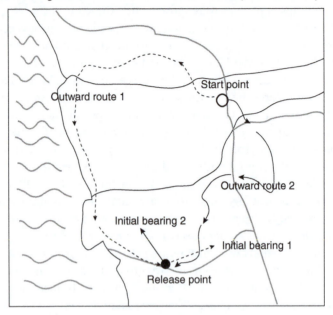

Source: From Baker (1980).

Paolo Ioalè and colleagues carried out a more direct test of the odor hypothesis (Ioalè et al., 1990). These researchers kept a group of pigeons in an aviary where fans blew air containing an odorous chemical (benzaldehyde) across the pigeons (left side of Figure 7.7). This smelly artificial wind came from the north. Later the pigeons were taken to a distant site, benzaldehyde was painted onto their noses, and they were released. All of these pigeons headed off in a southerly direction – approximately the opposite direction from which the benzaldehyde had come in their home cages (right side of Figure 7.7). This makes sense in terms of an odor map. If one smell predominates in winds from the north and the birds are released with that smell on their noses, then they may reasonably conclude that since the smell is at high levels of intensity, they must be north of their home cage and should therefore head south to return home.

For each of the possible navigational strategies considered here, sun-compass, magnetic compass, and odor maps, contradictory studies exist. Particularly older and more experienced birds continue to navigate successfully under conditions where manipulations of one or other navigational system should throw them off course. The obvious answer to this apparent paradox is that, with increasing experience, homing pigeons learn to integrate navigational information from more than one source, and consequently, if one type of information is unreliable, the other types are given a heavier weighting in choosing a course home. Homing in pigeons remains an area of interest to many scientists, many of whom now utilize computer tracking technology

Figure 7.7   *Experimental pigeons kept in a home aviary (left-hand diagram) through which an odor of benzaldehyde is blown by fans*

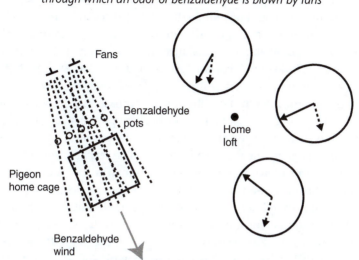

Notes: The three circles indicate the release bearings of birds from three different sites. The solid dot between the three circles indicates the direction of the home aviary from each of these three release sites. For the control birds, those not previously exposed to benzaldehyde (solid lines), the home bearings are accurate from all three release sites. The experimental birds, however (dashed lines), all headed in a southerly direction.

Source: From Wallraff (1990).

and brain imaging devices to more deeply understand the mechanisms behind this ability (Pecchia et al., 2013).

Bees foraging

The brain of the bee is only about 1 millimeter cubed in size – about the size of a single grain of sand. And yet the cognitive feats of bees in flying up to 2 kilometers (over a mile) from the hive to forage on flowers before finding the correct direction to fly home are certainly not trivial. As we shall see in Chapter 11, once back at the hive, they can also communicate the location and distance of the feeding site to their hive mates.

The first trick that bees have in their navigational toolbox is the sun-compass, already discussed above. Just like Boy Scouts and pigeons, bees are able to use the position of the sun, combined with a knowledge of time of day, to estimate the points of the compass.

The next strategy available to foraging bees is an awareness of how far they have traveled – or *dead reckoning*. The bee knows how far it has traveled, not through how much energy it has expended in flying nor in the sensation of air moving past it, but on the basis of the visual image moving past its eyes. This was demonstrated in experiments in wind tunnels in which bees were not confused by different head and tail winds that changed the amount of energy they had to expend in flying and the sensation of air moving past them. However, the bees were confused about the distance they had to fly if the patterning on the walls of the wind tunnel was changed so that it looked as though they had covered more ground than they really had (Srinivasan et al., 1996).

But dead reckoning, even aided by a sun-compass, is an inexact business. Small errors at the beginning of a journey become progressively larger as a trip continues, and then to reverse the process to fly home means that errors could be dangerously large by the time the hive should be reached. For more accurate navigation, bees also have an ability to use landmarks that they see along the route. Exactly how they do this is still the subject of some controversy.

It is clear that bees flying to and from the hive use landmarks such as rows of trees, hills, or other salient features to find their way. It seems that, as they fly out, bees commit scenes to memory that they then use to guide themselves on future trips. This has been demonstrated by experiments in which bees were captured and then released in the vicinity of landmarks but out of sight of the hive or foraging site. Experiments with a landmark that could be moved by the experimenters (a car) point to a similar conclusion (see Menzel et al., 1996).

A claim that bees use landmarks in a far more complex way was made by James Gould (1986). Gould proposed not only that bees recognize how landmarks look when they are heading to or from a foraging site but that bees' representations of landmarks are integrated into a proper cognitive map. A true map is something much more than just a set of landmarks with information about which way you should head as you pass by them. I can find my way to an unfamiliar spot if I am given information such as 'turn right at the lights by the vet'; 'head straight past the football field'. However, if I get lost or want to approach this unfamiliar spot from a different direction, then this route-sketch method is completely ineffective. If I have a proper map, on the other hand, I should be able to find my way even if I take a wrong turn, and I can find my way no matter which direction I am coming from. A true map is a far superior instrument to a route sketch, but it is also far more complex – is it really possible within the sand-grain sized brain of the bee?

Gould found that after being captured and displaced by experimenters, bees were able to correct their course for their goal when released – even when route-based rules could not be used; therefore, he reasoned, bees must be using cognitive maps. For several years, other researchers attempted to replicate Gould's results without success. Finally, the explanation for Gould's success and other researchers' failures seems to have been found.

Imagine you are traveling in a car using a route sketch to find your way somewhere. Now you are displaced off your route and have to find your way back. In general, you will be completely lost. However, if your route sketch includes things like 'head for the mountains' or 'keep the cliffs on your left', you may well be able to find your way even after quite large displacements. It seems that this was the situation for Gould's displaced bees. They were still able to see some relevant landmarks from their displaced positions. A better test of whether bees have mental maps involves displacing them to a position where landmarks are definitely not visible. In a test of this type, shown in Figure 7.8, the displaced bees were completely unable to find their way (see Dyer, 1996).

There is still much to be learned about just how the sand-grain brain of the bee integrates sun-compass, dead reckoning, and landmark information flexibly and reliably to find its way to and from sources of food (and communicates this

Figure 7.8   *Evidence that bees do not have a proper cognitive map*

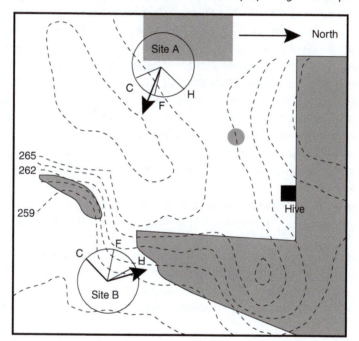

Notes: Shaded areas are trees; open areas are grass. Contour lines show elevation in meters. Circles show the release bearings of bees that were heading from the hive toward a feeder placed at the other site when they were captured. From each release site, bees might fly toward the hive (shown as H in the circle diagram), the feeding site (F), or the compass direction they were heading when caught (C). From site A, bees could see the landmarks that had been visible from their original foraging flight and so corrected their paths successfully and flew predominantly in the direction of the feeder they had originally been heading for. From site B, however, the landmarks of their original foraging route were not visible, and so they were unable to correct for the displacement that they had been exposed to, and when released, they headed predominantly homeward (H).

Source: From Dyer (1991).

information to its hive mates), but it seems that a proper cognitive map is not one of a bee's abilities.

Distractions, side biases, and other considerations

A pioneer of animal cognition, Wolfgang Köhler (1925), was interested in the question of how different species coped with detour problems. He used a fairly informal method in which members of different species were placed in front of barriers of various shapes, behind which he placed a desired food item. One of Köhler's barrier problems is shown in Figure 7.9.

The subject was placed at the starting point S: desired food was placed at point G. The barrier marked in Figure 7.9 was a transparent one made from a wire fence. The question of interest was, what would the animal do to get to the food? A dog placed in this arena immediately ran around the fence to get the food. However, on a subsequent test, when the food was placed closer to the fence, Köhler suggested that the dog could not bring itself to move away from the meat in order to get around the barrier to its ultimate goal. Köhler went on to report that a girl of just over one year old could also solve this problem though not without some hesitancy at having first to move away from the goal object before ultimately reaching it; hens also had a great deal of difficulty moving away from the desired objective in order to be able to progress around the fence.

While performances on detour tasks and several other classic tests of spatial navigation have often been used as an indicator of a species' spatial reasoning skills (and in some cases, as evidence for cognitive maps; Shettleworth, 2009), inconsistencies in the performance of individuals from a single species (especially when tested under slightly different conditions, as described above) may raise some red flags. When testing any aspect of cognition, it is important to ensure that other unintended variables, called *confounds*, can-

Figure 7.9 *Barrier problem set by Köhler*

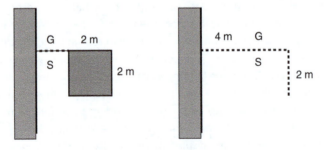

Note: S marks the starting point, and G the desired food.
Source: From Köhler (1925/1963).

not explain the behavior produced by the animal under test. We have already noted some ways that unintended cues (e.g., unintentional landmarks or bea-cons in the testing area) can make it appear that a species has a cognitive ability such as a cognitive map when it might not. However, the converse may also be true. A dog that refuses to move around a detour because meat is just out of reach on the opposite side of the fence has not lost its ability to navigate. In fact, dogs have passed many spatial cognition tests – includ-ing detour tasks – that would suggest that they may be good candidates for having cognitive maps. Instead it may mean that the presence of the meat is creating a motivational conflict – a desire to stay near the meat and a desire to obtain the meat (by going around the fence): unfortunately both cannot be accomplished simultaneously.

Other motivational conflicts – such as the *approach-avoidance conflict* – can influence the outcome of spatial navigation research as well (Montgomery, 1955). For example, a rat placed in a maze may be motivated to find the shortest route to a piece of cheese but may wish to avoid being picked up by the scientist at the end of the trial. As a result, the rat may move more slowly or take a less direct route to the cheese, even when it knows a faster, more direct route. Some studies have found that even the simple repetitive nature of repeatedly partici-pating in a test or running a maze can slow a rat's approach to a goal (Heathers, 1940), a fact that, if not carefully considered, could also confound data and influence interpretations of rats' spatial reasoning skills.

It is important to recognize that if Köhler had tested dogs with meat only at the closer distance in the detour task, he might have come to the incorrect conclusion that they were not capable of solving detour problems. It is there-fore critical that scientists interpret negative results (results that might suggest a species cannot do something) with care. More recent experiments on detour problems in animals have broadened the range of species shown capable of spa-tial reasoning on this task and have also identified some of the conditions that make detour problems easy or difficult for different species to solve.

Bruno Poucet and colleagues systematically examined the ability of cats to contend with detours of different types (Poucet et al., 1983). One of their detour problems is shown in Figure 7.10.

The cats started at the point marked S in the figure; food was placed at point G. To ensure they had an appreciation of the shape of the barrier and the rela-tive distances involved in the testing area, each cat was given two opportunities to explore the area without any food reward present. Once the cat had explored both sides of the barrier, it was removed to the starting point, and food was placed at the goal point, G, in such a way that the cat could see it being placed there. The question now was, would the cat choose the ultimately shorter route to the goal (route A in the figure), or would it choose route B, which, though longer overall, enabled the cat to stay closer to the goal object on its way? Poucet and colleagues found that the answer to this question depended on whether

Figure 7.10 *One of the barrier problems used by Poucet et al.*

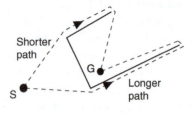

Note: S marks the cats' starting point and G shows where the food was placed.

Source: From Poucet et al. (1983).

the barrier was transparent or opaque. With an opaque barrier, the cats were far more likely to take the shorter route, *A*, than the longer one. However, with a transparent barrier, the cats' choice of routes was about 50/50. As well as pinpointing the importance of transparency in identifying whether cats will take the shortest route, Poucet and colleagues also explored the degree to which the necessary detour diverges from the most direct route to the goal object. These researchers found that cats were more likely to take a shorter detour if it was closer to the direct route to the goal; if the shorter detour route diverged too greatly from the direct route to the goal object, then the cats were more likely to take a longer route.

Nicole Chapuis and colleagues (including Bruno Poucet; Chapuis et al., 1983) performed a similar series of studies on dogs (Breton spaniels). Like the cats, Chapuis and coworkers' dogs preferred the shorter detour to a goal object when the barrier between their starting point and the object was opaque. When the barrier was transparent, however, the dogs, just like the cats, preferred the longer detour if that enabled them to stay closer to the desired object.

Köhler's early work indicating the difficulties chicks have in finding their way to desired objects by going around barriers has inspired an interesting series of more recent studies by Lucia Regolin and colleagues. Replicating Köhler's results and in line with the modern research on dogs and cats, Regolin and colleagues found that two-day-old chicks would more readily reach a goal object around a detour if the barrier was opaque rather than transparent (Regolin et al., 1994). Additionally, in the case of a transparent barrier, the chicks were more successful if the desired object was farther away than if it was directly behind the barrier. In further tests, Regolin and coworkers demonstrated that the chicks' problems with transparent barriers had less to do with the fact that they could see the desired goal object and were due more to the chicks' inability to comprehend that a transparent object could be a barrier (Regolin et al., 1995).

Angelo Bisazza and colleagues assessed the ability of poeciliid fish to swim around a barrier to obtain a desired goal object (Bisazza et al., 1997). Five related species of fish were tested in a very simple procedure. The males were separated from the females and given the opportunity to swim along a narrow channel until they reached a transparent barrier. Behind the barrier four adult females of the same species were held captive in a transparent glass cylinder. All the fish tested were able to swim around the barrier to get to the females, but interestingly, each species had a distinct preference for swimming around either the left or right side of the barrier. Similar lateral biases have been found for quokkas (small marsupials found in Western Australia) presented with a barrier task. As the barrier lengthened and the cost of laterality went up, however, the quokkas gave up their side preference in favor of the shortest route to food. While the reach of its influence appears to be limited to low-cost scenarios, side bias should be considered another possible source of variation in navigation research.

MIGRATION

> Not I, nor anyone else can travel that road for you.
> You must travel it by yourself.
> It is not far. It is within reach.
> Perhaps you have been on it since you were born, and did not know.
> From *Leaves of Grass*, Walt Whitman (1855 edition, p. 58)

The story of migration, a long journey to a distant land of promise, has inspired the work of artists, storytellers, and scientists alike. Occasionally such a tale resolves with the image of a child reaching the end of the journey alone, concluding the path that she was born on and entering the land that her parents would never see. This is the story of the monarch butterfly. Monarchs are the only species of butterflies to migrate north and south on the basis of the season (much in the same way that many bird species do). One population of monarchs is known to travel over 2,000 kilometers (1,500 miles) between the volcanic mountains of Mexico (in the winter) and the northern United States and Canada (in the summer). However, unlike most birds, the lifespan of a butterfly is very short – often less than two months once the adult form is taken – meaning that a single individual never makes the whole round-trip journey. Often it is the third or fourth generation that finally arrives in Canada, as earlier-generation females lay eggs and then die along the path. Despite the fact that not a single remaining individual will have made the trip before, it is a new generation of butterflies that reaches Mexico the following year to begin again (Brower, 1995).

FOCUS ON THE DATA: WHEN FIRE FACILITATES LIFE

Figure 7.11   *Density of eggs and larva on milkweed plants after prescribed summer burning*

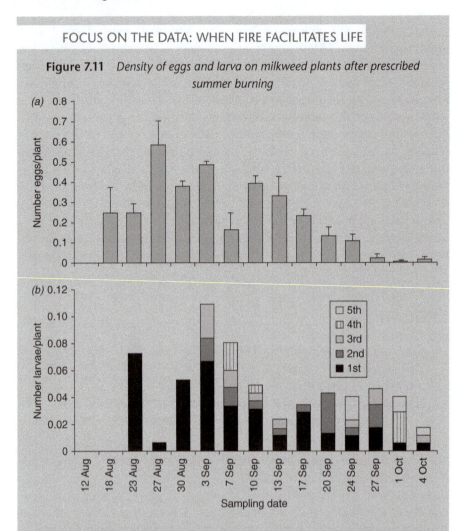

Source: Reprinted with permission from Baum & Sharber (2012). Fire creates host plant patches for monarch butterflies. *Biology Letters.*

Fire is often thought of as a destructive force, but in some instances it can allow new life to thrive. Because monarch butterflies must reproduce along their migration path, availability of food sources for larva can be a key factor in migration patterns and for survival. Milkweed is a common host plant to monarch butterflies. While many milkweed plants in Oklahoma are past their prime in late summer months, prescribed fires in the summer can allow for new growth and tender leaves in premigration months so that a new generation of butterflies will have time make it to their southern wintering grounds. Part (a) of the above graph (Figure 7.11) shows the density of eggs located in milkweed plants in areas with a summer prescribed fire. Baum and Sharber (2012) found not only that summer fires led to an increase in the number of milkweed plants available for use in the late summer months, specifically in August and September, but that monarchs were readily taking advantage of this renewed resource. August 27 showed the greatest density of eggs on these plants, as shown by the tallest gray bar on the graph. Part (b) of the graph shows the density of monarch larvae by their instar stage of development. The prevalence of young larvae is greatest in late August and early September, just after the peak in egg density, suggesting that many of these eggs did indeed hatch and began the progression to adulthood. The findings of this study suggest that carefully timed prescribed fires along the migration path of monarch butterflies could allow for additional breeding success in areas that might otherwise be short on food or host plant resources.

Read the full article: Baum, K. A. and Sharber, W. V. (2012) Fire creates host plant patches for monarch butterflies. *Biology Letters*. doi:10.1098/rsbl.2012.0550

Migration as a biological phenomenon can be found in every major branch of the animal kingdom (Dingle & Drake, 2007). Whether by sea, land, or air this distant, often seasonal movement is a fitting celebration of the mobility found across most animal species by a select subgroup who put navigation to the ultimate test.

Recently Hugh Dingle and V. Alistair Drake (2007) proposed that migration could best be defined in terms of four related concepts (incorporating both the behavior of the individual animal and unified movements made by the group):

1. A persistent form of locomotion that is direct, straight, and unwavering.
2. A movement of much longer duration or a significantly greater scale than typically seen in day-to-day activities.
3. A seasonal movement, where the different environmental endpoints serve different functions (e.g., one location serves as a breeding ground, and the other a birthing ground).
4. A movement that results in the spatial redistribution of a population.

Bird migrations, in which large flocks of individuals move in unison from their winter to summer homes, are but the best known of a very large group of such movements. Amphibians such as newts, salamanders, frogs, and toads are reported to migrate relatively short distances (a few kilometers) to and from breeding ponds in spring (Elewa, 2005). Spiny lobsters migrate down the coast of islands in the Bahamas every fall (Kanciruk & Herrnkind, 1978). Locust swarms migrate many thousands of kilometers (though they never retrace their steps) (Nevo, 1996). European eel larvae migrate from their hatching grounds in the Sargasso Sea off the Central American coast to their adult homes in Europe or Africa over a three-year journey (Ginneken et al., 2005). While many species of fish migrate, salmon have one of the most intriguing migration patterns identified to date.

Salmon spawn in fall and winter in freshwater lakes and streams before heading out into the ocean. Two or more years later, mature salmon return to their spawning grounds to breed. This migration is an exceptional feat for multiple reasons. First, most fish species are specialized for either saltwater or freshwater. Most saltwater fish that find themselves suddenly surrounded by freshwater (possibly at the hand of a well-meaning child who acquires a pet fish while at the beach and plops it in his freshwater tank at home) will bloat and die quite rapidly. This is because in a saltwater environment the saltwater fish's cells (which have higher levels of salts and other chemicals than freshwater fish) are well balanced with their surroundings. When a saltwater fish is placed in freshwater, however, its cells become an area of high salt concentration, contrasting with the water around it. Water begins to flow in from the new environment to dilute the salt (through osmosis); the cells bulge and expand in size, often bursting. The opposite happens for freshwater fish placed in saltwater.

Salmon are *anadromous*, which means they can survive in both saltwater and freshwater environments; this adaptation likely has to do with their lifecycle and migrational path from their freshwater place of birth to a saltwater adulthood and back again. Not only does their behavior change to accommodate their new environment (including the behavior of their cells, which pump salt and water in and out as needed), but their body changes as well. For one, the brilliant pink or red color we think of when we picture salmon begins to fade as they reach the ocean; as they grow mature enough for the journey back to their birthplace to lay eggs, they are often silver gray in color. Once back in freshwater, the fish have to fight to travel upstream to their spawning grounds, often leaping over rocks and climbing waterfalls along the path. Again the change back to freshwater takes a toll on their bodies. Now only mutants of their former magnificent form, the adult salmon turn darker gray, develop scraggly teeth, a crooked jaw, and often a hump on the back. Beaten and bruised, most fish that complete the journey will die within a few days or weeks of spawning.

Second, while literally fighting the environmental elements and experiencing changes to their own form, adult salmon must navigate back to the very streambed where they themselves hatched. The round-trip journey of some species of salmon (e.g., sockeye) can span thousands of kilometers, from the North American west coast to Japan or even Siberia. While it is not fully understood how salmon accomplish this, evidence has been found for the use of both olfactory and visual cues (or landmarks); this may include star-based navigation (Quinn, 1980). Recently it has been proposed that salmon, which show sensitivity to magnetic fields, may be able to use a magnetic compass (much like pigeons). By imprinting to the magnetic field of their native riverbed at birth, they may gain a constant bearing back home independent of where their adult ocean journey takes them (Lohmann et al., 2008).

Turtles are the record holders among migrating reptiles (see Figure 7.12). For example, the green sea turtle covers a round trip of nearly 2,000 kilometers

Figure 7.12 *Migration path of green turtles tracked by satellite from Redang Island in West Malaysia*

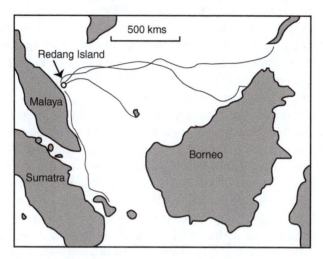

Source: From Papi and Luschi (1996).

between its breeding grounds on Ascension Island, (in the middle of the southern North Atlantic) and the Brazilian coast (Bowen et al., 1989). Much like salmon, individual turtles return to breed on the exact same beach every three years, and as with salmon, how they achieve this remains in large part a mystery. Some have speculated that the navigational methods used by sea turtles and salmon may be similar, consisting of a combination of olfactory, visual, and magnetic cues (Lohmann et al., 2008). Similar cues may in fact account for the migration patterns of many species that travel long distances, including the monarch butterflies described at the beginning of this chapter. Monarchs, of course, do not have the chance to experience landmarks or cues associated with the goal location firsthand; however, they may instead be born with a predisposition to head toward a specific bearing as guided by the position of the sun (sun-compass) and their biological clock (Merlin et al., 2009) or a light-based magnetic compass (Gegear et al., 2010). One of the best-known parts of the sea turtles' journey, however, occurs just after hatching: orienting and navigating toward the sea. While turtles may use both geographical and light cues given off by the reflection of the moon to locate and move toward the water upon hatching (Salmon & Witherington, 1995), conservation efforts have drawn attention to the impact that man-made sources of illumination can have on the initial journey of young sea turtles, interfering with visual cues provided by the moon and causing the turtles to move toward street lamps and buildings instead of toward the ocean (e.g., Bertolotti & Salmon, 2005). Reducing nighttime light pollution in these areas during turtle-hatching season seems to limit such occurrences, but this remains an ongoing effort.

Among mammals, the record for longest migration also goes to an aquatic family – the whales (Rasmussen et al., 2007). Whales, such as the gray whale, migrate each year between their warmer breeding grounds and cooler summer feeding areas. The route and timing is predictable enough that along a popular migratory path off the coast of Oregon permanent road signs mark whale-watching points. Sure enough, at the right time of year, a stop at such a spot almost guarantees a view of some of the 18,000 migrating gray whales (Moore, 2008) – among other species – as they travel by.

Some land-based mammals are quite accomplished migrators, too, such as elks, gnu, moose, caribou, and zebras; however, changes in landscape due to increased human populations have prompted conservation efforts here as well (Berger, 2004). These species move annually between feeding grounds that differ in their productivity at different times of the year. The caribou of Canada, for example, spend summers in the more northern areas, where they can feed on leaves of low trees, but move south around 500 kilometers in winter to feed on lichens and grasses (Duquette & Klein, 1987). African elephants tracked by GPS have been found to travel distances of 625 kilometers over the course of just a few months. One heard of elephants was tracked traveling distances of up to 60 kilometers every four days during the dry season to locate isolated water holes (Berger, 2004).

CONCLUSIONS

Humans, as a species, are actually quite hopeless at true navigation (despite the assurances of those who routinely refuse to pull over at a filling station for a map). While most of us can find our way to the corner shop and back, finding our way across an ocean or a desert is something we have found a way to do reliably only in the last couple of hundred years through the development of complex pieces of technology. Without these devices – stuck on a boat on an ocean without radio, compass, or Global Positioning System device – those of us without extensive survival training would feel completely helpless. However, many other species have exceptional navigation abilities, traveling both short and long distances with ease, sometimes from points never visited before.

The perceptual world and memory of a species can greatly influence the amount and kinds of tools available to navigation efforts. Animals that can see polarized light or readily localize smells often utilize this information as they travel, whereas other species (like humans) may be limited to other visual cues in the environment, such as landmarks or beacons.

Many of the perceptual and navigational abilities of the homing pigeon, such as use of a sun-compass, sensitivity to polarization of sunlight, magnetic sense, and odor guidance, have also been demonstrated in several migrating species, including turtles, salmon, and possibly monarch butterflies. Some species that migrate at night may also make use of the stars to navigate, as ancient mariners did. Sylviid warblers and indigo buntings have been tested under planetarium domes. These experiments demonstrated that star patterns alone are sufficient to enable these night-migrating species to find their migratory direction. When the stars in the planetarium were turned off, the birds were confused as to which direction they should head (Emlen, 1970). As a rule, most species can use more than one mode of navigation – allowing them to be flexible as the environment or the context of travel changes.

While the distance and nature of migration can vary dramatically, every major category of animal has been found to migrate (although not every individual species within each group does). Even many animals that do not migrate still have to travel within their environment to find food, water, protection, or mates. Therefore, navigation plays a critical role in the survival and evolution of numerous species and continues to serve as a topic of interest to scientists dedicated to uncovering the many ways it might be accomplished. In the cognitive realm, the study of navigation not only has direct relevance to discussions of spatial reasoning but also contributes to our knowledge of memory, communication, learning, time, perception, and many other areas within the field as well.

FURTHER READING

Boles, L. C., & Lohmann, K. J. (2003). True navigation and magnetic maps in spiny lobsters. *Nature*, 421(6918), 60–63.

Menzel et al. (2005). Honey bees navigate according to a map-like spatial memory. *Proceedings of the National Academy of Sciences of the United States of America*, 102(8), 3040–3045.

Provides a deeper look at the current state of migration research.

Web sources

http://kisdwebs.katyisd.org/campuses/MRHS/teacherweb/hallk/Teacher%20 Documents/AP%20Biology%20Materials/Ecology/Animal%20Behavior/51_ A01s.swf

Find animation of Tinbergen's digger wasp experiment at this website, along with practice questions to assess conceptual material surrounding his findings.

http://www.ustream.tv/migratingcranes

This website features live video streams from cameras placed along animal migration paths (as well as other animal sites). Because it is live, it is more active at some times of the year and day than others.

http://videos.howstuffworks.com/animal-planet/28399-fooled-by-nature-monarch-butterfly-migration-video.htm

Find more information on the monarch butterfly migration at this website.

8 Social Cognition and Self-Awareness

A dog, crossing a bridge over a stream with a bone in his mouth, saw his own reflec-
tion in the water and took it for that of another dog, with a bone double the size of
his own. He immediately let go of his own, and fiercely attacked the other dog to get
the larger bone from him. He thus lost both: that which he grasped at in the water,
because it was a reflection; and his own, because the stream swept it away.

Aesop's Fables, translated by G. F. Townsend

Fourteen years ago I took a trip to a Masai village in Kenya, Africa. The children in the village clamored to meet the dozen or so American visitors, in part
because such groups often carried with them foreign trinkets and treasures that
they were willing to share with those who expressed interest. I will never forget
the moment one member of our group pulled out his old instant Polaroid camera, took several pictures, and then gave them to the children. As the images
slowly appeared on the self-developing film, a purposeful flurry of excitement
rose across the group. It quickly became clear that the children could not identify themselves in the photographs on their own; instead they took turns helping each other identify themselves in the ghostly pictures.

The ability to recognize one's own image is often taken for granted, but
in actuality this is a skill that not all animals – not even all humans – share.
Among humans, self-recognition and self-awareness can vary substantially on
the basis of culture, experience, social development, and age. How we define
'self' can pose an even greater challenge. For example, in some parts of Mexico
an image or reflection is considered a part of the self. In such cultures taking
a photograph of another person is often taboo, since capturing one's image
on film may be interpreted as trying to steal the subject's soul. This may catch
unsuspecting tourists off guard and, in some cases, can have serious repercus-
sions, including the confiscation or smashing of the camera in order to free the
spirits captured within.

The degree to which an individual, human or nonhuman, is self-aware or
conscious of their own mental state or the mental states of others is not an easy
thing to establish. Self-awareness undoubtedly goes beyond self-recognition, but
how far and to what degree? Can someone who fails to recognize his or her own
image be self-aware? What does one's perception of self really say about consciousness? The philosopher Daniel Dennett, in his optimistically titled book

171

Consciousness Explained, describes consciousness as 'the last surviving mystery'. Having discussed some difficult problems that have become at least a little more tractable in the twentieth century, he states:

> With consciousness, however, we are still in a terrible muddle. Consciousness stands alone today as a topic that often leaves even the most sophisticated thinkers tongue-tied and confused.
>
> Daniel Dennett, 1991, p. 22

Dennett, of course, is considering only human consciousness. If it is so difficult to come to grips with consciousness in humans, where we at least have some personal experience to guide us, how are we to consider consciousness in other species? It seems positively foolhardy for an animal psychologist to blunder in where even philosophers fear to tread. Sometimes, however, a question is interesting and important enough that, having been appraised of the risks, we still want to proceed. Several animal psychologists have taken up the challenge of trying to understand animal consciousness through use of a variety of experiments that appear to capture at least part of what consciousness means to us as human beings.

At their core, the studies considered in this chapter are concerned with assessing how much insight one animal has into its own actions and motivations and how much it understands about the motivations of others. Psychologists know this form of consciousness as theory of mind, or the theory of what underlies the behavior of another individual. Before addressing responses with regard to others, however, we will delve a bit further into what humans and nonhuman animals know about the self.

SELF-RECOGNITION: IS THAT ME? – STUDIES ON MIRROR RECOGNITION

What do you see when you look in the mirror? Yourself, probably. It was not always so, however. During the first year of life a baby does not recognize itself in a mirror. Only after their first birthday do children start to react to the image in a mirror as being of themselves. If the child's mother dabs a spot of rouge on the child's nose while he is sleeping and then shows him a mirror, the child will see the rouge in the mirror and wipe his nose clean. Children younger than about one year show no reaction. People born blind who later gain sight or those who are brought up without access to mirrors may also take a little while to recognize themselves in a mirror when they first see one. Several species of our closest relatives – the great apes – can also recognize themselves in a mirror. Chimpanzees, after an initial period of reacting to their mirror reflection as if it were another chimpanzee, readily learn that the mirror shows them themselves and then use it to inspect areas of their body that are not normally easily visible. Interestingly, self-recognition in mirrors has not been observed in chimpanzees younger than two and a half years of age –although it occurs more commonly after four years of age and, most curiously, appears to decline after around age fifteen (see Boysen & Himes, 1999, for a review) Orangutans can also recognize themselves in a mirror (Suarez & Gallup Jr., 1981), and hotly disputed claims and counterclaims for this ability have been made for dolphins (Reiss & Marino, 2001), elephants (Plotnik et al., 2006), and a gorilla (Parker et al., 1994). Most other species tested, including fish, dogs, cats, and parrots, typically react to themselves in a mirror (if at all) as if their reflection were another animal (Figure 8.1).

Figure 8.1   *A four-month-old dog looking at its image in a mirror*

An interesting test of mirror self-recognition in animals is the mark test, developed by Gordon Gallup. This is similar to the test for babies and small children described above, where a dot of rouge is applied to the baby's forehead while he is sleeping. In Gallup's test, the animal is first anesthetized. While it is sleeping, its forehead and ear are marked with dots of nonirritating ink. Once they awake, the animals show no awareness of the ink dots until they see themselves in a mirror, at which point they may touch them on their own body. Touching the mark in this way indicates that they recognize the mirror image as being themselves. Chimpanzees, orangutans, and (possibly) a gorilla have all passed Gallup's mark test, but more than a dozen species of Old and New World monkeys, as well as gibbons, have all failed the test (see Gallup, 1997).

What are we to make of these mirror-using apes? Gordon Gallup and other supporters of the importance of the mark test argue that it proves that the ape recognizes itself in the mirror, and furthermore, that this self-recognition is evidence of a self-concept. This self-concept, they argue, is similar to our human awareness of self, including the ability to see ourselves as others view us, and possibly even an understanding that the self is mortal. This viewpoint has not gone unchallenged, however. Cecilia Heyes has suggested that these mirror tests do not prove that the animal is recognizing itself – the apes may simply become bored with the mirror and return to grooming themselves (which is what they do most of the time anyway) while still keeping an eye on the mirror. This might then give the impression that the animals are using the mirror to see themselves as they groom. Heyes argues that we should not just take the word of these researchers who say that they can tell what an animal is thinking while it looks in a mirror (Heyes, 1998).

This suggestion seems to be countered effectively by the results of the mark test, which shows the animal making a directed response to its own face as a result of something it could have seen only in the mirror. However, in controlled studies that have compared the rate at which the ape touches the mark on its forehead with a mirror present with the rate of mark touching when the mirror is absent, the differences in rates with and without a mirror are not as great as the typical summary of this research implies. It is not the case that chimpanzees *never* touch the dye mark in the absence of the mirror and touch it energetically as soon as the mirror is introduced. In one of the few studies to report the frequency with which chimps touched their dye marks, it was reported that on average chimps touched their marks 2.5 times in 30 minutes in the absence of a mirror and only 3.9 times in 30 minutes with a mirror (Povinelli et al., 1993).

The bigger question that these studies raise is, Why should we consider the ability to recognize oneself in a mirror as an acid test for self-awareness? The longevity of this test may be due in part to confirmed presuppositions about who should pass it. For years it has been suggested that humans and select nonhuman apes may have a level of self-awareness that exceeds that of other species. Mirror self-recognition tests often confirm this belief, possibly point-ing to a shared cognitive skill unique to our ancestral lineage. However, what if it was discovered that even a pigeon, given some basic experience with mir-rors and marks, could pass this test? Would we still be as keen to suggest that mark-directed behavior in the presence of a mirror indicated a higher level of self-awareness or social intelligence?

Robert Epstein and colleagues conducted a study asking just this question in 1981. Before engaging in the mark test, pigeons were first exposed to two pretest phases. In one phase pigeons were trained to look at a mirror and watch for the reflection of a blue key, which lit up on the wall behind them and was turned off before the pigeons could turn around. Turning and pecking the previously lit key provided the pigeons with brief access to food from a hopper. In the second phase blue dot stickers were placed on the pigeons' feathers in locations where they could clearly be seen. The pigeons were then given food if they pecked at the blue dots located on their feathers. In the test phase, or mirror test, a blue dot sticker was placed on the pigeons' chest feathers, but this time a white bib was also placed around each pigeon's neck to block its view of the sticker. A mir-ror placed in the chamber now provided the only visual access to this blue dot, akin to the mark test conducted with human and nonhuman primates. Would the pigeons now be able to pass this classic test? Although a surprising outcome to some, the answer was ultimately yes. Similar to the self-directed behavior witnessed in select primates, the pigeons looked toward the mirror and began to peck at the blue dot on their chest (Epstein et al., 1981).

Although it might be argued that these findings are inherently different from those obtained with apes, because the pigeons required prior training to pass the mark test while the behavior of humans and nonhuman primates is often reported as being spontaneous, this may be to miss the point. The pigeons were never directly trained to locate blue dots on their body using a mirror, the actual skill under test. Epstein and colleagues acknowledged that experience with mirrors and experience locating marks on one's body may very well be necessary prior abilities for the skill of recognizing dots on one's body using a mirror not only for pigeons but also for other species, including humans.

I already mentioned that children do not typically pass mirror self-recogni-tion tests before one to two years of age. By that time many children have had ample exposure to mirrors and other reflective surfaces, as well as an unknown amount of encouragement to engage in self- and other-directed behaviors by parents and caretakers, well before participating in a mark test, even if explicit training has not occurred. In fact the presence of strong cultural differences indicates that environment and experience do play an important role in mir-ror self-recognition studies conducted with human children. In a recent study Tayna Broesch and colleagues (2011) compared the performance of children from Kenya, Fiji, Grenada, Saint Lucia, and Peru with children living in the

United States and Canada on a simple version of the mark test. In this test the experimenter covertly placed a sticker on each child's head during play and then later raised a mirror so the children could see themselves for 30 seconds. Only children who did not touch the sticker before the mirror was presented were included in the study. The researchers were interested in how many children from each culture would touch or remove the sticker after seeing their reflection. While 84 percent of the children from the United States and Canada (35–54 months of age) demonstrated self-directed behavior and removed the sticker in the presence of the mirror, a much lower percentage of children of the same age range engaged in self-directed behaviors in Fiji (0%), Peru (51%), Grenada (52%) and Saint Lucia (58%). In Kenya the results were also striking: out of 82 children only 2 showed any self-directed behavior in the presence of the mirror, and only 1 child successfully removed the sticker. Therefore, prior experience, even culture, may factor into success on mark tests using a mirror. Indeed, reports of other species successfully using mirrors in mark tests after prolonged exposure to reflective surfaces may suggest that, given the right environment, primates and pigeons may not be alone. A study by Diana Reiss and Lori Marino (2001) found that two dolphins living in a tank with reflective walls later demonstrated increased self-directed behavior in front of a mirror during a mark test; similar studies are presently ongoing with dogs, crows, magpies, and elephants.

However, conceding that experience influences performance on mirror-recognition tasks, even for humans, does not entirely resolve the original question: Is an individual's performance on a mirror-guided task a good measure of whether that individual is self-aware? Imagine a good friend of yours suffers a stroke. This stroke leaves her intellectually unaffected except in one respect – she can no longer recognize herself in a mirror. You have to help her comb her hair and apply lipstick because she is unable to do these things herself, but other than that, there are no symptoms to her syndrome. Her mental faculties are unaffected, and you have no reason whatever to doubt her sense of self, yet she can no longer pass the traditional mark test described above. While a strict interpretation of mirror self-recognition test performance might result in the conclusion that your friend does not display evidence of being self-aware, this is likely untrue.

In fact, there is a known syndrome, prosopagnosia, which leads to an inability to recognize familiar faces. Severe prosopagnosics are unable to recognize themselves in a mirror or in pictures, but nobody has suggested that they lack a healthy self-concept. Oliver Sacks describes a prosopagnosic in *The Man Who Mistook His Wife for a Hat* (1990). In this fascinating account, Sacks describes a music professor who loses the ability to recognize objects. Unfortunately, Sacks does not tell us how his patient, Dr. P., reacts to his own face in a mirror.

However, an earlier report of a case of prosopagnosia caused by a head injury states:

> In the early convalescent phase he frequently, especially when shaving, questioned whether the face gazing at him was really his own, and even though he knew it could physically be none other, on several occasions grimaced or stuck out his tongue 'just to make sure'.
>
> Macreae and Trolle (1956)

So there exists a neurological syndrome that can lead to failures on mirror self-recognition without any diminution of self-concept. Conversely, there are also syndromes that can lead to a disrupted self-concept without any effect on the ability to recognize oneself in a mirror. For example, autistic individuals are characterized as severely lacking in the ability to see themselves as others view them and in the ability to put themselves imaginatively into the situation of others. This lack of self-concept is measured in tests of the understanding of other people's intentions and thoughts. Although autistics' self-concept can be severely limited, for some the ability to recognize themselves in a mirror is quite normal. Many autistic children can use mirrors to inspect their bodies and to pass the mark test just as typically developing children do (Dawson & McKissick, 1984), although in some autistic individuals who do ultimately show mirror self-recognition, this ability takes longer to develop (Ferrari & Matthews, 1983).

Thus, there are people who are unable to recognize themselves in mirrors but whose self-concept is unaffected (prosopagnosics), and there are other people who are impaired in their self-concept but well able to recognize themselves in mirrors (autistic children). Consequently, the mirror test cannot be considered a foolproof test of an animal's (or human's) self-concept. In so far as self-recognition in a mirror demonstrates anything, it shows that an animal has what we might call an 'own-body' concept – it is able to differentiate between itself and the rest of the world. Now an own-body concept is something that most animals surely must have. The animal that knows when fighting that it should bite the other animal's limbs and not its own must have some sense of where its own body ends and the other animal's begins. Heyes suggests that even to be able to move through the environment without bumping into things implies an own-body concept of this type. Viewed in this way, the interesting question that the mirror-recognition experiments raise is, why are most animals able to recognize their own body in normal viewing, but rather few are able to recognize their own body in a mirror? This is a fascinating question, but it will not, I believe, be answered by pondering the deeper nature of a chimpanzee concept of self. Rather the question will be answered by looking at how the different species use vision to identify themselves and others under different circumstances.

In the previous edition of this book, it was suggested that one interesting line of study would be whether different species can recognize themselves in video images. Unlike reflections, TV projections are not mirror reversed, which might provide a simpler stimulus for species that, unlike humans, may not have extensive prior exposure to mirrors. One of the first studies of this type was conducted by Charles Menzel, Sue Savage-Rumbaugh, and Janet Lawson (1985) with two captive-born chimpanzees named Sherman and Austin. While not a typical self-recognition test, this study asked whether chimpanzees could use a video image of their arm to guide their hand to a hidden target. At the time of testing, the chimpanzee sat in a small room behind a solid opaque wall with a single arm-sized hole. Initially food was placed somewhere on the outside of the wall so that the chimpanzee could not see it but could reach it through the hole. A video camera was set up so that it recorded the outside wall during trials, showing the location of the food and any arm movements made by the chimpanzee in its attempts to grab the food. A TV located inside the chimpanzee's enclosure allowed the subject to watch the video feed in real time (Figure 8.2).

After sticking their arm through the opening and grasping around for the food for a while, the chimpanzees were able to use the video image to reliably

Figure 8.2 *The experimental layout as described in Menzel et al. (1985)*

Notes: Here a chimpanzee reaches its arm through a hole to obtain a food reward as guided by a live TV image of its movements.

Source: Image reprinted with permission from Menzel et al. (1985).

guide their hand to the reward. Later the food was replaced with a black ink dot to reduce the likelihood that the chimpanzee could locate the target through another means such as smell. Food was provided to the chimpanzees once they touched the dot with their hand. Again both chimpanzees were able to locate this target using the video feed provided on the monitor.

Indeed, when the image on the monitor was mirror reversed, both chimpanzees had a more difficult time locating the target. While this might at first appear to support the idea that mirror-reversed images pose more of a challenge in terms of bodily self-recognition than video images do, it should be noted that when given the opportunity to locate the target using a real mirror (instead of a mirror-reversed video image), both chimpanzees were able to do so accurately and quickly. While interesting, these findings are difficult to interpret. More research will need to be conducted before anything concrete can be said about the possible advantages or disadvantages of using video versus mirror images. Luckily, research utilizing the video guidance method seems to be gaining traction and may lead to interesting new directions for self-recognition research. For example, a study by Hirosi Toda and Takashi Watanabe (2008) demonstrated that pigeons not only recognized themselves in a video image but could do so even with a five- to seven-second delay in the video playback (three-year-old human children can do this as well, but only when the delay is less than two seconds).

SENSITIVITY TO THE ACTIONS OF OTHERS

In some ways measuring an individual's response to the behavior of others is simpler than assessing how that individual perceives its own image or movements. This may be due to the importance of the behavior of other members of one's own species in nature. Responding appropriately to the behavioral cues provided by an aggressive male or to the mating display of a receptive female may be critical to an individual's survival and fitness. On the other hand, a specific set of responses to one's own reflection may be less important.

One advantage of attending to the behavior of others may be the ability to obtain additional information that would otherwise not be directly accessible, like the location of a food source or the presence of possible threats. In some cases this information might be freely given by other individuals and intended for use by the recipient. This form of communication is formally called a *signal*. For example, if a jay spots a hawk overhead, it may let out a mobbing call that alerts other birds in the area to the presence of the hawk; recipients can then respond by taking cover or joining in the mobbing defense even if they cannot see the predator themselves. In some cases, however, the animal providing the information is not doing so intentionally. In this case the transmission of information is labeled a *cue*, and the observer is said to be *eavesdropping*. For example, an unsuspecting fox returning home might unwittingly lead a trailing coyote to her den of kits. In cases such as this the information communicated, which will likely result in increased risk of predation to her offspring, was no doubt unintentional (more on these forms of communication in Chapter 12). Nonetheless, in both accounts the individual attending to the behavior of another may gain a substantial benefit for doing so. Because the motivation and outcome of the two individuals involved in this type of scenario can be quite different, the term *demonstrator* will be used to describe the individual providing information (or the animal being watched), and the term *observer* will be applied to the individual that has the opportunity for information gain (or the animal doing the watching), independent of the presumed intent or outcome for either party. This terminology is also consistent with a related literature on social learning and imitation, which will be discussed in Chapter 9.

In recent years domestic dogs have become a popular model for understanding social sensitivity to the actions of others, both conspecifics (other dogs) and heterospecifics (humans). In fact, the domestic dogs' acute ability to interpret and respond appropriately to even the most subtle aspects of human behavior (for example, see Box 8.1) may contribute to their success as a species as well as the ubiquitous presence of pet dogs in human homes across the Western world (Udell & Wynne, 2008; Udell et al., 2010). One of the first formal tests of a dog's response to the actions of others was conducted by Adam Miklósi and colleagues in 1998, in a paradigm known as the object-choice task. In this test a human experimenter stood between two bowls, both of which smelled like food, but only one contained accessible food. A dog subject stood 3 meters back from the experimenter and watched as the human pointed to the bowl hiding the food reward. The dog was then allowed to approach one of the two bowls. If it approached the one indicated by the human first, it was allowed to eat the food treat; otherwise it would be shown the food at the other location but would not be allowed to eat it. All five dogs that participated in this original study reliably followed the human point to the correct container. The experimenter then made the task more challenging by providing a series of more subtle gestural stimuli: bowing or leaning over the correct bowl, nodding at the correct bowl, turning his head toward the correct bowl, and finally just glancing at it. While at least one dog was able to use each gesture to locate food, either initially or after additional trials, more subtle gestures, such as glancing, were more difficult for the dogs to follow (Miklósi et al., 1998). Nonetheless, pet domestic dogs have now participated in many versions of the object-choice task conducted by researchers all over the world, and it is clear that dogs living with humans are incredibly in-tune with the gestures of their two-legged companions, especially when following a human's movements results in a toy, treat, or other reward.

BOX 8.1 GUILTY OR SOCIALLY SENSITIVE?

In comparison with their wild canine relatives, domestic dogs are a very successful species. The dog population is likely over 1,000 times the size of the gray and red wolf populations combined, and this difference only appears to be increasing (Coppinger & Coppinger, 2001). What makes this success story even more fascinating, however, is that dogs could not have achieved it without a very important benefactor – humans! Domestic dogs are obligatory symbiotes, which means they would not exist and likely could not survive without mankind. This does not mean that all dogs are pets nor that they all should be. However, it does mean that without human assistance, dogs would not have the resources they need to survive, be it shelter, protection, or food such as table scraps and trash heaps. What's more, dogs' closest relatives –wolves – are often villainized by the same humans who are responsible for their cousin's success (think of 'Little Red Riding Hood' or 'The Three Little Pigs' or check the recent news about wide-scale wolf hunts in North America). While dogs may not be universally loved around the world – in fact, in much of the world they are more like tolerated pests than pets – in the Western world they are often considered family. For example, in the United States there are over 78 million dogs living in human homes whose owners collectively spend over 50 billion dollars on them yearly (APPA, 2012). So why do we choose to share our resources with such an unlikely companion? Some researchers suggest that it is dogs' uncanny ability to read our behavior and respond accordingly that allows them to reap the rewards of human civilization.

Of course nobody is perfect, and dogs do misbehave. What dog owner hasn't come home to an occasional mess on the floor or chewed slipper? Yet it is what the dog does next that might make all the difference. Head lowered, ears flat and back, tail low and wagging slowly, the dog skulks up to the owner, gives its best 'puppy eyes', and begs for our forgiveness (see Figure 8.3). How could anyone be mad, have a heart! The dog clearly feels guilty. Isn't that enough punishment after all? What the research suggests might surprise you.

The first hint that something might be off with the so-called guilty look (see Figure 8.3) of the dog came from an experiment conducted recently by Alexandra Horowitz (2009). In her study 14 dogs were left in a room with a piece of food that their owners had forbidden them to eat. Once their owners had left the room, each dog experienced one of four conditions: (1) The dog ate the treat (to ensure this result, the experimenter fed it to the dog), and when the owner returned, she was told the dog ate the treat and was instructed to scold the dog. (2) The dog ate the treat; however, when the owner returned, she was told the dog had not eaten it. (3) The dog did not eat the treat (to ensure this result, the experimenter removed it as soon as the owner left the room), but when the owner returned, she was told the dog ate the treat and was instructed to scold the dog. (4) The dog did not eat the treat, and when the owner returned, she was told the dog had not eaten it. Horowitz found that dogs tend to look guilty when they are being scolded, even if they were not guilty of the act. In fact, dogs tended to look even guiltier when they were punished for something they did not do.

Figure 8.3   *The classic guilty look*

Source: Photograph courtesy of Nathaniel Hall.

As it turns out, the topography of the guilty look is actually quite similar to how ethologists classify canine submission and may be more of an appeasement or fearful behavior displayed in the presence of an owner who, for lack of a better term, is showing signs of dominance. In other words, your dog may not be so guilty after all – instead it may just be responding to your scolding behaviors – the tone of your voice, the way your hands are placed on your hips just so, or the tap of your foot. Nonetheless, the guilty look works. A second study found that while owners are quite poor at telling whether or not their dogs have actually committed a forbidden act (despite their confidence to the contrary), owners are less likely to punish their dog once they spot the guilty look, whether the dog was guilty or not (Hecht et al., 2012). Success!

For almost a decade researchers interpreted dogs' ability to follow human gestures in object-choice task as entirely unique in the animal kingdom, claiming that this research provided evidence for a human-like social cognition in domestic dogs. In other words, some believed that dogs understood human gestures at a deeper level that did not require social experience or learning (Hare et al.,

2002; Riedel et al., 2008). After all, humans also follow points, and research-ers had encountered difficulties in demonstrating point-following behavior in other species, including nonhuman primates. Maybe the domestic dog's respon-siveness to human gestures was the result of domestication or even *convergent evolution* (the evolution of similar social abilities in response to the selective pressures associated with a shared environment) with humans. Proponents of this hypothesis suggested that other species, including our closest primate rela-tive, the chimpanzee, and dogs' closest relative, the wolf, not only performed poorly on social tasks but lacked the capacity to respond to human gestures independent of life experience.

However, contradictory results soon began to surface. Almost all early stud-ies investigating nonhuman primates had been done with laboratory chim-panzees, many of whom experienced little human interaction or enrichment outside of testing. This was in sharp contrast to the lifestyle of the pet dogs that were so successful in object-choice tasks. There were also multiple stud-ies demonstrating nonhuman primate success on human-guided object-choice tasks; however, in each case the subject was socialized to humans (see Tomasello & Call, 2004, for a review). Given the right early experience and environment, chimpanzees and other primates clearly did not lack the capac-ity for this behavior. As it turns out – much like recognizing oneself in a mir-ror – even human children typically do not track pointing gestures until their second year of life (Lempers, 1979; Murphy & Messer, 1977), and more unu-sual gestures often require additional experience and learning. So what about dogs? Are they really born with an acute responsiveness to human actions? More recent findings suggest that domestic dogs may be predisposed to attend to the actions of their social companions, be it dogs or humans, but that this ability is shared by wolves and other social animals as well. The more spe-cific response of following the gesture of a human to a target likely requires two things. First, dogs must learn that humans can be their social compan-ions. This likely occurs through exposure to humans during a sensitive period of social development early in life. Second, dogs must learn that following a human gesture can result in a desired outcome. In this way an outstretched arm can come to predict the presence of food or toys in that general direction (Udell et al., 2010). This idea, known as the Two-Stage Hypothesis for dogs' responsiveness to human gestures, is more consistent with the broader litera-ture on canine social behavior. It also allows for the possibility that different responses to human gestures are more appropriate for different populations of dogs. For example, researchers have found that the response of Ethiopian vil-lage dogs to an approaching human is quite unlike that of pet dogs (Ortolani et al., 2009). The most common response made by village dogs was to flee from the human (52%), an additional 11 percent responded to the approach-ing human with aggression, and only 4 percent of the surveyed population approached the human nonaggressively.

About three-quarters of the world's domestic dogs are not pets. Instead they exist as scavengers living at the fringes of human society, much like raccoons in North America. For these populations, sensitivity to human behavior is likely just as critical to survival, but the ideal behavior a dog should exhibit in response to a human in this environment is undoubtedly different from what benefits Fifi, the pampered lap dog living in a human home. This touches on an important consideration when assessing the origins of behavior in any species; rarely is the answer found in genetics, environment, or development alone. Instead the answer is most often found at the intersection of all three.

FOCUS ON THE DATA: DOMESTICATION AND SOCIALIZATION

Animal domestication refers to genetic, physiological, and morphological changes occurring over generations within a species living in close proximity to humans. In many cases domestication is intentionally accomplished through artificial selection; however, there is evidence that some species, including dogs (Coppinger & Coppinger, 2001), may have become domesticated through natural selection on the basis of their proximity to humans, their reliance on human resources, or other environmental factors. Domestication often contributes to changes in behavior (including rate and type of vocalizations produced, flight distance, and timing of reproduction) between wild-type and domesticated animals of the same or similar species (Price, 1984). However, when it comes to social behavior, genetic domestication is only part of the picture. For example, research has shown that canines, both genetically wild and domesticated, can be tamed by humans if they receive adequate exposure early in life – this process is called socialization. Conversely, if socialization to humans does not occur early in a canine's development, whether domesticated or wild, dog or wolf, that individual will most likely display fear and hostility toward humans for life (Scott & Fuller, 1965). If domestication alone does not automatically predict friendly behavior in pet dogs or individuals from other domesticated species, then what role does domestication play?

One of the longest-running scientific studies on canine domestication was begun by Dmitry Belyaev in Siberia, Russia, in 1959. Known by many as the Farm-Fox Experiment, this work still continues today. Silver foxes living on a fur farm were rated for tameness in response to human presence. Only the tamest 20 to 25 percent were selected to breed the next generation of tame fox kits – a group eventually termed the domesticated elite. Although only formally selected for tame behavior, these foxes quickly began to develop other characteristics identified with domestication as well, including piebald coat coloration, floppy ears, and curly tails. By the 10th generation of breeding, 18 percent of the experimental foxes were classified as domesticated, by the 20th generation this group made up about 30 percent of the population, and in 1999 the domestication elite made up 70 to 80 percent of the experimental population (Trut, 1999).

Figure 8.4 illustrates just one of the many important findings gleaned from decades of domesticating foxes: selection for tameness did not simply lead to one isolated behavioral change, tameness; instead it altered many aspects of development, including the timing of sensory development and

Figure 8.4   *Shifted developmental timing as a byproduct of domestication*

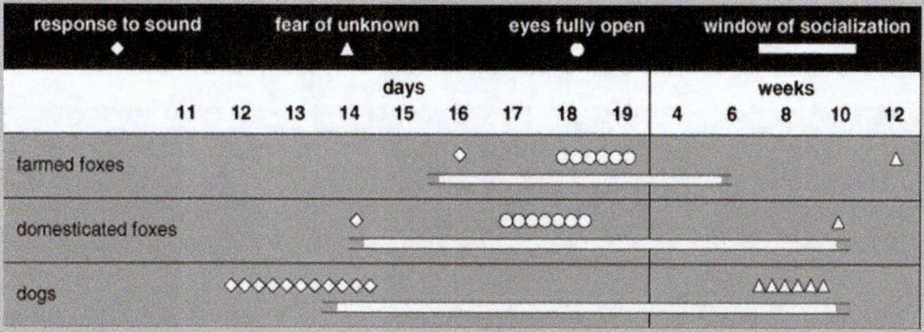

	response to sound ◆	fear of unknown ▲	eyes fully open ●	window of socialization ▬▬
		days		**weeks**
	11 12 13 14 15 16 17 18 19			4 6 8 10 12
farmed foxes	◇ (15) ●●●●●● (17–18)			△ (12)
domesticated foxes	◇ (14) ●●●●●●● (17)			△ (10)
dogs	◇◇◇◇◇◇◇◇◇◇◇ (11–13)			△△△△△ (8)

Source: Reprinted with permission from Trut (1999).

the onset of fear in the presence of novel stimuli. However, the most relevant aspect of the graph to the current discussion is the relative window of socialization across groups – denoted above by horizontal bars. Compared with the control group, the unselected farm foxes, the window of socialization in the domesticated foxes had become longer over many generations of socialization. In fact, the timing of this period for primary social experience and bonding began to look much more like that of a domesticated dog than a wild canid. Indeed, other wild canids also have short socialization windows. Wolves, for example, must be socialized to humans before six weeks of age, or the likelihood they will bond to humans is low (much like we might expect from the farmed foxes, represented in the graph above, whose window also closes at six weeks). While it may be socialization early in life that best predicts whether individuals of another species will show pro-social or friendly behavior toward humans, it turns out that domestication makes socialization more likely by extending the period of time available for these animals to form bonds with humans (or other species). In practice, it is quite easy to tame a puppy dog but very difficult to properly tame a wolf pup (never mind the many other wild-type behaviors that make wolves and other wild canids poor living companions). Therefore, it appears that the interaction of genetic (domestication) and lifetime (socialization and conditioning) processes may provide a more complete understanding of cross-species bonds than either process taken alone.

Read the full article: Trut, L. (1999) Early canid domestication: the farm-fox experiment. *American Scientist*, 87(2), 160. doi:10.1511/1999.2.160

A stronger emphasis on environmental context and the socialization history of animals participating in human-guided object-choice tasks has led to a growing body of studies that demonstrate that this skill is not limited to dogs and primates (Figure 8.5). Captive and hand-reared dolphins (Pack & Herman, 2004), fur seals (Scheumann & Call, 2004), wolves (Udell et al., 2008), bats (Hall et al., 2011), and horses (Maros et al., 2008) have all demonstrated the capacity to follow human points to a target among others, and the list of successful species is growing. It is possible that not all species will prove to be proficient on human-guided object-choice tasks. Indeed, many of the species currently

Figure 8.5 *In addition to dogs, bats, dolphins, and wolves are among a diverse group of species that have demonstrated the capacity to follow human points to a target in human-guided object-choice tasks. Early exposure to humans and relevant life experience appear to be important to the development of this behavior*

Source: Monique Udell.

passing this test demonstrate other important social and cognitive traits that have drawn the attention of scientists in their own right. For example, vampire bats have been found to reciprocally share blood meals with starving cave mates who have provided assistance in the past (Wilkinson, 1984), and fruit bats have been observed assisting in the birth of another's young (Kunz et al., 1994); so it may not be so surprising that megachoropterian bats are also sensitive to the actions of others, including humans, that can help them locate hidden food in an object-choice task (Hall et al., 2011). Nonetheless, the discovery that multiple species may share the responsiveness to humans once thought to be the exclusive domain of the domestic dog sheds light on the evolving nature of scientific progress. Sometimes a species may have the cognitive capacity for a particular behavior or skill like point following, but that capacity remains untapped or even untested by the scientific community. Therefore, claims that a behavior marks a unique inborn cognitive capacity in one species should be viewed with caution until considerable effort has been made to falsify that claim by exploring other species or conditions that might give rise to that same behavior in others. Certainly the behavior of pet domestic dogs is fascinating, and their gesture-following abilities may yet prove to be unique in range and degree. However, this behavioral repertoire appears to originate not through the evolution of a human-like cognition but through a capacity for social responsiveness shared with many species in combination with a unique history of associative conditioning in the human home (Udell & Wynne, 2008).

WHAT ARE YOU LOOKING AT? SENSITIVITY TO THE GAZE OF OTHERS

While more subtle than a point, for an attentive onlooker another potent source of information can be found in the eyes of a demonstrator. Yet while experts at gesture reading, pet dogs are not especially good at following a human's gaze to a target. A dog's vision does not allow it to see details as fine as the human eye can resolve, and it is possible that many dogs cannot detect the fine movement of the pupil in the human eye needed to track a directional gaze to the left or right without additional cues. While dogs perform a bit better using eye gaze with head movement, in general larger cues are more effective in guiding the behavior of dogs in the absence of training (Udell et al., 2008). On the other hand, many bird species can perceive and attend to very fine movements, making them more suitable candidates for tasks utilizing gaze cues.

Auguste Von Bayern and Nathan Emery (2009) asked whether human-raised jackdaws (a species of corvid) might prove better at following eye-gaze movement to a target location in a human-guided object-choice task than other species with less refined vision. Indeed the jackdaws were able to follow human gaze to the target as long as the experimenters' eye gaze moved back and forth between the subject and target. However, jackdaws were no more successful at following a static gaze or head turn cue than dogs or chimpanzees in previous studies. A few years earlier, Thomas Bugnyar, Stöwe and Heinrich (2004) found that hand-raised ravens often follow the gaze of a human experimenter even when no reward is available. In their study a human experimenter looked up, looked behind a barrier, or looked in the direction of the bird across multiple trials. Ravens often matched the directional gaze of the experimenter, looking up a third of the time and looking around the barrier half the time when the human did so despite the arbitrary nature of this behavior. Several species of great apes, including chimpanzees, have also been shown to follow this kind of human gaze (Bräuer et al., 2005; Povinelli & Eddy, 1996). In another study, it was demonstrated that domesticated goats living together in a zoo also appeared to match the gaze direction of conspecifics; however, these same individuals did not follow the gaze of a human, even when the gaze direction indicated the location of hidden food. Interestingly, these goats reportedly had little direct interaction with their human caretakers, which might suggest that the goats' relative familiarity or socialization to each species may have played a role in the development or expression of this response (Kaminski et al., 2005). More recently, it was demonstrated that a red-footed tortoise could reliably follow the gaze of a conspecific in a lookup task – suggesting that a proclivity for joint attention may extend beyond mammals and birds (Wilkinson et al., 2010).

In nature, however, following the gaze or actions of another individual to the location of food may not result in mutual benefit. Some species, including squirrels, jays, and wolves, cache, or bury, excess food to keep it contained and out of sight until it is needed. While the goal may be to protect this resource, others may locate and consume this food before the cacher returns – and this is especially likely if the second individual actually witnessed the hiding of the food. This type of eavesdropping can cost the demonstrator resources. However, in cases such as these, the ability to follow gaze can go both ways. For example, an individual that spots an onlooker gazing in its general direction may choose to recache its food if the original location has been compromised. Indeed multiple studies have suggested that this is what many birds do. In one study individual ravens were given the opportunity to cache meat in their aviary in the presence of two subordinate flock mates held in separate cages adjacent to the large enclosure. One of these individuals (the observer) had visual access to the caching event; the other individual (the nonobserver) had its view blocked by a curtain and thus could not see the location of hidden food. After caching the meat, the raven was removed from the area for five minutes. When allowed to reenter the aviary, he found himself either alone, with the observer, or with the nonobserver. The ravens were more likely to retrieve their caches in the presence of the observer than when alone or with the nonobserver, suggesting some understanding that this individual posed the greatest threat of pilfering (Bugnyar & Heinrich, 2005). Another study demonstrated that placement of cached food can be influenced not only by onlooking eyes but also by ears (Stulp et al., 2009). Stulp and colleagues found that when given a single opportunity to cache food in one of two locations, a 'noisy' tray filled with pebbles or a 'quiet' tray filled with soil, western scrub jays typically preferred to hide their food in the pebbles but with one exception: When an eavesdropper had auditory but not visual access to the caching event, the jays changed their behavior and cached in the quiet soil, concealing the location of the food.

Dogs also seem to be highly sensitive to the relationship between attentional state and the likelihood that food is available or unprotected. Originally a task used to assess perspective taking in nonhuman primates (Povinelli & Eddy, 1996), the begging task has been used to determine if dogs are attuned to who is looking at them and who is not. In one such study, dogs were given the opportunity to approach and beg from one of two women holding sandwiches. Two women faced the dog, one with a blindfold on her forehead and the other with a blindfold over her eyes. Dogs reliably chose to beg from the woman with the blindfold on her head – the one that could see them (Gácsi et al., 2003). In a second condition, the women again held sandwiches, only this time one woman faced the dog and tried to maintain eye contact without moving her head or body, while the other woman faced away from the dog and ignored it; dogs begged significantly more from the seeing, or attentive, individual than from the other woman (Gácsi et al., 2003). Two more recent studies add to these findings, demonstrating that dogs are also more likely to beg from an attentive individual than one reading a book; however, interestingly, dogs do not seem to make a distinction between a person looking at them and one wearing a bucket over her head (Cooper et al., 2003; Udell et al., 2011), a finding that will be discussed in more detail shortly. Nonetheless, these findings confirm what dog owners have suspected for a while: your dog does indeed know who the easy target is. These findings suggest that when begging from the dinner table, a dog will most likely hone in on the person casting glances toward it, ultimately increasing its chances of reward.

Possibly even more relevant to the day-to-day life of pet dogs is the forbidden food task. If you have ever owned a dog or know someone who has, you have likely experienced the following scenario: You return home with a large appetite after a long day and decide to make your favorite meal. After cooking for an hour, you put your food on the table, ready to indulge in the feast before you. But wait, you have forgotten a drink! You go to the fridge, only to return seconds later to find that all that remains on your plate is a slice of bread and a bit of dog slobber. Your dog sits a few feet away looking guilty, but with a telltale wag of satisfaction.

Research has shown that dogs can tell not only who is likely to respond to them positively, or who is willing to give a treat, but also who is in the position to tell them no. In the forbidden food task a piece of food is placed on the floor near the dog. The dog is instructed by its owner to 'leave' the food, essentially making it forbidden. As long as the owner maintains a clear view of both the dog and the food, most trained dogs will obey this command. However, if the human's eyes are closed, if the human's back is turned, if the human is distracted, if the human leaves the room, or if some barrier blocks the human's view of the food or the dog's approach to the food, all bets are off. Even well-trained dogs are likely to sneak the food under these conditions (Bräuer et al., 2004; Call et al., 2003). In other words, dogs can use their responsiveness to human gestures for good or for evil, at least from the human perspective. What this suggests is that dogs are not simply responding to human body language, gestures, orientation, and eye position in a cooperative fashion – they often use these cues to their advantage whether it benefits the human demonstrator or not.

So why is it important that birds or other species sometimes look where others look? Or that dogs know who is the most likely to provide reward or punishment on the basis of their orientation? The ability to identify the attentional state of another individual and respond advantageously brings us one step closer to the idea behind theory of mind – the ability to take the perspective of another individual. While following one's gaze to a target location, as in the previous examples, does not necessarily require theory of mind or knowledge about the mental state of the demonstrator (e.g., the jackdaw may simply move in the direction of the gaze because doing so has led to food in the past), perspective-taking tasks – which are designed to assess responsiveness to attentional state – have often been used as indicators for this cognitive ability.

THEORY OF MIND

According to a classic review by Heyes (1998), 'an animal with a theory of mind believes that mental states play a causal role in generating behaviour and infers the presence of mental states in others by observing their appearance and behaviour under various circumstances' (p. 102). Therefore, under the theory of mind framework a jackdaw following the gaze of a human to a target would do so not because it has located food that way in the past but because it interprets the human's stare as knowledge of the location of hidden food. Likewise, a scrub jay hiding food might not recache its store simply because it has lost food in the presence of onlooking scrub jays in the past but because it knows that the onlooking jays are eavesdropping with the intent to steal the food. Of course, such claims should not be made without proper scientific controls that would rule out simpler explanations, such as classical conditioning or trial and error learning.

To make the notion of theory of mind more concrete, however, let us first consider some examples from everyday human experience.

A friend phones you from a telephone booth to apologize for running late for dinner – she is having trouble finding your house. What would you do? You would ask her to describe where she is (what she can see from the booth) and then you would direct her to your house. Even though you are south of the river looking north and she is north of the river heading south, you succeed in putting yourself into her shoes and giving directions that are correct from her perspective. You have a theory of her mind – an idea of how the world looks from her perspective – and you are able to use this to provide helpful directions.

A crowd of people is gathered by the deli counter in the supermarket. What would you do? Most people would go over and see what the fuss is about. Whether consciously or not, you reason that these people may have discovered something at the deli counter (a really good special offer, perhaps) that you might like, too. You have an idea that their motivations may well be similar to your own motivations. You have a theory of their minds.

A colleague who you do not trust tells you of a way of impressing your boss and positioning yourself for promotion. You decide not to follow this advice. You reason that this colleague is not motivated toward anything but his own advancement, and therefore advice from him that appears to be to your benefit cannot be trusted. Again, you have a theory of your colleague's motivations – a theory of his mind.

As these examples show, theory of mind means having ideas about what goes on in the minds of other individuals. Another aspect of theory of mind is having ideas about one's own motivations. When you ask yourself, 'Why did I do that?' you are developing a form of reflective self-consciousness – a theory about your own mind – or self-awareness.

As one might imagine, the scientific study of theory of mind is challenging and even more so where nonhuman species are concerned. In studies with humans, subjects are often asked about their understanding of another's mental state directly – for example, 'What do you think Mary can see from where she is standing?' – a method that is impossible to replicate with animals that do not share our language. However, several scientific tests, some originating from the point and gaze following tasks discussed previously, have been developed to try to get at the same questions nonverbally – for example, does Mary's location reliably alter your behavior in ways that are consistent with an understanding of her perspective? However, some of the earliest proposed evidence for theory of mind in nonhumans came from observational reports.

Deceitful behavior is one type of action that suggests an understanding of others' minds. To be deceitful means to provide false information to one's own advantage. To know that placing a false belief in another's mind could be advantageous to oneself implies an understanding that others act on the information they receive – this implies a theory of others' minds.

Dorothy Cheney and Robert Seyfarth in their extensive study of vervet monkeys in West Africa observed some cases where monkeys appeared to act deceitfully in order to gain some advantage. Cheney and Seyfarth's work on the communicative system of these monkeys is discussed in more detail in Chapter 12. For now, it is sufficient to know that vervet monkeys can produce a range of alarm calls, each one depending on the predator they have seen.

Cheney and Seyfarth (1990) observed that one low-ranking male monkey, Kitui, was in the habit of uttering a leopard alarm call whenever a new male attempted to transfer into his group. Kitui was of such low rank that it was reasonable to assume that he would take a lower-ranked position to any new male monkey that might join the group. Consequently, Kitui would be motivated to prevent any new monkeys from joining his group if he could because a new member would increase the number of males he would have to compete with for food and access to females. When Kitui gave his leopard alarm, the monkeys – the other members of his group and the newcomer, too – all scattered into the trees, and the newcomer was kept at bay. This, then, might be evidence that Kitui had an understanding of the minds of other monkeys: He understood that any monkey hearing a leopard alarm call would think a leopard was nearby and would run into the trees for protection. If this was what Kitui was thinking, then it would imply that he had a theory of mind.

Kitui's subsequent behavior, however, makes this interpretation somewhat less likely. Once Kitui had frightened the intruding monkey into a tree with his leopard alarm, he would leave his own tree and cross over to make his alarm calls closer to the intruding monkey. Presumably Kitui wanted to be certain the intruding monkey got the message. However, if Kitui really had a theory of mind of the other monkey, he should have appreciated that by climbing down from his tree, he was showing that he did not really think there was a leopard in the vicinity. This weakens the account of Kitui's behavior in terms of a theory of mind and makes it more likely that Kitui had simply learned to associate alarm calls with monkeys getting into the trees. (Learning about the consequences of action is one of the kinds of associative learning considered in Chapter 5.) Perhaps once, when a new male was trying to join Kitui's group, there was a real predator threat that disrupted the new monkey's attempts to join the group. Perhaps Kitui was the first to notice the predator and gave the alarm. He then simply associated giving the leopard alarm with the consequence that the intruding monkey retreated into the trees. This would be a form of learning that did not imply a theory of mind on Kitui's part.

Another intriguing story of animal deceit comes also from Cheney and Seyfarth, this time from their studies on baboons. Among baboons, subordinate females typically raise their tails when approaching a more dominant animal. This seems to act as a gesture of submission and reflects the subordinate animal's anxiety at being in the vicinity of a more powerful individual. In one case, Cheney and Seyfarth observed a particular female baboon that attempted to press her rising tail down as she passed a dominant male animal. She may have done so because she recognized that her raised tail signaled anxiety and she wanted to conceal this from the dominant male. If this really were the reason why the female was pushing her tail down, then it might imply she had a theory of mind of the dominant male. But, as is so often the case, the anecdote raises more questions than it can answer. For example, if the subordinate female really had an understanding of how the male would interpret her rising tail, why didn't she hide it before she came into the male's view? How do we know that the female didn't just feel an itch in her tail at the point in time that she passed the male baboon? It is also not clear why the female would want to hide her submissive tail gesture from the more dominant male in the first place – submissive gestures usually function to reduce aggression in more dominant animals. Was the female baboon trying to get into strife with a more dominant troop member?

The problem with anecdotes from the wild is that they are always open to different interpretations. Those who believe that the animals under observation have a theory of mind can always pick the observations that best support their case. But others, who doubt the existence of theory of mind in animals, can always find an alternative interpretation for what was observed. Consequently, we need to move to experimental tests in order to gain a more detailed understanding of the possibility of nonhumans having a theory of mind.

DO YOU SEE WHAT I SEE?

Consider the following experiment. A chimpanzee sitting behind a screen observes a laboratory assistant hide food under one of two containers. This assistant leaves the room, and one of two distinctively dressed trainers enters the room. If the chimpanzee points out the location of the food to the *cooperative* trainer, this trainer will give the hidden food to the chimpanzee. If, however, the chimp points out the location of the food to the *competitive* trainer, this trainer keeps the food for himself. To get food when the competitive trainer enters the room, the chimpanzee must point out the empty container: Under these conditions the competitive trainer receives the empty food container, and the chimp receives the other container with the food in it. Gradually, the chimpanzees tested on this procedure were able to learn to obtain food in trials with both the cooperative and the competitive trainer. This result has been taken as evidence that the chimpanzee has an understanding of the minds of the two trainers. The chimp, it is argued, understands that one trainer is of a cooperative frame of mind, whereas the other is not. There are a couple of problems with this interpretation, however. For one thing, if I imagine myself as the chimp in this experiment, since I have a concept that the trainers have minds and attitudes, I think I would figure out almost immediately to be honest to the good guy (cooperative) trainer and to lie to the bad guy (competitive) trainer. I find it puzzling, therefore, that it took a large number of training trials (120) before any of the chimpanzees learned what to do here (Woodruff & Premack, 1979).

In addition, the experiment does not depend on the fact that two human trainers equipped with minds were involved. Imagine that instead of a cooperative and a competitive trainer, there are two lights in the room, one red and one green. The chimp's task is to point out the food location during the red light and to point to any other location during the green light. Now this is a fairly simple task – one that pigeons could solve. Nobody would suggest that the subject in a task like this would need to have a theory of the minds of the red and green lights!

In short, in order to learn to obtain food in this situation, the chimps did not need an understanding of the minds of other individuals; all they needed was an ability to learn to do different things to get food depending on what other stimuli were available in the room around them. As discussed in Chapter 5, all species that have been tested posses the ability to learn what stimuli predict rewards and what they need to do to obtain rewards. This perhaps simple-sounding talent gives many species an awesome ability to pick up on what is going on in the world. We looked in some detail at one of the most striking cases – that of Clever Hans – in Chapter 1.

However, one of the researchers involved in this cooperative-trainer versus competitive-trainer experiment, David Premack, suggested a follow-up experiment to answer some of these criticisms. This experiment was put into practice by Daniel Povinelli and his associates (Povinelli et al., 1990). Now there are four cups in front of the chimpanzee (see Figure 8.6). One of the four cups hides a piece of food that the chimpanzee is allowed to eat if she can find it. The chimp could not see which container the food was placed in because a screen was put between her and the containers. However, to help the chimp make her choice, two trainers point to one container each. One of the train-

Figure 8.6 *A chimpanzee choosing between the container pointed to by the guesser and that pointed to by the knower*

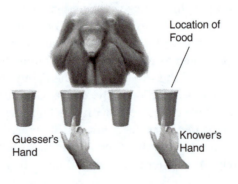

ers is the person who put the food into one of the cups – consequently, he is called the *knower*. A second trainer (the *guesser*) was not in the room at that stage. Will the chimp learn to choose the container that the knower points to and learn that the guesser is not a reliable source of information on where to find the food?

Two of the four chimpanzees tested on this task were ultimately able to learn to choose the cup pointed to by the knower and to ignore the cup chosen by the guesser.

Again it has been suggested that these chimpanzees operated with an understanding of what was going on in the minds of the two trainers – that they show evidence of a theory of mind. This experiment, however, is open to the same criticisms as the cooperative-trainer, competitive-trainer experiment. First, it took the chimpanzees far longer to master this task than seems consistent with the idea that they are applying knowledge of others' minds (at least 100 trials). Second, it is again possible that the chimps simply learned to attend to the actions of the knower because that is what consistently led to reward – just as a pigeon can learn to attend to certain colors because they predict reward. The difference in the guesser-knower experiment is that the factor that determines which trainer can accurately point to reward is whether he was in the room when the food cup was being baited – this makes the task more difficult but does not change its structure in principle.

In an attempt to answer these criticisms, Povinelli and associates changed the structure of the knower-guesser experiment a little for a final test. Now a third trainer baited one of the cups with food in the presence of the other two trainers – one of whom (the new guesser) had his eyes covered with a bag. The other trainer (the new knower) could clearly see what was going on. The chimp could see who was baiting the cup, who had a bag over his head, and who did not but could not herself see which cup was being baited because a screen was placed between her and the cups.

What were the results of this test, and what do they mean? In over 30 test trials of this type, three of the four chimpanzees developed a preference for the cup pointed to by the new knower. Though the learning was quicker than it had been on the original task, the performance was not perfect, and it was not present immediately. The chimps did not spontaneously recognize after their previous experience what to do under the changed conditions. Once again it is perfectly possible that the chimp simply learned that a person with a bag over his head is a poor predictor of where food is to be found, just as a pigeon learned that a blue light can be a poor predictor of food.

Povinelli, becoming less sure that chimpanzees possessed a theory of mind, then created one very simple but telling experiment: the begging task, which was described earlier in this chapter. Like the dogs, chimpanzees were offered a choice between begging for food from a person who could see them and one who could not. The chimps might be confronted by a person with a blindfold over her eyes and one with a blindfold over her mouth. Or the person who could not see might have a bucket over her head or her hands over her eyes, or she might be seated with her back to the chimpanzee. To the experimenters' surprise, the chimps were just as likely to ask for food from the person who could not possibly see them as from the person who could see clearly. With enough experience, the apes could gradually figure out whom they should ask for food, but they showed no spontaneous understanding that being unable to see would disqualify somebody from providing food (Povinelli & Eddy, 1996; Reaux et al., 1999).

In response to these findings, Brian Hare and colleagues (2000) suggested that it was the cooperative nature of Povinelli's research – the animals are expected to cooperate with a human trainer to obtain food – that resulted in failure on the task. Cooperation, Hare's group suggested, represents a highly unnatural situation for a chimpanzee. However, in situations where the animals *compete* for food, chimps might more readily demonstrate their understanding of the implications of what other individuals can and cannot see. In one such study, Hare and his associates placed one piece of food so that both a dominant and subordinate chimpanzee in adjoining cages could see it (and each could see that the other could see it). Another piece of food was placed so that only the subordinate animal could see it. The question of interest was, would the subordinate animal understand that the dominant animal would take the piece of food that he could see but leave the subordinate animal in peace with the food outside his visual field? This was indeed what Hare and colleagues found. Subordinate chimpanzees given a choice between a piece of food in sight of the dominant animal and another piece of food hidden from the dominant chimp preferred the piece that the dominant chimp could not see.

However, do either of these situations – the begging task or the competitor task – prove that the subjects understand the knowledge state of the other individual? Let's revisit the impressive performance of domestic dogs on the begging task. At least three studies have suggested that pet dogs prefer to beg from someone looking at them than from someone with obscured vision, at least in some cases (Cooper et al., 2003; Gácsi et al., 2003; Udell et al., 2011). However, more telling may be the instances where dogs and wolves do not choose correctly. As in previous begging studies, Udell et al. (2011) conducted an experiment where pet dogs, wolves, and dogs living in a shelter could choose to beg from either an attentive or an inattentive individual to obtain food; as in previous studies, all groups preferred to beg from someone looking at them compared with someone who had her back turned. However, only pet dogs preferred the attentive individual when the inattentive individual was reading a book (shelter dogs and wolves begged equally from both). Perhaps even more surprising, none of the groups strongly preferred the attentive individual when the inattentive individual held a bucket over her head and eyes (Udell et al., 2011). To humans this would easily have been a very obvious cue of inattention. This study challenges the perspective-taking interpretation of this task, because presumably if dogs truly understood the knowledge state of the humans, they would have been able to choose the attentive individual in all three conditions: back-turned, book, and bucket. Instead, a different pattern appeared. Pet dogs who often witness humans reading from books or magazines seemed to have learned that a human reading is no better than a human with her back turned – neither is likely to provide food. Wolves and dogs living in an animal shelter, where they have fewer opportunities to interact with reading humans, were indifferent to this cue. Despite a bucket being an even larger and more obtrusive way of blocking a person's vision, none of the groups appeared to recognize the occluding bucket as a cue of inattention. Of course in this case, none of the subjects could be expected to have much exposure to humans walking around donned in buckets, and this lack of experience seemed to be their downfall. Therefore, although dogs and other canines appear to readily learn about specific contexts or cues that predict the behavior of humans, this does not necessarily mean they fully understand or take our perspective (or even know what we can or cannot see). Instead, this skill, while impressive, seems to have its limits.

Clearly, the question of how much different species understand of the implications of what another individual is looking at is an area ripe for more research. However, the theory of mind debate remains ongoing across species, and no experiment has yet been identified that would serve as a foolproof test for this ability in nonhumans.

CONCLUSIONS

A number of chimps and a single gorilla will wipe a mark off their face that they can only see in a mirror. Some chimps have been trained to make different responses to get food depending on whether a cooperative or competitive trainer is in the room and have also learned which of two people can show them where food is hidden. This learning, however, was so slow that having a theory of mind does not seem necessary to explain how they learned. More recently dogs, dolphins, and even pigeons have also demonstrated similar behavior in different contexts. In all of these cases, however, associative learning of the type discussed in Chapter 5 cannot be ruled out – and in many cases seems like the most probable explanation.

Having a theory of mind enables humans, even very young ones, to learn almost instantly whom to trust, whom to ask for food, and whom to ignore or avoid. The argument has been made that, because they live in social groups, chimpanzees and some other species (like dogs and dolphins) must also have a theory of mind. Possession of a theory of mind is useful in a social context; therefore, it must have evolved, it is argued. This argument is not a strong one. Just because I might find a four-wheel-drive vehicle useful when I drive in the country, that does not mean that I own one! Even if other species share the same problems of social living that we do (and we know rather little about how other species manage their social lives), this need not imply that they would have evolved the same psychological mechanisms to cope with them as humans have.

An alternative approach to understanding theory of mind in nonhumans may come from a different, relatively simple, situation – that of learning by imitation – which will be discussed further in Chapter 9.

While theory of mind may be elusive and self-awareness even more so, we do gain from this research a better understanding of how species can use the behavior of others – or even their own image – to their benefit and thereby increase their chances of obtaining food or other rewards and avoiding punishment. The importance of these behaviors should not be overlooked even if the building blocks of the behavior can be explained through relatively simple mechanisms; even complex behaviors can have simple origins.

FURTHER READING

Heyes, C. M. (1998) Theory of Mind in Nonhuman Primates. *Behavioral and Brain Sciences*, 21(01), 101–114.
A good review and discussion of theory of mind research in primates, including commentary on methodology and interpretations.

Udell, M. A. R., Dorey, N. R. & Wynne, C. D. L. (2011) Can your dog read your mind? Understanding the causes of canine perspective taking. *Learning & Behavior*, 39(4), 289–302.
This article discusses possible mechanisms for theory of mind-like behaviors in dogs, followed by commentary addressing methodology and possible interpretations.

Van der Vaart, E., Verbrugge, R. & Hemelrijk, C. K. (2012) Corvid re-caching without 'theory of mind': a model. *PLoS ONE*, 7(3), e32904.
This article presents an alternative approach to recaching behavior in corvids.

Wynne, C. D. L. (2004) *Do Animals Think?* Princeton, N J: Princeton University Press.
Discusses self-awareness and mirror recognition, among other topics.

Web sources

http://www.scientificamerican.com/article.cfm?id=kids-and-animals-who-fail-classic-mirror
Find more on failing mirror self-recognition tests (both humans and nonhumans considered) on the Scientific American website.

http://www.pbs.org/wnet/nature/animalmind/consciousness.html
A very stimulating discussion of animal consciousness can be found on this PBS website.

http://plato.stanford.edu/entries/consciousness-animal
The Stanford Encyclopedia of Philosophy entry on animal consciousness, by Colin Allen, is available on this website.

9 Social Learning

One fine day two crabs came out from their home to take a stroll on the sand. 'Child,' said the mother, 'you are walking very ungracefully. You should accustom yourself, to walking straight forward without twisting from side to side.' 'Pray, mother,' said the young one, 'do but set the example yourself, and I will follow you.'
Aesop's Fables, translated by G. F. Townsend

Imagine walking down a busy street. All of a sudden everyone around you drops to the ground and covers their head with their hands as if to protect themselves from something falling from above. What do you do? If you are like most people, you probably duck and cover along with everyone else. Better safe than sorry! This predisposition to match the behavior of the crowd is called *social facilitation*. Social facilitation, or the tendency to engage in a behavior simply because others around you are doing it, may also cause you to overindulge in food and beverages at a party or unwittingly drive faster than you normally would when being passed by cars on a busy highway.

People, being highly social animals, seem to have a fairly spontaneous tendency to copy each other – even when the motivation behind the behavior of another individual is not well understood. These behaviors may be as simple as a yawn or form the basis of a cultural practice passed down across generations. What we eat, how we dress, even what we fear is continually colored by social influence. Many nonhuman animals, from rats to dogs, also show reliance on social information. In many cases the underlying processes that regulate socially mediated behavior appear to be quite similar across species. In this chapter I will discuss several forms of social influence, but the primary focus will be on categories of social learning, including imitation, emulation, and teaching.

SOCIAL INFLUENCE

There are many ways an individual or species can utilize social information, but only some are formally considered *social learning*. For social learning to occur, the behavior (1) must be a learned behavior, (2) it must be acquired through some form of social transmission, often by watching or interacting with another individual, and (3) it must persist even in the absence of the demonstrator. While this may seem self-explanatory at first, let's revisit one category of social influence often confused with social learning: social facilitation.

Social facilitation

Consider the delightful infectiousness of yawning and laughing, for example. It is strange how difficult it is, when sitting at a table surrounded by people laughing at jokes in a language you don't understand, not to join them in laughter – despite not having the faintest idea what they are laughing at. Many examples of copying or joint behavior in animals, such as birds feeding in flocks, fish schooling, or gazelles running in a herd, begin with the simple, automatic process of social facilitation. Unlike social learning, social facilitation does not require that the participants learn something new, nor does it require that the behavior continue in the future; it is simply an increase in a particular behavior that occurs in the presence of other individuals. While this might not seem particularly useful at first (e.g., a bird that is compelled to eat when surrounded by a dozen feeding birds will now have to compete for the same limited food supply), there may be real value in some types of conformity. Consider the following two examples:

> A herd of elk has been feeding, resting, and moving together in unison for days. All of a sudden one alert member of the group gives a deep call, gaining the attention of its other group members. He lifts his tail, exposing his white rump, and begins to run. Although the other elk do not see a predator, they quickly follow suit (social facilitation), lifting their tails and running as if they had experienced firsthand exposure to the threat.

By engaging in this joint behavior, the elk increase the likelihood that the whole herd will escape danger (as it creates confusion and makes it difficult for ambush predators to identify which of the elk have spotted them) as well as reduce their individual chance of becoming a target due to what is called the 'dilution effect' (1 moving elk that blends into a moving herd of 100 is much less likely to become dinner than a lone elk that didn't get on the bandwagon). Research has shown that the tendency to do as the herd does is strongly predicted by the benefits of shared vigilance and the dilution effect (Delm, 1990).

> It's the beginning of the rainy season, and a group of receptive male frogs begin to gather around a traditional breeding ground. At first, there is silence, but soon a characteristic chirping emerges from one of the males.

One mating call turns into two, and then two into many. The first few calls appear to trigger what becomes a loud chorus of reproductive cries.

Some species, including several species of frog, mate in large groups called leks. While there may be multiple advantages to members of a species gathering in one place at one time to mate (e.g., dilution effects, vigilance, increased likelihood of finding a mate), it has been more difficult to determine the factors that most accurately predict the onset of a lekking event. While not the only relevant factor, social facilitation has been found to play a role in the production of large choruses of mating calls in some species of male frogs. For example, one study found that playing a recording of calling males increased the likelihood that other males in the area would join the chorus; playing a recording of white noise had no such effect (Brooke et al., 2000).

Social facilitation may also contribute to other important survival and reproductive behaviors – including the initial migration of sea turtle hatchlings to the sea (Carr & Hirth, 1961), grooming repertoires (Palestis & Burger, 1998), and even the synchronous hatching of bird chicks from eggs in the same clutch (Vince, 1964) – demonstrating the diverse presence and importance of this evolutionary adaptation.

Stimulus and local enhancement

Another case of social influence falls just at the border of what is considered social learning: stimulus and local enhancement. As I type here in the front office of my home, it is not uncommon for Sybille, my cat, to jump up on my desk and try to get on the keyboard. As highly as I rate Sybille's intelligence, I cannot in all honesty claim that she is trying to imitate my typing activity, nor is she likely learning about the function of pressing the keys. It is much more likely that she simply finds the keyboard more interesting because she sees me interact with it so energetically. This is the essence of social enhancement – an increase in the tendency to interact with an object (stimulus enhancement) or approach a location (local enhancement) because of the presence and actions of another individual.

The first recognition of stimulus enhancement was made by the great Austrian ethologist Konrad Lorenz (1935). In 1973 Lorenz shared the only Nobel Prize ever awarded for research in animal behavior (with Niko Tinbergen and Karl von Frisch) for cofounding the discipline of ethology – the scientific study of animal behavior in the natural habitat. In a study he made on ducks, Lorenz observed that an individual duck was more likely to escape from a pen through a hole in the fencing if it happened to be near another duck in the act of jumping through the hole (Figure 9.1). Rather than making the tempting inference that the ducks were engaging in imitation (a form of social learning), Lorenz recognized that it was more likely that seeing a fellow duck jump through the

Figure 9.1 *Imitation in ducks*

Notes: The front duck has found a way through the fence. The two ducks behind it may be imitating their leader, but most likely they are just showing stimulus enhancement – their attention has been drawn to the gap by the action of the first duck.

hole pulled the other duck's attention to the hole – the other duck experienced stimulus enhancement of the hole.

In the case of stimulus and local enhancement, it can often be difficult to assess whether more complex social learning may be taking place, whether the observer is learning about the consequences of approaching an object or location or is simply drawn to it because of the presence of another individual. This has also led to challenges in interpreting research on social referencing, such as the canine pointing studies (object-choice tasks) discussed in Chapter 8. Although research shows that pet dogs are skilled at following a human point to a target location, such as a bowl where food can be obtained, it is not always clear whether the dog is responding to the referential nature of the gesture (the human point communicates something about the status of the bowl) or the human point results in stimulus enhancement of the nearby target (the bowl becomes attractive simply due to its proximity to the human hand). One argument in support of the local enhancement explanation is that dogs are generally more responsive to gestures that bring large portions of the human body closer to the target (full arm, leg, or torso) as opposed to gestures where the majority of the human form remains equidistant from two locations, moving only a small portion of the body in the desired direction (e.g., eye glance, head turn, or pointing with the elbow) (Udell et al., 2008). Dogs also show higher accuracy in following points when the human hand comes closer to the target (10 versus 50 centimeters) and remains in place throughout the dog's choice than when the hand is far from the target and presented only briefly (for a review, see Udell et al., 2010).

On the other hand, some pet dogs and human-socialized wolves have been found capable of responding to momentary distal points in which the human hand never comes closer than 50 centimeters to the target and is removed from the proximity of the target before the canine is allowed to make a choice (Udell et al., 2008). This suggests that while stimulus or local enhancement may account for point-following behavior in some instances – especially those where the human gesture remains in close proximity to the target throughout the testing trial – some of the reported successes on more challenging point-following tasks may implicate additional learning or cognitive mechanisms.

Affordance learning

While 'social' facilitation and 'social' enhancement center on social influence – but do not necessarily indicate learning – there are categories of learning that may appear to be governed by social influence but are not. One example is 'affordance learning', or learning about the environment through secondhand observation. Let's assume that a squirrel is sitting on the ground observing a second squirrel eating food from a hanging bird feeder (we will call the first squirrel the 'observer' and the second squirrel the 'demonstrator'). Within seconds the weight of the demonstrator squirrel causes the feeder to crash to the ground, releasing its seeds and providing a feast for both parties. Later, after the feeder is refilled and hung back in the tree, the observer squirrel is seen climbing onto the feeder and jostling it until, like the demonstrator, he too knocks the feeder down.

The temptation here might be to say that the observer learned from the demonstrator how to obtain a large amount of food from the feeder – a form of social learning. However, in the absence of experimental control, it is impossible to know for sure whether this is the case (we will see how critical controlled laboratory experiments have been in defining discrete categories of social learning and imitation later in this chapter). Let us assume we could rewind the scenario so that the observer squirrel never witnessed the demonstrator's actions. Instead the squirrel finds itself sitting on the ground looking up at a full bird feeder when a strong gust of wind knocks it out of the tree. The feeder falls to the ground, and the squirrel enjoys a feast. If later the squirrel is seen climbing onto the feeder and jostling it around until it knocks the feeder down, we can now be sure that if something was learned by the observing squirrel, it was not acquired through social means (in other words, the presence of the demonstrator squirrel was not required). Seeing the feeder fall – and possibly eating the food – was enough to alter the future behavior of the squirrel. This is affordance learning.

SOCIAL LEARNING: WHAT IS IT, WHY DO IT?

The fact that many behaviors can appear to be either social or learned (or both) when they are not adds an element of challenge to the study of social learning. Scientists must control for other possible sources of copying behavior, including social facilitation and local and stimulus enhancement, as well as nonsocial forms of learning (such as affordance learning and Pavlovian and instrumental conditioning). Box 9.1 shows one famous example of apparent copying behavior. However, social learning, as an adaptive mechanism, represents a significant leap forward in terms of an animal's ability to adjust to changing circumstances in its environment. While evolutionary selection favors traits that are important to the fitness of a generation, increasing the likelihood that individuals in the next generation will possess those traits as well, evolutionary change occurs slowly and cannot help, for example, a starving rodent whose typical food source has just been wiped out by a late winter freeze. If the animal is to survive, it must adapt to this environmental change immediately and find a new food source. As discussed in Chapter 5, one way this can be accomplished is through trial and error learning (nibbling on any foodlike substance encountered and adjusting feeding behavior accordingly). The problem here is that humans often consider rodents pests, and the creation of foodlike poisons intended to kill a rodent consumer at first bite makes up a substantial and lucrative industry. Therefore, a starving rodent that desperately eats from a novel plate of seeds left on the floor of a warm basement may become critically ill or even die after this first

Figure 9.2 *A mouse eating from a jar containing the same flavor food that a demonstrator had consumed*

Source: Monique Udell.

transgression. In other words, there is no guarantee that a rodent that makes a wrong choice will live to modify its behavior on future trials. As a result, many rodents avoid unfamiliar foods and rely instead on social experience to inform them of the relative safety of new food sources.

The social acquisition of food preferences in rodents has been well studied by scientists. In one such study, Craige Wrenn and colleagues (Wrenn et al., 2003) fed hungry demonstrator mice rodent chow flavored with either cinnamon or cocoa powder. The demonstrator was then placed in an interaction chamber with its hungry cage mates (observer mice) for 30 minutes while the number of muzzle sniffs directed toward the demonstrator by each observer was recorded. After a delay of 24 hours, each observer was placed in an individual cage with two jars of rodent chow – one flavored with cinnamon and the other with cocoa – for one hour (see Figure 9.2). Wrenn and his colleagues found that observer mice ate significantly more of the chow flavor that had been consumed by their demonstrator (e.g., if the demonstrator mouse was fed cinnamon-flavored chow, the observer ate the cinnamon chow as well; if the demonstrator ate cocoa, so did the observer). Furthermore, the amount of the same-flavored food eaten by the observer strongly coordinated with the number of times that the observer had the opportunity to sniff the demonstrator's muzzle the day before. Through this form of social or observational learning, individuals could acquire information about potential new food sources within their lifetime without engaging in a risky application of trial and error learning.

FOCUS ON THE DATA: THE CONNECTION BETWEEN SCENT AND FOOD SELECTION

Wrenn and colleagues (2003) found that mice showed a significant preference for food that matched the flavor previously smelled on a demonstrator's muzzle. Figure 9.3 illustrates this connection. Part A shows the average amount of food consumed (in grams) by the eight mice tested (n = 8). Mice ate significantly more of the demonstrator cued food than of the novel-smelling flavor. Part B of the graph shows the number of times each mouse (represented by a black dot) sniffed the muzzle of the dem-

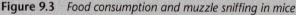

Figure 9.3   *Food consumption and muzzle sniffing in mice*

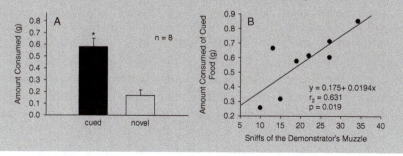

onstrator during the exposure phase of the social learning task, as well as the amount of cued food that the individual later consumed in the testing phase. The trend line shows a strong positive correlation ($r_2 = 0.631$) between the number of muzzle sniffs a mouse initiated and the amount of cued food consumed, suggesting that there was an important relationship between these two variables.

Read the full article: Wrenn, C. C., Harris, A. P., Saavedra, M. C. & Crawley, J. N. (2003) Social transmission of food preference in mice: methodology and application to galanin-overexpressing transgenic mice. *Behavioral Neuroscience*, 117(1), 21–31. doi:10.1037/ 0735–7044.117.1.21

Rodents may also learn about what foods to avoid through social means. In an experiment similar to the one conducted by Wrenn and colleagues (2003), Li-ann Kuan and Ruth Colwill (1997) fed one rat demonstrator cocoa-flavored food and another cinnamon-flavored food. However, in this study one of the two demonstrators was made ill immediately following food consumption. Both rats were then simultaneously placed in a cage with observers for 15 minutes. This time, observer rats showed a selective preference for the flavor of food consumed by the healthy demonstrator alone, avoiding the flavor consumed by the sick demonstrator. Although rats seem to have the capacity to develop food preference and avoidance on the basis of prior interactions with demonstrators, in practice rats more readily learn about smells that are consistent with safe food items than toxic ones. This may have to do with the degree of lethality of the toxic food substances they encounter in nature. When new food sources in a species' environment may lead only to mild illness, then trial and error learning is favored as the risk associated with eating novel items is limited. When the risk of consuming new foods is moderate, leading to noticeable illness and possibly death, social learning of both preference and avoidance may be the optimal strategy (as was found in the study by Colwill and colleagues). However, the poisons rats might encounter when consuming new foods outside of the laboratory are highly lethal, making it less likely that an observer would encounter many *living* demonstrators exposed to toxic food items. Because information about what is safe to consume is more prevalent in natural environments than what is unsafe, social transmission of food preferences (as opposed to avoidances) appears to be more adaptive and common in this species (Noble et al., 2001).

Social learning is not only useful for the identification of safe and nutritious food; it can also assist animals in navigation (Brown & Laland, 2001), courtship and reproduction (Freeberg, 2004), problem solving (Thornton & Malapert, 2009), and communication (Janik & Slater, 2000). As discussed in Chapter 5, there is also evidence that some animals acquire a proportion of their fears though social means – for example, monkeys learning to fear snakes after watching a video of another individual reacting with fear (Cook

& Mineka, 1990) – possibly sparing the observer direct exposure to a threat or predator. In 2001, a study conducted by Martin Kavaliers and colleagues (Kavaliers et al., 2001) investigated the degree to which naive mice would acquire fear of biting flies through observation alone. Mice that have not been exposed to flies show no fear or avoidance of them upon presentation; this is true for both harmless houseflies and biting flies. However, biting flies are capable of inflicting a painful bite; thus mice (as well as other species, including humans) tend to show signs of stress and avoidance in their presence once they have directly experienced them. In this study, fly-naive observer mice witnessed another mouse (a demonstrator) being attacked by biting flies in an adjacent holding area for 30 minutes. During this time the demonstrator engaged in defensive behaviors (ear flicking, face rubbing, and burrowing into the bedding) to avoid the painful bites, characteristic actions that an observer could associate with distress. After 24 hours the experimental group of observers was exposed to biting flies, and their behavior was recorded – however, before this test, the experimenters had altered the mouthparts of the flies so that they could no longer bite. Nonetheless, the observers responded with fear to the biting flies, engaging in defensive behavior just as they had observed the demonstrators doing – even though they had never directly experienced the painful bite for themselves. This study provided strong evidence not only that fears could be socially acquired but that active avoidance of a potentially dangerous stimulus could be socially transmitted through observation alone.

It is no coincidence that the term 'social learning' covers such a wide range of potential scenarios and behaviors. While many explanations for behavior fall outside the realm of social learning, it is still a broad category encompassing a wide range of learning processes that can occur when one animal is exposed to the behavior of another. In recent years controlled experiments have allowed scientists to identify and define two (of many) important forms of social learning with much more restricted criteria: imitation and emulation.

BOX 9.1   POTATO WASHING IN JAPANESE MACAQUES

In the early 1950s in Japan, scientists studying a wild population of macaques started providing them with potatoes to eat (Nishida, 1987). In September 1953, a young female monkey, Imo, was observed to wash one of these potatoes in the ocean before eating it (see Figure 9.4). This washing removed unpalatable sand from the potato. A month later, a second monkey was observed to wash potatoes in the same manner. Two more monkeys started washing potatoes two months later, and over the following few years many more monkeys took up the potato-washing habit. The questions of interest here are, was Imo the only monkey who learned to potato wash for herself, and did the others copy her because they saw what she was doing and wanted the beneficial consequences of potato washing (the sand-free potatoes) for themselves? Or did each monkey figure out for itself how to wash potatoes, perhaps encouraged but not directly enlightened by observing other monkeys taking potatoes to the water? The answer to this question is not straightforward. The original reports certainly claimed that social learning, maybe even imitation, had taken place among these monkeys. If so, then this would suggest that the monkeys understood each other's motivations. 'Why would she be washing a potato?' the observant monkey might ask itself, a question that implies a theory of mind.

Subsequent commentators on the potato-washing saga have been less convinced that true imitation learning (of the kind to be discussed in the next section) was taking place. One detail that proves to be important is just how many monkeys knew how to wash potatoes at any point in time and how quickly the habit spread. If imitation was taking place, then the

Figure 9.4 *A Japanese macaque washing potatoes in the ocean to get the sand off them*

Source: Picture courtesy of F. Kanchi.

habit should spread through the group of monkeys only slowly at first but increase in rate of transmission as time passes. The reason for this is that social transmission of a habit is similar to social transmission of a disease. At first, rather few individuals have the habit: Since you can catch the habit only by meeting with an individual who already has it, your chances of catching it are small, and the habit spreads slowly. As more individuals become infected with the habit, the chance of your meeting somebody who already has it goes up dramatically, and consequently, the rate of spread is much higher. Critics argue that the rate of spread of the potato-washing habit among the Japanese macaques did not show this slow-at-first, quicker-later pattern. Rather the rate of acquisition of the habit was fairly constant. This is more like the pattern that would be expected if the monkeys learned to wash potatoes independently of each other. The original research was done so long ago that it is unlikely now that a definitive answer to the question of whether the macaques really learned socially or independently will ever be reached.

IMITATION – THE SINCEREST FORM OF FLATTERY

Imitation might seem like a very simple thing to study. Just watch two animals, and observe if one copies what the other does. In reality the scientific study of imitation is quite challenging. For one thing, without careful experimental control, it can be very difficult to even be certain whether imitation has taken place. Take, for example, the famous case of the potato-washing Japanese macaques (Box 9.1). The original researchers were convinced that they had observed imitation in these animals. Subsequent, more skeptical scientists have demanded that these results be looked at more critically. The results obtained, they claim, are more compatible with the idea that each monkey learned independently. Furthermore, even once it is determined that learning through imitation has taken place, multiple explanations and interpretations of this behavior are possible. For example, to what degree do the observing animals understand the motivations of the demonstrator? Imitation becomes most interesting to an analysis of theory of mind when it shows evidence of an understanding of others' motivations.

As a result, identifying true imitation – where one animal imitates the behavior of another because it recognizes the relationship between the demonstrator's actions and obtaining something it would like for itself – is far more difficult than it would at first appear. Though we may observe two animals perform the same behavior, as with the Japanese macaques, without tight experimental control we cannot know what might have motivated one animal to perform the same action as another. In recent years, a number of cleverly designed experiments that attempted to control for the different reasons why two animals might behave the same way have shed light on the existence and implications of imitation in animals.

True imitation

True imitation is a form of social learning with very specific criteria: an animal must not only engage in goal-directed behavior based on the prior observation of another animal acting out that same behavior but must also match the topography of the demonstrator exactly (the behavior must look identical to the demonstrator's). Lets say you witness a friend checking his mailbox only to find a check for 100 dollars – however, before finding the check, the friend knocks three times and then opens the door with his teeth. For it to be said that you engaged in true imitation, you would also have to knock three times and open the mailbox door with your teeth (despite the fact that an easier solution – opening the door with your hand outright – may exist). Reaching the end goal, even if you find a check, is not evidence of true imitation (although it might be considered emulation, another category of social learning, which will be discussed in the following section). Instead it is important that the demonstrator's behavior and observer's behavior correspond exactly.

While this set of criteria – exact matching of even arbitrary or inefficient behaviors while achieving an end goal – may seem odd and even counterintuitive at first, the reasoning behind this distinction is powerful. If scientists could be sure that an animal was copying point for point all the behaviors of a demonstrator (even those that are not required and thus not individually reinforced), it might be possible to claim that the species under test is capable of transmitting and acquiring social *traditions* – one indicator of culture. Human cultures abound with both meaningful and arbitrary customs and traditions, influencing the behavior of individuals that come into contact with them (why is there no 13th floor in most buildings, or why do we bless someone who sneezes?). However, our ability to transmit information precisely across generations, even when the root of a behavior is unknown, also accounts for much of the exponential growth in knowledge and productivity that our species has achieved. In recent years scientists have begun to look for the evolutionary origins of cultural behavior in nonhuman animals in an attempt to identify species that demonstrate true imitative abilities.

In line with this goal, Cecilia Heyes and colleagues at University College in London developed what is now known as the 'bidirectional control' procedure to assess imitation in rats. This procedure, outlined in Box 9.2, enables a researcher to assess not only an animal's proclivity for social learning but also its tendency to imitate the arbitrary components of a demonstrator's behavior as well. If, as Heyes found, a rat pushes a joystick to the left after seeing another rat push that same joystick to the left (when a push in either direction would lead to a reward), this could be an indicator of true imitation in rodents.

BOX 9.2   METHODS FOR DETECTING TRUE IMITATION: THE BIDIRECTIONAL PROCEDURE AND TWO-ACTION TASK

In the bidirectional procedure, two subjects (rats in the original study) are put into a box containing two compartments separated by a transparent wall (Figure 9.5). The animal on one side of the transparent partition (the demonstrator) has a joystick, which it can operate by pushing to the left or right. Some demonstrators are trained to push the joystick to the left for a reward; others are trained to push it to the right. Once each demonstrator is reliably pushing the joystick in the assigned direction, a second animal – the observer – is placed in the other half of the box, where it can watch the demonstrator push the lever either to the left or to the right to receive a reward.

After a few sessions of watching the demonstrator perform, the observer is given a chance in the demonstrator's half of the box. The question to be tested is, Does the observer copy what it has seen the demonstrator do (does it operate the joystick, and if so, does it push it in the same direction as it saw a demonstrator push)? Heyes and Dawson (1990) found that rats that observed a demonstrator pushing the joystick to the left for a reward were indeed more likely to push the joystick to the left themselves – conversely, rats that observed the joystick pushed to the right were more likely to push right. This study was one of the first to demonstrate evidence for true imitation in a nonprimate species.

Figure 9.5   *Based on Heyes and Dawson's (1990) setup for the bidirectional control procedure. The demonstrator rat is pushing the pole to the left while the observer watches*

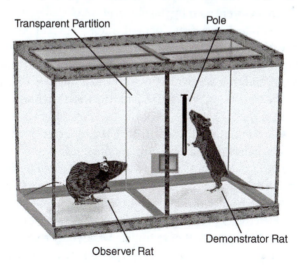

Transparent Partition   Pole

Observer Rat

Demonstrator Rat

However, it was later found that observer rats could have been influenced by odors or tastes left by the demonstrator on the side of the joystick that they had touched during demonstrations (Mitchell et al., 1999). In other words, rats might not have been imitating the direction-specific push of the demonstrator on the basis of visual observation after all – they might have simply contacted the side of the lever with the interesting smell or taste on it. Although it has now been confirmed that rats as well as other species, including dogs (Miller et al., 2009) and quail (Akins et al., 2002) do imitate directional lever or screen presses made by a demonstrator even in the absence of olfactory cues (Ray et al., 2000), this procedural criticism prompted scientists to again look for alternative methods for assessing true imitation in nonhumans.

Around the same period, Tom Zentall (1996) and his colleagues at the University of Kentucky advanced an alternative to the bidirectional procedure, the two-action task, originally used with birds such as pigeons and quail (see also Dawson & Foss, 1965, for an earlier use of this procedure). Birds were presented with a low treadle that they could operate either by stepping on or by pecking at. Zentall and colleagues found that the pigeons that observed a demonstrator step on the treadle to obtain food were more likely to step on than peck at the treadle. Similarly, pigeons that had observed the treadle being pecked for food reward were more likely to peck it themselves when their chance came. This was true despite the fact that depressing the treadle (independent of the body part used) was all that was required for obtaining the reward.

To take the two-action procedure (described in Box 9.2) one step farther, Chana Akins and Tom Zentall (1999) incorporated an extra condition into their work with quail. The experimenters exposed observer quail to one of four different types of demonstrators. As in their earlier work with quail, half the demonstrators pecked a treadle and the others stepped on it. However, this time only half of the demonstrators were seen by the observers to obtain reward; the other half were not seen to obtain reward (the demonstrator quail had been trained so that they did not expect reward every time they made an appropriate response and were happy to keep pecking or stepping on the treadle for five minutes at a time without reward). In other words, an observer quail might watch a demonstrator quail step on the treadle and get fed, step on the treadle without being fed, peck the treadle and get fed, or finally, peck the treadle and not get fed. The crucial question for Akins and Zentall was whether the observer quail would be more likely to copy the behavior of a demonstrator quail if the observers saw the demonstrator get a reward. Most interestingly, Akins and Zentall found that observers that watched a demonstrator receive food were indeed more likely to replicate the actions of the demonstrator (compared with quail who observed a demonstrator that did not get fed for its work). This suggests that, in quail at least, consequences are important in deciding whether to imitate what you see your comrade do.

Although imitative behavior has been reported for a number of species, differences in methodology – as well as the interpretation of results – may have a substantial impact on how the findings are reported. For example, a recent study conducted by Friederike Range and colleagues (Range et al., 2007) used a modified version of the two-action task to assess the imitative abilities of domestic dogs. In this study, a dog could depress a hanging rod by pushing downward with its paw or by pulling on it with its mouth (the latter was reported as the preferred method). The demonstrator was trained to use only its paw to depress the rod. Observers witnessed the demonstrator performing this act ten times under one of two conditions: for one group, the demonstrator had a ball in its mouth that prevented it from using the preferred method of pulling the rod; for the other group, the demonstrator's mouth was empty. There was also a control group of dogs that never saw the demonstrator. The researchers found that when observer dogs were given an opportunity to manipulate the rod for a reward themselves, only the group that witnessed the demonstrator use its paw to depress the rod while its mouth was empty preferentially used their paws to pull down the rod. Those that witnessed the demonstrator use its paw when its mouth was occupied (and the control group that never saw the demonstrator) preferentially pulled the rod with their mouth to obtain the reward. On the basis of these results, the researchers reported that dogs not only demonstrated imitative tendencies on a two-action task (by their willingness to engage in a less preferred action – using their paw –on the basis of prior demonstration) but selectively imitated the demonstrator only under conditions where the observed actions could not be justified by environmental circumstances (having a ball in one's mouth).

Though the results are intriguing, it should be noted that this study diverges from the majority of imitation studies in several ways. First, only one of the two target actions was demonstrated for the entire group of observers instead of two potential actions (pulling with paw only, instead of half pulling with mouth and half with paw). Second, the observers in this study had already been trained by their owners to operate the rod using both methods –their paws and their mouth. This second factor is especially noteworthy, as some researchers consider the novelty of the behavior to be imitated a definitive condition of true imitation (Heyes, 1994). Lastly, the dog subjects (including the observers) were prompted to push the rod by their owners during experimental trials (even though they were not instructed to use a specific method); therefore, the potential for social influence was not limited to the demonstrator dog but included the human as well. As a result, it is difficult to compare the study by Range and colleagues with those of previous imitation studies. In fact, with only a few exceptions (e.g., Miller et al., 2009), true imitation and even complex social learning has been difficult to establish in dogs (see Mersmann et al., 2011). More research is needed to determine whether conflicting reports of imitation in dogs, as well as other species, can be explained as a product of methodology or species capacity or by other factors.

Emulation

Another important category of social learning has been called 'emulation'. As with 'true imitation', the observer sets out to achieve some goal after witnessing a demonstrator obtain a reward. It is also assumed that the animal has learned something about the importance of a specific action or series of actions as they

Figure 9.6 *Young chimpanzee solving an opaque (a) and transparent (b) version of a puzzle box in a study conducted by Victoria Horner and Andrew Whiten (2005)*

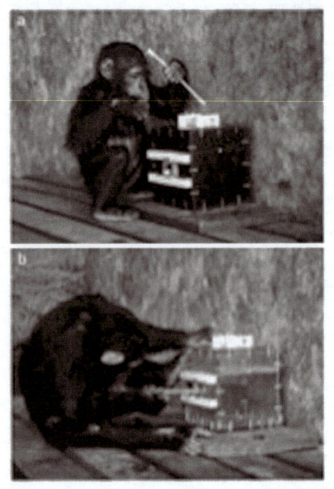

Notes: When the box was transparent chimpanzees could see that the additional steps taken by the demonstrator were pointless, and as a result they went straight for the reward.

Source: Reprinted with permission from Horner and Whiten (2005).

relate to obtaining the reward. However, in some cases an animal might not duplicate the exact actions of the demonstrator but might nonetheless set out to achieve the same goal, *or* an animal might precisely copy the actions of the demonstrator to achieve some other goal; for example, obtaining a reward that is qualitatively different from that of the demonstrator – or possibly to compete with the demonstrator for a single reward. I will consider each of these possibilities within the realm of emulation.

Same end, different means

A fascinating study by Victoria Horner and Andrew Whiten (2005) looked at how chimpanzees and three- to four-year-old human children utilize demonstrations by an adult human to solve a puzzle box for a food reward. While only one behavior was really necessary to obtain the food (pushing the food out of a hole with a stick), the adult demonstrator first engaged in a series of unnecessary behaviors, such as tapping on the puzzle box lid and pushing rods out of what appeared to be latches. Afterward the chimpanzee or child was given a turn with the stick (see Figure 9.6). To the surprise of many, both chimpanzees and children readily imitated the whole sequence of behaviors (both necessary and unnecessary) to obtain the reward when the box was opaque (which prevented them from seeing which actions were truly required to obtain the food). However, when a transparent Plexiglas box was used instead (allowing the observer to see which of the demonstrator's actions were pointless), the chimpanzees modified their behavior, skipping all the unnecessary steps in favor of the single action that led to reward (emulation). Children, on the other hand, continued to imitate the unnecessary actions, even when they could see that there was no relationship between the additional behaviors and obtaining the reward (true imitation).

Same means, different end

The game 'Simon says' may contribute to a human child's propensity for imitation; even in the absence of a tangible reward, the social rewards for precisely copying the behavior of another individual during this game might be sufficient to maintain a long chain of copying behaviors – even those as mundane as touching one's nose, waving a hand, or spinning in a circle. Scientists have begun to ask whether, with the right motivation, some nonhuman species might copy the behavior of others as well, even when the behavior being demonstrated is arbitrary or the goal unclear.

In 2006, József Topál and colleagues used a 'Do as I do' test to ask whether a trained service dog named Phillip would be able to analyze and reproduce a sequence of behaviors after observing a human demonstrator complete them (Topál et al., 2006). Prior to testing, the researchers built on the large number of behaviors that Phillip had previously been taught to assist his disabled owner; nine new behaviors were trained using operant conditioning methods (see Chapter 5), including a bow, jumping into the air, placing a bottle in a box, and turning around. However, instead of providing a verbal command for each new action, the trainer acted out the behavior and then said, 'Do it', and Phillip was rewarded with a favorite toy if he replicated the behavior. After Phillip could reliably reproduce all 9 behaviors under these conditions, the experimenters chose 16 other behaviors that Phillip already knew but that had never been included in the 'Do as I do' training. This is where the real test began: would Phillip be able to generalize his training to new behaviors; in other words, did Philip understand that the goal was to match any behavior produced by the demonstrator when he heard the command 'Do it'?

While Phillip did not copy every behavior every time, the study found that he was able to generalize his training to new behaviors, reproducing both familiar and novel human actions more often than would be expected by chance (67% of the time). It is important to note, however, that Phillip required a large amount of explicit training to achieve what, for humans, might be considered only an adequate level of performance on the task. A child playing 'Simon says', for example, would certainly not win praise for matching the leader's behavior only a little over half of the time. This might say something about the natural tendencies of dogs with respect to this form of social learning – copying sequences of behavior may not come as naturally to a dog as it does to humans, at least not in the way required here. That said, it is possible that dogs might be more inclined to copy the behavior of other dogs or would show improvement with the use of other training methods.

Furthermore, Phillip's motivation for copying the demonstrated action was not entirely a social one, nor was Phillip's reward for completing the behavior the same as for the human (Phillip completed each behavior to obtain his favorite toy; there was no indication that the action was rewarding in itself, nor did the actions directly produce the reward), making these findings more consistent with emulation than true imitation. Nonetheless, this study is an important one, as it sheds light on experiences that could contribute to the formation of imitative repertoires in species that might have the capacity but not a natural inclination for this form of learning.

The dog is not the only species that has been tested using the 'Do as I do' task. One of the first studies to use this method was conducted by Keith and Catherine Hayes (1952) with their home-raised chimpanzee named Viki. The Hayeses believed that if Viki was raised just like an infant child, she might take on human tendencies, including the ability to communicate using human language. While Viki learned to produce only four words verbally (mama, papa, up, and cup), her ability to imitate new behaviors after hearing 'Do this' met with more success. Hayes and Hayes (1952) reported that Viki learned to reproduce novel behaviors demonstrated by a humans readily with this procedure. More recent replications have supported the claim that chimpanzees will replicate arbitrary human actions to obtain a reward given the right training history (Custance et al., 1995).

Beyond primates, dolphins show exceptional promise on this task. Dolphins not only have been shown to copy the actions of another dolphin for a food reward but can do so even when they are blindfolded (Jaakkola et al., 2010). Some have suggested that the observer dolphin may accomplish this by using the sound produced by the motions of the other dolphin or perhaps through vocal communication occurring between the dolphins (but outside the range of human hearing). While more research is needed to identify the ways dolphins

Figure 9.7 *An elephant performing the same behavior as the human trainer*

Notes: Dorey (2011) found that Gay, an elephant, could be trained to present each behavior on command but did not imitate novel behaviors.

Source: Image courtesy of Nicole R. Dorey.

achieve this feat, there is mounting evidence that they are superb at copying the behavior of companions when they are instructed to do so.

Despite these successes, not all animals show a spontaneous tendency to copy the actions of a demonstrator. For example, Nicole Dorey (2011) replicated the 'Do as I do' task with an Asian elephant named Gay. A human trainer demonstrated a novel behavior (such as lifting a leg or shaking his head), after which the verbal command 'Do it' was given. If the elephant replicated the behavior, this was considered a success, and the next behavior was introduced. However, if Gay failed to copy the demonstrator, the behavior was shaped using operant conditioning (until it was reliably replicated after the demonstration and the command 'Do it') before moving on to the next behavior. Dorey (2011) found that while Gay could be trained to replicate the demonstrations on command, he did not spontaneously imitate any of the novel behaviors (Figure 9.7). The same was true in a second phase of the experiment in which the demonstrator presented novel combinations of the previously learned behaviors (e.g., lifting a leg while shaking his head); reproduction of the combinations could be trained but did not occur spontaneously. This outcome is not uncommon, as many studies have failed to find both imitation and emulation in a wide range of species, even in those known for their intelligence.

Same means, competitive end

Some species are notorious for their natural tendency to mimic. Lyre birds, for example, are known to replicate a wide range of sounds in their environment in an attempt to impress mates with their vocal flexibility. While many of these sounds are similar to what one might expect (e.g., the bird calls and songs of other species), it is not uncommon to hear cell phone rings, chain saws, or a car alarm projected from this great mimic's beak. Likewise, many species of parrots readily mimic sounds heard in their own environments, including human speech. Because parrots exist not only in the wild but also in captivity as pets and in zoos, you have likely witnessed this form of mimicry firsthand. This form of mimicry, also called vocal imitation, allows parrots to develop geographic dialects in the wild. Instead of being born with fixed vocalization patterns or songs, young parrots must learn what sounds to produce from other birds in their group – allowing them to identify their community and secure a proper mate.

Although vocal imitation does not necessarily imply the same goal-directed behavior as true imitation, scientists have questioned whether species that engage in vocal and behavioral mimicry in the wild might have an advantage on other tasks that require them to model a demonstrator's behavior. One long-term research project with an African gray parrot named Alex suggests that this might be the case. Using a procedure called the model-rival method (see Box 4.1 for an outline of this original training method), Irene Pepperberg trained Alex the parrot in a wide array of behaviors and responses, including the verbal labeling of items, the identification of the color and number of objects on a tray, and the issuing of requests. Alex appeared to learn quickly through modeling and was eager to produce responses to beat out his competition for rewards. More recently, other scientists have reported that even nonmimic species, including dogs, may be capable of learning new behaviors using this technique (McKinley & Young, 2003).

In some respects emulation makes more practical sense than true imitation. An animal with the ability to learn about a demonstrator's actions, as well as how they lead to a desired end goal, while maintaining the flexibility to improve upon the demonstrated strategy – or even to compete with the demonstrator for access to the reward in the future – would seem to have a more useful skill than repeated point-for-point copying. This might be especially true when some or all of the demonstrator's actions are inefficient or unnecessary (as in the study conducted by Horner & Whiten in 2005). However, emulation may not be without its costs. Time and energy may be spent modifying what could already be the perfect solution to a problem, and demonstrators might be wary of performing superior foraging strategies in the public eye if doing so repeatedly leads to competition from observers (see the discussion on eavesdropping in Chapter 8). Most importantly, the definition and criteria for emulation make research methodologies looking for this form of social learning less sensitive to the transmission of arbitrary responses that imitation researchers believe could be tied to the evolution of traditions – and perhaps culture. The difference between a child that imitates arbitrary behaviors unnecessarily and a chimpanzee that forgoes pointless steps in favor of efficiency is more significant than the obvious one – a chimp apparently outsmarting a human child. Instead it may indicate that imitation is more valuable to human children (because of human evolution, experience, and the potential for social reward) than just completing the task quickly to obtain the food reward. The opposite may be true for chimpanzees – imitation may simply be a means to an end (but only if it is the simplest means possible). In some respects the divide between true imitation and emulation may be more important to the researchers – who use these categories to ask questions about larger theoretical issues – than it is to the animals themselves. Nonetheless, this research has provided fruitful results and new directions for the way we think about social learning and the transmission of culture.

TEACHING

Individual gain, as might be achieved through social learning, imitation, or emulation, is not the only outcome possible when one animal shows sensitivity to the behavior of another. An awareness of the behavior of others might also allow for actions leading to mutual benefit, also known as cooperation, and in some rare cases might provide an opportunity to 'altruistically' assist others in need (or at least provide assistance unrewarded in the short term, with the expectation that the action will lead to personal or mutual gain in the long run). This kind of behavior has been widely studied and debated, especially with respect to the motivation one individual might have to sacrifice time, energy, or resources to the benefit of another, as well as to how the tendency for such behavior evolved in the first place. Some have even suggested that altruism might indicate higher-level emotions, such as empathy (de Waal, 2008). As it turns out, however, animals are more likely to engage in *altruistic behavior* when the individual they are assisting is a close relative (possibly indirectly contributing to their own fitness, or *inclusive fitness*, by helping another individual pass on shared genetic material) or when the individual they are assisting is likely to pay back the favor in the future (e.g., sharing a meal with a starving member of the group with the expectation that the individual assisted will reciprocate in the future, also known as *reciprocal altruism*). Species that live in large social groups with many related members, such as vampire bats, are especially likely to engage in behaviors that have often been called altruistic (Wilkinson, 1984, 1988).

Teaching is a special category of behavior where by definition one individual, a teacher, modifies her own behavior to benefit another individual, a pupil, often at a cost to herself. As a result, teaching has been included in scientific discussions of both altruism and social learning. For many years teaching was thought to be a uniquely human activity, but as with many areas of cognition, there is now evidence that the act of teaching may be more widespread than previously thought. Furthermore, teaching, like other seemingly altruistic behaviors, appears to be more common in species that live in highly social closely related groups.

Advancement in the scientific study of teaching behavior in nonhuman animals came with the proposal that research looking for teaching in nonhuman species was too reliant on ideas and definitions that described how human infants learned from adults. Furthermore, older definitions implied that the teacher must understand the mental state of the learner (i.e., show a theory of mind), which, as discussed in Chapter 8, has been difficult to demonstrate in many nonhuman species. However, in 1992 Tim Caro and Marc Hauser suggested three functional criteria for *teaching*:

1. The teacher must modify its behavior, specifically in the presence of naive individuals (but not knowledgeable individuals) to facilitate learning.
2. The teacher should not immediately benefit from the change in its own behavior. Instead the modification of behavior should benefit the learner

alone (sometimes at the immediate cost of the teacher). However, long-term payoff in the form of young that can feed themselves or now contribute to the group in some other way may still occur.

3. The pupil must learn a behavior it would not have otherwise learned, or it must learn the skill faster or earlier in life than it otherwise would have without the aid of the teacher.

Taken together, these criteria serve as a new, more inclusive, definition of teaching behavior. This definition is now considered the standard by most scientists working with nonhuman species (Caro & Hauser, 1992). It is important to note that while more inclusive than previous definitions of teaching, the criteria provided here are more exclusive than for other forms of social learning discussed in this chapter. To suggest that teaching has taken place, it is not enough for the observer to learn something by watching the actions of a demonstrator; instead the demonstrator, or teacher, must play an active role as well, modifying its own behavior specifically to benefit the observing pupil. This is not the case for other forms of social learning. For example, the behavior of a demonstrator rat that pushes a rod to obtain a reward or kicks up bedding to protect itself from the sting of biting flies is engaging in that behavior for its own benefit; in this form, unlike teaching, the presence of the observer does not make the demonstrator's behavior more likely and does not dictate its form.

Teaching in meerkats

Caro and Hauser (1992), on the basis of their new definition and criteria, noted that anecdotal evidence for teaching could be found for several species of mammals, most notably those that aid their young in early attempts to capture prey (including house cats, lions, cheetahs, and mongooses). For example, adult domestic cats (even pets) often hunt for prey if let outside. They move smoothly through a chain of predatory behaviors that, more often than not, result in the killing and consumption of an unlucky bird or rodent. However, once a female cat has kittens and those kittens become of age, her behavior changes. When hunting, she will capture her prey, but instead of consuming it, she will bring it back to her offspring, first dead and later alive, so that they may become exposed to potential future food items. If the prey escapes while a kitten is investigating it, the mother cat retrieves it and brings it back to her young. Eventually the mother allows her kittens to capture their own prey; she locates and stalks potential targets with them but lets her kittens go in for the kill (Caro & Hauser, 1992; Leyhausen, 1979). While this behavior certainly seems like teaching, with anecdotal accounts it is difficult to know for sure. For example, how can we know how much kittens are actually learning from the adult's behavior? Would kittens develop the motor patterns associated with hunting behavior on their own within the same timeframe even without the help of their mother (teaching criterion 3)?

As early as the 1960s, meerkats had been identified as another species that assists its young in the capture of prey in the wild (Ewer, 1963). Recently, however, a series of observations and experiments by Alex Thornton and Katherine McAuliffe (2006) have made it possible to go beyond the anecdotal evidence and scientifically evaluate whether these actions meet the criteria for teaching. When meerkat pups are around four weeks old, they begin to follow groups of adult foragers into the hunt, producing begging calls that prompt the adults to surrender their captured prey. However, the meerkat diet includes scorpions – which can produce a dangerous, if not deadly, sting when handled incorrectly – making it critical that young members of the group master proper handling of this creature early on. Adult meerkats have risen to this challenge. Instead of presenting whole living prey to pups, adults first present only dead prey to their offspring and then, as the pups get older, graduate them to live scorpions with stingers removed. This allows the pups to practice capturing scorpions without risking harm; it also allows for easy retrieval and re-presentation of the scorpion by adults should the pup lose the prey during the learning process. According to Thornton and McAuliffe's (2006) data, these actions do indeed allow the pups to learn the scorpion capture technique more quickly than they would on their own; the multistep approach was also more effective than providing pups only with dead scorpions. Furthermore, adults are only willing to help young individuals in this manner. Adults can identify the age of pups by the quality of their begging calls, and a playback experiment confirmed that adults modify their behavior in response to the age-specific calls that are being produced. Lastly, adults experience short-term costs (in terms of time, energy, and sacrifice of personal food) to the benefit of the learners; although clear long-term benefits (preserving the lives and health of offspring and increasing the rate at which they achieve foraging autonomy) are shared by all. As a result, this study was one of the first to demonstrate that prey capture assistance could indeed meet the criterion for teaching in a nonhuman species.

Teaching in ants

Again in 2006, another example of teaching behavior was identified, but this time in an unlikely subject: *Temnothorax albipennis*, a species of ant (Franks & Richardson, 2006). Ants of this species are known to engage in what is called *tandem running*. When a source of food is located by an ant, the next time it ventures out to the food source, it is accompanied by a second ant who can, in theory, learn the location of the food more quickly and help return the spoils to the group. To achieve this, the naive ant follows the leader, often placing its feelers on the legs or abdomen of the ant in front of it. However, as specified by the definition of teaching, the leader also modifies its behavior. When an inexperienced ant is present, the leader slows its progression toward the food location to allow the second ant to follow. If contact is lost, the leader will pause and wait for the follower to touch its legs or abdomen to signal its presence (Richardson et al., 2007). Although the actions of the leader are consistent with the definition of teaching, additional experiments are still needed to demonstrate what (or even whether) the pupil ant learns from the leader during this process (Leadbeater et al., 2006). Interestingly, while many accounts of teaching suggest that older members of the group primarily take the role of teacher, in ants it is prior experience – not age – that appears to be the best predictor of participation in tandem runs (as either the leader or follower). However, older more experienced ants move more slowly and are more accurate leaders than even the most experienced young (Franklin et al., 2012).

Teaching in apes

While it is commonly assumed that chimpanzees and other nonhuman apes teach their young, the scientific evidence is less clear. The example most often given in support of teaching in nonhuman apes comes from the behavior of a troop of West African chimpanzees whose behavior had been observed in the wild for over ten years. This troop engaged in characteristic nut cracking in which they used stones as an anvil (or hard base) that the nut could be placed upon and stones or branches as a hammer to smash open the nut. This behavior had been found only in select troops, implicating some form of social transmission within the unit. Chiristophe Boesch (1991) initially suggested that the behavior of the knowledgeable nut-cracking adults, as well as the learning style of their young, provided evidence for both social learning and active teaching.

In addition to modeling the behavior, chimpanzee mothers were more likely to leave their hammer unattended once they had offspring, providing opportunities for the young to practice nut cracking for themselves. Furthermore, mothers would occasionally leave the hammer and uncracked nuts by the anvil or even on the anvil itself, a tactic that appeared to stimulate nut-cracking behavior in their young in at least half of the observed cases. Chimpanzees without offspring were never observed to engage in these behaviors. Instead, nut-cracking tools were often protected or even carried around by childless chimpanzees as acquiring stones and branches of ideal size and shape could take substantial effort and leaving them behind could result in loss or theft. It is also true that the activity of the mother chimpanzees came at some cost. Not only did accommodating their young slow down their own rate of nut cracking and food consumption, but other actions, such as repeatedly providing hammers to young, which were subsequently lost or stolen, required them to spend additional time looking for replacements. However, beyond supplying the basic tools required for the task, there were only two recorded reports of a mother chimpanzee modifying her behavior in direct response to the actions of her young over the ten-year observation period.

In the first example, Sartre, a six-year-old male, took his mother's hammer in an attempt to open a very hard three-kernel nut for himself. After cracking one side of the nut and eating the first kernel, Sartre dropped the nut back on the anvil at an incorrect angle for a successful hit. In this instance his mother stopped him by removing the nut, cleaned off the anvil, and then positioned the nut correctly on the stone. Using the hammer, she cracked the nut again, obtaining the second kernel for herself. Although the onlooking Sartre may have indeed learned something from his mother's demonstration, this would not meet the current definition of teaching for two reasons. First, it is unclear how this demonstration changed Sartre's behavior. Second, in this instance it was the mother who immediately benefited from the demonstration (she ate the nut herself).

The second example, however, comes closer to our current definition of teaching. Nina, a five-year-old chimpanzee, was observed trying to crack open a nut unsuccessfully for eight minutes while her mother was resting nearby. After this period her mother came over, took the hammer, and slowly rotated it in her hands until it was oriented in a better nut-cracking position. She then cracked open ten nuts as Nina watched, providing Nina with at least a portion of each nut she cracked. Nina watched the whole episode carefully, and then resumed cracking nuts for herself using the new hammer position her mother had demonstrated. Nina went from cracking zero nuts in 8 minutes to cracking four nuts in 15 minutes, a measurable improvement. Furthermore, Nina's mother's refusal to demonstrate the behavior again, even when Nina whimpered and threw a 3-minute tantrum after she encountered some difficulty with the fifth nut, met the criterion for demonstrating teaching behavior only in the presence of naive individuals. While this episode appears to fall within the definition for teaching, it is worth noting how rare an occurrence this appears to be. Other researchers have also failed to find evidence of active teaching in wild chimpanzees (Inoue-Nakamura & Matsuzawa, 1997).

CONCLUSIONS

Learning from the actions of others can place an animal at a real advantage. Time and energy can be saved and risks mitigated by an observer who can adjust its behavior in accordance with the payoffs encountered by a demonstrator under similar conditions. However, not all behaviors that look socially learned really are. Laboratory studies have made it possible to control for alternative explanations for behavior that occurs in the presence of other individuals, including social facilitation and affordance learning, as well as to define specific categories of social learning that might inform significant theoretical questions, such as, can nonhuman animals socially transmit traditions or culture?

Imitation, emulation, and teaching are among the most stringently defined forms of social learning. The objective behind a large proportion of true imitation research is to identify willingness to copy arbitrary components of a demonstrator's behavior to achieve a like goal. Studies have shown that species such as pigeons, quail, mice, and rats are quite prepared to copy the actions of demonstrators precisely, using the same body parts to manipulate objects in their environment in an identical manner (even in the same direction) for food reward. In theory this could indicate the potential for cultural transmission of behavior across members of these species; for example, a nest of mice that socially transmit the tendency to push a lever to the left across generations might be said to have a cultural tradition for pushing left (despite the fact that pushing the lever right would lead to equal reward). Although cultural traditions appear to be much more complex in humans (when compared with left-pushing rats and foot-stomping pigeons), it is possible that at their root human traditions could have equally simple origins.

It is not just the presence of imitation in humans but their propensity for imitation that seems to go beyond that of most species. For example, in some studies human children have continued to imitate the actions of adults even when it was made obvious that the behaviors had no connection to obtaining the goal. Chimpanzees, on the other hand, appear to imitate only when the relationship between action and reward is unclear; once they can see that a demonstrator's actions are unnecessary, they stop imitating them. This might be partially due to experience as well as to the importance of social reinforcement in the lives of humans. For example, human children might respond differently than chimpanzees on this task because of their experience with rules and games that reward following the adult or leader independent of a material end goal. It is also possible that the ability or opportunity to express certain cultural tendencies, including some forms of tool use, may depend on reduced or shifted survival pressures. In some cases, superior reproduction of another's behavior (or imitation) may in itself serve as an indicator of biological fitness or attractiveness in a social species – perhaps in the same manner that vocal mimicry is used to attract mates by the lyre bird.

One of the most interesting trends in the realm of social learning research is the surprising cluster of species that are most often successful on social learning tasks. While it is generally assumed that chimpanzees, possibly followed by dogs, dolphins, and elephants, should outperform other species on many cognitive tasks (especially those thought to play a significant role in human cognition), in the case of social learning the opposite is often true. For example, evidence of imitation is strong in birds and rodents but has been difficult to demonstrate in nonprimate mammals, including dogs and elephants. While chimpanzees demonstrate the ability to imitate, they are quick to abandon it for an easier solution (emulation). Teaching has been demonstrated by meerkats and possibly one species of ants, but ten years of direct observation and decades of research on nonhuman primates have yielded only one anecdotal story of teaching-like behavior in a chimpanzee. This raises questions not only about the origins of these behaviors but also about the definitions and methodologies used to study them. It may take years of additional research to fully understand the roles that different forms of social learning play in the lives of a diverse range of species and perhaps longer to understand why these repertories are so easy to detect in some species but seemingly absent in so many others.

FURTHER READING

Cheney, D. L. & Seyfarth, R. M. (1990) *How Monkeys See the World*. Chicago: Chicago University Press.
This fascinating book contains very stimulating evidence for imitative behavior in primates in the wild.

Cornell, H. N., Marzluff, J. M. & Pecoraro, S. (2012) Social learning spreads knowledge about dangerous humans among American crows. *Proceedings of the Royal Society B: Biological Sciences*, 279(1728), 499–508.

Whiten, A., McGuigan, N., Marshall-Pescini, S. & Hopper, L. M. (2009) Emulation, imitation, over-imitation and the scope of culture for child and chimpanzee. *Philosophical Transactions of the Royal Society B: Biological Sciences*, 364(1528), 2417–2428.

Web sources

http://www.youtube.com/watch?v=VjE0Kdfos4Y
This video clip of the lyre bird's vocal mimicry is posted by the BBC.

http://robotic.media.mit.edu/projects/robots/leonardo/sociallearning/sociallearning.html
This website discusses interesting research on the possibility of robotic social learning and teaching.

http://video.pbs.org/video/1778560486/

In this Nova presentation of dolphin cognition research, joint behavior and possible social influence are demonstrated and discussed eight minutes in.

http://video.pbs.org/video/1778560467/

A Nova video in tribute to the late Alex the parrot. The model-rival technique is demonstrated and discussed beginning five minutes into the video. Other cognitive abilities, including communication, counting, and concept formation, are also discussed.

10 Remembering

I had a dog who was savage and averse to all strangers, and I purposely tried his memory after an absence of five years and two days. I went near the stable where he lived, and shouted to him in my old manner; he showed no joy, but instantly followed me out walking, and obeyed me, exactly as if I had parted with him only half an hour before. A train of old associations, dormant during five years, had thus been instantaneously awakened in his mind.

Darwin, 1989/1877, p. 74

Whenever the behavior of an animal in the present shows the influence of events in the past, memory of some kind must be implicated. Viewed in this way, it is clear that we have already considered many examples of memory. In Chapter 5, when discussing Pavlovian conditioning, for example, we saw many cases where an animal's behavior was altered by past experience. Even the marine snail that responds differently to the light touch to its mantle after training with a shock to its tail can be said to have a memory of the tail shocks. The Siamese fighting fish, which produces aggressive displays to a red light after the light has been paired with the presentation of a mirror, has a memory of that mirror. Instrumental conditioning also implies simple forms of memory. Take the queen triggerfish that learned to press a plastic rod in order to obtain a piece of food. She performed this action more frequently with training because she remembered that doing so could help her get food.

In Chapter 7, where navigation was under consideration, the ability of species like pigeons and bees to 'home' from distant sites implies a memory for where they have come from. Similarly, the migratory abilities of many hundreds of animal species imply a long-lasting memory for places. Even locusts, which journey over thousands of kilometers and never return from whence they came, must have some kind of memory of the direction they have come from in order to be able to avoid it in the future.

The ability to act now on the basis of experience in the past – the ability to use memory to guide action – must often bring with it significant biological advantages. Take, for example, a Hawaiian nectar-feeding honeycreeper, the amakihi, which feeds on mamane flowers. After an amakihi has taken the nectar from a flower, it takes the mamane about an hour to refill with nectar. Consequently, there is little point for the amakihi in returning to a mamane flower for about an hour. An amakihi that can remember which flowers it has collected nectar from and avoid returning to them for a time will have a significant advantage over a bird that wastes its time and energy repeatedly returning to flowers it has recently emptied. Sure enough, Alan Kamil (1978) found these birds avoid returning to clusters of flowers they have recently visited.

Memory is one of the most intensely studied areas of animal cognition, and it will not be possible in this chapter to provide more than a 'taster' of the wide range of research that is going on at present.

First, we consider the simplest forms of memory in the simplest organisms – the most elementary cases of past experience influencing present behavior. These simple forms of memory are also present in more complex organisms, including ourselves. Other forms of memory, those closer to our everyday meanings of that term, can be considered in many different ways. We shall follow the simplest categorizations of memory: short term and long term. Short-term memory refers to a limited capacity store, which usually lasts only a short time (perhaps a few minutes). Long-term memory refers to the storage of information that appears almost unlimited both in terms of the amount that can be retained and the length of time it can be remembered. Following this, we discuss the degree to which animals may be consciously aware of their memories.

SIMPLE MEMORIES

Around a hundred years ago, Herbert Jennings (1906) made a study of the behavior of the 'lower organisms', as he called them. Jennings studied the reactions of the barely visible unicellular animals that congregate in the sludge and slime at the bottom of ponds and other areas of still water. One genus that particularly attracted Jennings's interest was the *Stentor*, shown in Figure 10.1. Stentors usually attach to a firm base and feed by wafting water into their mouth with little hairs called cilia. If something nasty comes along, the stentor contracts into its tube to protect itself until the threat passes. Jennings found that the first time the stentor is stimulated with something that disturbs it but does no harm, such as a jet of water, it contracts into its tube, but with subsequent stimulations, it grows progressively less perturbed and eventually maintains its normal feeding posture. Here we see behavior, albeit very simple behavior, that is modified by experience. The response to later jets of water is not the same as the first jet. This simple change in response with repeated stimulation is called 'habituation', and we shall count this change in the stentor's behavior as the simplest form of memory. Habituation is found in all animals. The ability to ignore and sleep through the at first disturbing ticking of an unfamiliar clock is the same response the stentor shows to repeated stimulation with harmless water.

Pavlovian and instrumental conditioning also imply simple forms of memory. It used to be believed that such memories were only very brief. Take Pavlovian conditioning of the eye-blink reflex, for example. In this situation an animal learns

Figure 10.1   *A stentor*

to blink to a tone or other initially neutral conditioned stimulus (see Chapter 5) because it is repeatedly paired with a small shock close to the eye that evokes a reflex blink. In this situation the interval between the tone (conditioned stimulus) and the shock (unconditioned stimulus) must be very short (around half a second) for conditioning to progress well. Studies of this type led to the belief that the memories instilled in Pavlovian conditioning were always extremely short. Researchers in the 1970s, however, found situations where the interval between the conditioned and unconditioned stimuli can be very much longer.

John Garcia and colleagues (Garcia and Koelling, 1966) studied how rats learn about foods that cause sickness. In this form of Pavlovian conditioning, animals learn that an unfamiliar flavor is later followed by sickness. The conditioned stimulus is the unfamiliar flavor; the unconditioned stimulus is a poison to induce sickness. The unconditioned response to the poison is sickness. With experience a response develops to the novel flavor – this response is to avoid that flavor in the future. (Described in the clinical language of Pavlovian conditioning, this may sound like a strange scenario – it is, in fact, a very common experience. Who has not woken up in the morning feeling sick and with an intense aversion to whatever was eaten the night before – especially if exotic food was consumed?) What is interesting about this form of Pavlovian conditioning for our consideration of memory is that the conditioning was still effective with conditioned stimulus to unconditioned stimulus intervals of many hours. This demonstrates that the memories implied in Pavlovian conditioning can be far longer than was originally believed.

In instrumental conditioning, it is generally important that the consequence of an animal's behavior (the 'reinforcement') promptly follows the behavior. If a delay is imposed between, say, a rat choosing one or other arm of a T maze and obtaining its food reward, then even very short delays will cause the rate of learning to slow dramatically. Early experiments showed that a delay of as little as a second was enough to disrupt the learning of a rat (Grice, 1948). Later research has found that the animal's problem in instrumental conditioning experiments with delayed reinforcement is that the animal goes on to engage in a variety of behaviors after the one that is going to be reinforced. So how is the animal to know which of its behaviors is being reinforced? Subsequent studies have 'marked' the to-be-reinforced behavior with a neutral stimulus such as a tone or light (Lieberman et al., 1979). Under these conditions the animal is much better able to identify which of its behaviors is being reinforced, and a much longer memory can be demonstrated.

SHORT-TERM MEMORY

Short-term memory is, as its name implies, a relatively brief memory store. Though its duration varies in different experiments, a range of seconds or minutes is usual. As well as being of brief duration, short-term memory is also of limited capacity. For most humans seven items is about the limit for short-term memory (see Figure 10.1).

BOX 10.1   METHODS USED IN SHORT-TERM MEMORY RESEARCH

Two methods have become very popular in short-term (and some long-term) memory research because of their great flexibility. These are mazes (of various types) and the 'delayed matching to sample' method. Mazes of many kinds have been a part of the study of animal cognition since its earliest days as an experimental science. The first maze used in animal research was modeled on the Hampton Court maze from the garden of a royal palace outside London. These early attempts with very complex mazes were not particularly successful, and in modern times, simpler mazes have been more popular.

One of the most popular kinds of mazes in use today is the radial arm maze, developed by David Olton in the 1970s (see Olton, 1985). Rats are the most common subjects in radial arm mazes, though mice and other rodents are also used, and versions have been developed for use with fish and pigeons As was shown in Figure 5.9, the radial arm maze consists of a central area with a number of

Figure 10.2 *A rat in a water maze*

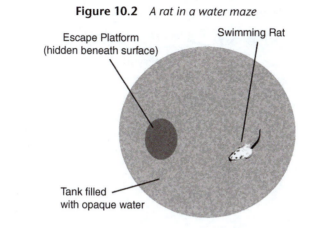

Escape Platform
(hidden beneath surface)

Swimming Rat

Tank filled
with opaque water

arms running off it. At the end of each arm, a small piece of food is hidden in
a food cup. The animal's task is to run down each arm and collect the hidden
food as efficiently as possible. Normally the food, once taken, is not replaced
by the experimenters; so the rat must remember which arms it has been down
in order not to waste time and energy returning to arms in which the cup has
already been emptied. Different numbers of arms can be attached to the central
area, but eight is a number commonly used in memory research. The animal
can be detained in the central area by means of small doors operated by remote
control by the experimenters. This enables the experimenters to test how long
the rats can remember which arms they have been down and allows them to
modify the apparatus in the middle of a trial (e.g., by moving arms or other
stimuli around) in order to test how the animal remembers where it has been
and where it still needs to go.

A highly original form of maze that has grown in popularity since its
invention by Richard Morris (1981) is the water maze (see Figure 10.2). This
'maze' is simply a circular vat of water (1.3 meters in diameter). The water is
made opaque by the addition of milk powder or white powder paint. Hidden
beneath the surface of the water is an escape platform. No food is used to
motivate the rat in this maze; the desire to escape from the water-filled vat
is motivation enough. Rats are competent but reluctant swimmers and are
highly motivated to find the hidden platform that saves them from having
to swim any longer. The ingenuity of this maze is that it gets round problems
of motivation (each time a rat is put in the water maze, it can be assumed
to be equally motivated to find the hidden platform; in a more orthodox,
food motivated maze, an animal may become less motivated as its hunger
abates). The water maze also removes all possibility of the rat finding its
way by using local information – for example, by scent marking the parts of
the maze it has already explored. The mazes internal featurelessness ensures
that the rats must be navigating solely on the basis of whatever is visible
outside the maze (doors, windows, and so on in the laboratory) and their
memory for where they have already swum in the maze.

The delayed matching to sample (DMTS) task is far simpler than its
rather convoluted name might suggest (Figure 10.3). It is similar to the
procedure described in Chapter 3 to demonstrate the development of
a concept of 'same'. A subject (this could be a human or a member of
a great many other species) is shown a sample stimulus. This stimulus

Figure 10.3   *The delayed matching to sample procedure*

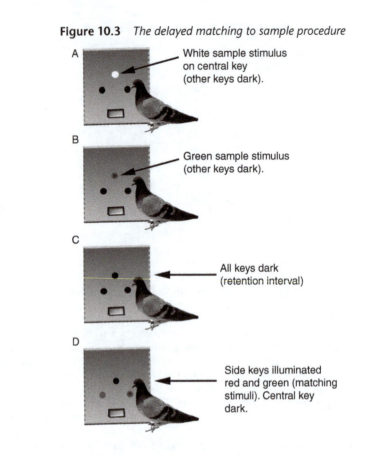

A — White sample stimulus on central key (other keys dark).

B — Green sample stimulus (other keys dark).

C — All keys dark (retention interval)

D — Side keys illuminated red and green (matching stimuli). Central key dark.

could be a picture, a sound, or an object of any kind. The stimulus is then removed and the subject left in peace for a period of time known as the retention interval. At the end of the retention interval the subject is shown two (or more) similar stimuli. One of these is the same as the originally presented sample stimulus – this is the matching stimulus; the other stimuli are distracters. The attraction of the DMTS procedure is that it is simple enough that it can be used with a wide range of species, thus permitting interspecies comparisons. But it is also flexible enough that almost any type of object can be used as the stimulus. Duration of memory can be ascertained simply by testing retention at longer and longer retention intervals, and other aspects of memory can be examined by judicious manipulation of the distracter stimuli presented in the matching phase of the procedure.

As it is commonly tested with pigeons, DMTS requires a standard operant chamber (see Chapter 5) with three pecking keys in a row. First, the central pecking key is lit up with white light to attract the pigeon's attention. After the pigeon has pecked the white light a couple of times, a sample stimulus is presented on the center key. This could be the color green. Usually the pigeon is required to peck this stimulus a couple of times, after which it is turned off. There then follows the retention interval, during which stimuli are not normally presented. After the retention interval, the two side keys are illuminated: one the same as the sample stimulus (green), the other a distracter (red, say). The position of these two stimuli is randomized across trials so that the pigeon cannot simply learn to always peck on one or other of the side keys. If the pigeon now pecks the matching (green) stimulus, it obtains a food reward. After an interval the central pecking key is lit up with white light again to indicate the start of the next trial.

Capacity

While long-term memory has an almost limitless capacity, short-term memory is a temporary store for just a few items at a time. The capacity of rat short-term memory can be readily tested in the radial arm maze by adding more and more arms until the rat starts to make errors. In a standard-sized radial maze of eight arms, rats rarely return to an arm they have already visited. Numerous control experiments have demonstrated that the rats really are using memory to keep track of which arms they have visited (they do not, for example, scent mark the arms they have been down). It has also been shown that rats do not simply go around the maze clockwise or counterclockwise – to a human observer their activity seems fairly random. If more than eight arms are used, accuracy starts to decline. Rats can still perform above chance level with 17 or 24 arms, but as the number of arms increases, they start to simplify the task by adopting new strategies, such as always turning to the right when leaving an arm.

Duration

Duration is perhaps a pointless subheading to consider under 'short-term memory', since if it lasts too long, it isn't 'short-term' any more! Nonetheless, there is value in considering how long an animal's memory of the kind demonstrated in these types of tasks can last. In one investigation, rats working in the eight-arm radial maze were removed from the maze after making their first four choices and returned to their home cage. After a delay lasting from 4 minutes to 24 hours, they were brought back to the maze to finish their task by collecting the food from the arms they had not yet visited. After a gap of up to 4 hours, the rats completed the task without error, but after 8 or more hours errors became frequent (Beatty & Shavalia, 1980).

Marcia Spetch and Werner Honig (1988) developed a task similar to the radial arm maze for use with pigeons (see also Spetch, 1990). The birds were tested singly in a room set up with eight possible food sites (Figure 10.4) constructed from modified two-liter milk cartons. A semicircular opening was cut in the side of each milk carton, and the tops were removed so that pigeons could see and peck inside the carton. At the bottom of the carton Spetch and Honig placed grit with a couple of seeds on top. The pigeons' task was to fly

Figure 10.4   *The layout used by Spetch and Honig to study pigeons'*
memory for locations in a room

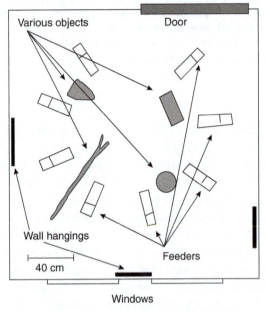

Source: From Spetch and Honig (1988).

around the room and collect the seeds from each milk carton as efficiently as possible.

The pigeons' memory was tested in conditions similar to those under which rats had been found capable of remembering for four hours which four arms of the radial maze they had already visited. Spetch and Honig allowed pigeons to collect the food from milk cartons positioned at four out of the eight possible locations shown in Figure 10.4 and then removed them to a holding cage. After periods ranging from 2 to 120 minutes the birds were allowed back into the room to complete their selection with cartons in all eight possible positions. Only the four food cartons that had not been visited in the initial phase of the experiment now contained food. These pigeons' memory of food location started to decay after half an hour, was still above chance level after one hour, but was down to chance level after two hours.

The delayed matching to sample procedure does not demonstrate such lengthy short-term memories as the radial maze does. For example, pigeons trained with different colors as stimuli could remember which of two matching colors to choose only when the delay between presentation of the sample and matching stimuli (the 'retention interval'; see Box 10.1) was less than three seconds – anything longer and there was no evidence of memory. In a heroic effort involving 17,000 training trials, Douglas Grant (1976) found that pigeons were able to remember stimuli over retention intervals of up to one minute. Even monkeys and dolphins have demonstrated memory duration of only a couple of minutes in the delayed matching to sample procedure (see Box 10.2 for a matching to sample task with bees). Clearly delayed matching to sample is a difficult task for most species.

Serial order effects

A phenomenon that was noticed long ago was that when humans attempted to memorize lists of items, the items at the beginning and end of a list tended to be better remembered than those in the middle. Better memory for the items at the start of the list is known as 'primacy', and better memory for the last items in a list is called 'recency'. Together these are known as 'serial order effects'. Recency can probably be explained by the fact that nothing comes after the last items in the list; they are the most recently seen and consequently the least likely to have decayed in memory or become confused. The existence of primacy is perhaps a little more surprising. Why should the first items in a list be better remembered than items in the middle? The reason probably has to do with the fact that there are no items before the first items that could become confused with them – this places them at an advantage to items in the middle of a list, which can be confused with both earlier and later items. In some cases, exposure to words at the beginning of a list may also allow for 'rehearsal', or repetition of the thing to be remembered, which is thought to increase the likelihood that the piece of information (the word) will make it into long-term memory – skirting the rapid decay associated with short-term memory.

Evidence of recency has repeatedly been found in nonhuman subjects tested for their memory of a list of items. Roger Thompson and Lou Herman (1977), for example, played dolphins a list of six sounds. At the end of the sequence the dolphins were presented with a test sound. Sometimes this sound was one of the six that had just been played; other times it was not. The dolphins' accuracy in identifying whether or not the test sound had been included in the sequence would provide an indication of their short-term memory. Their memory was strong for the fourth, fifth, and sixth sounds (recency) but very weak for the earlier ones.

FOCUS ON THE DATA: PRIMACY AND RECENCY

When humans are presented with a series of words flashed one at a time on a screen and then are asked to recall which words they have previously seen, they most accurately identify words presented near the beginning (primacy) or near the end (recency) of the word list. Words at the beginning of the list are most likely to be rehearsed and thus are stored in long-term memory,

Figure 10.5   *Serial order effect in monkeys*

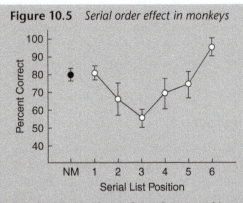

Source: Reprinted with permission from Castro and Larsen (1992).

while those presented most recently are likely still in short-term memory. However, words in the middle of a series are often forgotten.

Figure 10.5 illustrates the primacy and recency effect in monkeys engaged in a picture-based recall task. Carl Castro and Thomas Larsen (1992) first trained six captive rhesus monkeys on a same-different discrimination task using computer-generated images (pictures of animals, toys, vehicles, etc.). Pairs of items were presented one by one. When the two images matched, the monkeys could earn a food reward by touching the bottom object; when the images did not match, reward could be earned by touching a white box on the screen. Once the monkeys were reliably discriminating between matches and nonmatches, they were allowed to proceed to the memory recall task. Now the monkeys saw a sequence of images presented one at a time on the screen (similar to the word list presentations often used in human studies) followed by a final image that could be identified as a 'match' (if it had been seen in the previous sequence) or a nonmatch if it had not. The white dots in the above graph represent the mean percent of correct choices (accurately identified matches) for all six monkeys, depending on where the matching stimulus had been located in the previous sequence of images (presented first, second, or third and so on). The black dot represents the mean percent of correct choices made by the monkeys when the final stimulus was non-matching (had not been presented in the previous list). As you can see, the monkeys were quite accurate at identifying when the final image did not match any of the previous images (roughly 80% accuracy on average), and they were equally accurate at identifying that the final image was a match if the same image had been presented first in the prior sequence (primacy effect). However, monkeys were most accurate (almost 100%) at identifying a match if the final image was the same as the last image presented in the sequence (recency effect). This strong recency effect has also been easy to identify in a wide range of species. Note, however, that when matching images had been presented in the middle of the sequence, for example, as the third item in the list, performance was low (only identified as a match slightly over 50% of the time). This provides strong evidence for the serial order effect.

Read the full article: Castro, C. A. & Larsen, T. (1992) Primacy and recency effects in nonhuman primates. *Journal of Experimental Psychology: Animal Behavior Processes*, 18(4), 335–340. doi:10.1037/0097–7403.18.4.335

Evidence of primacy was initially more difficult to demonstrate in nonhuman subjects. However, Johan Bolhuis and Hendrik van Kampen (1988) were able to demonstrate primacy and recency in rats gathering food in a radial arm maze. These rats were trained in an eight-arm maze modified so that the experimenters could control access to the arms by the use of remote-controlled doors in the central area of the maze. First, the experimenters opened all the doors so that the rat could freely access all eight arms of the maze. After the rat had run down and collected the food from five of the arms (which typically took less than two minutes), the doors were lowered to block off all the arms, and the rat was removed from the apparatus and taken to its home cage. After delays ranging from 30 seconds to 60 minutes, the rat was returned to the central area of the radial arm maze, where all but two of the arms were blocked off. One of the two open arms was one the rat had been down before, the other it had not previously entered. The rat's task was to select the arm it had not already visited – only this arm contained food. Of course, to select the arm it had not already visited, the rat had to be able to remember where it had been. Bolhuis and van Kampen found that the rats were most successful in recollecting which of the two arms they had not already been down when the previously visited arm was one they had visited at the very beginning of the experiment (primacy) or one they had just visited (recency). Just as in the human case, Bolhuis and van Kampen found that primacy was more common when the retention interval (the length of time the rat was absent from the apparatus) was longer (greater than 16 minutes), and recency was more common at shorter retention intervals. This is consistent with the interpretation that information benefiting from the primacy effect is likely stored in long-term memory.

In recent years, both primacy and recency effects have been shown in several nonhuman species, including pigeons and baboons (Fagot & Cook, 2006), dogs (Craig et al., 2012), and monkeys (Basile & Hampton, 2010).

BOX 10.2   MEMORY IN HONEYBEES

While most research on animal memory has focused on a small group of vertebrate species, some researchers have studied the memory of an invertebrate – the honeybee. We saw in Chapter 5 that bees can be conditioned, which implies a simple form of memory. In addition, in Chapter 7 we discussed how bees can navigate to food sites and find their way home. This implies memory for the route they have flown to find food.

Research indicates that the memory of the bee extends not just to navigation but also to color. Michael Brown and his coworkers (1998) trained bees on delayed matching to sample of colored stimuli. The bees collected sugar solution on petri dishes placed on top of a horizontally mounted computer monitor. This monitor was programmed so that different-colored circles could appear directly beneath the glass dishes. In this way the bees were given sugar solution on one color and after a delay presented with a choice of two colors. Sugar solution was now available on the same color as it had been originally. It was found that the bees chose the originally rewarded color significantly more often than chance (though still making, it must be conceded, a high rate of errors).

More recently, Darrell Moore, Byron Van Nest, and Edith Seier (2011) further explored the honeybee's memory for time (also see Chapter 4). Like birds who estimate the ideal time to revisit a flower to obtain maximum nectar, bees also learn about sources of food that are available only within specific periods or times of day with much accuracy. Until recently, the duration of such memories were thought to extinguish (or decay) rapidly unless food was acquired at the source daily. This would allow the bee to move on and acquire new food sites, but it would also mean losing knowledge of a site that may have been a reliable source of food in the past and could continue to be in the future. However, Moore and colleagues (2011) demonstrated that the duration of memory a bee has for a food site (including the time food is available) is actually tied to the amount of experience and success the bee has had at that site in the past. For example, during periods of poor weather bees are able to retain memories about a food site for several days, even if attempts to find food go unrewarded, as long as prior experience (a long history of obtaining food at a site) or environmental circumstances (like poor weather, which could account for an unusual absence of food) predict that it could be advantageous to do so.

What causes forgetting?

Forgetting is just a failure to remember – right? Well perhaps, but recent research in animal (and human) memory suggests that there may be more to forgetting than just not remembering.

It seems very likely that a large part of the phenomenon of forgetting is due not to the decay of some kind of memory trace but to confusion arising from other things that an animal is trying to remember. This confusion is known as 'interference'. Interference can take two forms. Either information already in memory can interfere with new information – this is called 'proactive' interference. Alternatively, new information may interfere with what is already in memory – this is 'retroactive' interference. Primacy and recency effects suggest the existence of proactive and retroactive interference. Items in the middle of a list are not well remembered because they are subject to both proactive and retroactive interference. They are exposed to proactive interference from the items earlier in the list and are vulnerable to retroactive interference from the items that come after them. The items at the beginning of the list are better remembered because they experience only retroactive interference and no proactive interference. Conversely, the items at the end of the list are better remembered because they are exposed only to proactive interference, with no items following them that could cause retroactive interference.

It is quite easy to demonstrate the effects of proactive and retroactive interference directly. Proactive interference in the radial arm maze can be shown simply by requiring a rat to work through finding food in the eight arms of the maze several times in quick succession instead of just once per day. The first time a rat is tested each day, it performs very well. With each successive test on the same day, however, the rat's performance declines, presumably because of proactive interference from the previous trials run on the same day.

A simple demonstration of retroactive interference consists of testing an animal on delayed matching to sample but making a change in illumination during the retention interval between the sample and matching stimuli (see, e.g., Grant, 1976). Pigeons, dolphins, and monkeys have all been found to perform less well under these conditions, presumably because the illumination change interferes retroactively with their memory for the sample stimulus.

Recent studies have shown that the old view of forgetting as a passive decay of information over time is not accurate. Forgetting is better thought of as an active rejection of information no longer relevant to a situation. Adaptive forgetting is crucial to an efficient memory system. Without forgetting, the limited short-term memory capacity would become saturated and unable to absorb any new information.

William Maki and Donna Hegvik (1980) introduced an ingenious modification to the delayed matching to sample procedure for pigeon subjects. Immediately after being shown the sample stimulus, the birds were shown an additional stimulus. This could be either the 'remember cue' or the 'forget cue'. In trials where the sample stimulus was followed by the remember cue, the trial proceeded as normal, with a retention interval followed by two comparison stimuli – the pigeon had to choose the stimulus that matched the sample stimulus, just as in the normal procedure. In trials where the sample stimulus was followed by the forget cue, however, the comparison stimuli were not presented – there was no need to remember the sample stimulus. The question that Maki and Hegvik posed was, are pigeons capable of remembering or forgetting the sample stimulus on command – do they have active control over the memorization process? To test this, the researchers occasionally tricked the pigeons by introducing the comparison stimuli in trials that had started with the forget cue. Sure enough, on trials where the pigeons had not been expecting to have to remember the sample stimulus, their matching performance was poor. These results remain controversial and are the subject of ongoing studies attempting to resolve theoretical difficulties. However, more recent research has confirmed that evidence of *directed forgetting* (or active control over memory) can be found in pigeons when the procedures utilized limit interference that may be caused by the presentation of the 'forget' cue (Kaiser et al., 1997). When compared with methodologies that ask the subject to either remember or forget a single sample, predicting a test or no test, respectively (which could unintentionally cause the subject to ignore the unexpected prompt to match the sample after the forget cue on experimental trials), instructing a subject to forget one of two sets of stimulus presentations, requiring them to still remember and respond to the other, allows for a more accurate test of what the subject really remembers. If probed to respond to a sample that had been followed by the forget cue, pigeons will still engage in the trial; however, they perform worse than when prompted to match the sample followed by the remember cue. This suggests that pigeons can accurately shift their allocation of memory to hold the information that should be the most relevant to the task (Roper et al., 1995), actively forgetting information that they believe will not be tested. It has also been found that the function of the forget cue transfers to other tasks, suggesting that it may serve as a higher-order task instruction (Roper et al., 2005), much like the instruction 'forget it' can be applied to many different scenarios for humans.

Evidence for the active nature of memory and forgetting also comes from rats in the radial maze. Until recently it was assumed that an eight-arm radial maze requires a rat to remember seven arms (the first one is chosen at random; at the second arm the rat must remember to avoid one arm; at the third arm the rat must avoid two arms; by the eighth arm the rat has seven arms it must remember to avoid). On the other hand, if the rat has active control over its memory, it could make the task easier by remembering which arms it visited for the first four entries and then just remembering which arms it has *not* visited for the remaining four. That way it would never have to remember more than four arms at a time. Robert Cook and coworkers (1983) designed a simple test for whether rats are able to actively control their memory in this way. Using a radial arm maze with 12 arms, Cook and colleagues occasionally removed rats from the maze after their 2nd, 4th, 6th, 8th, or 10th choice. If the rats always remembered the arms they had visited (and not the arms they still had to visit), then this interruption should have been harder to deal with the later it came in their exploration of the maze. (During an interruption after just two arms have been visited, the rat has only two arms it must remember; during an interruption after its tenth choice, the rat has ten arms to remember.) On the other hand, if the rats start out by remembering which arms of the maze they have already visited but halfway through switch to remembering which arms they still need to visit, then by the time they have made their tenth choice, they have to remember only two more empty arms of the maze, and the inconvenience of being removed from the maze should be relatively easy to deal with. On this basis, the most difficult interruption would be after six arms have been visited, because here the rat would have to remember either the six arms it has visited or the six arms it has not yet been to. Sure enough, Cook and colleagues found that the rats made the most errors if they were removed from the maze midway through and fewer if they were removed toward the beginning or the end of their search through the maze.

It is common for people to complain about their failing memory as they age. Particularly common are complaints about forgetting the locations of objects – such as one's keys: in other words problems with spatial memory. Older people also complain about difficulties remembering new names or labels. Forgetting appears to increase with age in other animals as well, including dogs (Tapp et al., 2003); this appears to be especially true for working or short-term memory.

LONG-TERM MEMORY

Discussion of animal memory often evokes the saying ' An elephant never forgets,' and this may be for good reason. Long-term memory deals with memories that have progressed beyond the restricted capacity and duration of short-term memories (in humans this is typically accomplished through repeat exposure or rehearsal of the thing to be remembered); long-term memory can hold a much larger store of information for up to the lifetime of the animal. In animals that are both social and live a long life, including humans and elephants, this may be critical to long-term success or even survival.

In a review of recent field and experimental work on elephant memory, it was found that elephants, which can live to be over 60 years old in the wild, have an exceptional memory for social relationships and encounters. Young elephants show signs of remembering the smell of their mother – relying on the scent of her urine – even after decades of separation; adults (especially those in large families led by an old matriarch) can often recognize and remember the calls of over 100 other elephants from different clans and families (Hart et al., 2008). This is in addition to the impressive spatial memory of elephants mentioned in Chapter 7, which allows them to travel over great distances to previously visited watering holes with incredible precision. However, elephants are just one of many species that demonstrate the ability to remember large quantities of information over long periods of time.

Food-storing birds

Some of the most impressive feats of memory in the animal kingdom are those of the food-storing species of birds. Clark's nutcrackers, from the American Southwest, store up to 33,000 pine seeds in around 6,000 different sites in the late summer. Over the course of winter and into spring, the birds go back and recover their caches. Research we shall consider here indicates that they do this largely by remembering for months where they have put the seeds. On a smaller scale, English marsh tits and North American chickadees, when they find a rich source of food, instead of eating it all at once, take seeds away and store them nearby for consumption over the next few hours or couple of days. They may store over a hundred items under these conditions.

Marsh tits and chickadees

Richard Cowie and his colleagues (1981) gave marsh tits radioactive sunflower seeds (the seeds were only mildly radioactive – just enough that they could be found later with a Geiger counter). True to form, the marsh tits took the seeds and stored them in various places. The experimenters then found those seeds with the Geiger counter and placed other seeds either close to (within

10 centimeters) or far from (1 meter) each of the seeds the birds had stored. Cowie and colleagues found that all the seeds they added were less likely to be collected later by the marsh tits than the seeds the birds had stored themselves. This suggests that the marsh tits were not just looking for seeds in certain kinds of nooks and crannies but remembered to within ten centimeters where they had placed the seeds earlier.

Field studies can take us only so far in identifying for certain whether these birds use memory to find their stores of seeds and how they do so. In a sequence of experiments John Krebs, David Sherry, and Sara Shettleworth have investigated the role of memory in food storing by marsh tits and the related North American chickadees. One ingenious experiment that demonstrated definitively that marsh tits rely on memory to find cached seeds made use of the fact that each eye of the bird is connected to only one side (the opposite side) of the brain. By covering up one eye with an eye patch while the birds were hiding seeds and then letting them recover the seeds later with either the same or the other eye covered up, Sherry and colleagues (1981) found that only if the same eye was covered during caching and recovery were the birds able to find the seeds. This indicated that information stored in the bird's brain was crucial to finding the seeds again and, in addition, that this information is not transferred from one side of the brain to the other.

Sherry (1984) also performed an experiment on black-capped chickadees that suggests they use more distant, global cues to find seeds in preference to closer, local cues. Chickadees were tested in a 2 cubic meter enclosure (see Figure 10.6). This enclosure contained four identical artificial 'trees', into which 32 holes had been drilled for the birds to use as storage places for seeds. These holes were identically placed in each tree; so for each food storage site in one tree, there was an identical one in the other three trees so that the bird could not identify which tree was which. The experimenters placed a large colored shape on each wall of the enclosure (a global cue) and small colored cards next to each seed storage site (local cues). The birds were given an opportunity to store seeds with both the global and local cues present. Later they were allowed back into the enclosure to find their seeds under one of four conditions: the experimenters had left the enclosure as it had been when the birds stored their seeds (local and global cues present), had removed the local cues, had removed the global cues, or had removed both sets of cues. Perhaps surprisingly, the birds were most confused by the removal of the global cues – the large colored shapes on the walls. The removal of the local cues – the colored cards next to the food storage sites – had no significant effect on their success in recovering seeds. In a subsequent experiment, Sherry and his colleagues (Herz et al., 1994) found that if the global cues were rotated around the box by 90, 180, or 270 degrees, then the birds also looked for the seeds they had cached in positions respectively 90, 180, or 270 degrees from where they had originally hidden them.

Figure 10.6   *The environment in which Sherry and colleagues studied how birds rely on global cues to remember where they have stored food*

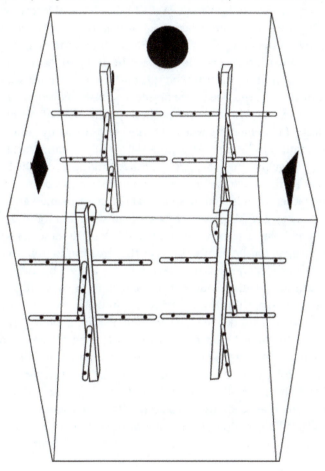

Source: From Sherry (1992).

Nutcrackers

Stephen Vander Wall (1982) allowed two Clark's nutcrackers to hide food separately in an indoor aviary. Each bird was given an opportunity to store before either was allowed back in to recover seeds. In a strong indication that the birds were relying on memory and not simply choosing parts of the aviary that looked good for hiding seeds, each bird accurately recovered its own seeds without disturbing the seeds that the other bird had hidden. Vander Wall discovered, however, that these birds were seriously disrupted in finding their seeds if significant objects in the aviary (such as logs and rocks) were moved around between the time they hid the seeds and the time they returned to look for them (for more on the role of landmarks and beacons in special reasoning, see Chapter 7).

In another experiment by Vander Wall (1982), all the objects (except the hidden seeds) on one side of an aviary were displaced 20 centimeters during the interval between the nutcrackers hiding the seeds and their recovery (shown in Figure 10.7). When they were allowed back in to try to recover the seeds, the birds were spot on in the undisturbed side of the aviary but missed their caches by 20 centimeters on the side where objects had been moved.

In all the above experiments, the possibility remains that the birds are making their task of remembering where they hid seeds easier by always placing the seeds in the same kind of spot each time. Rather like making the task of finding your car in a large parking lot easier by always parking under the largest tree in the lot. Alan Kamil and Russell Balda (1990) tested for this possibility by forcing Clark's nutcrackers to hide seeds in spots that the experimenters and not the birds had chosen. They gave the nutcrackers seeds to store in a room that contained 180 sand-filled holes. The experimenters could close up these holes so that only enough were open for the number of seeds the birds had to store. Even when the birds were forced to store seeds in holes arbitrarily chosen by the experimenters, they were still successful at finding their seeds 10 to 15 days later.

Another interesting finding by Kristy Gould, Amy Ort, and Alan Kamil (2012) suggests that Clark's nutcrackers demonstrate memory for what-when-where related to the location of food caches (episodic memory of this type will be discussed in more detail later in this chapter). The birds were allowed to cache red and blue colored seeds in sand-filled holes, where they returned after either a short period of time (three days) or a long period (nine days). During this interval seeds were replaced with either another edible seed or an inedible bead depending on the color of the original cache and the period of time that had passed. While nutcrackers were proficient in finding their

Figure 10.7   *The arena used by Vander Wall to test nutcrackers' memory of stored seed positions*

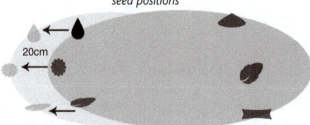

Notes: All the objects on one side of an aviary were displaced 20 centimeters between the nutcrackers storing seeds and their opportunity to recover them.
Source: Based on Vander Wall (1982).

caches after any delay, they were successful in collecting more seeds than beads after the longer durations alone. This may suggest that long-term memory and episodic-like memory in nutcrackers are linked, although how and why is less well understood.

There is evidence that food-storing birds such as black-capped chickadees and scrub jays use the sun-compass to find seeds they have hidden. (The sun-compass was introduced in Chapter 7.) This involves combining information about the time of day with the position of the sun to find compass directions. Since an animal's sense of time of day stems from when it observes sunrise and sunset, tests of a bird's use of the sun-compass system can be made by keeping the birds in an indoor aviary and turning the lights on either earlier or later than normal. In tests where scrub jays were woken up six hours later than normal, it was found that they searched for food in an octagonal aviary 90 degrees clockwise from where they should have – just as the use of a sun-compass would predict (Duff et al., 1998).

Pigeons

Russell Balda and Wolfgang Wiltschko (1995) tested pigeons under conditions rather similar to those that had been used with the food-storing species of birds mentioned above. Their pigeons were trained to dig up food that had been hidden by the experimenters in one of eight sand-filled plastic cups in a large (5-meter diameter) aviary. It was found that the pigeons easily learned to dig up the seeds, and having learned which of the eight cups had been baited, they could readily remember this for ten months. Balda and Wiltschko found no difference in the pigeons' memory whether they were tested hours or up to four days after the original training. Even after ten months, no pigeon made more than one false choice (out of eight possibilities) before identifying the correct cup.

Two studies have looked at the capacity of long-term memory in the pigeon. William Vaughan and Sharon Greene (1984) trained pigeons in Skinner boxes to discriminate 80 pairs of slides. In one experiment the slides had had random shapes ('squiggles') drawn on them; in another, the slides were photographs taken around the Cambridge, Massachusetts, area. In each experiment the pigeons were trained using a Go/Nogo procedure, where they were to respond to one stimulus in each pair (the positive stimulus) and refrain from responding to the other stimulus. Choice of which stimulus in each pair was positive and which negative was completely arbitrarily. With sufficient training (nearly 1,000 daily sessions for the squiggles, about 850 for the photographs), the birds reliably chose the positive stimulus in each pair. They were then given a break of eight months in the case of the squiggles and two years in the case of photographs before being retested. On retesting, they showed good memory for which were the positive and which were the negative stimuli. The slowness of the ini-

Figure 10.8 *A selection of the stimuli used by Fersen and Delius in their study of pigeons' rote memorization ability*

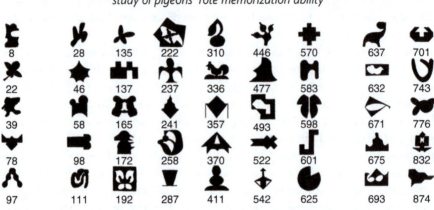

Source: From Fersen and Delius (1989).

tial learning of the distinction between these stimuli may in part be explained by the difficulty of some of the distinctions they were required to learn.

Lorenzo von Fersen and Juan Delius (1989) trained pigeons to discriminate between 100 positive stimuli and 625 negative stimuli using a concurrent discrimination method (Chapter 2). The stimuli Fersen and Delius presented were black designs on a white background (a sample is shown in Figure 10.8). The birds learned to reliably discriminate these objects over 224 sessions. In subsequent tests, Fersen and Delius replaced either the 100 positive or the 625 negative stimuli with novel items that the pigeons had never seen before. Their excellent performance under these test conditions indicates that they had memorized both the positive and the negative stimuli. In fact, the pigeons performed slightly better when the negative stimuli were replaced with novel items, suggesting that they were perhaps discriminating positive from negative stimuli on the basis of their familiarity.

After training, the pigeons were given a six-month break from the experiment. When they were returned to the experimental environment, unlike Vaughan and Greene's subjects, Fersen and Delius's pigeons did not immediately recognize the objects with which they had been trained earlier. However, after a few days of practice with a subset of the stimuli they had previously seen, they were reintroduced to the remaining stimuli (which had not been seen for over six months) and were able to categorize them correctly to a very high degree.

In studies of human long-term memory, people are often just asked whether they recognize an object or scene as one they have seen before (under which condition people have been shown capable of recognizing up to 10,000 pictures). This familiarity measure would seem to be an easier task than discriminating between negative and positive items, as Vaughan and Greene's and Fersen and Delius's pigeons were required to do. It also appears a more ecologically relevant task, as homebound pigeons often need to differentiate between familiar landmarks and unfamiliar territory. Darwin's account of his dog's long-term memory, quoted at the start of this chapter, is a case of using familiarity to test memory, and it shows a longer-lasting memory than has been demonstrated in any modern experiment.

More recently a study by Joël Fagot and Robert Cook (2006) demonstrated just how large and long pigeon (and baboon) long-term memory might really be when challenged. Two pigeons and two baboons were included in this study. All subjects participated in ongoing matching to sample tasks (where the presentation of a unique image corresponded with a correct choice as presented on the left or right of a computer screen). The number of new stimuli steadily increased over three to five years, stretching and testing the limits of each species long-term memory capacity. Over this time the pigeons demonstrated a memory for 3,037 and 1,978 total images (the underperforming pigeon may not have reached its full potential as it died prior to the end of the experiment). The baboons did even better, demonstrating a memory for 5,910 and 6,180 total images. While these numbers may be an overestimate of what any one individual can remember at a given time (the researchers suggest that a more accurate estimate for the capacity of pigeon picture memory may fall between 800 and 1,200 images; 3,500 and 5,000 for baboons), this is by far one of the most impressive demonstrations of the capacity of long-term memory in these species. For another impressive feat of memory see Box 10.3.

BOX 10.3   MEMORY DESPITE METAMORPHOSIS

Many animals undergo a metamorphosis – a complete change of body form – at some stage in their lives. Ralph Miller and Alvin Berk (1977) decided to investigate whether memory is preserved in the African claw-toed frog as it metamorphoses from tadpole to frog. Miller and Berk first trained tadpoles and frogs to avoid one compartment of a two-compartment chamber by placing a mild electric shock under one part of the chamber floor. This could be learned readily both by tadpoles and by adult frogs. Then they waited 35 days, during which time the tadpoles metamorphosed into frogs and the animals that were already frogs just grew older. Next all the subjects were tested again to see whether they could remember which compartment was the dangerous one. Miller and Berk found that, despite the great changes that the tadpoles had undergone in metamorphosing into frogs over these 35 days, they showed considerable memory for which side of the chamber was dangerous. Their memory was equivalent to that of the animals that had been adult frogs all along.

IMPLICIT AND EXPLICIT MEMORY

One of the many distinctions drawn in studies of human memory research is between implicit and explicit memory processes. Not all memory is conscious. Many memories show themselves even though there may be no conscious 'recollection' of the events in question. Motor skills, such as riding a bicycle, fall into this category of implicit memories. Experiments on people whose explicit memory has been impaired through brain damage suggest that many simple patterns of behavior are remembered without the need for conscious recollection. On the other hand, explicit memory is the remembering of things that we can describe in words, memories that we are conscious of. Explicit memory is the kind of memory activated when somebody asks you, 'Do you remember when...?' Unfortunately we cannot simply ask nonhuman animals whether they are aware of their memories or what dimensions of memory they have access to. However, with careful experimental design, it has been possible to gain some insight into what aspects of experience different species are capable of remembering and whether or not they are aware of remembering them.

Metamemory – knowledge of what one remembers

When considering animal memory, it is very difficult to judge whether we are dealing with explicit or implicit memory. Since there is no proven method of demonstrating consciousness in animals, it has often been assumed that animal memory must be implicit. We need not necessarily accept this argument, however. Though we cannot demonstrate that an animal is conscious, we can explore whether it can report on its own behavior – this would seem to be the fairest animal analogue of explicit memory. For example, Charles Shimp (1981, 1982) trained pigeons to report on the number or pattern of pecks they had just emitted. The pigeons were first trained to peck either quickly or slowly onto a central response key. Occasionally, two side keys would light up. A peck on one side key was rewarded if the previous response sequence on the center key had consisted of fast responses: A peck on the other side key would be rewarded if the previous center key response sequence had been slow. The pigeons became quite adept at reporting their memories of their own response patterns in this manner.

Explicit reporting or knowledge of one's own memories is often termed *metamemory*. In recent years scientists have developed ways to *ask* nonhuman species about what they can and cannot remember, in addition to reporting on memories of their own behavior. Several species of nonhuman primates, as well as humans, have been shown to share this capacity. One way this has been demonstrated is by allowing subjects to opt out of matching to sample memory tests, typically after some delay or in the absence of complete information, for a reduced reward. For example, at least one capuchin monkey tested by Kazuo

Fujita (2009) was found to reliably opt out of memory tests that it would have been likely to fail because there had been long delays between the presentation of the sample stimulus and the opportunity to make a choice response. In opting out, the monkey accepted a lesser but guaranteed reward. In trials where the monkey would be expected to get the answer correct, it appropriately chose to take the test and obtain the full reward. Similar results have been found for other nonhuman primates, including macaques (Beran et al., 2006), as well as for dolphins (Smith et al., 2003). In other tests of metamemory, apes, including chimpanzees, have been shown to seek additional information when they are unsure about their knowledge of the solution to a problem (Call, 2010).

The possibility of metamemory in pigeons has also been explored. In one study pigeons participated in a delayed matching to sample task (as in Box 10.1) in which they would receive six food pellets for pecking one of three keys that matched the sample stimulus or three pellets for pecking an alternative *safe* key (Sutton & Shettleworth, 2008). When available, the safe key could be used to obtain at least some reward, assuming the pigeon could not accurately recall or match the sample stimulus for the full six pellets; incorrect choices resulted in no pellets. Pigeons performed more accurately on matching to sample trials they chose to take than when they were forced to choose on all trials because no safe key was available. This finding was consistent with previous studies of metamemory in primates. However, in a second test – in which pigeons were required to choose the safe key or the memory test before they were given the choice array – pigeons appeared to choose the safe option too often. In other words, they often chose the safe key (accepting three pellets) even under conditions where they had reliably matched to sample (leading to six pellets) in the past. While this may show sensitivity to other factors, such as an aversion to risk, such behavior is not entirely consistent with the idea that the pigeons were accurately assessing what they could or could not remember at the time of the task – the cornerstone of metamemory (Sutton & Shettleworth, 2008).

Episodic memory – what, when, and where

Episodic memory is a category of explicit memory that relates to big-picture autobiographical events – or in other words, the ability to remember not only that something happened but roughly when and where it happened as well. Episodic memory is often considered uniquely human as it implies a higher level of awareness about past events. However, increased investigation into this topic has led to possible examples of episodic memory in nonhuman species. An experiment by Nicola Clayton and Anthony Dickinson (1998) suggested that scrub jays may have some form of explicit memory. Jays were given the opportunity to learn that 'wax worms' (wax moth larvae) – a highly preferred food – become unpalatable after a period of several hours. Next the jays were trained to take either wax worms or peanuts (an acceptable but less preferred food that does not become unpalatable for several days) and store them in trays of sand. Clayton and Dickinson found that, given a choice between retrieving cached wax worms or peanuts after just four hours (a period of time when the wax worms were still very palatable), the scrub jays would selectively recover the wax worms. Given the same choice after 124 hours (a long enough period for the wax worms to have decayed and become unpalatable), the jays recovered the peanuts instead. This result indicates that the jays were able to recall not just where they stored food but what food they had stored and when. More recently, a similar study conducted by Miranda Feeney, William Roberts, and David F. Sherry (2009) demonstrated that black-capped chickadees could utilize the what, where, and when dimensions of memory in a food-retrieval task as well. This is the kind of rich multidimensional memory that has been termed episodic memory when observed in humans.

Dogs, although not yet tested formally on all three components of episodic memory, have shown promise on tasks that require them to remember the what and where of previous experiences. In an innovative study conducted by Kazuo Fujita, Ayako Morisaki, Akiko Takaoka, Tomomi Maeda, and Yusuke Hori (2012), dogs were led to – and allowed to investigate – four food-baited containers (each a different size and shape) lined up in a testing room. However, they were allowed only to eat the food found in two of the four containers. After this exposure phase, the dogs were taken outside for a walk lasting at least ten minutes – owners were instructed to take their belongings and behave as if they were leaving to go home to remove any indication that the dog would return (adding a surprise element to the memory task). Simultaneously, the buckets in the room were replaced with identical ones, but this time none of the containers held food (to eliminate smell cues). The dog was then led back to the room by its owner and released at a spot equidistant from each of the four now empty containers. Eleven out of the 12 dogs tested visited one of the previously baited (but uneaten) containers on their first trial, suggesting that they were using memory of the previous experience to approach locations where food had been and should logically still be (since they had not been allowed to consume it). This is in contrast to a basic instrumental conditioning account because, as discussed in Chapter 5, in instrumental conditioning one would predict that the dog would revisit the containers for which approach had previously been rewarded (one of the two containers it had been allowed to eat from).

While this study demonstrated that dogs were capable of remembering where past items were located in an earlier encounter, a second experiment was required to assess if they also recalled what could be found in each container. This time Fujita and colleagues (2012) individually exposed 39 new dogs to four containers that varied in size and shape, just as in the first experiment. However, this time only two of the four containers contained food; a third container held a neutral object (a stone or plastic figurine), and the fourth container was empty. Again each dog was led to the four containers one at a time and allowed to investigate the contents; however, this time the dog was allowed only to eat food located in a single container. After a ten-minute walk the dog was returned to the testing room to find four identical (but new) containers. This time over half the dogs (20 out of 39) first approached the container that previously held uneaten food. Of the remaining dogs, 11 approached the uneaten food container second (most of these 'second choice' dogs had approached the container where they had previously eaten food first – as would be predicted by instrumental conditioning). This performance demonstrated that dogs not only remembered where they had previously seen and eaten food but also remembered what was located in each container. It would not have been enough to remember the location of places food was previously eaten to locate the container that should have been hiding the remaining food (as might have been possible in the first experiment); for a successful first choice the dog was also required to remember which of the remaining containers should contain food as opposed to an object or nothing at all. At least half the dogs demonstrated this capacity given only a single trial. More research will be needed to determine whether dogs demonstrate the full range of skills associated with episodic memory, but this study has provided a platform for future investigations into this topic.

CONCLUSIONS

This chapter has shown that there are many different types of memory. The unicellular stentor, which alters its response to a repeated innocuous stimulus, is obviously far removed from the Clark's nutcracker, which stores thousands of seeds in the autumn to keep it going through the winter, or the elephant that identifies the smell of its mother after decades of separation. Clearly an animal's lifestyle – its ecological niche – determines the kind of memory it will have. Though this statement is generally true when very different species are being considered, it has proven quite difficult to demonstrate differences in memory between more closely related species. Throughout the 1990s, Shettleworth, Krebs, and others compared the memorization abilities of food-storing birds (such as the nutcrackers, marsh tits, and chickadees considered above) with those of their nonstoring relatives, such as jays (which are related to nutcrackers) and titmice (which are related to chickadees and marsh tits). While it has been shown that birds that hoard food rely more on spatial information than do their nonhoarding cousins (nonhoarding species make more use of visual information and patterns), differences in their memorization abilities have proven harder to demonstrate. Krebs, Shettleworth, and their colleagues have suggested that food-storing birds (marsh tits) are less vulnerable to proactive interference than are nonstoring birds (blue tits) (see, e.g., Krebs et al., 1990). However, when Robert Hampton and colleagues (1998) compared the memory abilities of food-storing chickadees with those of dark-eyed juncos (nonstoring birds), it was the nonstoring juncos that showed less vulnerability to proactive interference.

Comparing the cognitive abilities of different species at more than a superficial level is always fraught with problems. Can we be sure that even closely related species see the world the same way? If their sensory and attentional abilities are not comparable, then their memories can hardly hope to be. In the case of memory, an additional complexity arises from our lack of knowledge about what any given species needs to remember. It is known that certain species of birds store food and use memory to find their caches later – but what about non-food-storing species of birds? Is it reasonable to assume that they do not have as much to remember? They may indeed remember where and when they have been foraging and where there are predators, as well as important social information such as where to find mates and avoid rivals – the list is potentially endless.

This may partly explain why laboratory tests have failed to find universal clear-cut distinctions between the memorization abilities of different classes of birds. The birds we classify as not storing food may have other substantial memory tasks to deal with in their lives of which we are simply unaware. The same is true for the myriad of other species that have been tested on memorization tasks (as well as those that remain untested). In interpreting results of memory research, it will continue to be important to consider what aspects of memory are most relevant to the species under test and what tasks would most reliably measure an animal's full potential. Identifying memory tasks that are appropriate to an animal's evolutionary history or contextual life experiences (as with Fujita's episodic memory test for dogs) may yield the most telling results in years to come.

FURTHER READING

Kamil, A. C. & Roitblat, H. L. (1985) The ecology of foraging behaviour: implications for animal learning and memory. *Annual Review of Psychology*, 36, 141–169.

Raby, C. R. & Clayton, N. S. (2010) Chapter 1 – the cognition of caching and recovery in food-storing birds. In T. J. R. H. Jane Brockmann (ed.), *Advances in the Study of Behavior* (Vol. 41, pp. 1–34). Academic Press.

These two contributions are very good reviews of the research on memory in food-storing birds.

Salwiczek, L. H., Watanabe, A. & Clayton, N. S. (2010) Ten years of research into avian models of episodic-like memory and its implications for developmental and comparative cognition. *Behavioural Brain Research*, 215, 221–234.

A review addressing several aspects of explicit memory in birds.

Web sources

http://news.nationalgeographic.com/news/2003/08/0822_030822_tvanimalmemory.html

This website summarizes the research of Clayton and Dickinson as well as other research looking for explicit memory in nonhuman animals.

http://games.lumosity.com/chimp.html

This website contains a video of Ayumu, the chimpanzee, performing on Inoue and Matsuzawa's (2007) short-term memory test, as well as a sample of the test that you can try for yourself.

11 Animal Communication in the Wild

The kites of olden times, as well as the swans, had the privilege of song. But having heard the neigh of the horse, they were so enchanted with the sound, that they tried to imitate it; and, in trying to neigh, they forgot how to sing.

Aesop's Fables, translated by G. F. Townsend

Communication is one of the most fascinating and often most conspicuous behaviors that animals engage in. The very fact that we hear sparrows sing, see peacocks lift their magnificent wing feathers, and sometimes smell the emissions of our canine friends itself raises interesting questions about the costs and benefits of communication. Why do so many animals accept the danger of revealing their location to predators in order to communicate? There must be a substantial corresponding advantage for such behavior to have evolved in so many diverse species.

Communication serves animals' needs to survive and reproduce and their ability to project their genes into future generations by aiding their close relatives. When a vervet monkey utters an alarm call, it is helping its relatives to survive by avoiding a snake in the grass. When a honeybee dances in the hive and communicates the location of a flower ripe with nectar, she is aiding the survival of her sisters in the hive and the further reproductive efforts of her mother, the queen (the worker bee herself is sterile and so can see her genes into the next generation only by aiding her sisters and mother). When a male cowbird sings his song, he is attending to his need to attract a female cowbird and get his genes into the next generation. In each of these cases there is a fitness advantage to the communicator.

Animals do not only communicate with their relatives. Prey also communicate with predators: as when a gazelle stots (jumps up suddenly in the air) to communicate to the lion stalking it that he has been spotted and thus is unlikely to catch the gazelle. They should both save themselves the bother of a pointless chase that will just waste their time and energy. Sometimes predators listen in on the communications of their prey – as when dolphins detect the sounds made by fish.

In discussing animal communication, it is customary to identify a signaler and the recipient of a signal. This does not imply that either individual is consciously aware or even unconsciously intends to send or receive the signal. An

259

older view construed communication as a cooperative activity in which a sender and receiver collaborated to get a message across. It is now understood that the picture can be much more complex. Receivers may eavesdrop on signals that the signaler would rather they did not pick up. Bats, for example, listen in on the mating calls of male frogs in order to locate and predate on them. Some species are sensitive to the presence of potential eavesdroppers and modify their signals accordingly. For example, many songbirds have 'quiet' songs that travel only short distances in order to prevent others of their own species from detecting their presence (Dabelsteen, 2004). Monkeys that raid farmers' crops have quiet alarm calls, known as 'conspiratorial whispers' (Dawkins & Krebs, 1978), that they use to warn each other of the arrival of the farmer. These calls are clear enough that the monkeys hear each other but quiet enough that the farmer does not detect them (Kavanagh, 1980). In other situations, an evolutionary arms race may develop in which signalers compete to get their message across with ever louder, larger, and brighter signals. It is thought that the large bright tail of the peacock evolved in this way, in an evolutionary arms race among male birds to impress the females.

The tail of the peacock is an example of an honest signal. The size and bright coloration of an impressive male's feathers indicate health, requiring adequate nutritious food, energy, and preening (grooming) to maintain (Loyau et al., 2005). Peacocks do not have the resources to fake their tails. Furthermore, having bright flashy feathers or a long train that might slow you down can come at the cost of being more susceptible to predators. A male that is fit enough to survive despite this potential handicap must surely be a catch for a lucky female (Zahavi, 1975). The deep notes of frogs' and toads' mating calls are also honest signals of their owner's size. The laws of physics impose a necessary relationship between the depth of a tone and the size of the body that produces it: big body means deep call. Although a recent study (Bee et al., 2000) showed that males of one species of green frog, *Rana clamitans*, may sometimes lower the dominant frequency of their calls during territorial contests in order to make the calls sound deeper and the frog seem larger than normal. In other words, not all signals are honest. Examples of dishonest signals include the behavior of mimics, which copy the behavior of another individual. For example, two species of fireflies emit similar patterns of flashes of light. Females of the *Photinus* species use their characteristic flashing pattern to attract mates. Females of the *Photuris* species mimic the flashing pattern of *Photinus* females so that they can lure *Photinus* males and eat them (Eisner et al., 1997).

The study of animal communication started with Darwin himself in *The Expression of Emotions in Man and Animals* (1872). In this richly illustrated work, Darwin considered the ability of animals to convey emotions and the many similarities in how they do so and how emotions are conveyed in people. For example, Darwin showed how a Celebes macaque revealed her teeth in a smile

Figure 11.1   *Darwin's dog Polly 'watching a cat on a table'*

when pleased by caresses and a chimpanzee pouted her lips when 'disappointed and sulky'. He compared these poses to the expressions of people of diverse ages and from many cultures when feeling the same emotions as he assumed the macaque and chimpanzee were feeling.

Some of the pictures in Darwin's *Expression of Emotions* are of his own terrier, Polly (see Figure 11.1). Polly outlived Darwin by only a few days and was buried at Down, where they lived and where Darwin had intended his own internment (he was actually buried at Westminster Abbey, next to Sir Isaac Newton). Emma Townshend (2009) offers a fascinating account of Darwin's love of dogs.

In 1923, Julian Huxley, (the grandson of Darwin's friend and key supporter Thomas H. Huxley) proposed that one of the ways that communicative behaviors could have evolved was through what he termed ritualization. According to this theory, a behavior that initially has some communicative potential becomes refined to be more efficient in the transfer of information through the simplification, exaggeration, repetition, or increasing stereotypy of the original behavior. Thus dogs necessarily bare their teeth before they bite. The baring of teeth can become a signal that on its own communicates the dog's unfriendly intent. The dog may come to bare its teeth in a more pronounced, exaggerated, and prolonged way than is necessary simply to be ready to bite. Teeth baring has become a ritualized signal.

Communication serves the overarching need of animals to survive, reproduce, and ensure the presence of their genes in future generations, and in doing so, it achieves several more short-term aims. Communication can enable species recognition, mate attraction, and the maintenance of pair bonds and other social connections, alarm warnings, and communication about resources such as food sources. Examples of all these types of communication follow in this chapter.

THE DANCE OF THE HONEYBEE

Honeybee navigation was considered in Chapter 7. If the navigational ability of this small insect seemed amazing enough, the system the bee uses to communicate (often called its 'dance language') is even more astonishing. In 1973, for his work in unraveling the dance communication system of the honeybee, the German behavioral biologist Karl von Frisch shared (with Konrad Lorenz and Niko Tinbergen) in the only Nobel Prize ever to be awarded for work on animal behavior.

When a forager bee returns to the hive after a successful foraging trip, she (all foraging bees are female) performs a dance on the vertical surface of a honeycomb. If the nectar source was relatively close (less than about 100 meters), the dance she performs is known as a round dance. The worker bee runs around in a circle to her left and then to her right, alternating back and forth as shown in Figure 11.2. This performance may continue for about half a minute. The sight of this dance makes the other worker bees very excited. First, they troop around behind the dancing bee, keeping their antennae close to her body in a sort of bee conga dance. Pretty soon they fly off to find the food themselves. In the case of the round dance, the excitement with which the forager bee dances her way around the honeycomb gives some indication of how good a source of nectar she has found, and the bees she recruits pick up the odor of the nectar source with their antennae and use this to find the right flowers.

The so-called waggle dance of the bee contains even more information. When the goal is more than about 100 meters from the hive, the returning bee changes her dance slightly but significantly. Instead of dancing around in an approximate circle, she now dances in a figure eight. As Figure 11.2 shows, the bee first dances a short vertical run before turning to the left and on the next time through turns to the right to create a figure eight. As she dances the middle

Figure 11.2 *The round (left) and waggle (right) dances of the honeybee*

section of the figure, the bee waggles her body from side to side energetically and makes a buzzing sound. As in the round dance, other bees start following the dancer around. They pick up odor with their antennae, but in addition, von Frisch identified that the waggle dance also communicates both the distance of the food source from the hive and the approximate bearing required to reach the food. Through an elegant series of experiments, von Frisch was able to demonstrate that the speed with which the forager bee danced the waggle dance indicated the distance of the food source from the hive.

Perhaps the most astonishing feature of the waggle dance is that it also signals the bearing needed to reach the food source. Von Frisch found that the forager bees do not always dance their figure eights with the central section strictly vertical. Rather, the angle to the vertical can vary substantially. Von Frisch was able to show that the angle of the central part of the waggle dance to the vertical is actually the bearing to the sun that will lead to the nectar source.

Some years after von Frisch's original observations, Adrian Wenner and Patrick Wells became skeptical of von Frisch's hypothesis that foraging bees rely on the dance to find nectar-bearing flowers. They pointed out that, in fact, rather few new bees are recruited to a nectar source by the performance of a dance and many bees make their way to the nectar without attending to the dance of a bee who has already been there (Wenner & Wells, 1990). Recruited bees are also in the air for much longer than they need to be for a direct flight to the nectar source if they really knew what direction it lay in. Additionally, bees continue to turn up at a nectar source in significant numbers even if every single arriving bee is killed or put in a box so that none can fly back to the hive to communicate with the others.

Wenner and Wells proposed instead that bees actually find food sources by relying on odor plumes. These are the diffuse clouds of aroma that emanate from a fragrant source. All that is communicated by returning forager bees to their hive mates is the odor of the source they have returned from.

The technology available to von Frisch permitted only somewhat indirect tests of what the forager bees were relying on to find new flowers. Von Frisch put out arrays of feeding stations in different locations and recorded whether recruited forager bees went to the same location as the dancing bee that they had been attending to in the hive. More recently, some more direct tests have been carried out using modern technology, and these have largely vindicated von Frisch's hypothesis.

Axel Michelson and colleagues (1992) designed and built an artificial, computer-controlled mechanical bee that they could program to dance according to their instructions. Forager bees were willing to attend to this robo-bee and were found to fly off in the direction it was indicating – though not in the same numbers or quite as accurately as foraging bees do in nature.

Figure 11.3   *Each line represents the flight path of a bee that attended to the waggle dance of a bee that started at the hive and found its way to the feeder. The diamond release points at the bottom left of the figure are where bees that were attempting to fly out of the hive were shifted to and then released. It can be seen that they fly out of the release points in the approximate direction and distance of the feeder*

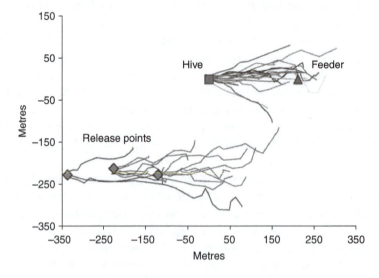

Source: Modified from Riley et al. (2005).

Another experiment utilizing modern technology also gave support to von Frisch's account of the function of the bee's dance. Joe Riley and colleagues (2005) attached passive radar transponders to the backs of bees. Although these transponders do not have the range of active radar or GPS devices, they are much lighter than these more powerful devices and so could be strapped onto the bees without any noticeable impact on their flying ability. And the passive radar transponders were sufficiently powerful to enable the researchers to identify the tracks taken by different bees around a large mowed field.

The researchers allowed forager bees to find a feeder they had provisioned with sugar water. The forager bees flew home and danced for other bees. These other bees were captured as they left the hive after following a dance and moved around 300 meters away to one of three other locations in the field before being released. The radar tracking devices showed that these bees flew off in what would have been the correct direction and approximate distance to reach the feeder had they still been in the hive. The paths of these bees are shown in Figure 11.3.

Another fascinating complex form of animal communication, bird song, is considered in Box 11.1.

BOX 11.1   BIRD SONG

Who has not been struck by the beauty of birdsong? And yet what possesses a blackbird to sit on a branch singing his heart out for hours on end? Clearly he does not do it for our benefit but for some purposes of his own.

About half of all bird species belong to the order Passeriformes – songbirds. The 'true' songbirds, or oscines, learn to sing by listening to a 'tutor', usually another male of their species – typically their father. Some species, including the canary, can learn new songs at any time of life, but others, such as the zebra finch, learn just one song early in life and do not change their song thereafter. Other species of singing birds, the suboscines, do not learn their song. Singing is also found in some other orders of birds such as parrots (Psittaciformes) and hummingbirds (Apodiformes). Most research has been carried out on the true songbirds, the oscines, especially zebra finches (small flocking birds from Australia) and white-crowned sparrows (North American songbirds). Particular research interest has focused on how birds learn their songs. This research has uncovered a fascinating trajectory that combines genetic information (nature) with the young bird's environment (nurture).

In zebra finches, chaffinches, and some other birds that share this developmental trajectory, the young male bird goes through a 'memorization phase' before he is yet singing himself. At this time of life, the young bird forms a memory of the song of his tutor. Later in life the bird starts to sing for himself and compares his own vocalizations with his memory of the song of his tutor. A young bird that does not hear a tutor will nonetheless sing as he reaches adulthood, but his song will be rough and crude. A bird that is deafened after he has heard his tutor sing will produce a better song but not as accurate a copy of the tutor's song as a bird that hears a tutor early in life and can hear himself sing when older and practicing his own song (Marler, 1976; Slater, 1983).

White-crowned sparrows show a different trajectory of song learning. In normal development, the young male sparrow hears the songs of his father and other adult male birds during his first summer and autumn. At this time, his own song is a primitive, rambling sequence of notes known as subsong. As he enters his first breeding season in late winter and early spring, his song becomes more organized and recognizable as the song of his species. This phase is called plastic song, and the bird continues to refine his song through his first breeding season until by the end of it he produces his crystallized song, which contains imitations of the songs of adult males he heard many months earlier (Marler, 1970; Marler & Tamura, 1964).

As shown in the following 'Focus on the data' box, young white-crowned sparrows reared in the laboratory so they cannot hear the songs of adult males of their species develop abnormal song. However, if they are exposed to recordings of the song of their species during the 10th to 50th days of life, their adult song is normal. Juvenile white-crowned sparrows must also hear themselves sing to develop normal song. Figure 11.4 includes the sonogram of a bird deafened at an early age. Its song is clearly abnormal. However, birds deafened after they have developed their crystallized adult song continue to sing normal song for at least a year after deafening (Konishi, 1965).

Experiments on song sparrows indicate that these birds go through two phases: a sensory phase, during which they learn and remember songs, and then later a sensorimotor phase, when they actually practice their songs and refine them. In the song sparrow, young males actually drop songs from their repertoire as their personal songs crystallize. Interestingly, they are most likely to drop songs that they do not hear sung by other birds around them. It is not entirely clear why they prefer to sing songs that they hear other birds sing. One hypothesis is that using shared songs may indicate that a young male is local to the vicinity and so perhaps less threatening to other males (Beecher & Brenowitz, 2005). This hypothesis is supported by observations that male sparrows that sing more local songs live longer lives than those that sing more 'foreign' songs (Wilson et al., 2000).

FOCUS ON THE DATA

Figure 11.4   *Sonograms of white-crowned sparrow song*

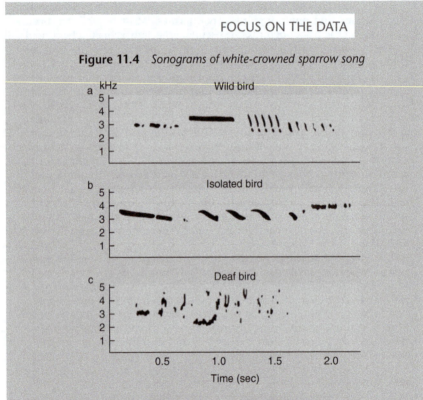

Source: From Konishi (1965).

Figure 11.4 shows sonograms – a way of representing sound in two visual dimensions. In each panel, the height of a mark up the plot shows the pitch of the sound – higher readings are higher frequencies. The thickness of a mark shows the amount of energy at that frequency (loudness). Time passes from left to right in each panel. These sonograms from white-crowned sparrow songs show the songs of birds reared under different conditions: (A) a bird reared under normal wild conditions; (B) a bird reared in social isolation in the laboratory so that he could not hear adult birds sing; (C) a bird deafened at an early age. From Konishi, 1965.

CHICKEN ALARM CALLS

Chickens may not be songbirds, but they do make sounds. In fact, they make two different kinds of alarm calls. Figure 11.5 shows the apparatus used to present videos of aerial predators to roosters and have hens listen to the roosters' calls.

One of the dangers of alarm calling is that it may reveal to a predator where a potential victim is located. Therefore, animals would do well to issue alarm calls only when there is an audience of their own species around to profit from the risk they take with their calling. Chris Evans and Peter Marler (1995) demonstrated that roosters call more often when they can see a hen (she doesn't have to be live: a video recording will do). And they call more to other chickens than to an audience of bobwhite quail (Karakashian et al., 1988).

Chickens do not only make alarm calls. Roosters will also call when they find food. This is the purpose of the familiar clucking sound of the chicken. Roosters are more likely to cluck when they find food and there are hens about; the clucking of the rooster attracts hens with whom he may then attempt courtship (Marler et al., 1986a, 1986b; Evans & Marler, 1994).

Figure 11.5 *Experimental arrangement for Evans and Marler's experiments on communication in chickens*

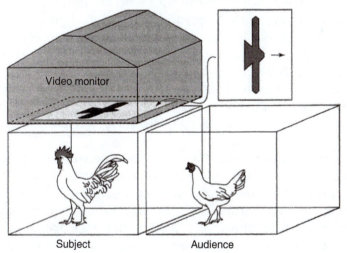

Notes: The video monitor was mounted above the cage containing the rooster subject so that the image on it was visible to the rooster but not to his audience (the hen in the next cage).

VERVET MONKEYS OF KENYA

One of the most thorough and fascinating studies of a spontaneous communication system in a nonhuman primate was carried out over many years by Dorothy Cheney, Robert Seyfarth and their coworkers on East African vervet monkeys (Cheney & Seyfarth, 1990). Similar results have subsequently been found on captive rhesus monkeys and Japanese macaques.

Cheney and Seyfarth built their research on an observation made by an earlier researcher. In 1963 Thomas Struhsaker spent a year among the vervet monkeys of Kenya's Amboseli National Park (Struhsaker, 1967). Over many thousands of hours of careful observation and audio taping, he transcribed 36 different kinds of vervet monkey sounds. He noted the contexts in which these different sounds were made so diligently that he was able to identify 21 of them as distinct messages that the monkeys made to each other. For example, vervet monkeys give distinct acoustic calls to three different major predators: leopards, eagles, and snakes. Each alarm call sounds different and produces a different response in the vervet monkeys who hear it.

The first step Cheney and Seyfarth took was to demonstrate that the monkeys were really responding to the acoustic alarm calls and not directly to the predator itself or the behavior of the monkey issuing the alarm call. To do this, the researchers taped alarm calls and then played them back to the monkeys when the predator was absent. The monkeys' distinctive response to each alarm call type in these playback experiments showed that they really were responding just to the acoustic calls.

Next Cheney and Seyfarth carried out a series of experiments attempting to uncover as much as possible about what the information these alarm conveyed to the vervet monkeys. Does the call made in response to a leopard, for example, mean something like 'Watch out, there's a leopard!', or is it more like 'Quick everybody, up into the trees!' Evidence that the calls really refer to the predator rather than the action that a monkey should take to avoid the predator comes from the observation that monkeys who hear the calls when they are in different places (on the ground, up a tree, and so on) will take different types of evasive action.

To understand exactly what the vervet monkey alarm calls convey to their audience, Cheney and Seyfarth (1990) developed an experiment out of the story of the boy who cried 'Wolf!' once too often. They played back an alarm call used by the vervet monkeys when another group of monkeys was getting close. This is a long trilling 'wrr'. The first time they played back this wrr with no other group present, the monkeys looked around them for about six seconds. By the time the experimenters had played the wrr tape eight times with no other group present, the monkeys looked up from what they were doing for just two seconds. They had learned that there was no other group approaching, and somebody was just 'crying wolf' (or rather, 'wrr'). The next thing Cheney and Seyfarth did was to switch the call on the tape to a short staccato chutter. This chutter sounds completely different from the wrr but is also used by vervet monkeys to signal the approach of another group. Now, if the monkeys were just listening to sounds, they would be expected to take renewed interest when the sound they heard changed and look around them much longer. On the other hand, if what they were doing was extracting the meaning of the wrr call, then the change to a chutter call does not involve a change in meaning, and so they would not be expected to pay any more attention to the chutter call than to the now discounted wrr call. This is exactly what was found. The first chutter call was paid even less attention than the last of the eight wrr calls – the monkeys looked around them for less than two seconds.

This is an important result because it indicates the calls of animals in the wild can be referential; that is to say, they can refer to things in the outside world. They are not just indications of the caller's state of mind. Doubtless if I stumbled across a snake in the woods and cried out 'snake' to my companions, they would be able to tell that I was very afraid – but my call would also be referential – it would describe the object of my fear. If I stumbled across an alligator, I would say something different, and my companions would again know not just that I was anxious but what I was anxious of. Cheney and Seyfarth's research on vervet monkeys was among the first to demonstrate that other species could be capable of referential calling.

The possibility that vervet monkeys' use of alarm calls in a possibly deceptive manner might imply a theory of mind is discussed in Chapter 8.

DIANA MONKEYS EAVESDROPPING ON OTHER SPECIES' SIGNALS

Diana monkeys live on the opposite (west) coast of Africa from vervet monkeys, but they share with their eastern cousins the habit of making distinct alarm calls to different threats. Just like vervet monkeys, Diana monkeys respond differently to calls that members of their troupe make to different kinds of threats (Zuberbühler, 2003). Diana monkeys also cease responding if the same alarm calls is repeatedly made in the absence of the threat to which it ought to refer. Interestingly, Diana monkeys also respond to the sounds made by other animals, and Klaus Zuberbühler and colleagues (1999) demonstrated that an alarm call has the same meaning to the monkeys as the sounds made by the threat itself. Zuberbühler and colleagues played the alarm call of the monkey to the threat of an eagle repeatedly without there being any eagle around until the monkeys no longer responded to the call. They then played the actual shrieking sound of an eagle. Monkeys that had learned to ignore monkey eagle alarm calls also ignored the eagle's own shriek. Zuberbühler and colleagues repeated the experiment with leopard alarms. They played the monkey's leopard alarm repeatedly till the monkeys ignored it and then played the growl of a leopard. Again, the monkeys ignored the growl of a leopard if they had just heard the alarm call repeated in the absence of any live threat. In a final control test, they found that if they played back the eagle alarm call repeatedly and then followed it with the leopard growl or the leopard alarm call repeatedly followed by the eagle shriek, the monkeys responded with a more typical magnitude of response to the eagle or leopard. They were not tired of all alarm calls; they had learned that just one particular call was a false alarm.

Diana monkeys that live near chimpanzees also make leopard alarm calls when they hear chimpanzees scream. Leopards also hunt chimpanzees, and it seems that the Diana monkeys that have chimpanzees for neighbors have learned that the screams of the chimps can imply danger for themselves. Interestingly, chimpanzees also hunt Diana monkeys, and if the monkeys detect hunting chimps (or humans), they do not make alarm calls but rather remain as silent and hidden as possible (Zuberbühler, 2000).

DOLPHINS

In the 1960s, the husband and wife pioneers of bottlenose dolphin research, David and Melba Caldwell, discovered that, in addition to the click sounds they use for echolocation (see Chapter 2), bottlenose dolphins produce relatively pure tone sounds. The Caldwells identified these pure tones as characteristic of the individual dolphin uttering them and therefore labeled them 'signature whistles' (Caldwell & Caldwell, 1965).

Studying how dolphins use their whistles to communicate is very challenging because dolphins move freely in an underwater environment where it is very difficult for people to keep up with them and see what they are doing. Indeed, it is precisely because vision is a relatively ineffective sense in water (and odor is also an ineffective means of communication in water) that dolphins rely so extensively on sounds for communication. An additional challenge to studying dolphin vocalizations comes from the fact that these animals do not open their mouth to emit their sounds; so it is not easy to spot which individual vocalized. Dolphin sounds are produced inside their head through a modified nostril. The sound waves are projected through a lens of tissue in their forehead straight into the water. Thus there do not even have to be any air bubbles appearing from their blowhole when they vocalize, making it all the more difficult to see what they are up to.

Notwithstanding these challenges, a lot has been learned about dolphin communicative vocalizations in the 50 years since the Caldwells discovered signature whistles.

Vincent Janik and Peter Slater (1998) found that dolphins were more likely to produce their signature whistles if they were separated from other members of their group than if they were close together. Rachel Smolker and colleagues (1993), studying bottlenose dolphins in Shark Bay, Western Australia, found that signature whistles were more frequent just before mothers and calves came back together after a separation and then declined in frequency once they found each other. These findings suggest a role for signature whistles in maintaining group cohesion.

The Caldwells found that captive bottlenose dolphins develop their characteristic signature whistles in the first two years of life (Caldwell & Caldwell, 1979). In captivity, the signature whistles of juvenile dolphins are quite different from those of their parents (Tyack & Sayigh, 1997). But studies of wild dolphins in Sarasota Bay, Florida, have found that only the signature whistles of female dolphins differ from those of their mother: male dolphins develop whistles at least initially more similar to those of their mother (Sayigh et al., 1995). It may not be as important for male dolphins to form signature whistles that are distinct from their mother's because they leave the mother's group quite early in life to form all-male groups. During this phase of life they modify their signature whistles to be more similar to those of their fellow group members (Smolker & Pepper, 1999).

Heidi Harley showed that bottlenose dolphins can discriminate the signature whistles of different dolphins by training captive individuals to press different levers when they heard different dolphins' whistles (Harley, 2008). Further evidence that dolphins can identify each other on the basis just of their whistles comes from a study by Laela Sayigh and colleagues (1999) in which dolphins were found to react more strongly to the whistles of close associates than those of unrelated individuals.

The Caldwells found that dolphins can spontaneously copy sounds (Caldwell & Caldwell, 1972), and Douglas Richards and colleagues found that captive dolphins can be trained to imitate the exact frequency of artificially created sounds (Richards et al., 1984). Peter Tyack (1997) demonstrated that captive dolphins sometimes imitate the signature whistles of other dolphins. These imitated signature whistles are usually those of their close social contacts. Copying of signature whistles has also been found in the wild (Janik, 2000). Stephanie Watwood and colleagues (2005) found that dolphins in Sarasota Bay, Florida, sometimes produce whistles similar to those of absent associates.

We already discussed how dolphins rely on sound to communicate because other means of communication used by mammals, such as sight and odor, are of very limited utility in water. But sound has limitations, too. Janik (2000b) demonstrated that under ideal circumstances a signature whistle could have a range of over ten miles. But Ester Quintana-Rizzo and colleagues (2006), studying dolphins in Sarasota Bay, Florida, observed that in water of 1.6 meters depth (approximately 5 feet) with sea grass growing on the bottom, signature whistle range was reduced to just around 200 meters (220 yards). Interestingly, mothers and calves stayed within calling range of each other.

Human activity is one major factor that affects the amount of noise in water and thus the range over which dolphins can hear each other's signature whistles. Kara Buckstaff (2004) observed that dolphins increase their rate of calling when a boat approaches, perhaps to give the group a chance to come together before the boat's engines are so noisy that they cannot maintain contact any more. Michelle Lemon and colleagues (2006) found that if the dolphins in a pod were already close together when a power boat approached, they did not increase their calling rates.

What could be the function of characteristic identifying signature whistles and their imitation by others? It seems likely that these whistles are an important means of ensuring group cohesion in a social animal that lives in an environment where visual contact cannot always be maintained. Emitting signature whistles is a bit like calling out 'I'm over here!' in a darkened or smoke-filled room.

The practice of imitating others' signature whistles might also act as a way of calling a group together – possibly to request the assistance of other group members. Peter Tyack reported how he and his colleagues temporarily captured a wild dolphin in order to attach an underwater microphone (Tyack, 1997). They kept this dolphin in their corral for an hour. During the first half hour, the dolphin produced its signature whistle 520 times and variant whistles 39 times, with no imitations of any other dolphin's whistle that the researchers could identify. In the second half hour, the captive dolphin quite suddenly started producing imitations of the signature whistle of the oldest dolphin in the group. Signature whistles dropped to 472, but imitations went up to 47, with just 6 variant whistles. Tyack interprets this as the captive dolphin calling for assistance from the oldest member of the group.

Though the dolphins' use of signature whistles is a very interesting example of a communicative system in the wild that is quite different from how animals on land communicate, the nature of that communication is not especially rich. Although, as we shall see in the next chapter, it has proved possible to teach dolphins a complex form of language with a characteristic grammar to which the dolphins are sensitive, there is no evidence of syntactical rules in the natural vocalizations of these animals (Ford, 1989).

THE FUNCTION AND EVOLUTION OF REFERENTIAL CALLS

The discovery that animal calls can refer to something concrete in the world and are not just reflections of the internal state of the animal is a very exciting one. As we shall see in the next chapter, the fact that animal calls can be referential is not enough on its own to make it equivalent to human language, but it is still very thought provoking. What does it tell us about the cognitive capacities of the animals involved?

Some would like to see in the referential calls of animals evidence that they possess a theory of mind. (This concept is explored in Chapter 8.) In brief, it implies that an individual has an understanding that others have minds. Thus one might argue that when a vervet monkey gives a call to alert fellow members of his troupe that there is a snake in the grass, he must have an awareness that the other monkeys are ignorant of the presence of the snake and would like to know about it. Similarly, the discovery that roosters are more likely to give alarm calls when there are hens around to hear them might imply that the roosters are considering the state of mind of the hens before they give their calls. These might be evidence for theory of mind.

But simpler explanations of animal calls are also possible. Dorothy Cheney and Robert Seyfarth, the authors of the research on vervet monkeys alarm calls we have discussed here, consider the underlying capacity that makes it possible for the monkeys to recognize so many different alarm calls and their relationship to many different threats to be an ability to link a sound (such as an alarm call) with a consequence (attack by a predator). This is Pavlovian conditioning (covered in Chapter 5). It is a very basic and widely dispersed form of learning. From the point of view of how the monkeys learn to respond to these sounds, it doesn't make any difference whether the sound comes from the predator itself (perhaps a cracking branch in the undergrowth that gives away the approach of a leopard) or from another member of the troupe. The first case we would just call vigilance, but the second case is communication. Nonetheless, in both cases the underlying cognitive mechanism, Pavlovian conditioning, is the same.

If listening to and acting on an alarm call can be readily understood as an example of Pavlovian conditioning, the production of an alarm call is somewhat more difficult to understand. Cheney and Seyfarth themselves noted that vervet monkeys are born with a repertoire of sounds that they are inclined to make and a tendency to make them in specific circumstances. The monkeys could probably refine their use of the calls they have available to them through associative learning (this time the learning would likely be operant, as the animals would be learning about the consequences of their actions), but it is very hard to see how they could develop a novel call if a new type of threat appeared in their world. Cheney and Seyfarth noted that the development of new alarm calls was rare to nonexistent, writing 'One suspects that many vervets – even many generations of vervets – would die before a new call, signaling a novel escape response, could be incorporated into their repertoire' (Seyfarth & Cheney, 1999, p. 410).

CONCLUSIONS

In the next chapter we shall consider attempts to teach animals forms of human language. In that context, the wild communication of animals may seem restricted. As we shall see in that chapter, there are several aspects of human communication that seem beyond the abilities of any other species. But this is to take an anthropomorphic perspective. Animals do not need the same forms of communication as we do – they needs ways of communicating with each other that solve the problems that they have in their daily lives. The natural systems of communication that we have considered in monkeys, dolphins, chickens, and bees are adapted to solving problems of group cohesion, finding food, and warning of predators. These are the kinds of communicative problems that are of critical importance for their survival.

FURTHER READING

Cheney, D. L. & Seyfarth, R. M. (1990) *How Monkeys See the World*. Chicago: University of Chicago Press.
The researchers who unwrapped the communication system of vervet monkeys summarize their findings in this fascinating book.

McGregor, P. K. (2005) Communication. In J. J. Bolhuis & L-A. Giraldeau (Eds), *The Behavior of Animals*. Oxford: Blackwell Publishing.
A very useful and thorough chapter on animal communication.

Slater, P. J. (2003) Fifty years of bird song research: a case study in animal behaviour. *Animal Behaviour*, 65, 633–639.
Slater summarizes the history of his own and other researchers' work in the understanding of birdsong.

von Frisch, K. R. (1967) *The Dance Language and Orientation of Bees*. London: Oxford University Press.
Von Frisch summarizes his lifetime's work on the communicative system of the honeybee in this fascinating volume.

Web sources

http://acp.eugraph.com/#
This rich site summarizes much research on communication in various species and also contains video and audio files of communication in progress.

http://www.pbs.org/wgbh/nova/bees/dances.html
This is an interactive website where you can learn more about the dance of bees.

http://www.birds.cornell.edu/AllAboutBirds/studying/birdsongs/
This very educational and informative site covers birdsong from many angles.

12 Language

A famished wolf was prowling about in the morning in search of food. As he passed the door of a cottage built in the forest, he heard a Mother say to her child, 'Be quiet, or I will throw you out of the window, and the Wolf shall eat you.' The Wolf sat all day waiting at the door. In the evening he heard the same woman fondling her child and saying: 'You are quiet now, and if the Wolf should come, we will kill him.' The Wolf, hearing these words, went home, gasping with cold and hunger. When he reached his den, Mistress Wolf inquired of him why he returned wearied and supper-less, so contrary to his wont. He replied: 'Why, forsooth! I gave credence to the words of a woman!'

Aesop's Fables, translated G. F. Townsend

Who has not dreamed of one day waking up and being able to understand what the animals around us are saying? Children's stories, adults' daydreams, and movies are full of speaking animals. Babe the pig, Flipper the dolphin, Mickey Mouse, and countless others speak to us with distinctive yet fully comprehensible voices. And don't imagine that the researchers whose ingenious work on the cognitive abilities of animals we have discussed in earlier chapters have not sometimes wished they could just ask their subjects directly: 'So, how many dots can you see?' 'Can you remember what I showed you yesterday?' How often have we looked our subjects in the eye and wished we could cut through the elaborate experimental designs and just ask them straight out.

In this chapter we will look at studies that have attempted to teach something like human language to other species.

On the one hand, attempts to teach human language to members of other species are a frankly anthropocentric project. Clearly it is only from the perspective of a human being that the question of whether any other species might be able to communicate as we do even arises. But it also has to be acknowledged that for centuries people have pondered what it is that makes us human, and one of the most striking and often-discussed distinctions between humans and other animals lies in our use of language. The seventeenth-century French philosopher René Descartes put this quite bluntly: 'It is very remarkable that there are none so depraved and stupid, without even excepting idiots, that they cannot arrange different words together, forming of them a statement by which they make known their thoughts; while, on the other hand, there is no other animal, however perfect and fortunately circumstanced it may be, which can do the same' (Descartes, 1976).

Because much of what needs to be covered in this chapter is controversial, it is prudent, before we consider the research that has looked at the language abilities of animals, to remind ourselves of some of the cautionary tales from Chapter 1 and of the impressive abilities of many animals to notice cause and effect relationships that we considered in Chapter 5.

In Chapter 1 we discussed Clever Hans, the horse who was too clever by half. Hans appeared to be able to perform complex arithmetic and solve other sorts of problems, too, but in reality his cleverness lay not in mathematical ability but in a skill that was almost as ingenious in a different way. Hans was able to detect tiny movements that the people around him made, movements so slight that they failed to notice they were making them. These movements told Hans when he had made enough hoof stomps to answer correctly the question that had been set him. In Chapter 5 we saw that abilities like Hans's are the norm rather than the exception throughout the animal kingdom. All the species that have been tested have shown an ability to learn about signals that predict when important things (like food) are going to happen; and they can also learn what actions they should perform to get food and other items that are important to them. When we look at the attempts to teach human language to other animals, we must keep in mind that these subjects are usually trained by the use of rewards (see Box 12.1), and we must ask ourselves, are these animals really learning language, or are they just learning which signals are followed by reward? Or are they learning which actions they have to perform to obtain reward (whether this is what their trainers intended or not)? Similarly, we must watch out for any human observers present who might be offering almost imperceptible cues to indicate what response is required – just as Clever Hans picked up on the slight cues made by the people around him.

Remember also Lloyd Morgan's canon. According to this precept, we should not ascribe a behavior to a more complex cognitive process if a simpler one is sufficient to account for what we observe. This is a basic principle of all science – without it we can never be sure that we are not over interpreting what we observe.

APE LANGUAGE STUDIES

Words

The earliest attempts to teach human language to apes involved adopting a chimpanzee and encouraging it to talk, just like one would a human baby. In 1931 Professor Winthrop Kellogg of Indiana University and his wife Luella adopted a chimpanzee, Gua, and raised her alongside their son Donald. Donald was 18 months of age when the project started and just beginning to speak. Gua was 2 months younger. The Kelloggs hoped that Donald's influence would cause little Gua to learn language, too, but they were to be disappointed. After 9 months all Gua could say was 'Papa' and that only after a lot of coaching from Winthrop (Wynne, 2004).

In the late 1940s another husband and wife team, Cathy and Keith Hayes, repeated the Kelloggs' experiment – though this time without a human child of their own. Their chimpanzee, Viki, was slightly more successful than Gua and over the course of four years learned to pronounce four words: Mama, Papa, cup, and up (Hayes, 1951).

Both the Kelloggs and the Hayeses noticed that, unlike human infants, their apes showed little inclination to imitate their caregivers and did not engage in the babbling play with sound that is typical of normally developing human children.

To most observers it appeared that the studies of Gua and Viki had demonstrated that apes are not capable of learning human language. But then in the late 1960s another husband and wife team, Beatrice and Allen Gardner, of the University of Nevada, proposed that the limitations of prior ape language studies had not lain in any fundamental inability to understand language on the part of the chimpanzees but on the method chosen to communicate with them. Many observers, starting with the English diarist Samuel Pepys in the seventeenth century, had noted that chimps appeared to try to communicate with hand gestures. The Gardners decided to attempt to teach an ape to communicate with the sign language used by deaf people in the United States, American Sign Language (ASL).

All subsequent studies of ape language have used one of two methods: ASL or a system of visual symbols, the best known of which is Yerkish – named after one of the early researchers in animal psychology, Robert Yerkes. Yerkish is a system of symbols, expressed by pressing keys on a keyboard. The methods used to train chimps words are detailed in Box 12.1.

BOX 12.1   TEACHING WORDS TO AN APE

The first people to attempt to teach a chimpanzee ASL were Allen and Beatrice Gardner, who adopted a wild-born female chimpanzee, Washoe, in 1966 when she was about one year old. Washoe was housed in a trailer in the Gardners' backyard and was accompanied by human trainers who communicated with each other and with her entirely in ASL at all times. They did not use spoken language even to communicate with one another when in Washoe's presence. The Gardners had hoped that Washoe would spontaneously imitate ASL signs, but in practice they mainly taught her to use signs by molding. Molding is a process of physically guiding the chimp's hand into the desired position. Later ASL was used by Francine Patterson to communicate with a gorilla named Koko. Unlike the Gardners with Washoe, Patterson also simultaneously spoke English with Koko, in the hope that using two communication systems might enhance Koko's language acquisition. Again, training was by imitation and molding of the correct signs. Herb Terrace's chimp, Nim Chimpsky (named in teasing reference to the linguist Noam Chomsky, who believed that only humans can learn language), was also trained in ASL in a similar manner to Washoe (Figure 12.1).

Figure 12.1   *Nim signing 'Me hug cat' to a human trainer*

Source: Courtesy of H. Terrace.

Yerkish was developed by Duane Rumbaugh and colleagues at the Yerkes Regional Primate Centre in Atlanta Georgia. Lana, a chimpanzee, was the first student of this system of communication. She was trained to press keys on large keyboards (Figure 12.2). The keys were of several different colors, and each key was embossed with a different lexigram. A lexigram is a diagram that has symbolic value in the language system. Just as the word 'apple' has nothing that looks, sounds, or tastes like an apple about it, so the Yerkish lexigram for apple (a blue triangle) is completely arbitrary, with no apple-like qualities. Lana was trained to press the keys in appropriate grammatical order by rewarding her with foods she liked when she got something right. First, she was required only to press one key at a time to obtain reward, but with more training, ever more complex sequences were required of her before she would be given a reward.

A simpler symbolic language was used by David Premack to communicate with a chimpanzee named Sarah. This language was also based on symbols, but these symbols were made from metal-based plastic chips of different shapes and colors. Again the appearance of the chip bore no resemblance to the item it named. The chips were stuck onto a magnetic board in sentences written vertically. Just like Lana, Sarah was rewarded with favorite foods for correctly responding to progressively longer and more complex instructions in the symbolic language.

Figure 12.2   *Lana operating a Yerkish keyboard*

Source: Courtesy of D. Rumbaugh.

All of the methods described in Box 12.1 have achieved some success in teaching some words to their subjects. For example, Washoe, the chimp trained in ASL by the Gardners, was able to produce 132 ASL signs when her training ended after nearly 5 years. Koko (the gorilla trained in Yerkish signs by Francine Patterson) attained a vocabulary of 250 signs after 4 years, and Nim (the chimp trained by Herb Terrace and colleagues) learned some 125 ASL signs in 3½ years. These numbers may seem quite impressive, but it is worth bearing in mind that a two-year-old child learns new vocabulary at an astonishing rate of about 10 new words every day! Koko's four year 250 sign vocabulary is less then one month's work for a typical human two-year-old. Figure 12.3 compares Nim's acquisition of ASL signs with that of a deaf child learning ASL and a hearing child learning English. Clearly there is a massive difference here. And apes are no longer unique among animals in the number of words they can understand.

Figure 12.3   *Growth of Nim's vocabulary over a 32-week period compared with that of a child just after her second birthday*

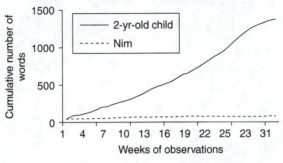

Box 12.2 outlines a recent study on a dog, Chaser, who comprehends over a thousand words of English.

BOX 12.2   ONE DOG'S VOCABULARY

John Pilley and Alliston Reid recently reported on a border collie, Chaser, who knows the names of over 1 000 different toys as well as a small number of verbs (Pilley & Reid, 2011). Julianne Kaminski and colleagues (2004) had previously presented tests on a dog (also a border collie) that knew the names of over 200 objects, but Pilley and Reid's study differed from that of Kaminski and colleagues not only in that Chaser knows the names of more objects but also in demonstrating more about how their dog learned these words and what she understood about the words being used.

One factor that differentiates Chaser from any other dog that has been reported to have a substantial vocabulary is that John Pilley, one of the scientists responsible for the study, trained Chaser himself. Thus the method of training is fully known (Chaser was mainly rewarded for collecting a named toy by being allowed to chase that toy), and Pilley and Reid reported on Chaser's rate of learning. As shown in Figure 12.4, Chaser's vocabulary grew at a very steady rate over the course of the three years that she was in training. There is nothing to suggest that Chaser was reaching the limit of the number of words she could learn when the study was terminated after 36 months.

Chaser's knowledge of vocabulary was tested periodically throughout her three years of training. A group of objects selected from all of those she had been trained on was placed on the floor, and Chaser was instructed to collect them one by one by name only. In routine tests during training, Chaser was required to collect one particular toy from eight different mixtures of toys. To collect the toy once from a group of eight might occur by chance one time in eight. To collect the correct toy from eight different groups of eight would be expected to occur by chance only one time in less than 16 million. Each month Chaser was also tested with five groups of 20 objects. In these tests Chaser and her trainer could not see each other as she went in another room to retrieve the named item. To be considered 'learned', Chaser had to get every single test with that object correct.

Figure 12.4   *Chaser on top of a pile of all the toys she knows the names of*

In addition to a large vocabulary, Chaser's training and testing also led to several further interesting results. The first was that, in addition to many nouns, Chaser was also taught three different verbs: take, paw, and nose. 'Take' indicated that Chaser should pick up an object; 'paw' and 'nose' meant that she should touch the object with the named part of her body. Pilley and Reid tested Chaser with three objects, each of which she was instructed to either take, paw, or nose. The order of commands was fully randomized over 14 trials. Chaser got every single one of them correct. This indicates two things. The first is that the object names really functioned as nouns for Chaser. Prior studies of animals with large vocabularies of object names had been criticized for not being able to demonstrate that the object names were truly nouns and not commands to fetch the object. Second, this experiment showed that Chaser could differentiate verbs from nouns.

Pilley and Reid also investigated whether Chaser had any comprehension for common nouns – words such as 'ball' and 'chair', which can refer to many different unique objects. Among the many items that Chaser had learned names for were many different balls and Frisbees. The remaining objects in Chaser's vocabulary were all toys. Using the same methods as in the original training, Pilley and Reid taught Chaser that each of these objects could also be referred to as balls, Frisbees, or toys. In tests, Chaser successfully discriminated the three classes of objects from each other, but she also discriminated between toys and non-toys: items around the house that she was not allowed to play with. This categorization is particularly interesting because objects that are toys are very diverse, and of course objects that are not toys have little if anything in common with each other beyond the fact that Chaser was not allowed to play with them.

Rico, the dog discovered and tested by Kaminski and colleagues (2004), had shown that she could appreciate that a novel name should apply to a novel object. Rico was instructed to collect an item with a name she had never heard before from a collection of objects, all of which she had been taught names for except one. Rico reliably returned with the novel object in these tests. Pilley and Reid also carried out these kinds of tests with Chaser. Chaser also learned in a single opportunity that a novel name must apply to a novel object and she could retain these newly learned object names for at least eight days.

Producing words or signs is one thing, but what about the use of these words? How much of what they were signing did the apes really understand? With the recent achievements of dogs such as Rico (Kaminski et al., 2004) and Chaser (Pilley & Reid, 2011), described in Box 12.2, apes no longer even hold the record for the largest number of human signs understood by a nonhuman. Can the claim be substantiated that by learning so many ASL or Yerkish signs, the apes were really understanding language?

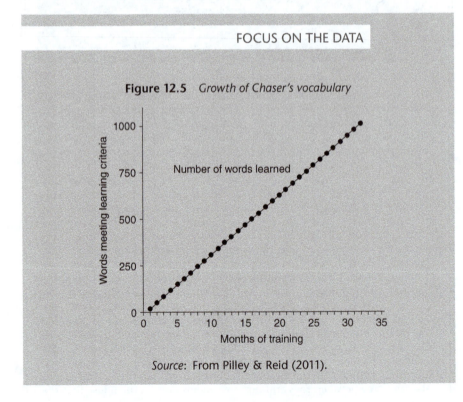

FOCUS ON THE DATA

Figure 12.5   *Growth of Chaser's vocabulary*

Number of words learned

Source: From Pilley & Reid (2011).

Figure 12.5 shows Chaser's success in learning new words over almost three years of training. It can be seen that her rate of learning new words showed no sign of slowing down over this extended period of training.

One phenomenon that has been pointed to as evidence that language-trained apes have a deeper understanding of the meanings of the signs they have been taught is the ability to come up with new words. The Gardner's chimp Washoe, for example, signed, 'water bird' apparently to indicate a swan; Lucy (a chimpanzee who had received two years of language training similar to Washoe's) signaled 'drink fruit' for watermelon; and Lana (a chimp trained in Yerkish symbols) signed, 'apple which-is orange-color' to identify the fruit orange. In each case the ape did not know the correct word for the item but seemed to come up with a suitable name from its available lexicon. Or did they? How do we know that Washoe was devising a new word for swan when she signed 'water bird'? Could she not just have likely been signing for the two things she could see, 'water' and 'bird'? What is the evidence that she intended these two signs to refer to the one thing, that she meant a type of bird, a water bird? Similarly, how do we know that Lucy meant 'drink fruit' as a name for watermelon rather than as a request to be allowed to drink the fruit? A ripe melon is a fruit with a great deal of fluid in it. The problem here is that anecdotes alone will not do the job – without carefully designed tests and complete contextual information judgment must be suspended. Anecdotes typically suffer from lacking critical background information, but they are also unreliable because of an insidious reporting bias. Anyone who observes the behavior of animals is inevitably most drawn to the interesting, curious, and exciting aspects of the animals' behavior. The thousands of times the dog fails to open the gate, the cat does not knock her food down from the shelf, or the ASL-trained chimp strings two signs together in a totally meaningless or repetitive fashion go unrecorded. Without a record of the frequency of these failures, however, the occasional anecdote of an interesting success is quite uninterpretable.

In the case of Lana signing 'apple which-is orange-color', a transcript is available (Rumbaugh & Gill, 1977):

In this exchange, Tim, the trainer is holding an orange, which he finally gives Lana at the end. There is no apple present, nor is Shelley (another trainer) in the testing area. Words linked by hyphens are one symbol in Yerkish, comments in italics were added by Rumabugh and Gill in the original publication to aid a reader's understanding of what was happening.

Tim: What color-of this?
Lana: Color-of this orange
Tim: Yes.

Lana: Tim give cup which-is red. *[This was probably an attempt to request the orange however, because a red cup was part of her object/color naming materials, Tim responded with the latter object.]*

Tim: Yes. *[Thereupon he gave her the cup, which she discarded.]*

Lana: Tim give which-is shut?

Shelley give?

Tim: No Shelley.

Lana: Eye. *[A frank error, probably.]*

Tim give which-is orange?

Tim: What which-is orange?

Lana: Tim give apple which-is green. *[At this point Lana frequently confused the keys for the colors orange and green.]*

Tim: No apple which-is green. *[In other words, 'I have no green apple to give.]'*

Lana: Tim give apple which-is orange. *[Thereupon she bounded with apparent enthusiasm to the door to receive 'the orange-colored apple.]'*

Tim: Yes. *[And he gave it to her.]*

Viewed in full, Lana's production of 'apple which-is orange' seems much less compelling. The trainer initiated the 'color-of' dialogue, and even the 'apple' was not Lana's spontaneous name for the object Tim was holding. She refers to it as 'cup' and 'shut' (and possibly 'eye') before she first mentions apple, and when she does, she calls it 'apple which-is green'. All of which is much more suggestive of her having learned that certain sequences of symbols are likely to lead to reward than that she really understands the meaning of these symbols at some deeper level.

An interesting example of the use of language in a novel way that suggests an understanding of the meaning of words was shown by Sarah, a chimpanzee trained by David Premack (1976) in another symbolic language. She was taught some new words by having their relation to existing words spelled out to her. Sarah was taught the symbol for the previously unknown color 'brown' with the sequence 'brown color-of chocolate'. The statements 'color-of' and 'chocolate' were already known to her, though there was no chocolate visible at the moment of training. Sarah was then presented with four different-colored disks and asked to select the brown one, which she did successfully. This demonstration is interesting not just for the novel use of an unknown word but also for the reference to an object (chocolate) that is not present. There is a problem here because Sarah was extensively drilled with 'color-of' constructions, and since she was using symbols on magnetic backgrounds (see Box 12.1), her trainers were able to restrict the number of symbols available to her so that the task was much easier than it might appear at first. Nonetheless, this is an interesting demonstration.

Another important quality of our human language is known as displaced reference – the ability to converse about things that are not immediately present. I am talking to you about chimpanzees. There are no chimps here in my office where I write, and I suspect that there are no chimps where you are as you read this, and yet we can converse about chimps. Talking about objects that are not present is something we do all the time, and it is a very significant part of what makes our human language so powerful. What is the evidence that this crucial feature of language is present in the ape language studies? In the above example of Sarah learning the color brown by reference to chocolate that was not physically present at that moment of time, we have a suggestion of displaced reference. Other examples, however, are hard to find. The apes in these language studies are almost always signing about objects that are physically present at the moment they are being asked to sign about them.

Sentences

Human language certainly involves a lot of words. Educated English speakers typically have a vocabulary of over 80,000 words. It is not, however, vocabulary alone that makes language so amazingly productive; rather it is the ability to string words together into sentences. Sentences link words together according to certain rules that determine their meaning – whether they mean anything at all and what that meaning is. The ability to build sentences turns language from a tool able to express 80,000 ideas into something that can be used to express any idea at all. The number of possible sentences in English or any other language is

Figure 12.6 *Change in length of utterance for Nim, a deaf child, and a hearing child*

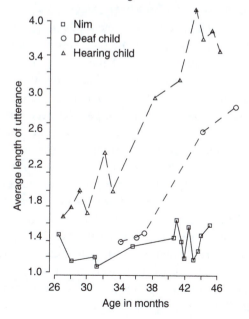

potentially unlimited. Is there any evidence from the ape language studies that any of their subjects are able to build anything akin to sentences?

The first item we can consider is the length of the expressions that the apes uttered. The vast majority of Nim's productions during the last year of his training were of just one word. Figure 12.6 shows how Nim's mean length of utterance increased compared with that of deaf and hearing children. Where the children's curves show a rapid spurt of longer and longer expressions used in the second and third years of life, Nim just plods along using utterances with a mean length around 1.2 (Terrace, 1983). The other scientists working with other ASL-trained apes have offered no evidence that their charges were producing longer utterances.

But of course length of utterance is not everything. These apes have all occasionally made longer utterances than just one or two symbols. Nim's longest utterance was 'Give orange me give eat orange me eat orange give me eat orange give me you.' While not exactly hard to understand, it was not evidence of much grammatical sense either (Terrace, 1979).

Suppose your two-year-old son said to you, 'Please mummy give me an M&M.' Assuming you are the child's mother, you would have every right to be pleased – that is a fairly advanced sentence for a two-year-old. In comparison, let's consider an utterance of Lana's: 'Please machine give M&M period.' At first glance this would seem to suggest that Lana has an understanding of words and can formulate grammatical sentences with a high level of expertise. Before we leap to this conclusion, however, we should inform ourselves about what Lana is actually doing and how she achieved this feat.

As Box 12.1 describes, Lana was trained to press keys on a keyboard in order to obtain rewards from a machine. At first, Lana only had to press the key for the reward (in this case an M&M). Next she was trained to prefix her request with a key that her trainers labeled 'please' and follow it with a key labeled 'period' before her request would be granted. When your two-year-old remembers to say 'please', you are probably happy to see that he is beginning to understand some basic social niceties. However, when Lana learned to press a key her trainers called 'please', there is no reason to assume that she had learned anything other than that this key was necessary if the 'M&M' key was going to function for her to get an M&M. Similarly, as Lana was trained to add the key her trainers labeled 'machine' between the 'please' key and the 'M&M' key, there is simply no reason to assume that this key meant anything to Lana at all. During this training the machine connected to Lana's keyboard was the only thing offering M&Ms; so Lana was not discriminating between the machine and anything else that might have given her a candy. The 'machine' key was just another key that had to be pressed in the right order to obtain a reward. Remember also that these 'sentences' of Lana's are not spontaneous productions or imitations of the actions of her trainers, as a child's language typically is, but rather the result of thousands of trials of explicit training. Over and over again, Lana was required to press keys in the desired order to get the reward she wanted. As seen in several previous chapters, most notably Chapter 4, chimpanzees are very adept at pushing a large number of keys in order to obtain reward.

Interestingly, human infants do not appear to be given much direct training on grammar at all. Parents are much more concerned with praising their children for honest, accurate speech than grammatically correct utterances. Children do not usually respond very effectively to direct grammatical training. McNeill (1970, pp. 106–107) gives the following delightful example:

> *Child*: Nobody don't like me.
> *Mother*: No, say 'nobody likes me.'
> *Child*: Nobody don't like me.
> [Eight repetitions of the above exchange]
> *Mother*: No, now listen carefully; say 'nobody likes me.'
> *Child*: Oh! Nobody don't likes me.

Psychologists interested in the development of language puzzle over how, when parents are so concerned with truth and so little with grammar, the process usually results in children who tell lies that are grammatically correct!

Overall, the evidence for grammatical structure in the spontaneous utterances of any of the language-trained apes is very slight. As we have seen, most of the spontaneous statements made by these animals have been extremely short (typically less than two signs long), leaving little room for grammatical development. Some preferred patterns of word order have been found in these studies. For example, the Gardners reported that in combinations of 'you', 'me', and an action sign, Washoe preferred to put the sign for the subjects before the sign for the action. She also preferred to put the sign for 'you' in front of the sign for 'me' in utterances that combined those two signs (Gardner and Gardner, 1971). Patterson (1978) reported that Koko usually put the sign 'more' in first position in most of the utterances that contained it. However, syntax is not a set of rules about where specific words or signs appear in a sentence but about the ordering of different types of words. Imagine if I placed the word 'more' at the beginning of every sentence that contains it. More would that be grammatical? Obviously not. In English it is usual to place subject, action, and object in that order. Consequently, in this simple sentence structure, the word 'more' would belong at the beginning of a sentence only if it refers to the subject of the sentence ('More water flooded into houses'). If I wanted 'more' to refer to the object of the sentence, then it would belong toward the end ('Water flooded into more houses'). A habit for putting one word or another at some position in a sentence is not itself grammatical.

Kanzi

By the early 1980s the great excitement generated among those interested in the possibilities of language in other species by Washoe, Lana, Nim, and the other apes in language training had given way to disappointment as the problems with these animals' performances became apparent. It was around this time that a new species entered the ape language arena. Kanzi is a bonobo – previously known as pygmy chimpanzee. Bonobos are a little smaller than chimpanzees. Kanzi was trained by Duane Rumbaugh and Sue Savage-Rumbaugh to express himself with Yerkish symbols, but they communicate with him in spoken English. Kanzi's mother, Matata, was the object of a study, and he just hung around and watched while she was trained. Matata was not a successful language student and was dropped from the project after about two years. At the end of this time it was found that Kanzi quickly picked up how to use the Yerkish keyboard to indicate things that he wanted, and he could also 'name' things he was shown by pressing the correct symbol.

Kanzi shows displaced reference when he uses symbols to indicate places he would like to be taken, places that are obviously not physically present until he is taken to them.

Sue Savage-Rumbaugh and colleagues (1993) carried out on Kanzi the most thorough tests of grammatical comprehension of any of the ape language studies. They tested Kanzi with 310 different sentences; for example, 'Would you please carry the straw?' Of these 310, Kanzi responded correctly to 298. First off, Savage-Rumbaugh and colleagues acknowledged that there was no evidence to suggest that words such as 'would', 'please', 'the', and so on, carried any meaning for Kanzi. They maintained, however, that Kanzi did understand the syntax in the remaining words. That Kanzi could understand, to take an example that was not used in the study, that 'Dog bites man' means something different from 'Man bites dog.' The problem with this interpretation is that very few of the commands on which Kanzi was tested were at all ambiguous as to what could be done to what. Consider the example given above, 'Would you please carry the straw?' Kanzi could carry a straw, but could a straw carry Kanzi? Certainly not. Kanzi correctly responded to 'Grab Jeannine' and 'Give the trash to Jeannine.' In the first, Jeannine is the object of the sentence (the thing grabbed); in the second she is the subject (the person to whom the trash should be given): Did Kanzi understand this grammatical distinction when he responded correctly to these two commands? The most likely answer is no. In the first example, the verb 'grab' does not permit any other interpretation than to grab the thing named. In the second example, Kanzi could hardly give Jeannine to the trash instead of the trash to Jeannine!

Kanzi was presented with just 21 pairs of commands that could form a test of grammatical comprehension; the pairs of instructions were offered in two different forms, such as 'Make the [toy] doggie bite the [toy] snake,' and 'Make the [toy] snake bite the [toy] doggie.' Although Savage-Rumbaugh and colleagues reported that Kanzi got 57 percent of these items correct, a reanalysis of the original results indicated that Savage-Rumbaugh and colleagues' grading of Kanzi's responses had been extremely generous (Wynne, 2004). Rescored to eliminate overinterpretation, Kanzi actually achieved fewer than 30 percent correct responses to these critical commands that demand grammatical comprehension for their correct completion.

Interestingly, Kanzi's spontaneously utterances remain extremely short: The vast majority of them (94 %) are just a single sign (Savage-Rumbaugh et al., 1986).

To summarize, the claims of their advocates notwithstanding, the ape language projects have generated very little evidence of linguistic comprehension or production. The labeling of the signs produced by chimpanzees and gorillas with English words has obscured a great deal more than it has uncovered. Convincing evidence for even rudimentary features of what could be considered language understanding, such as displaced reference (using a sign to refer to an object that is not present), is extremely scarce. As for syntax and grammar, the typical ape's one- or two-word utterance hardly offers much scope for grammatical prowess, and very little has been observed.

LANGUAGE TRAINING WITH OTHER SPECIES

Communicating with Dolphins

Aquatic mammals have sparked a lot of interest among psychologists because of their highly developed brains. In addition, as discussed in the previous chapter, dolphins and other species of cetaceans spend a lot of time making noises at each other that indicate some system of communication among themselves. Though vocal mimicry has been demonstrated in dolphins, the technical problems in processing their very high pitched vocalizations have, up to the present, prevented anybody from training them to produce sounds on demand that could then be tested for language qualities. Louis Herman and colleagues (1984) at the University of Hawaii carried out a fascinating study on language comprehension in dolphins that we shall consider here. (A report on a similar study carried out by Robert Gisiner and Ronald Schusterman on sea lions was published in 1992.) Herman studied the comprehension of commands by two bottle-nosed dolphins, Akeakamai and Phoenix. Phoenix was trained on noises generated by computer; Akeakamai was trained to follow gestural commands.

Here we follow Akeakamai's training to understand a gestural language. A trainer standing at the side of the pool (and wearing goggles so that her eyes could not give anything away) signed certain gestures and then rewarded Akeakamai if she followed the instructions correctly. Figure 12.7 shows some of the commands that Akeakamai was taught. In total, she learned over 50 signs. This is a relatively small number compared with that of the ape language projects, but these signs were carefully chosen so that interesting tests of displaced reference and syntax could be carried out. In displaced reference tests, Akeakamai was given a command that related to an object that was out of view, and she had to find it before she could carry out the command. She was successful in completing most of these tests.

Although the gestural language on which Akeakamai was trained had relatively few words, it had a strict grammar, and so a number of sentences could be constructed with meaning depending on the ordering of the words. Akeakamai

Figure 12.7 *Some of the commands used to train Akeakamai*

was tested on 193 novel sentences and performed 85 percent of the commands successfully. For example, in Akeakamai's gestural language, 'Pipe hoop fetch' means 'Take the hoop to the pipe', whereas 'Hoop pipe fetch' means 'Take the pipe to the hoop'. Akeakamai was clearly successful in differentiating these two commands and on similar sentences up to four words long. In further tests, Akeakamai was also presented some semantically nonsensical commands, such as, 'Person water fetch', which means to take the stream of water to the person. Akeakamai ignored such impossible requests while carrying out novel but possible commands of equivalent complexity without difficulty.

Irene Pepperberg and Alex

Alex, the African gray parrot who was in training with Irene Pepperberg for over two decades, has been mentioned before (in Chapters 4 and 9). Pepperberg exploited the wonderful vocal mimicry for which parrots are famous and trained Alex to speak (broken) English. Using her 'model/rival' technique (see Box 4.2), Alex was trained at first simply to name objects, but in subsequent studies he learned successfully to identify the color, shape, material, and even number of objects. Latterly, Alex has correctly answered questions of a high degree of complexity, such as, 'What shape is the green wood?' Alex's need for human company makes it difficult to completely rule out his picking up the correct answers from subtle cues his human companions may give out, much as Clever Hans did. However, the very wide range of responses that Alex can produce make this less likely than in the case of Hans, who just stomped his foot. Pepperberg has not pursued the questions of the Alex's understanding of grammar, preferring to exploit the parrot's language skills as a tool in uncovering other cognitive abilities.

CONCLUSIONS

In the past 30 years, several attempts to teach sign language to chimpanzees have generated a lot of excitement, but in reality it is unlikely that anything approximating human language capacity has been demonstrated in any nonhuman species. Many of the claims made on behalf of these animals have been exaggerated. Viewed in an evolutionary perspective, it isn't really surprising that other species do not share our language. Modern human language probably came into being sometime between 100,000 and 500,000 years ago. The human ability to make precise movements of the mouth in order to form word sounds has been linked to a gene called FOXP2 (Marcus and Fisher, 2003), which it is estimated became widespread in human populations only 200,000 years ago (Enard et al., 2002). In comparison, human evolution went on its own way from that of our closest living relative, the chimpanzee, about five or six million years ago. Though five million years is also not a long time in evolutionary terms, it is well before we developed language.

In recent years discussion of the possibilities for language in nonhumans has moved away from consideration of the traditional structures of speech like grammar, syntax, vocabulary, and so on toward a novel consideration of what makes human language different from other forms of communication. Marc Hauser and colleagues (2002) proposed that the capacity for language can be separated into two sets of skills. What they called the 'faculty of language in the broad sense' (FLB) includes many cognitive abilities that are used in human language but are not unique to it. This includes capacities such as memory, attention, the ability to create sounds, and so on. These abilities, as we have seen elsewhere in this text, are clearly not unique to human beings. But Hauser and colleagues also delineated what they called the 'faculty of language in the narrow sense' (FLN). According to Hauser and colleagues (2002) the FLN consists of just one critical ability – recursion. In a later paper the same authors (Fitch et al., 2005) somewhat softened their original position and indicated that FLN contains many skills, none of them unique to humans. Rather, the uniqueness of humans lies in adapting these cognitive abilities to the function of communication.

Hauser and colleagues (2002) focused research interest on the question of recursion. Recursion is a property of sequences of symbols – usually in language the symbols we are considering are words, but they don't have to be to understand recursion. In general, recursion just means the embedding of something inside itself. Thus a simple example is a picture of an object that includes a copy of the picture of the object. For example, a box of breakfast cereal that includes on its cover a picture of the box of cereal being poured into a bowl is an example of recursion. Another example of recursion is the nesting Russian dolls, each one of which contains a smaller version of the doll hidden inside itself.

In language, recursion refers to the way that sentences can be embedded within other sentences to make longer sentences. For example, the sentence 'John was dancing' can be embedded within the sentence 'John was singing' to make the longer sentence 'John, while dancing, was singing.' This is distinct from the possibility of just stringing two sentences together with 'and' ('John was singing and dancing'), which does not require recursion.

The jury is presently still out on the importance of recursion to human language, but interest in this question has prompted a number of interesting studies both on humans and other species. One study that produced evidence that an understanding of recursion is not unique to humans was carried out by Kentaro Abe and Dai Watanabe (2011). Abe and Watanabe chose Bengalese finches as their subjects. These songbirds are inclined to sing back at songs they hear and will sing more to songs that strike them as novel and unfamiliar than to songs they have become familiar with. Abe and Watanabe familiarized the birds to songs that contained recursion. These songs were made up of three different kinds of song syllables that they labeled A, C, and F. A typical recursive song went A A C F F. This song is recursive because of the way the C syllable is tucked inside the A and F syllables. Abe and Watanabe exposed the birds to novel songs, some of which respected the recursive grammar even though they contained new elements or were longer than the songs the birds had first been exposed to, and other songs that did not respect the recursive grammar. The researchers found that the finches sang back more to nongrammatical songs than to novel songs that were grammatically correct, indicating that these birds do possess a sensitivity to recursion.

The popular media have encouraged the belief that animal psychologists have achieved Dr. Doolittle's prowess with at least some other species, such as chimpanzees and dolphins. It is often claimed, for example, that dolphins have a complex communicative system, and there are even those who claim to understand what dolphins are saying. This is a case where reality is a little less exciting. In the case of dolphins, no serious attempt has been reported of two-way communication with people. Certainly dolphins can be trained to carry out simple commands, but then so can dogs (dolphins' understanding of syntax has never been demonstrated in dogs, but it has never been attempted either).

Some of the early attempts to teach human language to apes look in retrospect somewhat misguided. It is far more informative to consider what structural aspects of language make it interesting (e.g., displaced reference, syntax, or recursion) and to focus study on those components. Dolphins do appear to understand a simple syntax; some chimpanzees and dolphins have shown an understanding that symbols can refer to things that are not present. Some birds are sensitive to recursion.

The idea of teaching something like our language to animals and uncovering direct evidence about their minds just by asking them has a deceptive simplicity to it. In fact, interpreting what they say is very difficult. This may be what the Austrian philosopher Ludwig Wittgenstein meant when he said, 'If a lion could speak, we could not understand him'.

FURTHER READING

Hess, E. (2008) *Nim Chimpsky: The Chimp Who Would Be Human*. London: Bantam. Hess gives an evenhanded account of Nim's life and the controversies that swirled around him.

Premack, D. & Premack, A. (1983) *The Mind of an Ape*. New York: Norton.
Savage-Rumbaugh, S. (1994) *Kanzi*. New York: Oxford University Press.
Terrace, H. (1979) *Nim*. New York: Knopf.
These three books provide fascinating personal accounts of teaching chimps to use sign language.

Wallman, J. (1992) *Aping Language*. Cambridge, UK: Cambridge University Press.
Wallman gives a detailed and highly critical account of the ape language studies.

Wynne, C. D. L. (2006) *Do Animals Think?* Princeton, NJ: Princeton University Press.
This book, by one of the present authors, extends the discussion of ape language studies and other forms of animal communication.

Web sources

http://epsych.msstate.edu/adaptive/vikiVideo/
This website includes a large selection of movies of the Hayeses' chimp Viki showing what she could do.

http://www.psy.fsu.edu/history/wnk/ape.html
This web page outlines Kellogg's experiment with Gua, the first chimpanzee used in language training. However, it does not include any movie footage. Several interesting movies can be found on YouTube by searching for 'Kellogg, Gua, chimpanzee'.

http://www.dolphin-institute.org/resource_guide/animal_language.htm
This website, set up by Louis Herman, the researcher who studied Akeakamai and Phoenix, is an excellent summary of that research project.

Several original movies of Washoe in language training have been uploaded to YouTube by J. Patrick Malone. They can be found by searching for 'Washoe Malone'.

13 Conclusions and Comparisons

A Man and a Lion were discussing the relative strength of men and lions in general. The Man contended that he and his fellows were stronger than lions by reason of their greater intelligence. 'Come now with me', he cried, 'and I will soon prove that I am right.' So he took him into the public gardens and showed him a statue of Hercules overcoming the Lion and tearing his mouth in two.

'That is all very well,' said the Lion, 'but proves nothing, for it was a man who made the statue.'

Aesop's Fables, translated G. F. Townsend

How do animals differ psychologically from each other, and from us? This question has fascinated comparative psychologists for over a century. It is not, unfortunately, a question that has proved easy to find a way of answering. Evolution teaches us to expect similarities in the psychology of closely related species and differences in the psychology of distantly related species, but it does not tell us what the appropriate measures of psychological similarity and dissimilarity might be. Evolution also teaches us that every species has adapted over generations to thrive in a particular part of the world – that species' ecological niche. The fact that every species is adapted to its own niche with its own adaptive problems to deal with means that it is difficult to meaningfully compare the cognitive talents of different species. As the interaction between the man and the lion quoted above from Aesop's Fables indicates, each species is well adapted to its chosen environment, and comparisons can be unhelpful and even offensive.

Though the task of comparing psychological abilities in different species may be difficult both philosophically and practically, it is important enough to be worth making the attempt. Consequently, in this final chapter we review various ways of comparing the cognitive abilities of different species.

BRAIN SIZE

All behavior starts in the nervous system. Consequently, one might expect the size of the brain to have some impact on the complexity and intelligence of behavior that an animal can achieve. A simple ranking of animals in terms of their brain size, however, would place elephants and whales, with brains often in excess of five kilograms, at the top of the list. This does not sound right at all. Though we do not know much about the cognitive abilities of

Figure 13.1 *Brain mass against body mass for several different species of vertebrates*

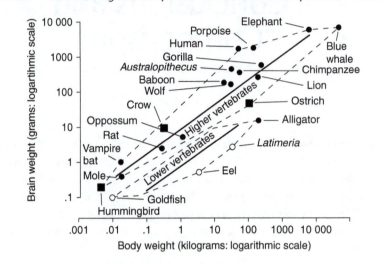

Source: From Jerison (1973).

elephants and whales, we have nothing to suggest that they are more intelligent than some of the smaller-brained species discussed here (like jays and crows). Surely they have the largest brains at least in part because they have the largest bodies. All the organs of the body change size in proportion: feet, legs, arms, head, and brain, too. An animal with a larger body will typically have a larger brain in proportion to that body. Figure 13.1 shows the relationship between brain weight and body weight in many different species of vertebrates. Heavier animals typically have heavier brains. It is also clear that not all animals have the same relationship between their brain weight and their body weight. The heavy line shows the typical relationship between brain weight and body weight. Some species, like humans and porpoises, fall above the line – this means they have larger than average brains for their body sizes. Other species, like eels and alligators, have smaller than average brains for their body sizes – they fall below the line.

What we need is a measure of brain size *after taking account of* the differences in body mass. Such a measure is the *cephalization index*. The cephalization index (known as *K*) measures how big an animal's brain is after taking into account its body size. Higher K values mean the animal has a larger than average brain for its body size, and smaller Ks imply a smaller brain than the norm. In effect, K is a measure of how far an animal is from the solid line in Figure 13.1.

As shown in Figure 13.2, for 'simple' mammals, K values around 0.1 are typical. Many mammals have K values around 0.2. Primates and whales have K values in the 0.2 to 0.3 range. Higher up this scale, dolphins have a cephalization index of 0.64, and humans are at the top of the class at 0.89.

Figure 13.2   *Cephalization indexes of several species*

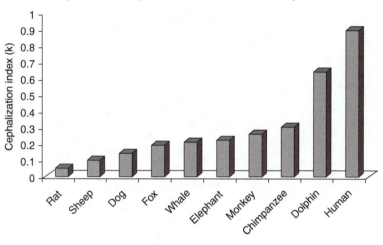

Source: Data from Russell (1979).

The simplicity of K is attractive, and K values also generally coincide with popular conceptions of the intelligence of different species (Beren et al., 1999). This simplicity brings with it serious drawbacks, however. There are many factors beside behavioral complexity that influence the size of brain a particular creature will have (Kaas, 2000). For birds that fly, for example, weight is a very critical concern, just as it is for machines that fly. Consequently, birds may have evolved smaller brains for their body size than land-based animals not because of any limitations in their psychological processes but because they have evolved a more compact brain under the evolutionary pressure to keep weight down. At the other end of the scale, dolphins may have evolved their exceptionally large brains not because of the cognitive demands of their lifestyles but because in water the weight of a large brain is relatively unimportant. Consequently, the brain has grown without the constraint that gravity imposes on land-dwelling animals.

In any case, all brain is not created equal. Much brain tissue is taken up with controlling breathing, movement, digestion, and other essential but not very cognitive activities. To compare total brain sizes, even after allowing for different body sizes, is still to confuse many different things with the psychological questions we are interested in. The part of the brain that is particularly well developed in humans is the neocortex. It has been argued that the size of the neocortex reflects advanced intelligence. Figure 13.3 shows a typical human brain compared with the brains of some other animals. You can see that the neocortex shows characteristic folds. This is because, in our brains, the neocortex has become so large that it can fit inside our skulls only by folding. In most other species, the neocortex is much smaller compared with the rest of the brain and consequently needs much less folding to fit inside the animal's head.

Figure 13.3 *Human brain compared with that of a reptile, fish, bird, and rat*

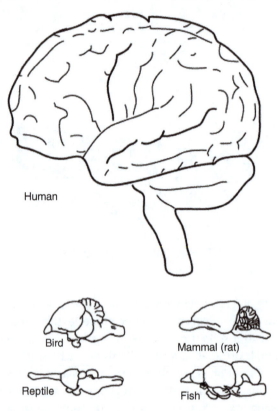

In lowly insectivores, the neocortex is only 13 percent of total brain weight; in rodents it is around 30 percent and in primates above 50 percent; in the human case, the neocortex makes up a magnificent 80 percent of total brain volume.

But even this measure has problems. For one thing, only mammals have a neocortex. Bird brains, for example, have taken a different track in evolution and have no neocortex at all. How, then, can we compare the size of different parts of the brain when different species have different brain designs? Furthermore, how much can we learn from crude measures of the size of different parts of brains? One thing that would seem important in reckoning the processing power of a brain is the number of nerve cells that brain contains. Brain cells can vary greatly in size and in how densely they are packed, and consequently, the size of a piece of brain tissue tells us little, if anything, about the number of brain cells it contains. Take the neocortex of the dolphin. Dolphins and other cetaceans (ocean mammals like whales and porpoises) have particularly large neocortexes. As I mentioned above, in the human case, the neocortex is so large that it has to be folded to fit inside the skull. The amount of folding is such that a human neo-cortex, when removed from the skull and spread out, occupies more than twice the surface area it had when folded up inside the skull. In dolphins, the neocortex is even more intensely folded; it takes up over five times as much space when spread out flat than when folded in the skull. But this does not mean that dolphins have more nerve cells in their neocortex. Recent studies have found that the density of nerve cells in the neocortex of sea-living mammals like dolphins and whales is only a quarter of the density of cells in the neocortex of land-based mammals. Consequently, a dolphin's brain does not have nearly as many nerve cells as its large size would have led us to expect (Deacon, 1990).

In summary then, measures of brain size, even after allowing for body size and even if we try and consider just parts of the brain that might be more important for behavioral complexity, are not going to enable us to compare the intelligence and cognition of different species of animals. Our knowledge of the brains of different species is just too primitive and limited, and new discoveries are being made every day. Add to this the limited state of our understanding of the cognition of any species and the relationship between cognition and brain structures, and it is clear that such an indirect approach is not likely to bear fruit for a long time to come.

LEARNING SET

For many years, researchers interested in animal cognition struggled to find a standard test of cognitive ability or intelligence that would enable the direct comparison of different species. One task that for some time seemed to offer promise of a means of such a simple comparison is known as 'learning set'. Learning set is a higher-order type of learning – a form of learning about learning.

Consider this very simple problem: A subject has a choice between a triangle stimulus and a square. It has to select the triangle to obtain a small food reward – selection of the square leads to no reward. This is a simple form of instrumental conditioning (Chapter 5) known as a concurrent discrimination, and a great many different species can successfully solve a problem of this type. Once our subject has mastered this problem, it is presented with a new discrimination: perhaps circle versus hexagon. Again, the subject is trained until it masters this task and is then presented another and then another, and so on, for dozens or possibly hundreds of similar discrimination problems. The point of this long series of repetitions of very similar problems is to look into how much the subject improves with each new problem. In learning the very first problem, for example, our subject might make 20 errors before it was consistently selecting the triangle. In learning the second problem, our subject might make 15 errors before it consistently selects the circle. To learn the third problem, the subject might make slightly fewer errors again, and so on, making slightly fewer errors on each problem over the series of dozens or hundreds that are presented to it. The critical questions of interest are, what is the highest level of performance that a subject can reach after extensive training, and how long does it take to reach that level?

For a subject that is capable of extracting the principle that all these discrimination problems have in common, there is no need to make more than one error on each problem. On the first trial, the subject must choose at random (there is no way it could know in advance whether the triangle or square is going to be rewarded), but as soon as it has experienced the consequences of that first trial, there is no logical reason why it need ever make a mistake again. In our example, an animal that chooses the triangle on the first trial and gets rewarded should always choose the triangle from then on. Conversely, an animal that chooses the square on the first trial, should never choose the square again. This ability to extract the principle at work in these experiments is a simple form of concept learning. An animal's success or failure in extracting this principle can most easily be seen by plotting performance on the second trial of each problem. On the first trial, an animal must choose at random, but in theory, an animal can reach correct response levels of 100 percent on the second trial.

At first, obviously, animals have little idea what is required of them and perform around chance (50 percent) on the second trial of each new problem. With more experience, however, some species begin to pick up the principle underlying the task, and their performance on trial 2 progressively improves. Figure 13.4 shows performance on trial 2 for several different species trained on many successive problems in this way.

From this figure it can be seen that rats and squirrels barely improve on trial 2, even after 1,800 different but similar problems have been presented. Rhesus monkeys, at the other extreme, reach a level of nearly 90 percent correct responses after 400 problems. Other species, such as cats, marmosets, and squirrel monkeys, attain levels of trial 2 performance that are above chance but still include substantial numbers of errors. Part of the attraction of learning set as a method of comparing different species is the fact that the performances shown in Figure 13.4 correlate well with the relative brain sizes (as measured with the index K; see Figure 13.2) of the species shown.

Figure 13.4   *Percentages of correct responses on trial 2 of different discrimination problems plotted against successive problem number for several different species*

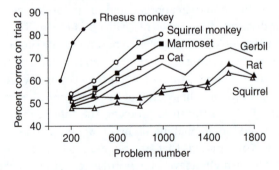

Source: From Passingham (1981).

There are, however, several problems with such a seemingly simple method of directly comparing the intelligence of different species. The first is that data collected in my laboratory by Kathryn Bonney flatly contradict this neat account. Bonney's study animal is a small marsupial called the fat-tailed dunnart (see Figure 13.5). Dunnarts are nocturnal mouselike creatures that live throughout arid southern parts of Australia in a variety of habitats where they hunt small invertebrates and insects. Bonney studied the learning set ability of dunnarts in a simple apparatus in which the animal was given a choice of two tunnels with different visual stimuli at the ends. For the first problem, the dunnart had to learn to approach an empty circle (like a doughnut) and not a uniform gray square in order to obtain a mealworm food reward; for problem 2, the dunnarts were given a choice between a white square and a black square – and so on, for 36 different

Figure 13.5   *Picture of dunnart next to trial 2 performance on 36 successive problems*

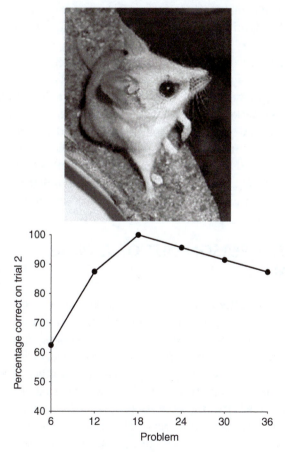

Source: Courtesy of K. Bonney.

discrimination problems. The dunnarts' performance on trial 2 of each of these problems is shown in Figure 13.5. Clearly, these animals are improving on the second trial of each problem even faster than the rhesus monkeys in Figure 13.4. Dunnarts were achieving over 90 percent correct choices on trial 2 within just 18 different discrimination problems. The brain of the dunnart, however, is very small. Their cephalization index, K, is around 0.07, a lower value than that of any of the animals listed in Figure 13.2 (Darlington et al., 1999). Their small brain also contains only a small amount, around 20 percent, of the part of the brain assumed to underlie advanced problem solving, the neocortex.

The most likely reason for the exceptional performance of dunnarts lies in their flexible lifestyles. Fat-tailed dunnarts are one of the few small marsupial species that forage in open areas, where predation from the air is a much greater danger than it is in woodlands, which offer protection. Catching fast-moving insects and small invertebrates in an arid and dangerous environment probably demands an ability to learn quickly about signals in the environment.

More generally, the learning set task – indeed the whole notion of a 'magic bullet' task that would enable the direct comparison of the intelligence of different species – has lost favor for a number of reasons. For one, it has been found that performance can vary greatly depending on relatively minor procedural alterations. Dolphins, for example, were found to be completely incapable of forming learning sets with visual discriminations but were well able to form learning sets with auditory stimuli (Herman & Arbeit, 1973). Since there are inevitable procedural differences between the ways in which members of different species are tested for the ability to form learning sets, these differences, rather than any more meaningful species differences, may be the reason for the varying results obtained from different species. There are also problems in assuming that the different species tested possess equivalent perceptual abilities or similar motivational states when they are tested under what may appear to us to be similar conditions.

TAKING THE PERSON OUT OF ANIMAL PERSONALITY

Emotion and personality are other areas where animals may be expected to have noteworthy differences from one another and from humans. As humans each of us has certain characteristic traits that remain relatively consistent over time and across contexts; our friends, family, and those we work with come to identify these traits as a part of our *personality*. As with many other areas of cognition, studying personality is a particular challenge when considering the behavior of nonhuman animals. First, the term itself – *person*ality – implies the quality or essence of humanity; as a result, personality research conducted with animals is often automatically subject to criticisms of anthropomorphism. On the other hand, those who own animals or work with them often remark on unique but persistent qualities or traits of a particular animal. Could refusing to recognize such consistency in nonhuman species be viewed as equally egocentric? One challenge is that personality is often linked with the study of other internal and cognitive states that have proved difficult to assess, including emotion, and that are responsible for centuries of heated debate (see Box 13.1).

BOX 13.1   THE PROBLEM OF EMOTION

Charles Darwin contemplated the emotions of animals, from his own pet dog Poly to a fear-ridden hippopotamus giving birth to its young (Darwin, 1872). Yet even a century later it is difficult to know whether other animals really experience emotions in the same way that humans do.

This is not to claim that animals are devoid of feelings or even something like emotion, but with wildly different perceptual worlds it would be naive to assume that something that looks like fear, excitement, or joy to us feels the same way to an animal – or stirs up the same human-defined emotions that we experience. In some cases, the animal's experience may be heightened and more refined (since feelings of what we call 'fear' might be closely tied to the presence of actual danger for wild animals and thus might be higher on the scale of responses that humans might identify as fear); in other cases, they might be dampened (some behavior patterns that look incredibly expressive to humans – such as the guilty look considered in Chapter 8 – might not be wrought with feeling or emotion at all. Instead they might simply be a conditioned or even automatic response to a stimulus that has resulted in positive outcomes in the past). In humans a condition known as synesthesia often leads to a crossing of perceptual information, resulting in individuals who may *hear* tones when they see colors or *see* sound. People with this syndrome sometimes report experiencing emotion as color or visual auras. For such individuals 'positive emotions tend to elicit synesthetic colours of pink, orange, yellow, and green, whereas words associated with negative emotions elicit synesthetic colours of brown, grey, and black' (Ward, 2004, p. 768). While most humans may have no way to conceive of this potential dimension of emotional experience, the perception of color may be an integral part of what emotion is to others. Furthermore, many people can cry on cue or fake a smile if the situation warrants it. Given these problems in interpreting the emotional experience of other members of our own species from their outward behavior, how can we be confident that we are making fair judgments about the experiences of other species? Nonetheless, attributions of emotional experience to animals on the basis of external features or behaviors are quite common. In a study conducted by Paul Morris and colleagues (2008), pet owners were asked to report on the emotional life of one of their pets. Owners completed a survey in which they were asked whether their animal ever displayed the following emotions: anger, fear, surprise, joy/happiness, sadness, disgust, interest, love/affection, anxiety, and curiosity (traditionally classified as first- or lower-order emotions), as well as empathy, shame, pride, guilt, jealousy, embarrassment, and grief (second-order emotions). The percentage of owners reporting the presence of a subset of these emotions in their pets (by species) can be found in Figure 13.6.

Figure 13.6   *Owner's ratings of the emotions they believe their pets display*

% of positive owner reports by species					
Emotion	Dog (N=337)	Cat (N=272)	Horse (N=69)	Bird (N= 75)	Hamster (N=34)
Primary					
Sadness	**87**	68	78	72	58
Anger	65	**82**	80	76	73
Joy	99	96	**100**	97	91
Fear	93	96	**100**	95	89
Secondary					
Guilt	**74**	35	36	24	15
Empathy	64	57	**67**	12	2
Pride	58	62	**81**	54	8
Jealousy	**81**	66	79	67	15

Note: Bold values indicate the species with the highest owner ratings for each emotion.

Source: Based on data collected by Morris, Doe, and Godsell (2008).

It could be assumed that the expectation of higher-level emotions in animals is based on an intuitive perception of their underlying cognitive complexity; perhaps it is right to assume that a pet dog has a more complex emotional life than a pet bird or hamster. On the other hand, perhaps we simply perceive a dog as more expressive because we see more similarities in the behavior and form of the dog, a fellow mammal, and thus we can more easily draw comparisons between what we are seeing and how we might feel if we looked that way. Even more similarities might be found in the facial movements and postures of other primates. However, a very meaningful wing flap of a bird, the burying behavior of a hamster, or the gill expansion of a fish might be more difficult for us to relate to, making it less likely that we would interpret them as signs of complex emotion. However, as we have seen, rodents, birds, fish, and insects are in some cases capable of cognitive and perceptual feats that dogs and humans cannot match (e.g., the long distance navigation strategies discussed in Chapter 7). Thus our ratings of the emotional lives of animals may be biased in ways that do not correspond well with the cognitive capabilities of different species.

Like consciousness or theory of mind, the study of emotions – especially second-order emotions such as jealousy, guilt, and pride – is a captivating topic. However, it has proven difficult to assess the presence of such emotions in animals directly. This makes experimental studies comparing species or even individuals within a species very hard to design and carry out. In addition, the majority of studies that *have* been conducted on animal emotion have focused on humans and nonhuman primates; thus claims that primates are the only species that show evidence of secondary emotions are not surprising – but such findings also tell us little about the abilities, cognitions, or internal states of other species (Morris et al., 2008). This does not mean that all attempts to study emotion in animals should be abandoned; instead it suggests that claims about an animal's emotional world should be made carefully and humbly, especially in the absence of scientific evidence. Until then there will continue to be temptations to paint a picture of animal emotion and personality in ways that we understand but that actually prevent us from conceptualizing the rich diversity of experience that could exist among other species than our own.

Modern personality research, however, may provide a different approach to classifying patterns of behavior in individual animals. Instead of taking the stance that the personality of an animal is an unobservable internal mechanism driving observable behavior, many researchers in this field have embraced 'temperament' as a term for the biological predispositions of an animal, and 'personality' as a generally consistent but moderately adaptable product of the interactions between an animal's behavioral predispositions and its environment. These definitions fit well within the framework of a wide range of animal behavior and cognition research and can be tested, replicated, and evaluated directly in ways that not only lead to predictions about an animal's behavior, but also allow for control. For example, an animal that is labeled *bold* on the basis of actively approaching new objects in the past should be expected to approach if a new object is added to the environment by an experimenter. This is not only useful in improving our basic scientific understanding of animal minds but can lead to practical applications. For example, in some animal shelters efforts are being made to link personality scores of humans (who fill out a questionnaire before choosing a pet to adopt) with the available animals (who undergo a personality and behavior assessment before going up for adoption). Personality trait labels might also be useful in predicting outcomes on other cognitive tests, especially those that require the presence of other animals or stimuli. For example, a *bold* animal might be expected to behave or perform differently than one who has been labeled *fearful*. Without such measures, factors that predict characteristic responses of an individual – independent of the cognitive task – might be overlooked or wrongly attributed to the relative intelligence of the individual or species.

However, the comparative study of animal personality has its challenges. Both a squid and a dog might be labeled aggressive, for example, but it would take some understanding of the behavior of both species to know what actions this label might predict for each. Without knowledge of the natural function of species-specific behaviors, the temptation to compare the form of these behaviors to human actions and intentions could lead again to anthropomorphism. Furthermore, personality is intended to define behavioral patterns of individuals within a species – it is not clear that the same approach can be taken to compare different species or even breeds within a species. If an entire strain or species contrasts with another on a trait, this may not be due to personality at all. In fact, most studies of animal personality focus on differences between individuals within a species and not differences between the species themselves (Gosling, 2001).

ARE THERE REALLY DIFFERENCES BETWEEN SPECIES?

So difficult has it proved to test and identify differences in the performances of different species that cannot be reduced to motivational or perceptual factors that it has been seriously suggested that there may be *no* differences in the intelligence of *any* nonhuman species. Euan MacPhail has proposed that with the exception of humans, whose intelligence is extended by the possession of language, all other species have approximately equal levels of intelligence (MacPhail, 1987). Much, of course, depends here on how one defines 'intelligence'. MacPhail's assessment of intelligence emphasizes the kinds of learning ability that we considered in Chapter 5 – learning about cause and effect. It certainly is the case that there is a surprising consistency across species of ability in this domain. As discussed in Chapter 5, a wide range of species has been found capable of learning about the consequences of their actions and of learning about the relationship between signals and things signified in the environment around them. More detailed studies, not reviewed here in any detail but discussed by MacPhail, show that a wide variety of species appears to learn about these things in similar ways.

But what about other forms of animal cognition covered elsewhere in this book? What about social learning, reasoning, memory, communication, and the great variety of cognitive skills we have discussed: can it really be argued that there are no (or minimal) species differences in these areas, too?

Abstract conceptual abilities (Chapter 3) provide one point of comparison where a range of diverse species has been tested, including pigeons, rats, monkeys, and chimpanzees. In addition, studies of object permanence have been performed on cats and dogs and other bird and mammal species. Most species tested succeed on the visible displacement task (where an object is hidden in full view of the subject), but only four species are widely accepted as successful on the hidden displacement task (where the object is hidden from view while in an opaque container). These four are humans, chimpanzees, gorillas, and dogs. Were it not for the presence of dogs in this list, we would be dealing with a small group of very closely related animals. As things stand, however, there is no obvious pattern – either in terms of evolutionary relatedness or ecological niche – that can explain why these four species should be the only ones to succeed on the invisible displacement task. Perhaps studies on more species will make the pattern clearer.

Research on animals' sense of time and number suggests that these abilities are fundamental to a wide range of species. Time of day seems to be something that a great many species are aware of, and evidence for an ability to time shorter intervals also appears to be very widespread. Though few systematic studies have been carried out, few reports suggest differences in timing abilities across species. Research on sensitivity to number has not been carried out in a wide range of species, but there is evidence that a variety of animals are sensitive at least to relative and absolute number. Species that have been studied in this regard include birds (such as pigeons, crows, and parrots) and mammals (rats, a raccoon, and several primates). More advanced number skills that contribute to counting have been demonstrated in chimpanzees and a parrot. It seems unlikely that counting skills could be restricted just to these two species. Further research will hopefully show what the counting abilities of some other species are like.

Memory (Chapter 10) is one area of research where differences in ability based on ecological specialization have been found. Birds that store food over winter in many separate caches can remember many more locations than closely related birds that do not store food. Apart from these differences in memory capacity, it has not proven possible to demonstrate that food-storing birds have memory systems that function differently from the memory systems of other birds. Even pigeons, which are used in memory research only out of experimental convenience, prove to have quite prodigious abilities to memorize hundreds of arbitrary stimuli. Another species intensively used in memory research because it is easy to house and test – the rat – also has excellent memorization abilities. A handful of other species, including invertebrates (honeybees) and primates, has been tested on memory tasks. Tests on various species are usually different enough that comparisons across species are very hard to make; yet what evidence we have suggests that, though capacity may vary, the ways in which different species memorize things do not vary dramatically.

This problem of different species being tested in completely different ways makes it especially difficult to draw comparative conclusions from the research that has been carried out on reasoning in different species (Chapter 6). Though the range of species that have been studied on spatial reasoning tasks, for example, is commendably broad (from Australian spiders to chimpanzees), rarely have the same methods been used on more than one species. Similar problems beset consideration of tool use. Serial learning, on the other hand, has been studied using fairly similar methods in pigeons, rats, monkeys, chimpanzees, and humans. The results here indicate that transitive inferential reasoning (where a subject has to go beyond the evidence given to deduce relationships that have not been presented directly) may be solved in very similar ways by all the species that have been tested. On linear ordering tasks, on the other hand, (where a subject is trained to respond to keys in a set order and then tested on subsets of those keys), monkeys are far more successful than pigeons. It would be very interesting to have results from more species on this problem so that we could see which other species behave like pigeons and which like monkeys.

Research on communication (Chapters 11 and 12) presents a very varied and eclectic picture. Different species communicate in many different ways. In terms of the spontaneous communicative abilities of animals observed in the wild, the most complex communicative system would have to be that of the honeybee. Honeybees, remember, are tiny flying insects with a brain of the most modest size. And yet the waggle dance of a honeybee communicates three different things to its hive mates: distance, direction, and the quality of a food source. No other species, not even other great apes (except humans, of course) communicates so much information to others. Vervet monkeys can communicate which of several different types of danger is approaching, but they do not have any system for communicating more than that one dimension of information.

Human language, of course, enables us to communicate any number of dimensions of information. Attempts to teach human language to other species, though they may not have led to much mastery of language as such, have enabled these animals to communicate several dimensions of experience. Even Alex the parrot identified the number, color, and identity of objects placed in front of him. Since it is unlikely that animals demonstrate in the laboratory abilities they would never use in the wild, this demonstration makes it possible that examples of more complex communication in the wild will be found once we have developed better methods to study them.

Overall then, a comparative analysis of animal cognition presents superficially great diversity. Looking at this diversity more closely, however, provides, at the present time, few examples of clear broad-stroke differences between species. This may be because too few species have been studied on many questions; where multiple species have been studied, the methods adopted are often too varied to permit meaningful comparisons. Certainly, in cases where comparable methods have been used, at least some clearly differing results have been found (e.g., in mirror self-recognition, visible and invisible object displacements, and communication). On the other hand, the reason why so few clear differences between species have been found could be because nonhuman species differ rather little in their cognitive abilities. This conclusion may seem intuitively unlikely, but the evidence is not strong enough at the moment to reject it. It is also possible that what differs between some species is not the capacity for certain cognitive skills but how the species has adapted and modified its cognitive potential to meet the needs encountered in its current environment. Thus some behaviors, both simple and complex, that appear wildly different on the surface may tie back to cognitive capabilities shared by many species. Of course, the genetic endowments of an individual are unequivocally tied to development and life experience as well, all of which are colored by the unique perceptual world of a species (or even individual). Thus it is not hard to imagine how even small cognitive differences could appear much larger on the surface, possibly accounting for much of the rich diversity we see in nature that allows species to thrive in their particular niche. On the other hand, it is possible that further differences exist in the cognitive capacities of different species or groups that are yet to be identified.

Animal cognition as a science is still a relatively new and growing field. The vast quantity of unanswered questions that remain and the inadequate methods for testing some of the more challenging ideas and theories that have been presented can be a frustration to those of us who want to find answers to them. There is one attraction to this state of affairs, however. It does mean that contributing to the big questions in animal cognition is something any reader of this book could do. You don't need fancy or expensive equipment – just access to some animals, an inquiring and critical mind, a lot of patience, and plenty of respect for your animals. We sincerely hope some are inspired to join us in the struggle to understand animal minds.

FURTHER READING

Blumberg, M. S. & Wasserman, E. A. (1995) Animal mind and the argument from design. *American Psychologist*, 50, 133–144.

A now slightly older but still very thought-provoking article on how to think about animal minds.

Gosling, S. D. & Vazire, S. (2002) Are we barking up the right tree? Evaluating a comparative approach to personality. *Journal of Research in Personality*, 36, 607–614.

An interesting consideration of personality in nonhuman animals.

MacPhail, E. M. (1987) The comparative psychology of intelligence. *Behavioral and Brain Sciences*, 10, 645–695.

MacPhail summarizes his argument that nonhuman species do not differ in their intelligence in this article, which is also accompanied by commentaries by many other leading scientists in the field.

Penn, D. C., Holyoak, K. J. & Povinelli, D. J. (2008) Darwin's mistake: explaining the discontinuity between human and nonhuman minds. *Behavioral and Brain Sciences*, 31, 109–130, 169–178.

A controversial assessment of the differences between human and nonhuman minds.

Roth, G. & Dicke, U. (2005) Evolution of the brain and intelligence. *Trends in Cognitive Sciences*, 9(5), 250–257. doi:10.1016/j.tics.2005.03.005

An interesting article on the brain size and intelligence debate.

Web sources

Learn more about the animal and human personality matching initiatives used at the ASPCA.

http://www.aspca.org/adoption/meet-your-match/meet-the-puppy-alities.aspx

Notes

CHAPTER 1

1. People are animals, too. However, for ease of reading, we stick to the tradition of calling humans 'humans' and the rest 'animals'.

CHAPTER 2

1. 'Hz' stands for hertz – the standard unit of frequency. One hertz is one vibration per second. One kHz is a thousand Hertz.
2. The abbreviation 'nm' stands for nanometer. One nanometer is one-billionth part of a meter.

References

Abe, K., & Watanabe, D. (2011). Songbirds possess the spontaneous ability to discriminate syntactic rules. *Nature Neuroscience*, 14, 1067–1074.

Able, K. P. (1996). The debate over olfactory navigation by homing pigeons. *Journal of Experimental Biology*, 199, 121–124.

Adamczewska, A. M., & Morris, S. (2001). Ecology and behavior of Gecarcoidea natalis, the christmas Island Red Crab, during the annual breeding migration. *The Biological Bulletin*, 200(3), 305–320.

Akins, C. K., Klein, E. D., & Zentall, T. R. (2002). Imitative learning in Japanese quail (Coturnix japonica) using the bidirectional control procedure. *Animal Learning & Behavior*, 30(3), 275–281.

Akins, C. K., & Zentall, T. R. (1999). Imitation in Japanese quail: the role of reinforcement of demonstrator responding. *Psychonomic Bulletin & Review*, 5, 694–697.

APPA (2012). National Pet Owners Survey: Industry Statistics & Trands. American Pet Products Association. Retrieved July 19, 2012, from http://www.americanpet-products.org/press_industrytrends.asp

Au, W. W. L. (1997). Echolocation in dolphins with a dolphin-bat comparison. *Bioacoustics*, 8, 137–162.

Aust, U., & Huber, L. (2006). Picture-object recognition in pigeons: evidence of representational insight in a visual categorization task using a complementary information procedure. *Journal of Experimental Psychology: Animal Behavior Processes*, 32, 190–195.

Aust, U., & Huber, L. (2010). Representational insight in pigeons: comparing subjects with and without real-life experience. *Animal Cognition*, 13, 207–218.

Aydin, A., & Pearce, J. M. (1994). Prototype effects in categorization by Pigeons. *Journal of Experimental Psychology: Animal Behavior Processes*, 20, 264–277.

Bagotskaia, M. S., Smirnova, A. A., & Zorina, Z. A. (2010a). [Corvidae are able to understand the logical structure in string-pulling tasks]. *Zhurnal vyssheĭ nervnoĭ deiatelnosti imeni I P Pavlova*, 60(5), 543–551.

Bagotskaia, M. S., Smirnova, A. A., & Zorina, Z. A. (2010b). [Comparative study of the ability to solve a string-pulling task in Corvidae]. *Zhurnal vyssheĭ nervnoĭ deiatelnosti imeni I P Pavlova*, 60(3), 321–329.

Baker, R. R. (1980). Goal orientation by blindfolded humans after long-distance displacement: possible involvement of a magnetic sense. *Science*, 210(4469), 555–557.

Balda, R. P., & Wiltschko, W. (1995). Spatial memory of homing pigeons, Columba livia, tested in an outdoor aviary. *Ethology*, 100, 253–258.

Barth, J., & Call, J. (2006). Tracking the displacement of objects: a series of tasks with great apes (Pan troglodytes, Pan paniscus, Gorilla gorilla, and Pongo pygmaeus) and young children (*Homo sapiens*). *Journal of Experimental Psychology*, 32, 239–252.

Barreto, G. R., & MacDonald, D. W. (1999). The response of water voles, Arvicola terrestris, to the odours of predators. *Animal Behaviour*, 57, 1107–1112.

Basile, B. M., & Hampton, R. R. (2010). Rhesus monkeys (*Macaca mulatta*) show robust primacy and recency in memory for lists from small, but not large, image sets. *Behavioural Processes*, 83(2), 183–190.

Baum, K. A., & Sharber, W. V. (2012). Fire creates host plant patches for monarch butterflies. *Biology Letters*.

Beatty, W. W. & Shavalia, D. A. (1980) Rat spatial memory: resistance to retroactive interference at long retention intervals. *Animal Learning and Behavior*, 8, 550–552.

Bee, M. A., Perrill, S. A., & Owen, P. C. (2000). Male green frogs lower the pitch of acoustic signals in defense of territories: a possible dishonest signal of size? *Behavioral Ecology*, 11, 169–177.

Beecher, M. D., & Brenowitz, E. A. (2005). Functional aspects of song learning in songbirds. *Trends in Ecology & Evolution*, 20, 143–149.

Begall, S., Červený, J., Neef, J., Vojtčch, O., & Burda, H. (2008). Magnetic alignment in grazing and resting cattle and deer. *Proceedings of the National Academy of Sciences*, 105, 13451–13455.

Beran, M. J., David, J., Redford, J. S., & Washburn, D. A. (2006). Rhesus macaques (*Macaca mulatta*) monitor uncertainty during numerosity judgments. *Journal of Experimental Psychology: Animal Behavior Processes*, 32(2), 111–119.

Beren, M. J., Gibson, K. R., & Rumbaugh, D. M. (1999) Predicting hominid intelligence from brain size. In M. C. Corballis & S. E. G. Lea (Eds), *The Decent of Mind: Psychological Perspectives on Hominid Evolution* (pp. 88–97). Oxford UK: Oxford University Press.

Berger, J. (2004). The last mile: how to sustain long-distance migration in mammals. *Conservation Biology*, 18(2), 320–331.

Bertolotti, L., & Salmon, M. (2005). Do embedded roadway lights protect sea turtles? *Environmental Management*, 36(5), 702–710.

Berton, F., Vogel, E., & Belzung, C. (1998). Modulation of mice anxiety in response to cat odor as a consequence of predators diet. *Physiology and Behavior*, 65, 247–254.

Bhatt, R. S., Wasserman, E. A., Reynolds, W. F., & Knauss, K. S. (1988). Conceptual behavior in pigeons: categorization of both familiar and novel examples from four classes of natural and artificial stimuli. *Journal of Experimental Psychology: Animal Behavior Processes*, 13, 219–234.

Bicknell, A. T., & Richardson, A. M. (1973). Comparison of avoidance learning in two species of lizards, Crotaphytus collaris and Dipsosaurus dorsalis. *Psychological Reports*, 32(3c), 1055–1065.

Biebach, H., Gordijn, M., & Krebs, J. R. (1989). Time-and-place learning by garden warblers, *Sylvia borin*. *Animal Behaviour*, 37, 353–360.

Bird, C. D., & Emery, N. J. (2009). Rooks use stones to raise the water level to reach a floating worm. *Current Biology*, 19(16), 1410–1414.

Biro, D., & Matsuzawa, T. (1999). Numerical ordering in a chimpanzee (Pan troglodytes): planning, executing, and monitoring. *Journal of Comparative Psychology*, 113, 178–185.

Biro, D., & Matsuzawa, T. (2001). Use of numerical symbols by the chimpanzee (Pan troglodytes): cardinals, ordinals, and the introduction of zero. *Animal Cognition*, 4, 193–199.

Bisazza, A., Pignatti, R., & Vallortigara, G. (1997). Laterality in detour behaviour: interspecific variation in poeciliid fish. *Animal Behaviour*, 54, 1273–1281.

Bloch, S., & Martinoya, C. (1982). Comparing frontal and lateral viewing in the pigeon. I. Tachistoscopic visual acuity as a function of distance. *Behavioural Brain Research*, 5, 231–244.

Blough, D. S., & Blough, P. M. (1997). Form perception and attention in pigeons. *Animal Learning and Behavior*, 25, 1–20.

Bluff, L. A., Troscianko, J., Weir, A. A. S., Kacelnik, A., & Rutz, C. (2010). Tool use by wild New Caledonian crows Corvus moneduloides at natural foraging sites. *Proceedings of the Royal Society B: Biological Sciences, 277*, 1377–1385.

Boesch, C. (1991). Teaching among wild chimpanzees. *Animal Behaviour, 41*(3), 530–532. doi:10.1016/S0003-3472(05)80857-7.

Boles, L. C., & Lohmann, K. J. (2003). True navigation and magnetic maps in spiny lobsters. *Nature, 421*(6918), 60–63.

Bolhuis, J. J., & van Kampen, H. S. (1988). Serial position curves in spatial memory of rats: primacy and recency effects. *Quarterly Journal of Experimental Psychology. B, Comparative and Physiological Psychology, 40*, 135–149.

Bovet, J. (1995). Homing red squirrels (Tamiasciurus hudsonicus): the importance of going straight. *Ethology, 101*, 1–9.

Bowen, B. W., Meylan, A. B., & Avise, J. C. (1989). An odyssey of the green sea turtle: Ascension Island revisited. *Proceedings of the National Academy of Sciences of the United States of America, 86*(2), 573–576.

Boysen, S. T. (1992). Counting as the chimpanzee sees it. In W. K. Honig & J. G. Fetterman (Eds), *Cognitive Aspects of Stimulus Control* (pp. 367–383). Hillsdale, NJ: Lawrence Erlbaum Associates.

Boysen, S. T., & Berntson, G. G. (1989). Numerical competence in a chimpanzee (Pan troglodytes). *Journal of Comparative Psychology, 103*, 23–31.

Boysen, S. T., & Himes, G. T. (1999). Current issues and emerging theories in animal cognition. *Annual review of psychology, 50*, 683–705.

Brannon, E. M., & Terrace, H. S. (2000). Representation of the numerosities 1–9 by Rhesus Macaques (Macaca mulatta). *Journal of Experimental Psychology: Animal Behavior Processes, 26*, 31–49.

Bräuer, J., Call, J., & Tomasello, M. (2004). Visual perspective taking in dogs (Canis familiaris) in the presence of barriers. *Applied Animal Behaviour Science, 88*(3–4), 299–317.

Bräuer, J., Call, J., & Tomasello, M. (2005). All great ape species follow gaze to distant locations and around barriers. *Journal of Comparative Psychology, 119*(2), 145.

Breland, K., & Breland, M. (1961). The misbehavior of organisms. *American Psychologist, 16*(11), 681–684.

Brines, M. L., & Gould, J. L. (1979). Bees have rules. *Science, 206*(4418), 571–573.

Broesch, T., Callaghan, T., Henrich, J., Murphy, C., & Rochat, P. (2011). Cultural variations in children's mirror self-recognition. *Journal of Cross-Cultural Psychology, 42*(6), 1018–1029.

Brooke, P. N., Alford, R. A., & Schwarzkopf, L. (2000). Environmental and social factors influence chorusing behaviour in a tropical frog: examining various temporal and spatial scales. *Behavioral Ecology and Sociobiology, 49*(1), 79–87.

Brooks, W. R. (1988). The influence of the location and abundance of the sea anemone Calliactis tricolor (Le Sueur) in protecting hermit crabs from octopus predators. *Journal of Experimental Marine Biology and Ecology, 116*(1), 15–21. doi:10.1016/0022-0981(88)90242-0

Brooks, W. R. (1989). Hermit crabs alter sea anemone placement patterns for shell balance and reduced predation. *Journal of Experimental Marine Biology and Ecology, 132*(2), 109–121.

Brosnan, S. F., & Waal, F. B. M. de. (2003). Monkeys reject unequal pay. *Nature, 425*(6955), 297–299.

Brower, L. P. (1969). Ecological chemistry. *Scientific American, 220*(2), 22–29.

Brower, L. P. (1995). Understanding and misunderstanding the migration of the monarch butterfly (*Nymphalidae*) in North America: 1857–1995. *Journal of the Lepidopterists' Society, 49*, 304–385.

Browne, J. (2003). *Charles Darwin: The Power of Place*. Princeton, NJ: Princeton University Press.

Brown, C., & Laland, K. (2001). Social learning and life skills training for hatchery reared fish. *Journal of Fish Biology*, 59(3), 471–493.

Brown, M. F., McKeon, D., Curley, T., Weston, B., Lambert, C., & Lebowitz, B. (1998). Working memory for color in honeybees. *Animal Learning and Behavior*, 26, 264–271.

Buckstaff, K. C. (2004). Effects of watercraft noise on the acoustic behavior of bottlenose dolphins, Tursiops truncatus, in Sarasota Bay, Florida. *Marine Mammal Science*, 20, 709–725.

Bugnyar, T., & Heinrich, B. (2005). Ravens, *Corvus corax*, differentiate between knowledgeable and ignorant competitors. *Proceedings of the Royal Society B: Biological Sciences*, 272(1573), 1641–1646.

Bugnyar, T., Stöwe, M., & Heinrich, B. (2004). Ravens, *Corvus corax*, follow gaze direction of humans around obstacles. *Proceedings of the Royal Society B: Biological Sciences*, 271(1546), 1331–1336.

Caldwell, D. K., & Caldwell, M. C. (1972). *The World of the Bottlenosed Dolphin*. Philadelphia, PA: Lippincott Co.

Caldwell, M. C., & Caldwell, D. K. (1965). Individualized whistle contours in bottlenosed dolphins (Tursiops truncatus). *Nature*, 207, 434–435.

Caldwell, M. C., & Caldwell, D. K. (1979). The whistle of the atlantic bottlenosed dolphin (Tursiops truncatus): ontogeny. In H. E. Winn & B. L. Olla (Eds), *Behavior of Marine Animals: Current Perspectives in Research: Vol. 3. Ceteceans* (Vol. 3, pp. 369–401). New York, NY: Plenum Press.

Call, J. (2001). Object permanence in orangutans (Pongo pygmaeus), chimpanzees (Pan troglodytes), and children (Homo sapiens). *Journal of Comparative Psychology*, 115, 159–171.

Call, J. (2010). Do apes know that they could be wrong? *Animal Cognition*, 13(5), 689–700.

Call, J., Bräuer, J., Kaminski, J., & Tomasello, M. (2003). Domestic dogs (*Canis familiaris*) are sensitive to the attentional state of humans. *Journal of Comparative Psychology*, 117(3), 257–263.

Camlitepe, Y., Aksoy, V., Uren, N., Yilmaz, A., & Becenen, I. (2005). An experimental analysis on the magnetic field sensitivity of the black-meadow ant *Formica pratensis* Retzius (Hymenoptera: Formicidae). *Acta Biologica Hungarica*, 56, 215–224.

Cannicci, S., Dahdouh-Guebas, F., Anyona, D., & Vannini, M. (1995). Homing in the mangrove swimming crab Thalamita crenata (Decapoda: Portunidae). *Ethology*, 100, 242–252.

Cantlon, J. F., & Brannon, E. M. (2006). Shared system for ordering small and large numbers in monkeys and humans. *Psychological Science*, 17, 401–406.

Cantlon, J. F., & Brannon, E. M. (2007). Basic math in monkeys and college students. *PLoS Biology*, 5, e328.

Carew, T. J., Hawkins, R. D., & Kandel, E. R. (1983). Differential classical conditioning of a defensive withdrawal reflex in Aplysia californica. *Science*, 219, 397–400.

Caro, T. M., & Hauser, M. D. (1992). Is there teaching in nonhuman animals? *The Quarterly Review of Biology*, 67(2), 151–174.

Carr, A., & Hirth, H. (1961). Social facilitation in green turtle siblings. *Animal Behaviour*, 9(1–2), 68–70.

Castro, C. A., & Larsen, T. (1992). Primacy and recency effects in nonhuman primates. *Journal of Experimental Psychology: Animal Behavior Processes*, 18(4), 335–340.

Cerella, J. (1980). The pigeon's analysis of pictures. *Pattern Recognition*, 12, 1–6.

Chapuis, N., & Scardigli, P. (1993). Shortcut ability in hamsters (Mesocricetus auratus): the role of environmental and kinesthetic information. *Animal Learning and Behavior*, 21, 255–265.

Chapuis, N., Thinus-Blanc, C., & Poucet, B. (1983). Dissociation of mechanisms involved in dogs' oriented displacements. *Quarterly Journal of Experimental Psychology. B, Comparative and Physiological Psychology*, 35B, 213–219.

Chapuis, N., & Varlet, C. (1987). Short cuts by dogs in natural surroundings. *Quarterly Journal of Experimental Psychology. B, Comparative and Physiological Psychology*, 39B, 49–64.

Cheney, D. L., & Seyfarth, R. M. (1990). *How Monkeys See the World*. Chicago, IL: University of Chicago Press

Cheng, K. (1989). The vector sum model of pigeon landmark use. *Journal of Experimental Psychology: Animal Behavior Processes*, 15(4), 366–375.

Cheng, K., & Sherry, D. F. (1992). Landmark-based spatial memory in birds (*Parus atricapillus and Columba livia*): the use of edges and distances to represent spatial positions. *Journal of Comparative Psychology*, 106(4), 331–341.

Church, R. M. (1978). The internal clock. In S. H. Hulse, M. Fowler, & W. K. Honig (Eds), *Cognitive Processes in Animal Behavior* (pp. 277–310). Hillsdale, NJ : Lawrence Erlbaum.

Church, R. M., & Deluty, M. Z. (1977). Bisection of temporal intervals. *Journal of Experimental Psychology: Animal Behavior Processes*, 3, 216.

Clayton, N. S., & Dickinson, A. (1998). Episodic-like memory during cache recovery by scrub jays. *Nature*, 395, 272–274.

Coemans, M. A. J. M., Vos Hzn, J. J., & Nuboer, J. F. W. (1990). No evidence for polarization sensitivity in the pigeon. *Naturwissenschaften*, 77, 138–142.

Collett, T. S., Cartwright, B. A., & Smith, B. A. (1986). Landmark learning and visuospatial memories in gerbils. *Journal of Comparative Physiology A: Neuroethology, Sensory, Neural, and Behavioral Physiology*, 158(6), 835–851.

Collier-Baker, E., Davis, J. M., & Suddendorf, T. (2004). Do dogs (Canis familiaris) understand invisible displacement? *Journal of Comparative Psychology*, 118, 421–433.

Connor, R. C., Richards, A. F., Smolker, R. A., & Mann, J. (1996). Patterns of female attractiveness in Indian ocean bottlenose dolphins. *Behaviour*, 133, 37–69.

Cook, M., & Mineka, S. (1990). Selective associations in the observational conditioning of fear in rhesus monkeys. *Journal of Experimental Psychology: Animal Behavior Processes*, 16(4), 372–389.

Cook, R. G. (1992). The visual perception and processing of textures by pigeons. In W. K. Honig & J. G. Fetterman (Eds), *Cognitive Aspects of Stimulus Control* (pp. 279–299). Hillsdale, NJ: Lawrence Erlbaum Assoc.

Cook, R. G., Brown, M. F., & Riley, D. A. (1983). Flexible memory processing by rats: use of prospective and retrospective information in the radial maze. *Journal of Experimental Psychology: Animal Behavior Processes*, 11, 453–469.

Cooper, J. J., Ashton, C., Bishop, S., West, R., Mills, D. S., & Young, R. J. (2003). Clever hounds: social cognition in the domestic dog (*Canis familiaris*). *Applied Animal Behaviour Science*, 81(3), 229–244.

Coppinger, R., & Coppinger, L. (2001). *Dogs: A Startling New Understanding of Canine Origin, Behavior & Evolution* (1st edn). Scribner. New York.

Corcoran, A. J., Barber, J. R., Hristov, N. I., & Conner, W. E. (2011). How do tiger moths jam bat sonar? *The Journal of Experimental Biology*, 214, 2416–2425.

Couvillon, P. A., & Bitterman, M. E. (1992). A conventional conditioning analysis of 'transitive inference' in pigeons. *Journal of Experimental Psychology: Animal Behavior Processes*, 18, 308–310.

Cowie, R. J., Krebs, J. R., & Sherry, D. F. (1981). Food storing by marsh tits. *Animal Behaviour*, 29(4), 1252–1259.

Craig, M., Rand, J., Mesch, R., Shyan-Norwalt, M., Morton, J., & Flickinger, E. (2012). Domestic dogs (*Canis familiaris*) and the radial arm maze: spatial memory and serial position effects. *Journal of Comparative Psychology*, 126(3), 233–242.

Custance, D. M., Whiten, A., & Bard, K. (1995, September). Can young chimpanzees (Pan troglodytes) imitate arbitrary actions? Hayes & Hayes (1952) revisited. *Behaviour*, 132(11/12), 837–859.

Dabelsteen, T. (2004). Strategies that facilitate or counter eavesdropping on vocal interactions in songbirds. *Anais da Academia Brasileira de Ciências*, 76, 274–278.

D'Amato, M. R., & Colombo, M. (1988). Representation of serial order in monkeys (Cebus apella). *Journal of Experimental Psychology: Animal Behavior Processes*, 14, 131–139.

D'Amato, M. R., & Van Sant, P. (1988). The person concept in monkeys (Cebus apella). *Journal of Experimental Psychology: Animal Behavior Processes*, 14, 43–55.

Darlington, R. B., Dunlop, S. A., & Finlay, B. L. (1999). Neural development in metatherian and eutherian mammals: variation and constraint. *Journal of Comparative Neurology*, 411, 359–368.

Darwin, C. (1859). *On the Origin of Species by Means of Natural Selection*. London: John Murray.

Darwin, C. (1965). *The Expression of Emotions in Man and Animals*. Chicago, IL: University of Chicago Press (original work published 1872).

Darwin, C. (1989) *The Descent of Man and Selection in Relation to Sex*. Pickering & Chatto, London (original work published 1877).

Darwin, C. (1987). *Charles Darwin's Notebooks, 1836–1844*. Edited by P. H. Barnett, P. J. Gautrey, S. Herbert, D. Kohn & S. Smith. British Museum (Natural History) and Cornell University Press, Ithaca, NY.

Davis, H. (1984). Discrimination of the number three by a raccoon (Procyon lotor). *Animal Learning and Behavior*, 12, 409–413.

Davis, H. (1992). Transitive inference in rats (Rattus norvegicus). *Journal of Comparative Psychology*, 106, 342–349.

Davis, H., & Albert, M. (1986). Numerical discrimination by rats using sequential auditory stimuli. *Animal Learning and Behavior*, 14, 57–59.

Davis, H., & Bradford, S. A. (1986). Counting behavior by rats in a simulated natural environment. *Ethology*, 73, 265–280.

Davis, H., & Bradford, S. A. (1991). Numerically restricted food intake in the rat in a free-feeding situation. *Animal Learning and Behavior*, 19, 215–222.

Davis, H., MacKenzie, K. A., & Morrison, S. (1989). Numerical discrimination by rats (Rattus norvegicus) using body and vibrissal touch. *Journal of Comparative Psychology*, 103, 45–53.

Davis, H., Taylor, A. A., & Norris, C. (1997). Preference for familiar humans by rats. *Psychonomic Bulletin & Review*, 4, 118–120.

Dawkins, R., & Krebs, J. R. (1978). Animal signals: information or manipulation. *Behavioural Ecology: An Evolutionary Approach*, 282–309.

Dawson, B. V., & Foss, B. M. (1965). Observational learning in budgerigars. *Animal Behaviour*, 13(4), 470–474.

Dawson, G., & McKissick, F. (1984). Self-recognition in autistic children. *Journal of Autism and Developmental Disorders*, 14(4), 383–394.

de Blois, S. T., & Novak, M. A. (1994). Object permanence in Rhesus monkeys (Macaca mulatta). *Journal of Comparative Psychology*, 108, 318–327.

de Blois, S. T., Novak, M. A., & Bond, M. (1998). Object permanence in orangutans (Pongo pygmaeus) and squirrel monkeys (Saimiri sciureus). *Journal of Comparative Psychology*, 112, 137–152.

de Waal, F. B. M. (2008). Putting the altruism back into altruism: the evolution of empathy. *Annual Review of Psychology*, 59(1), 279–300.

Deacon, T. W. (1990). Rethinking mammalian brain evolution. *American Zoologist*, 30, 629–705.

Deecke, V. B. (2012). Tool-use in the brown bear (Ursus arctos). *Animal Cognition*, 15(4), 725–730.

Delius, J. D., & Hollard, V. D. (1987). Orientation invariance of shape recognition in forebrain-lesioned pigeons. *Behavioural Brain Research*, 23, 251–259.

Delius, J. D., Perchard, R. J., & Emmerton, J. (1976). Polarized light discrimination by pigeons and an electroretinographic correlate. *Journal of Comparative and Physiological Psychology*, 90, 560–571.

Delm, M. (1990). Vigilance for predators: detection and dilution effects. *Behavioral Ecology and Sociobiology*, 26(5), 337–342.

Dennett, D. C. (1991). *Consciousness Explained*. Back Bay Books, Little, Brown: Boston, MA.

Descartes, R. (1976). 'Animals are machines.' In T. Regan & P. Singer (Eds), *Animal Rights and Human Obligations*. Englewood Cliffs: NJ: Prentice Hall, pp. 60–66.

Dickinson, A., & Mackintosh, N. J. (1978). Classical conditioning in animals. *Annual Review of Psychology*, 29(1), 587–612.

Dingle, H., & Drake, V. A. (2007). What is migration? *BioScience*, 57(2), 113–121.

Dorey, N. (2011). *Experimental investigation of social learning in domestic animals and non-human primates*. (Doctoral Thesis). University of Exeter, Exeter, UK. Retrieved from http://hdl.handle.net/10036/47016

Dorey, N. R., Rosales-Ruiz, J., Smith, R., & Lovelace, B. (2009). Functional analysis and treatment of self-injury in a captive olive baboon. *Journal of Applied Behavior Analysis*, 42(4), 785–794.

Duff, S. J., Brownlie, L. A., Sherry, D. F., & Sangster, M. (1998). Sun compass and landmark orientation by black-capped chickadees (Parus atricapillus). *Journal of Experimental Psychology: Animal Behavior Processes*, 24, 243–253.

Dumas, C., & Wilkie, D. M. (1995). Object permanence in ring doves (Streptopelia risoria). *Journal of Comparative Psychology*, 109, 142.

Duquette, L. S., & Klein, D. R. (1987). Activity budgets and group size of caribou during spring migration. *Canadian Journal of Zoology*, 65(1), 164–168.

Dyer, F. C. (1991). Bees acquire route-based memories but not cognitive maps in familiar landscape. *Animal Behavior*, 41, 239–46.

Dyer, F. C. (1996). Spatial memory and navigation by honeybees on the scale of the foraging range. *Journal of Experimental Biology*, 199, 147–154.

Eckerman, D. A. (1999). Scheduling reinforcement about once a day. *Behavioural Processes*, 45, 101–114.

Edwards, C. A., Jagielo, J. A., Zentall, T. R., & Hogan, D. E. (1982). Acquired equivalence and distinctiveness in matching to sample by pigeons: mediation by reinforcer-specific expectancies. *Journal of Experimental Psychology: Animal Behavior Processes*, 8, 244.

Eisner, T., Goetz, M. A., Hill, D. E., Smedley, S. R., & Meinwald, J. (1997). Firefly 'femmes fatales' acquire defensive steroids (lucibufagins) from their firefly prey. *Proceedings of the National Academy of Sciences*, 94, 9723–9728.

Elewa, A. M. T. (2005). *Migration of Organisms: Climate. Geography. Ecology*. Heidelberg, Germany: Springer.

Emlen, S. T. (1970). Celestial rotation: its importance in the development of migratory orientation. *Science*, 170, 1198–1201.

Emmerton, J. (1998). Numerosity differences and effects of stimulus density on pigeons' discrimination performance. *Animal Learning and Behavior*, 26, 243–256.

Emmerton, J., Lohmann, A., & Niemann, J. (1997). Pigeons' serial ordering of numerosity with visual arrays. *Animal Learning and Behavior, 25*, 234–244.

Enard, W., Przeworski, M., Fisher, S. E., Lai, C. S., Wiebe, V., Kitano, T., Monaco, A. P., et al. (2002). Molecular evolution of FOXP2, a gene involved in speech and language. *Nature, 418*, 869–872.

Epstein, R., Kirshnit, C. E., Lanza, R. P., & Rubin, L. C. (1984). 'Insight' in the pigeon: antecedents and determinants of an intelligent performance. *Nature, 308*, 61–62.

Epstein, R., Lanza, R. P., & Skinner, B. F. (1981). 'Self-awareness' in the pigeon. *Science, 212*(4495), 695–696.

Evans, C. S., & Marler, P. (1994). Food calling and audience effects in male chickens, Gallus gallus: their relationships to food availability, courtship and social facilitation. *Animal Behaviour, 47*, 1159–1170.

Evans, C. S., & Marler, P. (1995). Language and animal communication: parallels and contrasts. In H. L. Roitblat & J.-A. Meyer (Eds), *Comparative Approaches to Cognitive Science* (pp. 341–382). Cambridge, MA, MIT Press.

Ewer, R. F. (1963). The behaviour of the meerkat, Suricata suricatta (Schreber). *Zeitschrift für Tierpsychologie, 20*(5), 570–607.

Fagot, J., & Cook, R. G. (2006). Evidence for large long-term memory capacities in baboons and pigeons and its implications for learning and the evolution of cognition. *Proceedings of the National Academy of Sciences, 103*(46), 17564–17567.

Feeney, M., Roberts, W., & Sherry, D. (2009). Memory for what, where, and when in the black-capped chickadee (*Poecile atricapillus*). *Animal Cognition, 12*(6), 767–777.

Ferrari, M., & Matthews, W. S. (1983). Self-recognition deficits in autism: syndrome-specific or general developmental delay? *Journal of Autism and Developmental Disorders, 13*(3), 317–324.

Fersen, L. von, & Delius, J. D. (1989). Long-term retention of many visual patterns by pigeons. *Ethology, 82*, 141–155.

Fersen, L. von, & Delius, J. D. (2000). Acquired equivalences between auditory stimuli in dolphins (Tursiops truncatus). *Animal Cognition, 3*, 79–83.

Fersen, L. von, & Lea, S. E. G. (1990). Category discrimination by pigeons using five polymorphous features. *Journal of the Experimental Analysis of Behavior, 54*, 69–84.

Fersen, L. von, Wynne, C. D. L., Delius, J. D., & Staddon, J. E. R. (1991). Transitive inference formation in pigeons. *Journal of Experimental Psychology: Animal Behavior Processes, 17*, 334–341.

Finn, J. K., Tregenza, T., & Norman, M. D. (2009). Defensive tool use in a coconut-carrying octopus. *Current Biology, 19*(23), R1069–R1070.

Fitch, W. T., Hauser, M. D., & Chomsky, N. (2005). The evolution of the language faculty: Clarifications and implications. *Cognition, 97*, 179–210.

Fitzke, F. W., Hayes, B. P., Hodos, W., Holden, A. L., & Low, J. C. (1985). Refractive sectors in the visual field of the pigeon eye. *Journal of Physiology, 369*, 33–44.

Ford, J. K. (1989). Acoustic behaviour of resident killer whales (Orcinus orca) off Vancouver Island, British Columbia. *Canadian Journal of Zoology, 67*, 727–745.

Franklin, E. L., Robinson, E. J. H., Marshall, J. A. R., Sendova-Franks, A. B., & Franks, N. R. (2012). Do ants need to be old and experienced to teach? *The Journal of experimental biology, 215*(Pt 8), 1287–1292.

Franks, N. R., & Richardson, T. (2006). Teaching in tandem-running ants. *Nature, 439*(7073), 153–153.

Freeberg, T. M. (2004). Social transmission of courtship behavior and mating preferences in brown-headed cowbirds, Molothrus ater. *Animal Learning & Behavior, 32*(1), 122–130.

Fujita, K. (2009). Metamemory in tufted capuchin monkeys (*Cebus apella*). *Animal Cognition, 12*(4), 575–585.

Fujita, K., Morisaki, A., Takaoka, A., Maeda, T., & Hori, Y. (2012). Incidental memory in dogs (Canis familiaris): adaptive behavioral solution at an unexpected memory test. *Animal Cognition*, 15(6), 1055–1063.

Fullard, J. H., Simmons, J. A., & Saillant, P. A. (1994). Jamming bat echolocation: the dogbane tiger moth Cycnia tenera times its clicks to the terminal attach calls of the big brown bat Eptesicus fuscus. *Journal of Experimental Biology*, 194, 285–298.

Gácsi, M., Miklosi, A., Varga, O., Topal, J., & Csanyi, V. (2003). Are readers of our face readers of our minds? Dogs (*Canis familiaris*) show situation-dependent recognition of human's attention. *Animal Cognition*, 7(3).

Gagnon, S., & Doré, F. Y. (1994). Cross-sectional study of object permanence in domestic puppies (Canis familiaris). *Journal of Comparative Psychology*, 108, 220–232.

Gallistel, C. R. (1993). *The Organization of Learning*. MIT Press.

Gallup, G. G. (1997). On the rise and fall of self-conception in primates. In J. G. Snodgrass & R. L. Thompson (Eds), *The Self across Psychology: Self-recognition, Self-awareness, and the Self Concept* (pp. 73–82). New York: NY: New York Academy of Sciences.

Garcia, J., & Koelling, R. A. (1966). Relation of cue to consequence in avoidance learning. *Psychonomic Science*, 4, 123–124.

Gardner, B. T., & Gardner, R. A. (1971). Two-way communication with an infant chimpanzee. In A. M. S. Schrier (Ed.), *Behavior of Nonhuman Primates* (Vol. 4, pp. 117–184). New York, NY: Academic Press.

Gaulin, S. J. C., & FitzGerald, R. W. (1986). Sex differences in spatial ability: an evolutionary hypothesis and test. *The American Naturalist*, 127(1), 74–88.

Gegear, R. J., Foley, L. E., Casselman, A., & Reppert, S. M. (2010). Animal cryptochromes mediate magnetoreception by an unconventional photochemical mechanism. *Nature*, 463(7282), 804–807.

Gill, F. B. (1988). Trapline foraging by hermit hummingbirds: competition for an undefended, renewable resource. *Ecology*, 69, 1933–1942.

Gillan, D. J., Premack, D., & Woodruff, G. (1981). Reasoning in the chimpanzee: I. Analogical reasoning. *Journal of Experimental Psychology: Animal Behavior Processes*, 7, 1–17.

Ginneken, V. van, Antonissen, E., Müller, U. K., Booms, R., Eding, E., Verreth, J., & Thillart, G. van den. (2005). Eel migration to the Sargasso: remarkably high swimming efficiency and low energy costs. *The Journal of Experimental Biology*, 208(7), 1329–1335.

Gisiner, R., & Schusterman, R. J. (1992). Sequence, syntax, and semantics: responses of a language-trained sea lion (Zalophus californianus) to novel sign combinations. *Journal of Comparative Psychology*, 106, 78–91.

Goerlitz, H. R., ter Hofstede, H. M., Zeale, M. R. K., Jones, G., & Holderied, M. W. (2010). An aerial-hawking bat uses stealth echolocation to counter moth hearing. *Current Biology*, 20, 1568–1572.

Gosling, S. D. (2001). From mice to men: what can we learn about personality from animal research? *Psychological bulletin*, 127, 45–86.

Gould, K. L., Ort, A., & Kamil, A. (2012). Do Clark's nutcrackers demonstrate what-where-when memory on a cache-recovery task? *Animal Cognition*, 15(1), 37–44.

Gould-Beierle, K. L., & Kamil, A. C. (1996). The use of local and global cues by Clark's nutcrackers, Nucifraga columbiana. *Animal Behaviour*, 52(3), 519–528.

Gould, J. L. (1980). The case for magnetic sensitivity in birds and bees (such as it is). *American Scientist*, 68, 256–267.

Gould, J. L. (1986). The locale map of honey bees: do insects have cognitive maps? *Science*, 232, 861–863.

Goulet, S., Doré, F. Y., & Lehotkay, R. (1996). Activation of locations in working memory in cats. *Quarterly Journal of Experimental Psychology. B, Comparative and Physiological Psychology,* 49B, 81–92.

Goulet, S., Doré, F. Y., & Rousseau, R. (1994). Object permanence and working memory in cats (Felis catus). *Journal of Experimental Psychology: Animal Behavior Processes,* 20, 347–365.

Grant, D. S. (1976). Effect of sample presentation time on long-delay matching in the pigeon. *Learning and Motivation,* 7, 580–590.

Grice, G. R. (1948). The relation of secondary reinforcement to delayed reward in visual discrimination learning. *Journal of Experimental Psychology,* 38, 1–16.

Griffin, D. R. (1986). *Listening in the Dark: The Acoustic Orientation of Bats and Men.* Ithaca, NY: Cornell University Press.

Griffin, D. R., & Galambos, R. (1941). The sensory basis of obstacle avoidance by flying bats. *Journal of Experimental Zoology,* 86, 481–506.

Grossetête, A., & Moss, C. F. (1998). Target flutter rate discrimination by bats using frequency-modulated sonar sounds: behavior and signal processing models. *Journal of the Acoustical Society of America,* 103, 2167–2176.

Hall, K. R. L., & Schaller, G. B. (1964). Tool-using behavior of the California sea otter. *Journal of Mammalogy,* 45(2), 287–298.

Hall, N. J., Udell, M. A. R., Dorey, N. R., Walsh, A. L., & Wynne, C. D. L. (2011). Megachiropteran bats (*Pteropus*) utilize human referential stimuli to locate hidden food. *Journal of Comparative Psychology,* 125(3), 341–6.

Hamm, J., Matheson, W. R., & Honig, W. K. (1997). Mental rotation in pigeons (Columba livia)? *Journal of Comparative Psychology,* 111, 76–81.

Hampton, R. R., Shettleworth, S. J., & Westwood, R. P. (1998). Proactive interference, recency, and associative strength: comparisons of black-capped chickadees and dark-eyed juncos. *Animal Learning and Behavior,* 26, 475–485.

Hanggi, E. B. (1999). Categorization learning in horses (Equus caballus). *Journal of Comparative Psychology,* 113, 243–252.

Hare, B., Brown, M., Williamson, C., & Tomasello, M. (2002). The domestication of social cognition in dogs. *Science,* 298(5598), 1634–1636.

Hare, B., Call, J., Agnetta, B., & Tomasello, M. (2000). Chimpanzees know what conspecifics do and do not see. *Animal Behaviour,* 59, 771–785.

Harley, H. E. (2008). Whistle discrimination and categorization by the Atlantic bottlenose dolphin (Tursiops truncatus): a review of the signature whistle framework and a perceptual test. *Behavioural processes,* 77, 243–268.

Hart, B. L., Hart, L. A., & Pinter-Wollman, N. (2008). Large brains and cognition: where do elephants fit in? *Neuroscience & Biobehavioral Reviews,* 32(1), 86–98.

Hauser, M. (2000). What do animals think about numbers? *American Scientist,* 88, 144–151.

Hauser, M. D., Chomsky, N., & Fitch, W. T. (2002). The faculty of language: what is it, who has it, and how did it evolve? *Science,* 298, 1569–1579.

Hayes, C. (1951). *The Ape in our House.* Harper. New York.

Hayes, K. J., & Hayes, C. (1952). Imitation in a home-raised chimpanzee. *Journal of Comparative and Physiological Psychology,* 45(5), 450–459.

Heathers, G. L. (1940). The avoidance of repetition of a maze reaction in the rat as a function of the time interval between trials. *The Journal of Psychology,* 10(2), 359–380.

Hecht, J., Miklósi, Á., & Gácsi, M. (2012). Behavioral assessment and owner perceptions of behaviors associated with guilt in dogs. *Applied Animal Behaviour Science,* 139(1–2), 134–142.

Henderson, J., Hurly, T. A., Bateson, M., & Healy, S. D. (2006). Timing in free-living Rufous hummingbirds, Selasphorus rufus. *Current Biology,* 16, 512–515.

Herman, L. M., & Arbeit, W. R. (1973). Stimulus control and auditory discrimination learning set in the bottlenose dolphin. *Journal of the Experimental Analysis of Behavior, 19*, 379–394.

Herman, L. M., Richards, D. G., & Wolz, J. P. (1984). Comprehension of sentences by bottlenosed dolphins. *Cognition, 16*, 129–219.

Herrnstein, R. J., & De Villiers, P. A. (1980). Fish as a natural category for people and pigeons. In G. H. Bower (Ed.), *The Psychology of Learning and Motivation: Advances in Research and Theory* (Vol. 14, pp. 60–97). San Diego: Academic Press.

Herrnstein, R. J., Loveland, D. H., & Cable, C. (1976). Natural concepts in pigeons. *Journal of Experimental Psychology: Animal Behavior Processes, 2*, 285–302.

Herz, R. S., Zanette, L., & Sherry, D. F. (1994) Spatial cues for cache retrieval by black-capped chickadees. *Animal Behaviour, 48*, 343–351.

Heth, G., Todrank, J., & Johnston, R. E. (1999). Similarity in the qualities of individual odors among kin and species in Turkish (Mesocricetus brandti) and golden (Mesocricetus auratus) hamsters. *Journal of Comparative Psychology, 113*, 321–326.

Heyes, C. (2012). Simple minds: a qualified defence of associative learning. *Philosophical Transactions of the Royal Society B: Biological Sciences, 367*(1603), 2695–2703.

Heyes, C. M. (1994). Social learning in animals: categories and mechanisms. *Biological reviews of the Cambridge Philosophical Society, 69*(2), 207–231.

Heyes, C. M. (1998). Theory of mind in nonhuman primates. *Behavioral and Brain Sciences, 21*, 101–134.

Heyes, C. M., & Dawson, G. R. (1990). A demonstration of observational learning in rats using a bidirectional control. *Quarterly Journal of Experimental Psychology. B, Comparative and Physiological Psychology, 42*, 59–71.

Hill, M. E. (2006). Research article: the effect of aposematic coloration on the food preference of *Aphelocoma coerulescens*, the Florida scrub jay. *BIOS, 77*(4), 97–106.

Holland, R. A., Kirschvink, J. L., Doak, T. G., & Wikelski, M. (2008). Bats use magnetite to detect the earth's magnetic field. *PLoS ONE, 3*, e1676.

Hollis, K. L., Dumas, M. J., Singh, P., & Fackelman, P. (1995). Pavlovian conditioning of aggressive behavior in blue gourami fish (Trichogaster trichopterus): winners become winners and losers stay losers. *Journal of Comparative Psychology, 109*(2), 123–133.

Hollis, K. L., Pharr, V. L., Dumas, M. J., Britton, G. B., & Field, J. (1997). Classical conditioning provides paternity advantage for territorial male blue gouramis (Trichogaster trichopterus). *Journal of Comparative Psychology, 111*, 219–225.

Hood, B. M., Hauser, M. D., Anderson, L., & Santos, L. (1999). Gravity biases in a non-human primate? *Developmental Science, 2*, 35–41.

Horner, V., & Whiten, A. (2005). Causal knowledge and imitation/emulation switching in chimpanzees (Pan troglodytes) and children (Homo sapiens). *Animal cognition, 8*(3), 164–181.

Horowitz, A. (2009). Disambiguating the 'guilty look': salient prompts to a familiar dog behaviour. *Behavioural Processes, 81*(3), 447–452.

Horowitz, A. (2012). Fair is fine, but more is better: limits to inequity aversion in the domestic dog. *Social Justice Research, 25*(2), 195–212.

Hoyer, W. J. (1973). Discontinuous shock and discriminated-avoidance learning by tadpoles (Rana pipiens). *Psychological Reports, 33*(1), 143–146.

Hume, D. (1739/1978). *A Treatise of Human Nature: Book I Of the Understanding.* Oxford, UK: Oxford University Press.

Hunt, G. R., & Gray, R. D. (2004). The crafting of hook tools by wild New Caledonian crows. *Proceedings of the Royal Society B: Biological Sciences, 271*(Suppl_3), S88–S90.

Huxley, J. S. (1923). Courtship activities in the red-throated diver (Colymbus stellatus Pontopp.); together with a discussion of the evolution of courtship in birds. *Journal of the Linnean Society of London, Zoology, 35*, 253–292.

Inoue, S., & Matsuzawa, T. (2007). Working memory of numerals in chimpanzees. *Current Biology*, 17, R1004–R1005.

Inoue-Nakamura, N., & Matsuzawa, T. (1997). Development of stone tool use by wild chimpanzees (Pan troglodytes). *Journal of Comparative Psychology*, 111(2), 159–173.

Ioalè, P., Nozzolini, M., & Papi, F. (1990). Homing pigeons do extract directional information from olfactory stimuli. *Behavioral Ecology and Sociobiology*, 26, 301–305.

Irie-Sugimoto, N., Kobayashi, T., Sato, T., & Hasegawa, T. (2008). Evidence of means–end behavior in Asian elephants (*Elephas maximus*). *Animal Cognition*, 11(2), 359–365.

Jaakkola, K., Guarino, E., & Rodriguez, M. (2010). Blindfolded imitation in a bottlenose dolphin (Tursiops truncatus). *International Journal of Comparative Psychology*, 23, 671–688.

Janik, V. M. (2000). Whistle matching in wild bottlenose dolphins (Tursiops truncatus). *Science*, 289, 1355–1357.

Janik, V. M., & Slater, P. J. B. (1998). Context-specific use suggests that bottlenose dolphin signature whistles are cohesion calls. *Animal Behaviour*, 56, 829–838.

Janik, V. M., & Slater, P. J. B. (2000). The different roles of social learning in vocal communication. *Animal Behaviour*, 60, 1–11.

Jennings, H. S. (1906). *Behavior of the Lower Organisms*. New York, NY: Columbia University Press.

Jerison, H. J. (1973). *Evolution of the brain and intelligence*. New York, NY: Academic Press.

Jones, R. B., & Roper, T. J. (1997). Olfaction in the domestic fowl: a critical review. *Physiology and Behavior*, 62, 1009–1018.

Jordan, K. E., & Brannon, E. M. (2006). Weber's law influences numerical representations in rhesus macaques (Macaca mulatta). *Animal Cognition*, 9, 159–172.

Kaas, J. H. (2000). Why is brain size so important: design problems and solutions as neocortex gets bigger or smaller. *Brain and Mind*, 1, 7–23.

Kaiser, D., Sherburne, L., & Zentall, T. (1997). Directed forgetting in pigeons resulting from the reallocation of memory-maintaining processes on forget-cue trials. *Psychonomic Bulletin & Review*, 4(4), 559–565.

Kamil, A. C. (1978). Systematic foraging by a nectar-feeding bird, the amakihi (Loxops virens). *Journal of Comparative & Physiological Psychology*, 92, 388–396.

Kamil, A. C., & Roitblat, H. L. (1985). The ecology of foraging behaviour: implications for animal learning and memory. *Annual Review of Psychology*, 36, 141–169.

Kamil, L. J., & Balda, R. P. (1990). Differential memory for different cache sites by Clark's nutcrackers. *Journal of Experimental Psychology: Animal Behavior Processes*, 16, 162–168.

Kamin, L. J. (1968). 'Attention-like' processes in classical conditioning. In M. R. Jones (Ed.), *Miami Symposium on the Prediction of Behavior: Aversive Stimulation* (pp. 9–31). Miami. FL: University of Miami Press.

Kaminski, J., Call, J., & Fischer, J. (2004). Word learning in a domestic dog: evidence for 'fast mapping'. *Science*, 5677, 1682–1683.

Kaminski, J., Riedel, J., Call, J., & Tomasello, M. (2005). Domestic goats, Capra hircus, follow gaze direction and use social cues in an object choice task. *Animal Behaviour*, 69(1), 11–18.

Kanciruk, P., & Herrnkind, W. (1978). Mass migration of spiny lobster, Panulirus Argus (Crustacea: Palinuridae): behavior and environmental correlates. *Bulletin of Marine Science*, 28(4), 601–623.

Karakashian, S. J., Gyger, M., & Marler, P. (1988). Audience effects on alarm calling in chickens (Gallus gallus). *Journal of Comparative Psychology*, 102, 129–135.

Kastak, C. R., Schusterman, R. J., & Kastak, D. (2001). Equivalence classification by California sea lions using class-specific reinforcers. *Journal of the Experimental Analysis of Behavior*, 76, 131.

Kavaliers, M., Choleris, E., & Colwell, D. D. (2001). Learning from others to cope with biting flies: social learning of fear-induced conditioned analgesia and active avoidance. *Behavioral Neuroscience*, 115(3), 661–674.

Kavanagh, M. (1980). Invasion of the forest by an African Savannah monkey: behavioural adaptations. *Behaviour*, 73, 238–260.

Kawai, N., & Matsuzawa, T. (2000). Numerical memory span in a chimpanzee. *Nature*, 403, 39–40.

Keeton, W. T. (1971). Magnets interfere with pigeon homing. *Proceedings of the National Academy of Sciences*, 68(1), 102–106.

Killeen, P. R., & Fetterman, J. G. (1988). A behavioral theory of timing. *Psychological Review*, 95, 274–295.

Klug, H., Lindström, K., & St. Mary, C. M. (2006). Parents benefit from eating offspring: Density-dependent egg survivorship compensates for filial cannibalism. *Evolution*, 60, 2087–2095.

Koay, G., Heffner, R. S., & Heffner, H. E. (1998). Hearing in a megachiropteran fruit bat (Rousettus aegyptiacus). *Journal of Comparative Psychology*, 112, 371–382.

Koehler, O. (1951). The ability of birds to 'count'. *Bulletin of Animal Behaviour*, 9, 41–45.

Köhler, W. (1925). *The Mentality of Apes*. London: Kegan Paul Trench & Trubner (trans. E. Winter).

Köhler, W. (1963/1921). *Intelligenzprüfungen an Menschenaffen: Mit einem Anhang: Zur Psychologie des Schimpansen* (Heidelberger Taschenbücher) (2nd edn), durchges. Aufl. 1921. Unveränd. Nachdruck.). Berlin: Springer.

Konishi, M. (1965). The role of auditory feedback in the control of vocalization in the white-crowned sparrow. *Zeitschrift für Tierpsychologie*, 22, 770–783.

Konishi, M. (1973). How the owl tracks its prey: experiments with trained barn owls reveal how their acute sense of hearing enables them to catch prey in the dark. *American Scientist*, 61, 414–424.

Krebs, J. R., Healy, S. D., & Shettleworth, S. J. (1990). Spatial memory of Paridae: comparison of a storing and a non-storing species, the coal tit, Parus ater, and the great tit, Parus major. *Animal Behaviour*, 39, 1127–1137.

Kreithen, M. L., & Keeton, W. T. (1974). Detection of changes in atmospheric pressure by the homing pigeon, Columba livia. *Journal of Comparative Physiology*, 89, 73–82.

Kruczek, M. (1998). Female bank vole (Clethrionomys glareolus) recognition: preference for the stud male. *Behavioural Processes*, 43, 229–237.

Kuan, L., & Colwill, R. M. (1997). Demonstration of a socially transmitted taste aversion in the rat. *Psychonomic Bulletin & Review*, 4(3), 374–377.

Kunz, T. H., Allgaier, A. L., Seyjagat, J., & Caligiuri, R. (1994). Allomaternal care – helper-assisted birth in the Rodrigues fruit bat, Pteropus-Rodricensis (*Chiroptera, Pteropodidae*). *Journal of Zoology*, 232, 691–700.

Leadbeater, E., Raine, N. E., & Chittka, L. (2006). Social learning: ants and the meaning of teaching. *Current Biology*, 16(9), R323–R325.

Lemon, M., Lynch, T. P., Cato, D. H., & Harcourt, R. G. (2006). Response of travelling bottlenose dolphins (Tursiops aduncus) to experimental approaches by a powerboat in Jervis Bay, New South Wales, Australia. *Biological Conservation*, 127, 363–372.

Lempers, J. D. (1979). Young children's production and comprehension of nonverbal deictic behaviors. *The Journal of Genetic Psychology*, 135, 93–102.

Levey, D. J., Londoño, G. A., Ungvari-Martin, J., Hiersoux, M. R., Jankowski, J. E., Poulsen, J. R., Stracey, C. M., et al. (2009). Urban mockingbirds quickly learn to identify individual humans. *Proceedings of the National Academy of Sciences*, 1728, 499–508.

Lewis, K., Jaffe, S., & Brannon, E. (2005). Analog number representations in mongoose lemurs (Eulemur mongoz): evidence from a search task. *Animal Cognition*, 8, 247–252.

Leyhausen, P. (1979). *Cat Behavior: The Predatory and Social Behavior of Domestic and Wild Cats* (B. A. Tonkin, trans.) (1st ed.). Taylor & Francis / Garland STPM Press.

Lieberman, D. A., McIntosh, D. C., & Thomas, G. V. (1979). Learning when reward is delayed: a marking hypothesis. *Journal of Experimental Psychology: Animal Behavior Processes*, 5, 224–242.

Limongelli, L., Boysen, S. T., & Visalberghi, E. (1995). Comprehension of cause-effect relations in a tool-using task by chimpanzees (Pan troglodytes). *Journal of Comparative Psychology*, 109, 18–26.

Lohmann, K. J., Lohmann, C. M. F., & Endres, C. S. (2008). The sensory ecology of ocean navigation. *Journal of Experimental Biology*, 211(11), 1719–1728.

Lohmann, K. J., Putman, N. F., & Lohmann, C. M. F. (2008). Geomagnetic imprinting: a unifying hypothesis of long-distance natal homing in salmon and sea turtles. *Proceedings of the National Academy of Sciences*, 105(49), 19096–19101.

Lorenz, K. (1935). Der Kumpan in der Umwelt des Vogels: Der Artgenosse als auslösendes Moment sozialer Verhaltungsweisen. *Journal für Ornithologie*, 83, 137–213; 289–413.

Lorenz, K. (1952). *King Solomon's Ring*. New York, NY: Thomas Y. Crowell.

Loyau, A., Saint Jalme, M., Cagniant, C., & Sorci, G. (2005). Multiple sexual advertisements honestly reflect health status in peacocks (Pavo cristatus). *Behavioral Ecology and Sociobiology*, 58, 552–557.

Macphail, E. M. (1987). The comparative psychology of intelligence. *Behavioral and Brain Sciences*, 10, 645–695.

Macreae, D., & Trolle, E. (1956). The defect of function in visual agnosia. *Brain*, 77, 94–110.

Maki, W. S., & Hegvik, D. K. (1980). Directed forgetting in pigeons. *Animal Learning and Behavior*, 8, 567–574.

Marchant, J (1975). *Alfred Russel Wallace: Letters and Reminiscences*. New York, NY: Arno Press. Vol. 1, p 243.

Marcus, G. F., & Fisher, S. E. (2003). FOXP2 in focus: what can genes tell us about speech and language? *Trends in Cognitive Sciences*, 7, 257–262.

Marler, P. (1970). A comparative approach to vocal learning: song development in white-crowned sparrows. *Journal of Comparative and Physiological Psychology*, 71, 1–25.

Marler, P. (1976). An ethological theory of the origin of vocal learning. *Annals of the New York Academy of Sciences*, 280, 386–395.

Marler, P., Dufty, A., & Pickert, R. (1986a). Vocal communication in the domestic chicken: I. Does a sender communicate information about the quality of a food referent to a receiver? *Animal Behaviour*, 34, 188–193.

Marler, P., Dufty, A., & Pickert, R. (1986b). Vocal communication in the domestic chicken: II. Is a sender sensitive to the presence and nature of a receiver? *Animal Behaviour*, 34, 194–198.

Marler, P., & Tamura, M. (1964). Culturally transmitted patterns of vocal behavior in sparrows. *Science*, 146, 1483–1486.

Maros, K., Gácsi, M., & Miklósi, Á. (2008). Comprehension of human pointing gestures in horses (Equus caballus). *Animal Cognition*, 11(3), 457–466.

Martinoya, C., & Delius, J. D. (1990). Perception of rotating spiral patterns by pigeons. *Biological Cybernetics*, 63, 127–134.

McFadden, S. A., & Reymond, L. (1985). A further look at the binocular visual field of the pigeon (Columba livia). *Vision Research,* 25, 1741–1746.

McGonigle, B. O., & Chalmers, M. (1977). Are monkeys logical? *Nature,* 267, 694–696.

McKinley, S., & Young, R. J. (2003). The efficacy of the model–rival method when compared with operant conditioning for training domestic dogs to perform a retrieval–selection task. *Applied Animal Behaviour Science,* 81(4), 357–365.

McLean, I. G., Schmitt, N. T., Jarman, P. J., Duncan, C., & Wynne, C. D. L. (2000). Learning for life: training marsupials to recognise introduced predators. *Behaviour,* 137(10), 1361–1376.

McNeill, D. (1970). *The Acquisition of Language: The Study of Developmental Psycholinguistics.* New York, NY: Harper and Row.

Mechner, F. (1958). Probability relations within response sequences under ratio reinforcement. *Journal of the Experimental Analysis of Behavior,* 1, 109.

Meck, W. H., & Church, R. M. (1983). A mode control model of counting and timing processes. *Journal of Experimental Psychology: Animal Behavior Processes,* 9, 320–334.

Menzel, R., & Erber, J. (1978). Learning and memory in bees. *Scientific American,* 239(1), 102–110.

Menzel, R., Geiger, K., Chittka, L., Joerges, J., Kunze, J., & Müller, U. (1996). The knowledge base of bee navigation. *Journal of Experimental Biology,* 199, 141–146.

Menzel, R., Greggers, U., Smith, A., Berger, S., Brandt, R., Brunke, S., Bundrock, G., Hülse, S., Plümpe, T., Schaupp, F., Schüttler, E., Stach, S., Stindt, J., Stollhoff, N., & Watzl, S. (2005). Honey bees navigate according to a map-like spatial memory. *Proceedings of the National Academy of Sciences of the United States of America,* 102(8), 3040–3045.

Menzel, E. W., Savage-Rumbaugh, E. S., & Lawson, J. (1985). Chimpanzee (Pan troglodytes) spatial problem solving with the use of mirrors and televised equivalents of mirrors. *Journal of Comparative Psychology,* 99(2), 211–217.

Merlin, C., Gegear, R. J., & Reppert, S. M. (2009). Antennal circadian clocks coordinate sun compass orientation in migratory monarch butterflies. *Science,* 325(5948), 1700–1704.

Mersmann, D., Tomasello, M., Call, J., Kaminski, J., & Taborsky, M. (2011). Simple mechanisms can explain social learning in domestic dogs (Canis familiaris). *Ethology,* 117(8), 675–690.

Michelson, A., Andersen, B. B., Storm, J., Kirchner, W. H., & Lindauer, M. (1992). How honeybees perceive communication dances, studied by means of a mechanical model. *Behavioral Ecology and Sociobiology,* 30, 143–150.

Miklósi, Á., Polgardi, R., Topál, J., & Csányi, V. (1998). Use of experimenter-given cues in dogs. *Animal Cognition,* 1(2), 113–121.

Miller, H. C., Gipson, C. D., Vaughan, A., Rayburn-Reeves, R., & Zentall, T. R. (2009). Object permanence in dogs: invisible displacement in a rotation task. *Psychonomic Bulletin & Review,* 16, 150–155.

Miller, H. C., Rayburn-Reeves, R., & Zentall, T. R. (2009). Imitation and emulation by dogs using a bidirectional control procedure. *Behavioural Processes,* 80(2), 109–114.

Miller, R. R., & Berk, A. M. (1977). Retention over metamorphosis in the African claw-toed frog. *Journal of Experimental Psychology: Animal Behavior Processes,* 3, 343–356.

Mínguez, E. (1997). Olfactory nest recognition by British storm-petrel chicks. *Animal Behaviour,* 53, 701–707.

Miskovic, V., & Keil, A. (2012). Acquired fears reflected in cortical sensory processing: a review of electrophysiological studies of human classical conditioning. *Psychophysiology,* 49(9), 1230–1241.

Mistleberger, R. E., & Rusak, B. (2004). Biological rhythms and behavior. In J. J. Bolhuis & L.-A. Giraldeau (Eds), *The Behavior of Animals: Mechanisms, Function and Evolution* (pp. 71–96). Hoboken, NJ: Wiley-Blackwell.

Mitchell, C. J., Heyes, C. M., Gardner, M. R., & Dawson, G. R. (1999). Limitations of a bidirectional control procedure for the investigation of imitation in rats: odour cues on the manipulandum. *The Quarterly Journal of Experimental Psychology Section B*, 52(3), 193–202.

Montgomery, K. C. (1955). The relation between fear induced by novel stimulation and exploratory drive. *Journal of Comparative and Physiological Psychology*, 48(4), 254–260.

Moore, D., Van Nest, B., & Seier, E. (2011). Diminishing returns: the influence of experience and environment on time-memory extinction in honey bee foragers. *Journal of Comparative Physiology A: Neuroethology, Sensory, Neural, and Behavioral Physiology*, 197(6), 641–651.

Moore, S. E. (2008). Marine mammals as ecosystem sentinels. *Journal of Mammalogy*, 89(3), 534–540.

Morgan, C. L. (1894). *Introduction to Comparative Psychology*. London, UK: Scott.

Morris, P. H., Doe, C., & Godsell, E. (2008). Secondary emotions in non-primate species? Behavioural reports and subjective claims by animal owners. *Cognition & Emotion*, 22, 3–20.

Morris, R. G. M. (1981). Spatial localization does not require the presence of local cues. *Learning and Motivation*, 12, 239–260.

Mossman, C. A., & Drickamer, L. C. (1996). Odor preferences of female house mice (Mus domesticus) in seminatural enclosures. *Journal of Comparative Psychology*, 110, 131–138.

Mouritsen, H., & Frost, B. J. (2002). Virtual migration in tethered flying monarch butterflies reveals their orientation mechanisms. *Proceedings of the National Academy of Sciences of the United States of America*, 99, 10162–10166.

Murphy, C. M., & Messer, D. J. (1977). Mothers, infants and pointing: a study of a gesture. In H. R. Schaffer (Ed.), *Studies in Mother-Infant Interaction*. London: Academic Press.

Nagel, T. (1974). What is it like to be a bat? *Philosophical Review*, 83, 435–450.

Natale, F., Antinucci, F., Spinozzi, G., & Potí, P. (1986). Stage 6 object concept in nonhuman primate cognition: a comparison between gorilla (Gorilla gorilla gorilla) and Japanese macaque (Macaca fuscata). *Journal of Comparative Psychology*, 100, 335.

National Pet Owners Survey: Industry Statistics & Trends (2012). *American Pet Products Association*. Retrieved July 19, 2012, from http://www.americanpetproducts.org/press_industrytrends.asp

Neiworth, J. J., Steinmark, E., Basile, B. M., Wonders, R., Steely, F., & DeHart, C. (2003). A test of object permanence in a new-world monkey species, cotton top tamarins (Saguinus oedipus). *Animal Cognition*, 6, 27–37.

Nelson, B. S., & Stoddard, P. K. (1998). Accuracy of auditory distance and azimuth perception by a passerine bird in natural habitat. *Animal Behaviour*, 56, 467–477.

Nevo, D. (1996). The desert locust, *Schistocerca gregaria*, and its control in the land of israel and the near east in antiquity, with some reflections on its appearance in Israel in modern times. *Phytoparasitica*, 24(1), 7–32.

Nicol, C. J. (1996). Farm animal cognition. *Animal Science*, 62(03), 375–391.

Nishida, T. (1987). Local traditions and cultural transmission. In B. B. Smuts, D. L. Cheney, R. M. Seyfarth, R. W. Wrangham, & T. T. Stuhsaker (Eds), *Primate Societies* (pp. 462–474). Chicago, IL: University of Chicago Press.

Noble, J., Todd, P. M., & Tucif, E. (2001). Explaining social learning of food preferences without aversions: an evolutionary simulation model of Norway rats.

Proceedings of the Royal Society of London. Series B: Biological Sciences, 268(1463), 141–149.

Oldham, C. (1930) The shell-smashing habit of gulls. *Ibis*, 72(2), 239–243.

Olton, D. S. (1985). A comparative analysis of memory. *Journal of Experimental Psychology: Learning, Memory, and Cognition*, 11, 480–484.

Ophir, A. G., & Galef, B. G. (2003). Female Japanese quail affiliate with live males that they have seen mate on video. *Animal Behaviour*, 66, 369–375.

Ortolani, A., Vernooij, H., & Coppinger, R. (2009). Ethiopian village dogs: behavioural responses to a stranger's approach. *Applied Animal Behaviour Science*, 119(3–4), 210–218.

Pack, A. A., & Herman, L. M. (2004). Bottlenosed dolphins (*Tursiops truncatus*) comprehend the referent of both static and dynamic human gazing and pointing in an object-choice task. *Journal of Comparative Psychology*, 118(2), 160–171.

Palacios, A. G., & Varela, F. J. (1992). Color mixing in the pigeon (Columba livia) II: a psychophysical determination in the middle, short and near-UV wavelength range. *Vision Research*, 32, 1947–1953.

Palestis, B. G., & Burger, J. (1998). Evidence for social facilitation of preening in the common tern. *Animal Behaviour*, 56(5), 1107–1111.

Papi, F., & Luschi, P. (1996). Pinpointing 'Isla Meta': the case of sea turtles and albatrosses. *Journal of Experimental Biology*, 199, 65–71.

Parker, S.T., Mitchell, R.W. & Boccia, M.L. (1994). *Self-Awareness in Animals and Human: Developmental Perspectives*. New York, NY, US: Cambridge University Press.

Parr, L. A., Winslow, J. T., Hopkins, W. D., & De Waal, F. B. M. (2000). Recognizing facial cues: individual discrimination by chimpanzees (Pan troglodytes) and rhesus monkeys (Macaca mulatto). *Journal of Comparative Psychology*, 114(1), 47–60.

Passingham, R. E. (1982). *The Human Primate*. Oxford, UK: W. H. Freeman.

Patterson, F. G. (1978). The gestures of a gorilla: language acquisition in another pongid. *Brain and Language*, 5, 72–97.

Pecchia, T., Gagliardo, A., Filannino, C., Ioalè, P., & Vallortigara, G. (2013). Navigating through an asymmetrical brain: lateralisation and homing in pigeon. In D. Csermely & L. Regolin (Eds), *Behavioral Lateralization in Vertebrates* (pp. 107–124). Springer Berlin Heidelberg.

Pepperberg, I. M. (1987). Evidence for conceptual quantitative abilities in the African gray parrot: labeling of cardinal sets. *Ethology*, 75, 37–61.

Pepperberg, I. M. (1988). An interactive modeling technique for acquisition of communication skills: separation of 'labeling' and 'requesting' in a psittacine subject. *Applied Psycholinguistics*, 9(01), 59–76.

Pepperberg, I. M. (1994). Numerical competence in an African gray parrot (Psittacus erithacus). *Journal of Comparative Psychology*, 108, 36–44.

Pepperberg, I. M., Willner, M. R., & Gravitz, L. B. (1997). Development of Piagetian object permanence in grey parrot (Psittacus erithacus). *Journal of Comparative Psychology*, 111, 63–75.

Pfiester, M., Koehler, P. G., & Pereira, R. M. (2008). Ability of bed bug-detecting canines to locate live bed bugs and viable bed bug eggs. *Journal of Economic Entomology*, 101, 1389–1396.

Pfungst, O. (1911/1965). *Clever Hans: (The Horse of Mr. von Osten)*. New York, NY: Holt, Rinehard and Winston, Inc.

Piaget, J. (1952). *The Origins of Intelligence in Children*. New York, NY: International Universities Press (Trans. M. Cook. Originally published 1936).

Pilley, J. W., & Reid, A. K. (2011). Border collie comprehends object names as verbal referents. *Behavioural Processes*, 86, 184–195.

Pizzo, M., & Crystal, J. (2002). Representation of time in time-place learning. *Learning & Behavior*, 30, 387–393.

Platt, J. R., & Johnson, D. M. (1971). Localization of position within a homogeneous behavior chain: effects of error contingencies. *Learning and Motivation*, 2, 386–414.

Plotnik, J. M., de Waal, F. B. M., & Reiss, D. (2006). Self-recognition in an Asian elephant. *Proceedings of the National Academy of Sciences of the United States of America*, 103(45), 17053–17057.

Poucet, B., Thinus-Blanc, C., & Chapuis, N. (1983). Route planning in cats, in relation to the visibility of the goal. *Animal Behaviour*, 31, 594–599.

Povinelli, D. J., & Eddy, T. J. (1996). What young chimpanzees know about seeing. *Monographs of the Society for Research in Child Development*, 61, v-247.

Povinelli, D. J., Nelson, K. E., & Boysen, S. T. (1990). Inferences about guessing and knowing by chimpanzees (Pan troglodytes). *Journal of Comparative Psychology*, 104, 203–210.

Povinelli, D. J., Rulf, A. B., Landau, K. R., & Bierschwale, D. T. (1993). Self-recognition in chimpanzees (Pan troglodytes): distribution, ontogeny, and patterns of emergence. *Journal of Comparative Psychology*, 107, 347–372.

Powell, R. W. (1967). Avoidance and escape conditioning in lizards. *Psychological Reports*, 20(2), 583–586.

Premack, D. (1976). *Intelligence in Ape and Man*. Oxford, England: Lawrence Erlbaum Assoc.

Premack, D., & Woodruff, G. (1978). Chimpanzee problem-solving: a test for comprehension. *Science*, 202, 532–535.

Price, E. O. (1984). Behavioral aspects of animal domestication. *The Quarterly Review of Biology*, 59(1), 1–32.

Quinn, T. P. (1980). Evidence for celestial and magnetic compass orientation in lake migrating sockeye salmon fry. *Journal of Comparative Physiology A: Neuroethology, Sensory, Neural, and Behavioral Physiology*, 137(3), 243–248.

Quintana-Rizzo, E., Mann, D. A., & Wells, R. S. (2006). Estimated communication range of social sounds used by bottlenose dolphins (Tursiops truncatus). *The Journal of the Acoustical Society of America*, 120, 1671–1683.

Raby, C. R., & Clayton, N. S. (2010). Chapter 1 – the cognition of caching and recovery in food-storing birds. In T. J. R. H. Jane Brockmann (Ed.), *Advances in the Study of Behavior* (Vol. 41, pp. 1–34). London, UK: Academic Press.

Range, F., Horn, L., Viranyi, Z., & Huber, L. (2008). The absence of reward induces inequity aversion in dogs. *Proceedings of the National Academy of Sciences*, 106, 340–345.

Range, F., Viranyi, Z., & Huber, L. (2007). Selective imitation in domestic dogs. *Current Biology: CB*, 17(10), 868–872.

Rasmussen, K., Palacios, D. M., Calambokidis, J., Saborío, M. T., Rosa, L. D., Secchi, E. R., Steiger, G. H., et al. (2007). Southern hemisphere humpback whales wintering off Central America: insights from water temperature into the longest mammalian migration. *Biology Letters*, 3(3), 302–305.

Ray, E. D., Gardner, M. R., & Heyes, C. M. (2000). Seeing how it's done: matching conditions for observer rats (Rattus norvegicus) in the bidirectional control. *Animal Cognition*, 3(3), 147–157.

Real, P. G, Iannazzi, R., & Kamil, A. C. (1984). Discrimination and generalization of leaf damage by blue jays (Cyanocitta cristata). *Animal Learning & Behavior*, 12, 202–208.

Reaux, J. E., Theall, L. A., & Povinelli, D. J. (1999). A longitudinal investigation of chimpanzees' understanding of visual perception. *Child Development*, 70, 275–290.

Regolin, L., Vallortigara, G., & Zanforlin, M. (1994). Perceptual and motivational aspects of detour behaviour in young chicks. *Animal Behaviour,* 47, 123–131.

Regolin, L., Vallortigara, G., & Zanforlin, M. (1995). Object and spatial representations in detour problems by chicks. *Animal Behaviour,* 49, 195–199.

Reid, S. L., & Spetch, M. L. (1998). Perception of pictorial depth cues by pigeons. *Psychonomic Bulletin & Review,* 5, 698–704.

Reiss, D., & Marino, L. (2001). Mirror self-recognition in the bottlenose dolphin: a case of cognitive convergence. *Proceedings of the National Academy of Sciences,* 98(10), 5937–5942.

Remy, M., & Emmerton, J. (1989). Behavioral spectral sensitivities of different retinal areas in pigeons. *Behavioral Neuroscience,* 103, 170–177.

Rescorla, R. A. (1967). Pavlovian conditioning and its proper control procedures. *Psychological Review,* 74, 71–80.

Richards, D. G., Wolz, J. P., & Herman, L. M. (1984). Vocal mimicry of computer-generated sounds and vocal labeling of objects by a bottlenosed dolphin, Tursiops truncatus. *Journal of Comparative Psychology,* 98, 10–28.

Richardson, T. O., Sleeman, P. A., McNamara, J. M., Houston, A. I., & Franks, N. R. (2007). Teaching with evaluation in ants. *Current Biology,* 17(17), 1520–1526.

Riedel, J., Schumann, K., Kaminski, J., Call, J., & Tomasello, M. (2008). The early ontogeny of human-dog communication. *Animal Behaviour,* 75(3), 1003–1014.

Riley, J. R., Greggers, U., Smith, A. D., Reynolds, D. R., & Menzel, R. (2005). The flight paths of honeybees recruited by the waggle dance. *Nature,* 435, 205–207.

Rilling, M., & McDiarmid, C. (1965) Signal detection in fixed-ratio schedules. *Science,* 148 (Whole No. 3669), 526–527

Roberts, S. (1981). Isolation of an internal clock. *Journal of Experimental Psychology: Animal Behavior Processes,* 7, 242–268.

Roeder, K. D., & Treat, A. E. (1961). The detection and evasion of bats by moths. *American Scientist,* 49, 135–148.

Romanes, G. J., (1884) *Animal Intelligence.* London, UK: Kegan, Paul, Trench & Co.

Roper, K., Chaponis, D., & Blaisdell, A. (2005). Transfer of directed-forgetting cues across discrimination tasks with pigeons. *Psychonomic Bulletin & Review,* 12(6), 1005–1010.

Roper, K., Kaiser, D., & Zentall, T. (1995). True directed forgetting in pigeons may occur only when alternative working memory is required on forget-cue trials. *Learning & Behavior,* 23(3), 280–285.

Rumbaugh, D. M., & Gill, T. V. (1977). Lana's acquisition of linguistic skills. In D. M. Rumbaugh (Ed.), *Language Learning by a Chimpanzee: The LANA Project* (pp. 165–192). New York: NY: Academic Press.

Russell S. (1979) Brain size and intelligence: a comparative perspective. In D. A. Oakley and H. C. Plotkin (Eds), *Brain, Behavior and Evolution,* (pp. 126–153). London, UK: Methuen.

Sacks O. (1990) *The Man Who Mistook His Wife for a Hat.* New York: HarperCollins Publishers.

Saigusa, T., Tero, A., Nakagaki, T., & Kuramoto, Y. (2008). Amoebae anticipate periodic events. *Physical Review Letters,* 100(1), 018101.

Salmon, M., & Witherington, B. E. (1995). Artificial lighting and seafinding by loggerhead hatchlings: evidence for lunar modulation. *Copeia,* 1995(4), 931–938.

Salwiczek, L. H., Watanabe, A., & Clayton, N. S. (2010). Ten years of research into avian models of episodic-like memory and its implications for developmental and comparative cognition. *Behavioural Brain Research,* 215, 221–234.

Savage-Rumbaugh, S., McDonald, K., Sevcik, R. A., Hopkins, W. D., & Rubert, E. (1986). Spontaeous symbol acquisition and communicative use by Pygmy Chimpanzees (Pan paniscus). *Journal of Experimental Psychology: General,* 115, 211–235.

Savage-Rumbaugh, E. S., Murphy, J., Sevcik, R. A., Brakke, K. E., Williams, S. L., & Rumbaugh, D. M. (1993). Language comprehension in ape and child. *Monographs of the Society for Research in Child Development*, 58, v–252.

Sayigh, L. S., Tyack, P. L., Wells, R. S., Scott, M. D., & Irvine, A. B. (1995). Sex difference in signature whistle production of free-ranging bottlenose dolphins, Tursiops truncates. *Behavioral Ecology and Sociobiology*, 36, 171–177.

Sayigh, L. S., Tyack, P. L., Wells, R. S., Solow, A., Scott, M., & Irvine, A. B. (1999) Individual recognition in wild bottlenose dolphins: a field test using playback experiments. *Animal Behaviour*, 57, 41–50.

Scheumann, M., & Call, J. (2004). The use of experimenter-given cues by South African fur seals (Arctocephalus pusillus). *Animal Cognition*, 7(4), 224–230.

Schloegl, C., Schmidt, J., Boeckle, M., Weiß, B. M., & Kotrschal, K. (2012). Grey parrots use inferential reasoning based on acoustic cues alone. *Proceedings of the Royal Society B: Biological Sciences*, 279(1745), 4135–4142.

Schmidt-Koenig, K., Ganzhorn, J. U., & Ranwaud, R. (1991). The sun compass. In P. Berthold (Ed.), *Orientation in Birds* (pp. 1–15). Basel, Switzerland: Birkhauser Verlag.

Schrier, A. M, Angarella, R., & Povar, M. L. (1984) Studies of concept formation by stumptailed monkeys: concepts humans, monkeys, and letter A. *Journal of Experimental Psychology: Animal Behavior Processes*, 10, 564–584.

Schusterman, R. J., & Kastak, D. (1998). Functional equivalence in a California sea lion: relevance to animal social and communicative interactions. *Animal Behaviour*, 55, 1087–1095.

Scott, J. P., & Fuller, J. L. (1965). *Genetics and the Social Behavior of the Dog* (1st ed.). Chicago, IL.: University Of Chicago Press.

Seyfarth, R. M., & Cheney, D. L. (1999). Production, usage and response in nonhuman primate vocal development. In M. D. Hauser & M. Konishi (Eds), *The Design of Animal Communication* (pp. 391–417). Cambridge MA: MIT Press.

Sherry, D. F. (1982). Food storage, memory and marsh tits. *Animal Behaviour*, 30, 631–633.

Sherry, D. F. (1984). Food storage by black-capped chickadees: memory for the location and contents of caches. *Animal Behaviour*, 32, 451–464.

Sherry, D. F. (1992) Landmarks, the hippocampus, and spatial search in food-storing birds. In W. K. Honig and J. G. Fetterman (Eds), *Cognitive Aspects of Stimulus Control* (pp. 184–201). Mahwab, NJ: Lawrence Erlbaum.

Sherry, D. F., Krebs, J. R., & Cowie, R. J. (1981). Memory for location of stored food in marsh tits. *Animal Behaviour*, 29, 1260–1266.

Shettleworth, S. J. (2009). *Cognition, Evolution, and Behavior* (2nd ed.). Oxford University Press, USA.

Shimp, C. P. (1981). The local organization of behavior: discrimination of and memory for simple behavioral patterns. *Journal of the Experimental Analysis of Behavior*, 36, 303–315.

Shimp, C. P. (1982). On metaknowledge in the pigeon: an organism's knowledge about its own behavior. *Animal Learning and Behavior*, 10, 358–364.

Simmons, J. A., Ferragamo, M. J., & Moss, C. F. (1998). Echo-delay resolution in sonar images of the big brown bat, Eptesicus fuscus. *Proceedings of the National Academy of Sciences*, 95, 12647–12652.

Skinner, B. F. (1948). 'Superstition' in the pigeon. *Journal of Experimental Psychology*, 38, 168–172.

Skinner, B. F. (1962). Two 'synthetic social relations'. *Journal of the Experimental Analysis of Behavior*, 5, 531–533.

Skinner, B. F. (1972). *Cumulative Record* (3rd ed.). New York: N.Y.: Appleton Century Crofts.

Slater, P. J. B. (1983). Bird song learning: theme and variations. In A. H. Brush & G. A. Clark, (Eds), *Perspectives in Ornithology* (pp. 475–499). Cambridge, England: Cambridge University Press.

Smith, J. D., Shields, W. E., & Washburn, D. A. (2003). The comparative psychology of uncertainty monitoring and metacognition. *The Behavioral and Brain Sciences*, 26(3), 317–339; discussion 340–373.

Smolker, R., & Pepper, J. W. (1999). Whistle convergence among allied male bottlenose dolphins (Delphinidae, Tursiops sp.). *Ethology*, 105, 595–617.

Smolker, R., Mann, J., & Smuts, B. (1993). Use of signature whistles during separations and reunions by wild bottlenose dolphin mothers and infants. *Behavioral Ecology and Sociobiology*, 33, 393–402.

Spetch, M. L. (1990). Further studies of pigeons' spatial working memory in the open-field task. *Animal Learning and Behavior*, 18, 332–340.

Spetch, M. L., & Honig, W. K. (1988). Characteristics of pigeons' spatial working memory in an open-field task. *Animal Learning and Behavior*, 16, 123–131.

Spetch, M. L., & Friedman, A. (2006). Pigeons see correspondence between objects and their pictures. *Psychological Science*, 17(11), 966–972.

Srinivasan, M. V., Zhang, S. W., Lehrer, M., & Collett, T. S. (1996). Honeybee navigation en route to the goal: visual flight control and odometry. *Journal of Experimental Biology*, 199, 237–244.

Staddon, J. E. R. (1970). Effect of reinforcement duration on fixed-interval responding. *Journal of the Experimental Analysis of Behavior*, 13, 9–11.

Staddon, J. E. R., & Higa, J. J. (1999). Time and memory: towards a pacemaker-free theory of interval timing. *Journal of the Experimental Analysis of Behavior*, 71, 215–251.

Staddon, J. E. R., & Simmelhag, V. L. (1971). The 'superstition' experiment: a reexamination of its implications for the principles of adaptive behavior. *Psychological Review*, 78, 3–43.

Struhsaker, T. T. (1967). Auditory communication among vervet monkeys (Cercopithecus aethiops). In S. A. Altmann (Ed.), *Social Communication among Primates*. Chicago, IL: University of Chicago Press.

Stulp, G., Emery, N. J., Verhulst, S., & Clayton, N. S. (2009). Western scrub-jays conceal auditory information when competitors can hear but cannot see. *Biology Letters*, 5(5), 583–585.

Suarez, S. D., & Gallup Jr., G. G. (1981). Self-recognition in chimpanzees and orangutans, but not gorillas. *Journal of Human Evolution*, 10(2), 175–188.

Suboski, M. (1992). Releaser-induced recognition learning by amphibians and reptiles. *Learning & Behavior*, 20(1), 63–82.

Sutton, J. E., & Shettleworth, S. J. (2008). Memory without awareness: pigeons do not show metamemory in delayed matching to sample. *Journal of experimental psychology: Animal Behavior Processes*, 34(2), 266–282.

Suzuki, S., Kuroda, S., & Nishihara, T. (1995). Tool-set for termite-fishing by chimpanzees in the Ndoki forest, Congo. *Behaviour*, 132(3–4), 219–235.

Swaisgood, R. R., Lindburg, D. G., & Zhou, X. (1999). Giant pandas discriminate individual differences in conspecific scent. *Animal Behaviour*, 57, 1045–1053.

Tapp, P. D., Siwak, C. T., Estrada, J., Holowachuk, D., & Milgram, N. W. (2003). Effects of age on measures of complex working memory span in the Beagle dog (*Canis familiaris*) using two versions of a spatial list learning paradigm. *Learning & Memory*, 10(2), 148–160.

Taylor, A. H., Elliffe, D. M., Hunt, G. R., Emery, N. J., Clayton, N. S., & Gray, R. D. (2011). New Caledonian crows learn the functional properties of novel tool types. *PLoS ONE*, 6(12), e26887.

Taylor, A. H., Medina, F. S., Holzhaider, J. C., Hearne, L. J., Hunt, G. R., & Gray, R. D. (2010). An investigation into the cognition behind spontaneous string pulling in New Caledonian crows. *PLoS ONE*, 5(2), e9345.

Terrace, H. (1979). *Nim*. New York, NY: Knopf.

Terrace, H. S. (1983), Apes who 'talk': language or projection by their teachers? In J. De Luce & H. T. Wilder (Eds), *Language in Primates: Perspectives and Implications* (pp. 19–42). New York, NY: Springer Verlag.

Terrace, H. S. (1993). The phylogeny and ontogeny of serial memory: list learning by pigeons and monkeys. *Psychological Science*, 4, 162–169.

Thinus-Blanc, C., & Scardigli, P. (1981). Object permanence in the golden hamster. *Perceptual and Motor Skills*, 53, 1010.

Thompson, R. K. R., & Herman, L. M. (1977). Memory for lists of sounds by the bottlenosed dolphin: convergence of memory processes with humans? *Science*, 195, 501–503.

Thorndike, E. L. (1898). Animal intelligence: an experimental study of the association processes in animals. *Psychological Review Monograph*, 2 (Whole no., 8).

Thorndike, E. L. (1911). *Animal Intelligence: Experimental Studies*. New York, NY: Macmillan.

Thornton, A., & Malapert, A. (2009). Experimental evidence for social transmission of food acquisition techniques in wild meerkats. *Animal Behaviour*, 78(2), 255–264.

Thornton, A., & McAuliffe, K. (2006). Teaching in wild meerkats. *Science*, 313(5784), 227–229.

Thouless, C. R., Fanshawe, J. H., & Bertram, B. C. R. (1989). Egyptian Vultures Neophron percnopterus and Ostrich Struthio camelus eggs: the origins of stone-throwing behaviour. *Ibis*, 131, 9–15.

Tinbergen, N. (1948). Social releasers and the experimental method required for their study. *Wilson Bulletin*, 60, 6–51.

Tinbergen, N. (1963). On aims and methods of ethology. *Zeitschrift für Tierpsychologie*, 20, 410–433.

Tinbergen, N. (1972). On the orientation of the digger wasp Philanthus triangulum. *The Animal in its World*, 1, 103–127.

Toda, K., & Watanabe, S. (2008). Discrimination of moving video images of self by pigeons (Columba livia). *Animal Cognition*, 11(4), 699–705.

Tolman, E. C., & Honzik, C. H. (1930). 'Insight' in rats. *University of California Publications in Psychology*, 4, 215–232.

Tolman, E. C., Ritchie, B. F., & Kalish, D. (1946). Studies in spatial learning. I. Orientation and the short-cut. *Journal of Experimental Psychology*, 36, 13–24.

Tomasello, M., & Call, J. (2004). The role of humans in the cognitive development of apes revisited. *Animal Cognition*, 7(4), 213–215.

Tomonaga, M. (1999). Establishing functional classes in a chimpanzee (Pan troglodytes) with a two-item sequential-responding procedure. *Journal of the Experimental Analysis of Behavior*, 72, 57.

Tomonaga, M., & Matsuzawa, T. (2002). Enumeration of briefly presented items by the chimpanzee (Pan troglodytes) and humans (Homo sapiens). *Learning & Behavior*, 30, 143–157.

Topál, J., Byrne, R. W., Miklósi, A., & Csányi, V. (2006). Reproducing human actions and action sequences: 'Do as I Do!' in a dog. *Animal Cognition*, 9(4), 355–367.

Townshend, E. (2009). *Darwin's Dogs: How Darwin's Pets Helped Form a World-Changing Theory of Evolution*. London, UK: Frances Lincoln.

Trut, L. (1999). Early Canid domestication: the farm-fox experiment. *American Scientist,* 87(2), 160.

Tyack, P. L. (1997). Development and social functions of signature whistles in bottlenose dolphins Tursiops truncatus. *Bioacoustics,* 8, 21–46.

Tyack, P. L., & Sayigh, L. S. (1997). Vocal learning in cetaceans. In C. T. Snowdon & M. Hausberger (Eds), *Social Influences on Vocal Development* (pp. 208–223). Cambridge: Cambridge University Press.

Udell, M. A. R., Dorey, N. R., & Wynne, C. D. L. (2008). Wolves outperform dogs in following human social cues. *Animal Behaviour,* 76(6), 1767–1773.

Udell, M. A. R., Dorey, N. R., & Wynne, C. D. L. (2010). What did domestication do to dogs? A new account of dogs' sensitivity to human actions. *Biological Reviews,* 85(2), 327–345.

Udell, M. A. R., Dorey, N. R., & Wynne, C. D. L. (2011). Can your dog read your mind? Understanding the causes of canine perspective taking. *Learning & Behavior,* 39(4), 289–302.

Udell, M. A. R., Giglio, R. F., & Wynne, C. D. L. (2008). Domestic dogs (*Canis familiaris*) use human gestures but not nonhuman tokens to find hidden food. *Journal of Comparative Psychology,* 122(1), 84–93.

Udell, M. A. R., & Wynne, C. D. L. (2008). A review of domestic dogs' (*Canis familiaris*) human-like behaviors: or why behavior analysts should stop worrying and love their dogs. *Journal of the Experimental Analysis of Behavior,* 89(2), 247–261.

Uexküll, J. von. (1957). A stroll through the world of animals and men. In C. H. Schiller (Ed.), *Instinctive Behavior: The Development of a Modern Concept* (pp. 5–80). New York: NY: International Universities Press (trans. C. H. Schiller).

Urcuioli, P. J., Zentall, T. R., Jackson-Smith, P., & Steirn, J. N. (1989). Evidence for common coding in many-to-one matching: retention, intertrial interference, and transfer. *Journal of Experimental Psychology: Animal Behavior Processes,* 15, 264–273.

Vallortigara, G., Regolin, L., Rigoni, M., & Zanforlin, M. (1998). Delayed search for a concealed imprinted object in the domestic chick. *Animal Cognition,* 1, 17–24.

Van der Vaart, E., Verbrugge, R., & Hemelrijk, C. K. (2012). Corvid re-caching without 'Theory of Mind': a model. *PLoS ONE,* 7(3), e32904.

Vander Wall, S. B. (1982). An experimental analysis of cache recovery in Clark's nutcracker. *Animal Behaviour,* 30, 84–94.

Varela, F. J., Palacios, A. G., & Goldsmith, T. H. (1993). Color vision of birds. In H. P. Zeigler & H.-J. Bischof (Eds), *Vision, Brain, and Behavior in Birds* (pp. 77–98). Cambridge, MA: MIT Press.

Vaughan, W. J., & Greene, S. L. (1984). Pigeon visual memory capacity. *Journal of Experimental Psychology: Animal Behavior Processes,* 10, 256–271.

Vince, M. A. (1964). Social facilitation of hatching in the bobwhite quail. *Animal Behaviour,* 12(4), 531–534.

Visalberghi, E., & Limongelli, L. (1994). Lack of comprehension of cause-effect relations in tool-using capuchin monkeys (Cebus apella). *Journal of Comparative Psychology,* 108, 15–22.

von Bayern, A. M. P., & Emery, N. J. (2009). Jackdaws respond to human attentional states and communicative cues in different contexts. *Current Biology,* 19(7), 602–606.

von der Emde, G., Schwarz, S., Gomez, L., Budelli, R., & Grant, K. (1998). Electric fish measure distance in the dark. *Nature,* 395, 890–894.

Vowles, D. M. (1954). The orientation of ants. *Journal of Experimental Biology,* 31, 356–375.

Walcott, C. (1991). Magnetic maps in pigeons. In P. Berthold (Ed.), *Orientation in Birds* (pp. 38–51). Basel, Switzerland: Birkhauser Verlag.

Walcott, C. (1996). Pigeon homing: observations, experiments and confusions. *Journal of Experimental Biology*, 199(1), 21–27.

Walker, M. M., & Bitterman, M. E. (1985). Conditioned responding to magnetic fields by honeybees. *Journal of Comparative Physiology A-Sensory Neural & Behavioral Physiology*, 157, 67–71.

Walker, M. M., & Bitterman, M. E. (1989a). Honeybees can be trained to respond to very small changes in geomagnetic field intensity. *Journal of Experimental Biology*, 145(1), 489–494.

Walker, M. M., & Bitterman, M. E. (1989b). Attached magnets impair magnetic field discrimination by honeybees. *Journal of Experimental Biology*, 141(1), 447–451.

Wallace, A. R. (1869). Principles of geology [review]. *Quarterly Review* 126, 359–394.

Wallraff, H. G. (1980). Olfaction and homing in pigeons: nerve-section experiments, critique, hypotheses. *Journal of Comparative Physiology*, 139, 209–24.

Wallraff, H. G. (1990). Navigation by homing pigeons. *Ethology, Ecology and Evolution*, 2, 81–115.

Ward, J. (2004). Emotionally mediated synaesthesia. *Cognitive Neuropsychology*, 21, 761–772.

Ward, J. F., MacDonald, D. W., & Doncaster, C. P. (1997). Responses of foraging hedgehogs to badger odour. *Animal Behaviour*, 53, 709–720.

Wasserman, E. A. (1993). Comparative cognition: toward a general understanding of cognition in behavior. *Psychological Science*, 4, 156–161.

Wasserman, E. A., & Bhatt, R. S. (1992). Conceptualization of natural and artificial stimuli by pigeons. In W. K. F. Honig (Ed.), *Cognitive Aspects of Stimulus Control* (pp. 203–223). Hillsdale, NJ: Lawrence Erlbaum Assoc.

Watanabe, S., Sakamoto, J., & Wakita, M. (1995). Pigeons' discrimination of painting by Monet and Picasso. *Journal of the Experimental Analysis of Behavior*, 63, 165–174.

Watwood, S. L., Owen, E. C., Tyack, P. L., & Wells, R. S. (2005). Signature whistle use by temporarily restrained and free-swimming bottlenose dolphins, Tursiops truncatus. *Animal Behaviour*, 69, 1373–1386.

Weir, A. A. S., Chappell, J., & Kacelnik, A. (2002). Shaping of hooks in New Caledonian crows. *Science*, 297, 981.

Wenner, A. M., & Wells, P. H. (1990). *Anatomy of a Controversy: The Question of a 'Language' among Bees*. New York: NY: Columbia University Press.

White, D. J., Ho, L., Santos, G. D. L., & Godoy, I. (2007). An experimental test of preferences for nest contents in an obligate brood parasite, Molothrus Ater. *Behavioral Ecology*, 18, 922–928.

Whitman, W. (2008). *Leaves of Grass: The First Edition (1855)*. Digireads.com Publishing.

Wilkinson, A., Mandl, I., Bugnyar, T., & Huber, L. (2010). Gaze following in the red-footed tortoise (Geochelone carbonaria). *Animal Cognition*, 13(5), 765–769.

Wilkinson, G. S. (1984). Reciprocal food sharing in the vampire bat. *Nature*, 308(5955), 181–184.

Wilkinson, G. S. (1988). Reciprocal altruism in bats and other mammals. *Ethology and Sociobiology*, 9(2–4), 85–100.

Wilson, P. L., Towner, M. C., & Vehrencamp, S. L. (2000). Survival and song-type sharing in a sedentary subspecies of the song sparrow. *The Condor*, 102, 355–363.

Wiltschko, R. (1996). The function of olfactory input in pigeon orientation: does it provide navigational information or play another role? *Journal of Experimental Biology*, 199, 113–119.

Wiltschko, W., & Wiltschko, R. (1996). Magnetic orientation in birds. *Journal of Experimental Biology*, 199, 29–38.

Woodruff, G., & Premack, D. (1979). Intentional communication in the chimpanzee: the development of deception. *Cognition, 7*, 333–362.

Wrenn, C. C., Harris, A. P., Saavedra, M. C., & Crawley, J. N. (2003). Social transmission of food preference in mice: methodology and application to galanin-overexpressing transgenic mice. *Behavioral Neuroscience, 117*(1), 21–31.

Wright, A. A., Cook, R. G., Rivera, J. J., Sands, S. F., & Delius, J. J. (1988). Concept learning by pigeons: matching-to-sample with trial-unique video picture stimuli. *Animal Learning and Behavior, 16*, 436–444.

Wright, A. A., Shyan, M. R., & Jitsumori, M. (1990). Auditory same/different concept learning by monkeys. *Animal Learning and Behavior, 18*, 287–294.

Wyatt, T. D. (2003). *Pheromones and Animal Behaviour: Communication by Smell and Taste*. Cambridge, UK: Cambridge University Press.

Wynne, C. D. L. (1998). A minimal model of transitive inference. In C. D. L. Wynne & J. E. R. Staddon (Eds), *Models for Action* (pp. 269–307). Hillsdale, N.J: Lawrence Erlbaum Assoc.

Wynne, C. D. L. (2004). *Do Animals Think?* Princeton, N. J.: Princeton University Press.

Wynne, C. D. L. & McLean, I. G. (1999). The comparative psychology of marsupials. *Australian Journal of Psychology, 51*, 111–116.

Young, M. E., Peissig, J. J., Wasserman, E. A., & Biederman, I. (2001). Discrimination of geons by pigeons: the effects of variations in surface depiction. *Animal Learning & Behavior, 29*, 97–106.

Zahavi, A. (1975). Mate selection – a selection for a handicap. *Journal of Theoretical Biology, 53*, 205–214.

Zentall, T. R. (1996). An analysis of imitative learning in animals. In C. M. Heyes & B. G. J. Galef (Eds), *Social Learning in Animals: The Roots of Culture* (pp. 221–243). New York, NY: Academic Press.

Zuberbühler, K. (2000). Causal knowledge of predators' behaviour in wild Diana monkeys. *Animal Behaviour, 59*, 209–220.

Zuberbühler, K. (2003). Referential signaling in non-human primates: cognitive precursors and limitations for the evolution of language. In P. J. B. R. Slater (Ed.), *Advances in the Study of Behavior* (Vol. 33, pp. 265–307). Amsterdam: Elsevier.

Zuberbühler, K., Cheney, D. L. & Seyfarth, R. M. (1999). Conceptual semantics in a nonhuman primate. *Journal of Comparative Psychology, 113*, 33–42.

Index

339

Printed and bound by CPI Group (UK) Ltd, Croydon, CR0 4YY